Option Pricing: Black-Scholes Made Easy

NOTE TO THE READER:

The original edition of this book contained a companion CD-ROM, the content of which is now available only on this web site: **www.wiley.com/go/marlow**. On this web site page, click on the "Download" tab.

Option Pricing: Black-Scholes Made Easy

A Visual Way to Understand Stock Options, Option Prices, and Stock-Market Volatility

Jerry Marlow

John Wiley & Sons, Inc.

New York • Chichester • Weinheim • Brisbane • Singapore • Toronto

Copyright © 2001 by Jerry Marlow. All rights reserved.

Published by John Wiley & Sons, Inc.

Published simultaneously in Canada.

Library of Congress Cataloging-in-Publication Data

Marlow, Jerry, 1949-

    Option pricing : black-scholes made easy : a visual way to understand stock options, option prices, and stock-market volatility / Jerry Marlow.

      p. cm. — (Wiley trading)

    Includes index.

    ISBN 0-471-43641-0 (cloth : alk. paper)

     1. Stock options.   2. Options (Finance)—Prices.   I. Title.   II. Series.

HG6042 .M39 2001

332.63'228—dc21   2001024904

10 9 8 7 6 5 4 3 2

To Wendy, Nancy, Larry,
Lynne, Lianna, Maxine, and Zoe

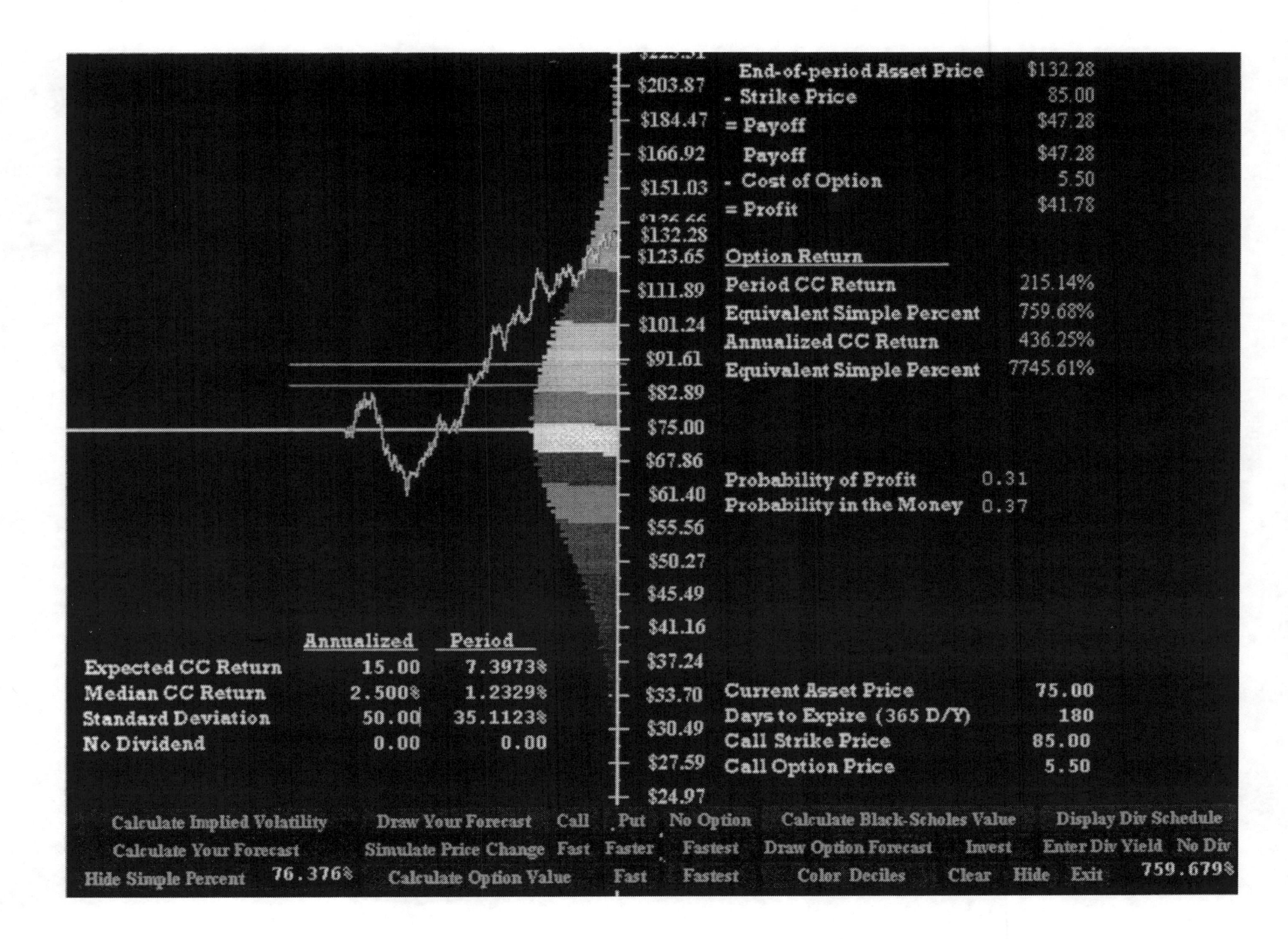

The great thing about investing in options is that
you can make money when the market's going up,
when it's going down, and—if you have the courage
to sell options—when the market isn't going anywhere at all.

—Hedge Fund Manager

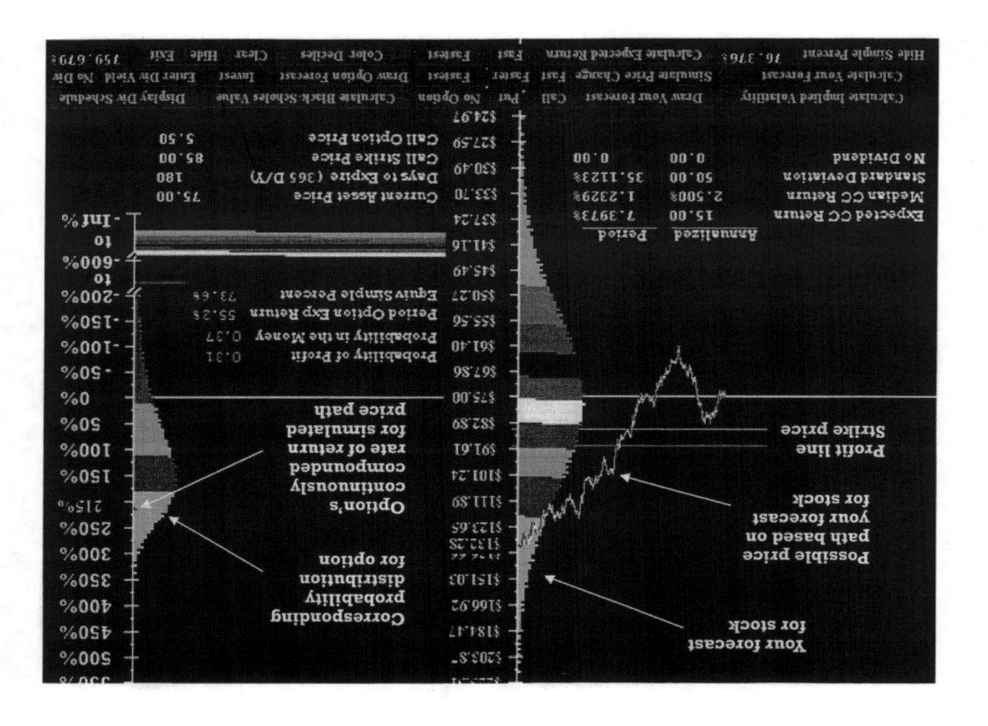

"The true logic of this world is in the calculus of probabilities."

—James Clerk Maxwell

A few years ago, a senior strategist at one of the world's leading investment firms told me something quite profound. "Many people," he said, "gain some understanding of the stock market. Then they apply that way of thinking to the options market. Usually these people do not fare very well."

"A much smaller group of people gain a sophisticated understanding of options-pricing theory. They then apply this way of thinking to the options market *and to the stock market.* These people have a superior understanding of both markets. They tend to fare extremely well."

In 1997, the Nobel Prize in Economics was awarded for the work that led to Black-Scholes Options-Pricing Theory. Black-Scholes has become the fundamental way of understanding the relationships among options prices, stock forecasts, and expected stock-market volatility.

Black-Scholes Options-Pricing Theory is based in the mathematics of probability distributions. Unfortunately, because of the way Black-Scholes usually is presented, many people find the theory's advanced mathematics daunting.

Option Pricing: Black-Scholes Made Easy makes this sophisticated way of thinking accessible to people who do not have the backgrounds necessary to do Nobel-Prize-winning mathematics.

Black-Scholes Made Easy shows you animations and simulations that you can understand easily and intuitively. The mathematics of Black-Scholes and probability distributions is behind the screen driving the animations and simulations.

Animations and simulations review the basics of how options work. They show you the relationships among option prices, stock-market volatility, and financial forecasts.

Animations show you that every financial forecast is a probability distribution and what that means. Simulations give you a clear understanding of what investment professionals mean when they talk about *expected return.* The expression may not mean what you think!

Once you have worked through the book and animations, you will understand how market-equilibrium forecasts are embedded in option prices. Using the animations, you will be able to extract from option prices the market-equilibrium forecasts of stocks you are interested in. You will see how, if you disagree with any of those forecasts, you can use options to leverage your expected return.

Based on your forecast, the animation calculates the expected return, probability of profit, and probability of being in the money for options you hold to maturity. You can simulate potential payoffs of investments you have in mind.

Black-Scholes Options-Pricing Theory revealed that investing in options is a probability game. *Black-Scholes Made Easy* shows you your odds.

Jerry Marlow

New York City
June 2001

Jerry Marlow is a freelance financial writer and marketing consultant. For investment firms, he creates marketing and educational presentations that bridge the gap between how sophisticated financial managers think about investing and how the firms' clients think about investing. He holds an MBA in Marketing from New York University where he also did post-MBA work in finance.

jerrymarlow@jerrymarlow.com

Acknowledgments

I have had the good fortune to have as friends and clients some very smart and savvy people. They have taught me a great deal about stock options, investment strategies, investor psychology, and investor education. For inspiring and enlightening me, I especially thank Josh Weinreich, Rich Marin, Peter Lengyel, and Al Bellino.

Black-Scholes Made Easy is not only a book. It also is a computer animation that contains roughly 10,000 lines of computer code. It is written in Macromedia Director's™ Lingo™. For his lucid and well-organized books on Lingo, I thank Gary Rosenzweig.

For testing the software from a naive investor's point of view and suggesting ways to make working with the animation a smooth interaction, I thank Lianna Sugarman.

For cajoling and encouraging me to address content issues I would've found it easier not to, I thank my gracious and diplomatic editor at John Wiley & Sons Claudio Capanzano.

For alerting me to points on which academicians are apt to attack any work on Black-Scholes, I thank New York University Professor of Mathematics Jonathan Goodman.

For developing Black-Scholes Options Pricing theory in the first place, I thank Myron Scholes, Robert Merton, and the late Fischer Black.

The details may be the devil's home stomping grounds, but in this work he has found his match—Danielle Lake of North Market Street Graphics, the project's copy editor. Thank you, Danielle.

For adapting John Wiley & Sons's scholarly style guidelines to this venture in new media and to a writing style geared to oral and informal presentation, I thank Robin Factor.

For allowing me to plug in my laptop at *Once Upon A Tart*, thank you Jerome.

Contents

Option Outcomes, Probability Distributions, and Expected Returns

Option Pricing

Black-Scholes Assumptions (Part II)

Value of Early Exercise of American Options
Black's Approximation for Valuing American Options

Sensitivity of Option Values to Changes in Volatility, Spot Price of
Underlying, Time to Expiration, and Risk-Free Rate

Using Options to Leverage Your Expected Return

Black-Scholes Assumptions (Part III)

Using the Animations to Assess Option Opportunities

Getting Up and Running

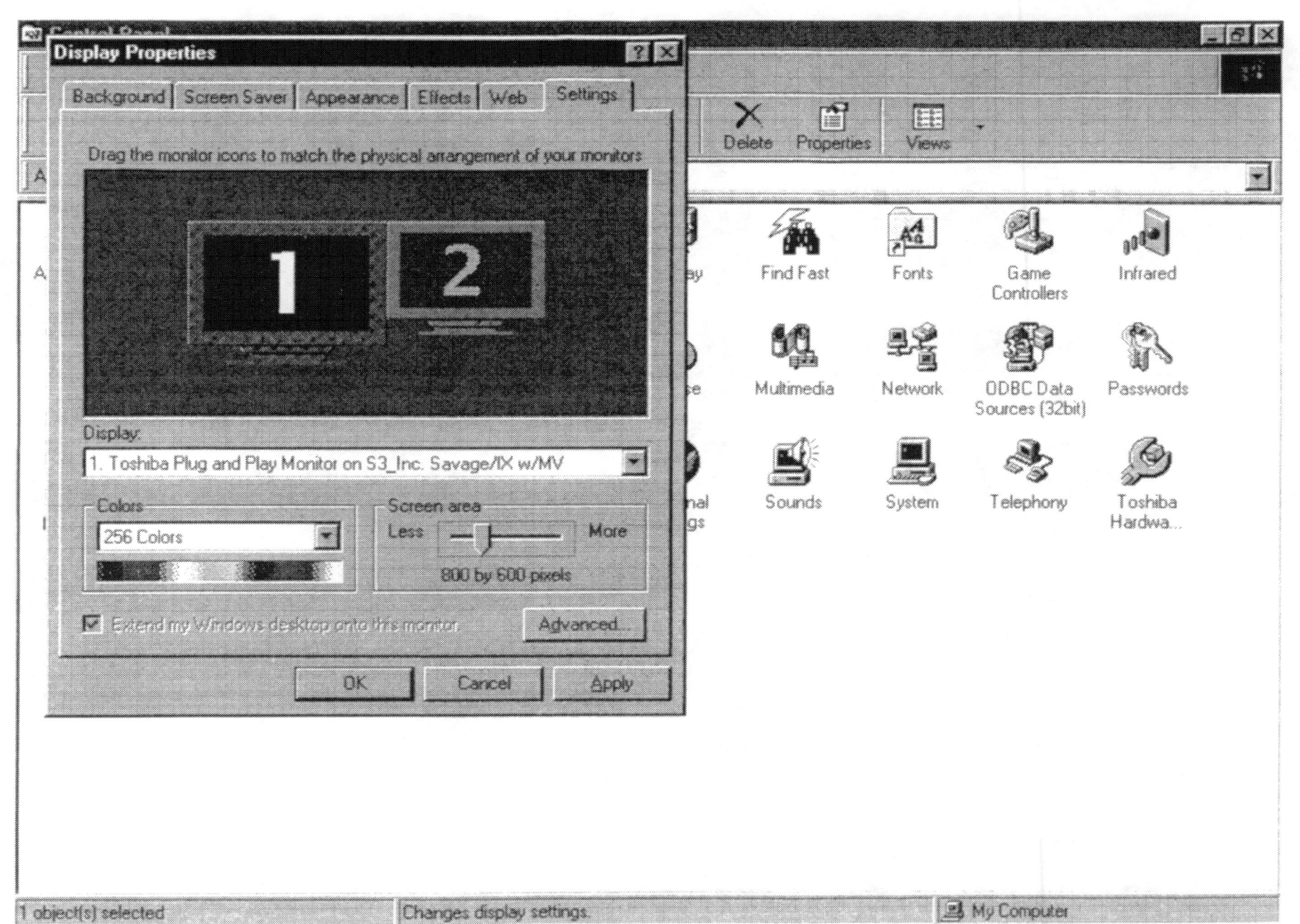

Display Properties

Background | Screen Saver | Appearance | Effects | Web | Settings |

Drag the monitor icons to match the physical arrangement of your monitors

Display:

1. Toshiba Plug and Play Monitor on S3_Inc. Savage/IX w/MV

Colors
256 Colors

Screen area
Less ——————— More
800 by 600 pixels

☑ Extend my Windows desktop onto this monitor   Advanced...

OK   Cancel   Apply

Find Fast   Fonts   Game Controllers   Infrared

Multimedia   Network   ODBC Data Sources (32bit)   Passwords

Sounds   System   Telephony   Toshiba Hardwa...

1 object(s) selected   Changes display settings.   🖳 My Computer

To fill your computer screen with the animation, set your computer's screen resolution to 800 × 600. To run the animation in a window, set your computer's resolution higher.

Black-Scholes Made Easy runs on Windows at a screen resolution of 800 × 600.

If you want the animation to fill up the entire computer screen, set your screen resolution to 800 × 600.

If, while you're running the animation, you also want to see on-screen other software you have running, then set your screen resolution higher than 800 × 600.

If you know how to set the resolution of your computer, go ahead and do so. Otherwise, follow these steps:

1. To bring up the Windows menu, simultaneously press the Control (Ctrl) key and the Escape (Esc) key.

2. Roll your mouse cursor up to the Settings icon.

3. Click on Control Panel.

4. Double-click on the Display icon.

5. At the top of the selection, click on Settings.

6. Set the resolution to 800 × 600 or higher. (If your computer only supports a screen resolution of 640 × 480, you'll have to use with a different computer.)

7. Click on OK.

8. Exit the Control Panel.

To run Black-Scholes Made Easy, double-click on BSMadeEasyFullScreen.exe or on BSMadeEasyInAWindow.exe.

www.wiley.com/go/marlow

To run the animation full screen, double-click on BSMadeEasyFullScreen.exe.

To run the animation in a window, double-click on BSMadeEasy-InAWindow.exe.

(To register as a user of *Black-Scholes Made Easy*, double-click on RegisterBlackScholesMadeEasy.htm. For links to the author's websites and e-mail address, double-click on StayIn-Touch.htm. For links to Tech Support, double-click on TechSupport.htm.)

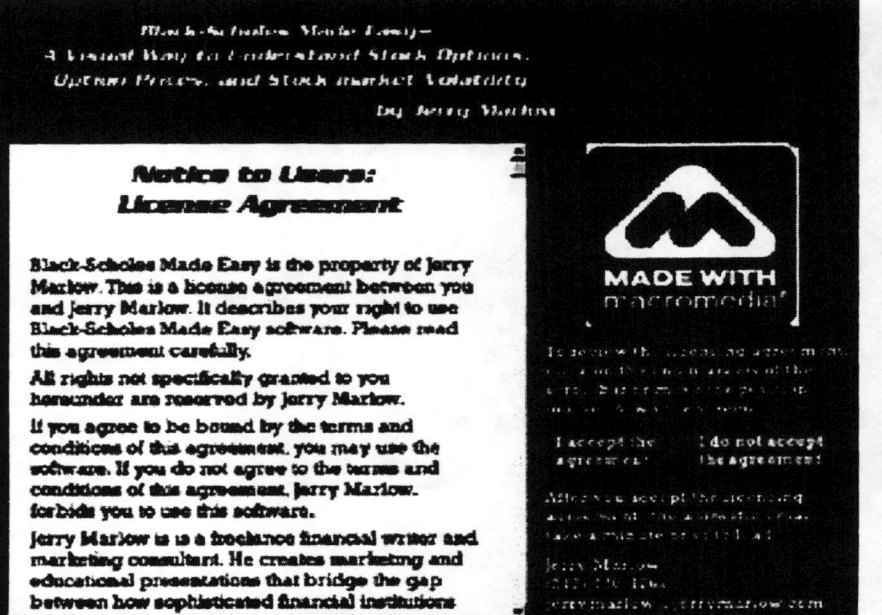

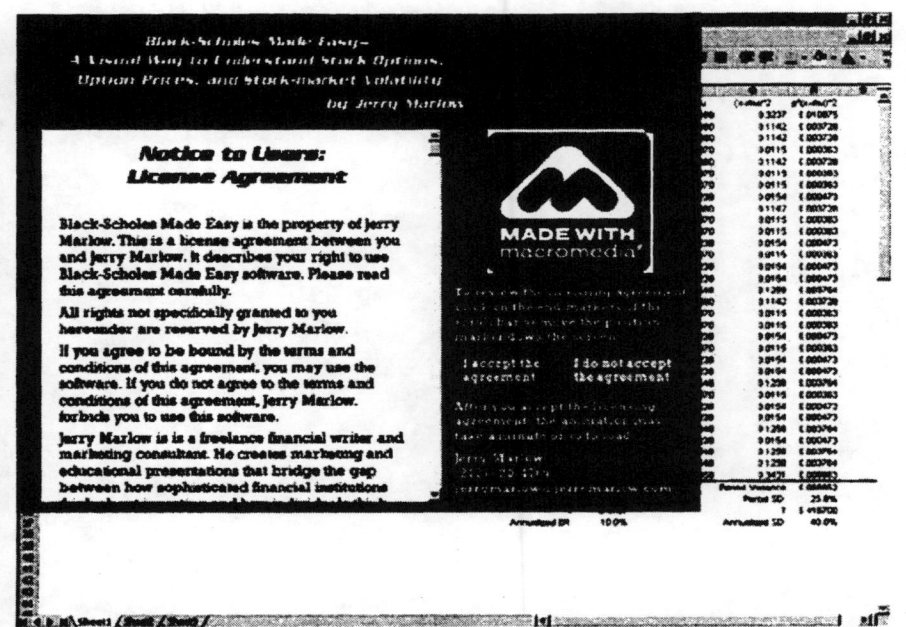

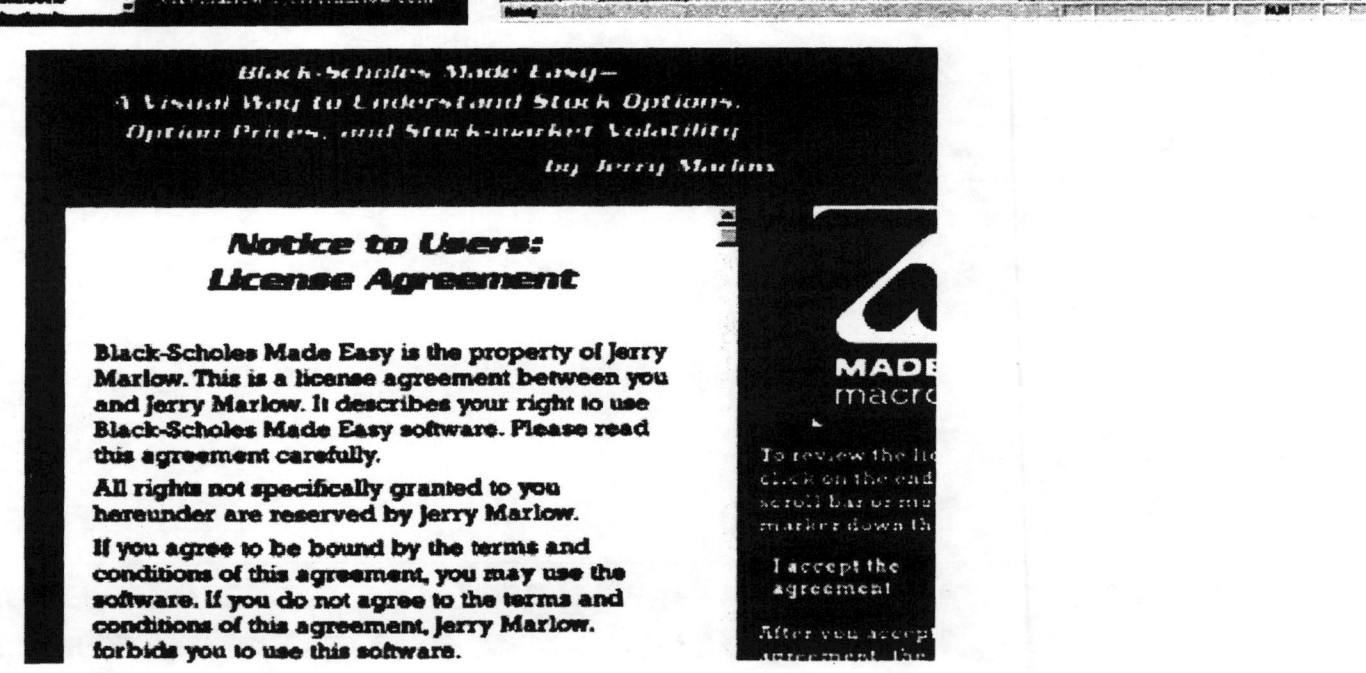

If the screen resolution is set correctly, the first screen will look like one of the two on top.

The first screen that the animation lands on should look like one of the images on top.

If it does, great.

If, however, the first screen of the animation looks like the bottom image, then the resolution of your computer is set too low.

If the screen resolution is not set correctly, hit the Esc key on your keyboard. Go through the instructions for screen resolution on page 2.

After you accept the licensing agreement, the animation may take a minute or so to load.

Black-Scholes Made Easy—
A Visual Way to Understand
Stock Options, Option Prices,
and Stock-market Volatility

by Jerry Marlow

To continue beyond the title, click anywhere on the screen.

To make the command buttons visible, roll the mouse cursor around on the screen.

Roll your mouse cursor around on the bottom and top left of the screen. You'll see command buttons appear when you roll over them.

Depending on what's going on on the screen, the functions of some command buttons may change.

1. To make the buttons disappear, click the Hide button three times.

If you want to ignore the tutorial and just start clicking on buttons, first read the section at the end of the book entitled: Navigating through the Animations.

Maybe you don't like to read and just want to click on buttons. Fine. If that's the case though, before you get started you may want to take a quick look at the section on navigating through the animations. It shows you the design principles that govern when and how things come up on screen. Your trial-and-error adventure will be less puzzling and messy.

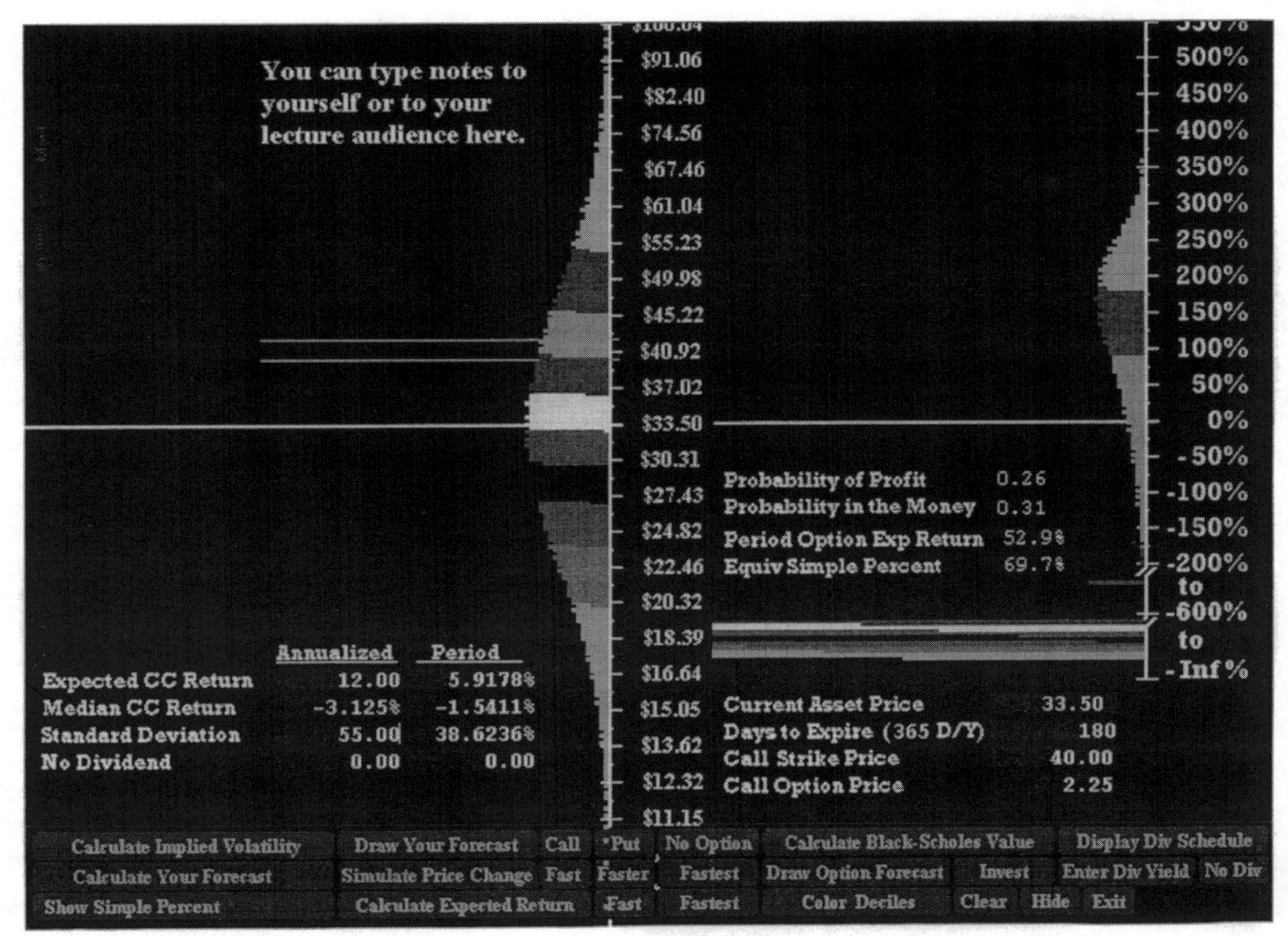

To save and print pictures of the simulations, use Print Screen and Ctrl+V to copy and paste screen captures into other software. Include notes to yourself.

The animation does not provide a direct way to save or print pictures of the simulations you create on the screen. Nonetheless, you easily can use programs such as Word, PowerPoint, and Excel to save and print pictures of the simulations. You can use graphics software to prepare screen captures for display on the Web.

1. To capture an image of a simulation you have on your screen, press the Print Screen key on your keyboard. It's usually near the F12 key on the top right of your keyboard. It may be abbreviated Print Scrn or Prt Sc.

2. Use your mouse or press Alt+Tab to go to a Word, PowerPoint, or Excel document that you have open.

3. In your Word, PowerPoint, or Excel document, hold down the Ctrl key and press the V key (Ctrl+V).

4. If you wish to modify a screen capture or use it on a web site, instead of pasting it into a document program, use Ctrl+V to paste the screen capture onto a 800 × 600 canvas in an imaging program such as Adobe Photoshop, Macromedia Fireworks, or Microsoft Photo Editor or Paint. In these programs, you can save screen captures as .gif files and import them into your documents and web sites.

The screen includes a field in which you can type notes to yourself or to your lecture audience.

5. To get to the field in which you can type notes, keep hitting the Tab key on your keyboard until the cursor appears in the top middle of the screen.

(The message field appears on-screen only when you have other data fields on screen.)

Volatility

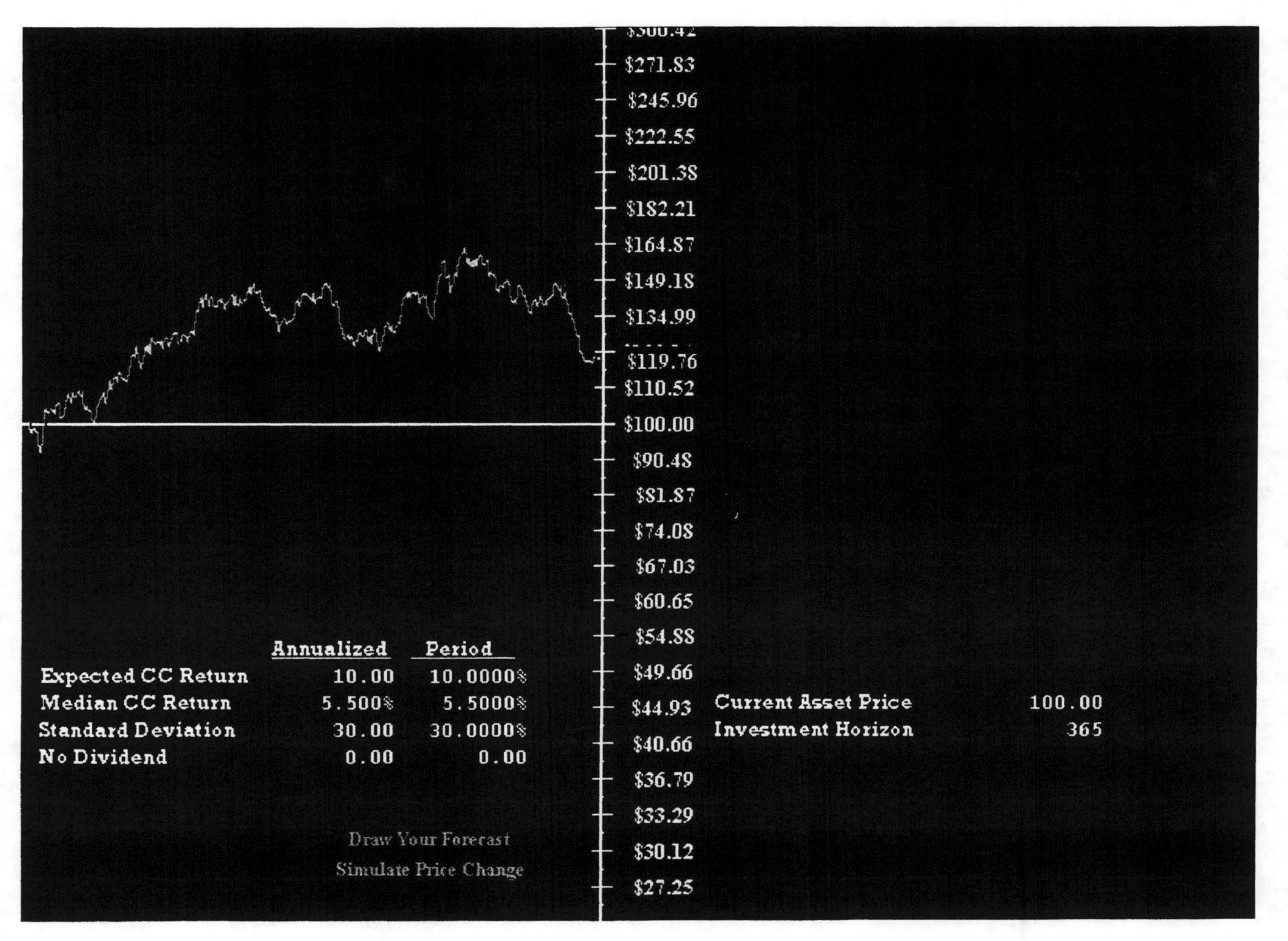

	Annualized	Period
Expected CC Return	10.00	10.0000%
Median CC Return	5.500%	5.5000%
Standard Deviation	30.00	30.0000%
No Dividend	0.00	0.00

Draw Your Forecast
Simulate Price Change

Current Asset Price	100.00
Investment Horizon	365

$300.42
$271.83
$245.96
$222.55
$201.38
$182.21
$164.87
$149.18
$134.99
$119.76
$110.52
$100.00
$90.48
$81.87
$74.08
$67.03
$60.65
$54.88
$49.66
$44.93
$40.66
$36.79
$33.29
$30.12
$27.25

Stock prices are volatile.

1. To zero out all the data fields, mouse around at the bottom right of the screen to find the Clear button and click on it three times.

2. To make anything you may have on-screen go away, click two or three times on Hide.

3. Click on Simulate Price Change.

Let's say you're thinking about buying a stock.

Today it is trading at $100.

4. Tab to the Current Asset Price field and enter 100.00. No dollar sign, please.

What's the price of this stock going to be one year from now?

We need a forecast.

Let's say that you believe in forecasts based on historical data.

You call up your broker and ask for the stock's historical performance. She says that, based on the past 10 years, the stock has an expected return of 10% with a standard deviation of 30%. The standard deviation is a measure of the stock's volatility.

We'll talk a lot more about expected return and standard deviation later. For now, let's just enter the historical performance into the animation as a forecast.

5. Click in or tab to the Expected Continuously Compounded Return field and enter 10.00.

6. For Standard Deviation, enter 30.00.

Our investment horizon is one year or 365 days.

7. For Investment Horizon, enter 365.

Given this forecast, we can simulate a potential price path.

8. Click again on Simulate Price Change.

There. That looks pretty reasonable, doesn't it?

One year from today, the stock might be worth the value at the end of the price path.

We see that, over the course of the 365 days, the price keeps changing. What's more, the direction of price change keeps changing. That's volatility.

Is this the only potential price path we can get from this forecast?

No.

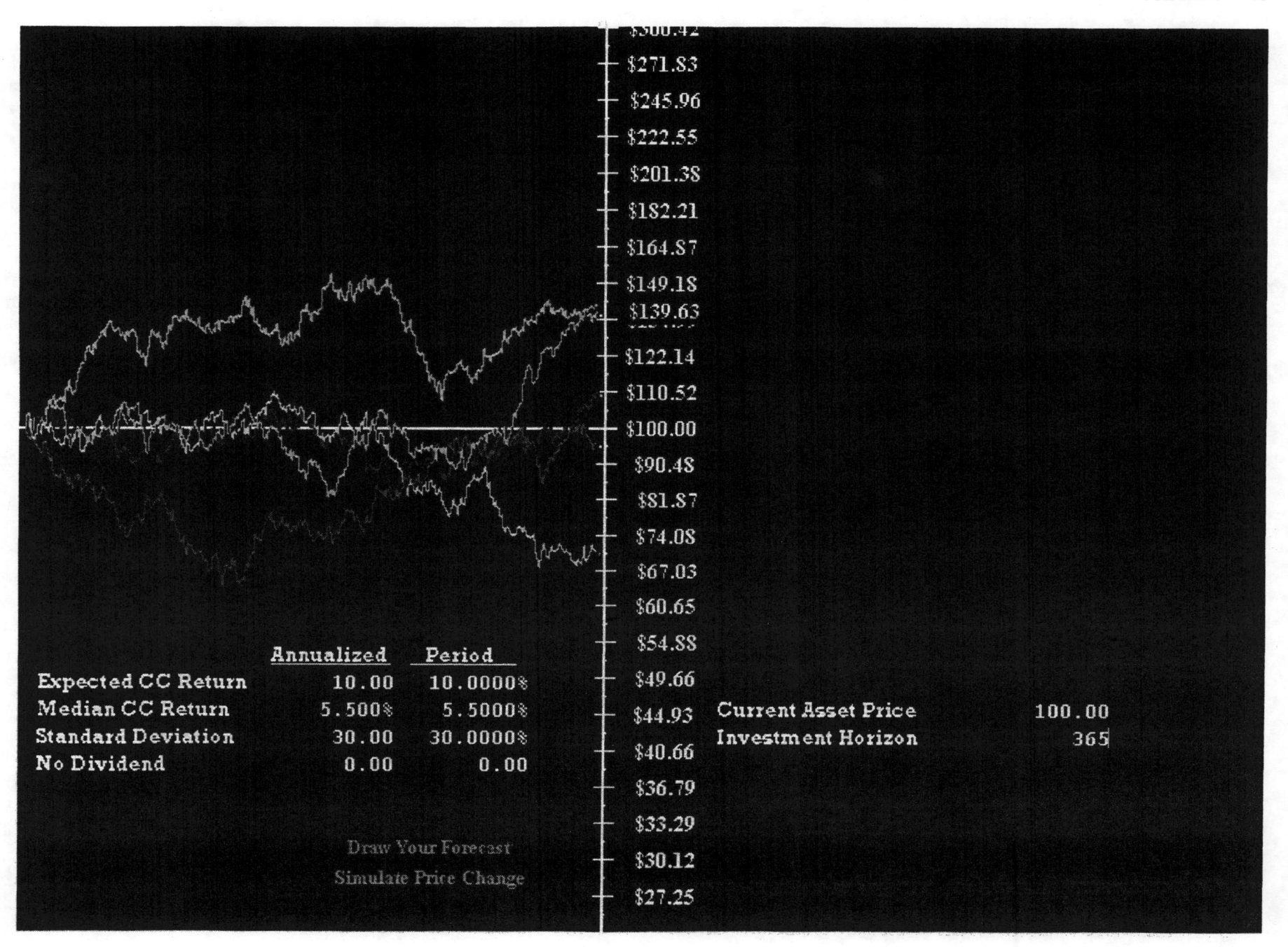

Volatility means that a stock's future price path is uncertain.

9. Click again on Simulate Price Change.

We get a different price path and a different outcome.

10. Click again on Simulate Price Change.

Same forecast. Different price path. Different outcome.

11. Click on Simulate Price Change a few more times. Each time, wait for the outcome.

All of these price paths, all of these outcomes, are allowed for in this one forecast. The volatility estimate allows for many different potential price paths.

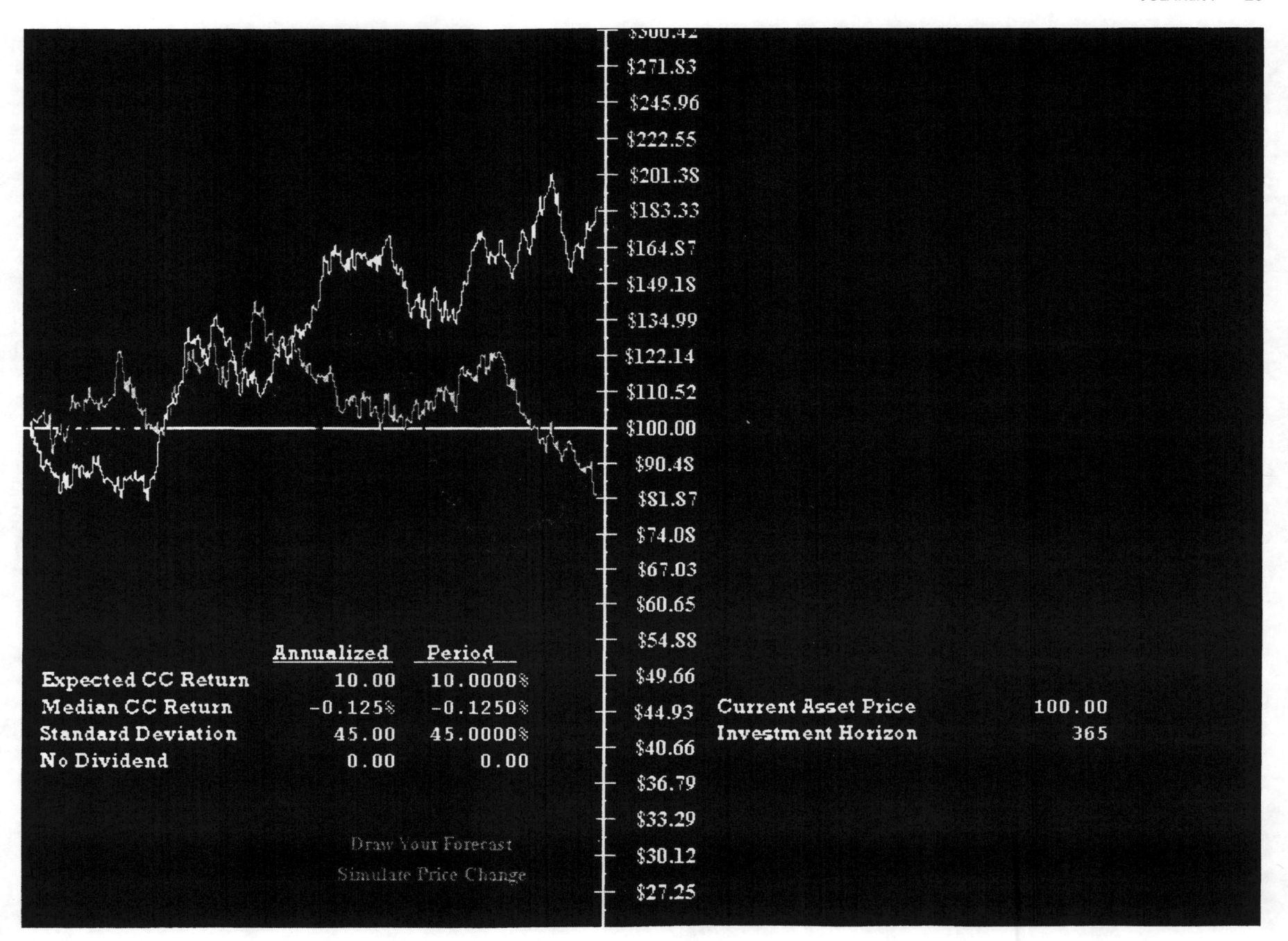

	Annualized	Period
Expected CC Return	10.00	10.0000%
Median CC Return	−0.125%	−0.1250%
Standard Deviation	45.00	45.0000%
No Dividend	0.00	0.00

Current Asset Price	100.00
Investment Horizon	365

Draw Your Forecast

Simulate Price Change

The more volatile a stock, the more uncertain its future value.

Let's see what happens to the potential price paths and outcomes if we change the volatility estimate.

If we put in a lower estimate of volatility, the animation draws a potential price path that has less volatility.

Let's see what a price path with a standard deviation of 20% looks like.

> 12. Click on Clear.
>
> 13. For Standard Deviation, enter 20.00.
>
> 14. Click on Simulate Price Change.

Not a straight line; but not a lot of volatility, either.

> 15. Click on Simulate Price Change a few more times. Each time, wait for the outcome.

With a volatility estimate of 20%, the potential price paths and outcomes stay in a fairly narrow band.

If our forecast has a volatility of zero, what does that look like?

> 16. For Standard Deviation, enter 0.00.
>
> 17. Click on Simulate Price Change.

The price path is a straight line—no volatility at all.

> 18. Click again on Simulate Price Change.

With no volatility, we always get the same price path and the same outcome.

If the volatility estimate is significantly larger, say a standard deviation of 45%, what do the price paths look like?

> 19. For Standard Deviation, enter 45.00.
>
> 20. Click on Simulate Price Change five times. Each time, wait for the outcome.

We see that, the greater a stock's volatility, the more uncertain is its future value.

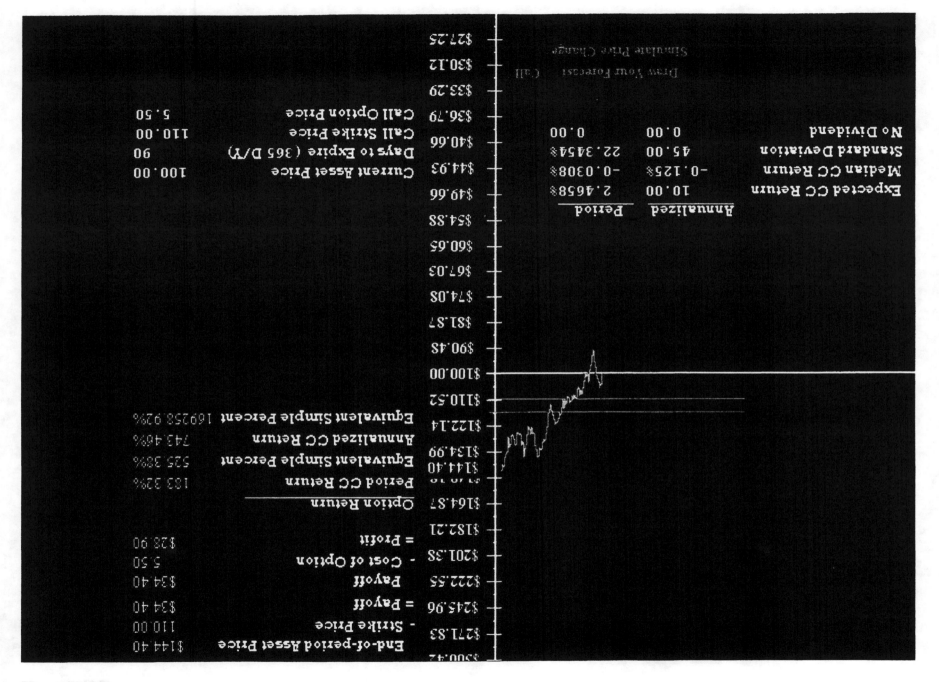

If you buy an option—depending on the price path the stock takes—you can make a ton of money or you can lose it all.

Right now, we're working with a stock that has an expected return of 10% and a volatility estimate of 45%.

Let's look at what might happen if you bought a call option on this stock and held the option until expiration.

A call gives you the right to buy a stock at a pre-set price called the strike price.

Let's say you buy a call that expires in 90 days. It has a strike price of $110.00. The option sells for $5.50.

> 21. Click on Clear.
>
> 22. Click on Call.
>
> 23. For Days to Expire, enter 90.
>
> 24. For Call Strike Price, enter 110.00.
>
> 25. For Call Option Price, enter 5.50.

The yellow line represents the strike price at $110. For the call to be in the money, the stock price has to be above the yellow line.

The distance from the yellow line to the green line represents the price of the option.

For you to make a profit from exercising the option, the stock price has to go above the green line.

Let's see what kind of results we might expect to get from buying this option and holding it until expiration.

> 26. Click on Simulate Price Change.

If the end-of-period price is above the strike price, the end-of-period price minus the strike price gives you your payoff.

The payoff minus the cost of the option gives you your profit.

If the price path goes your way, by investing $5.50 in the option, you can earn a very high return.

If the end-of-period price is below the strike price, the payoff is zero. Your "profit" is negative, and you lose all the money you invested in the option.

> 27. Click on Simulate Price Change a few times. Each time, wait for the outcome. Keep clicking until you get a couple of winners.

You see that, depending on the price path the stock takes, you can earn wildly different rates of return.

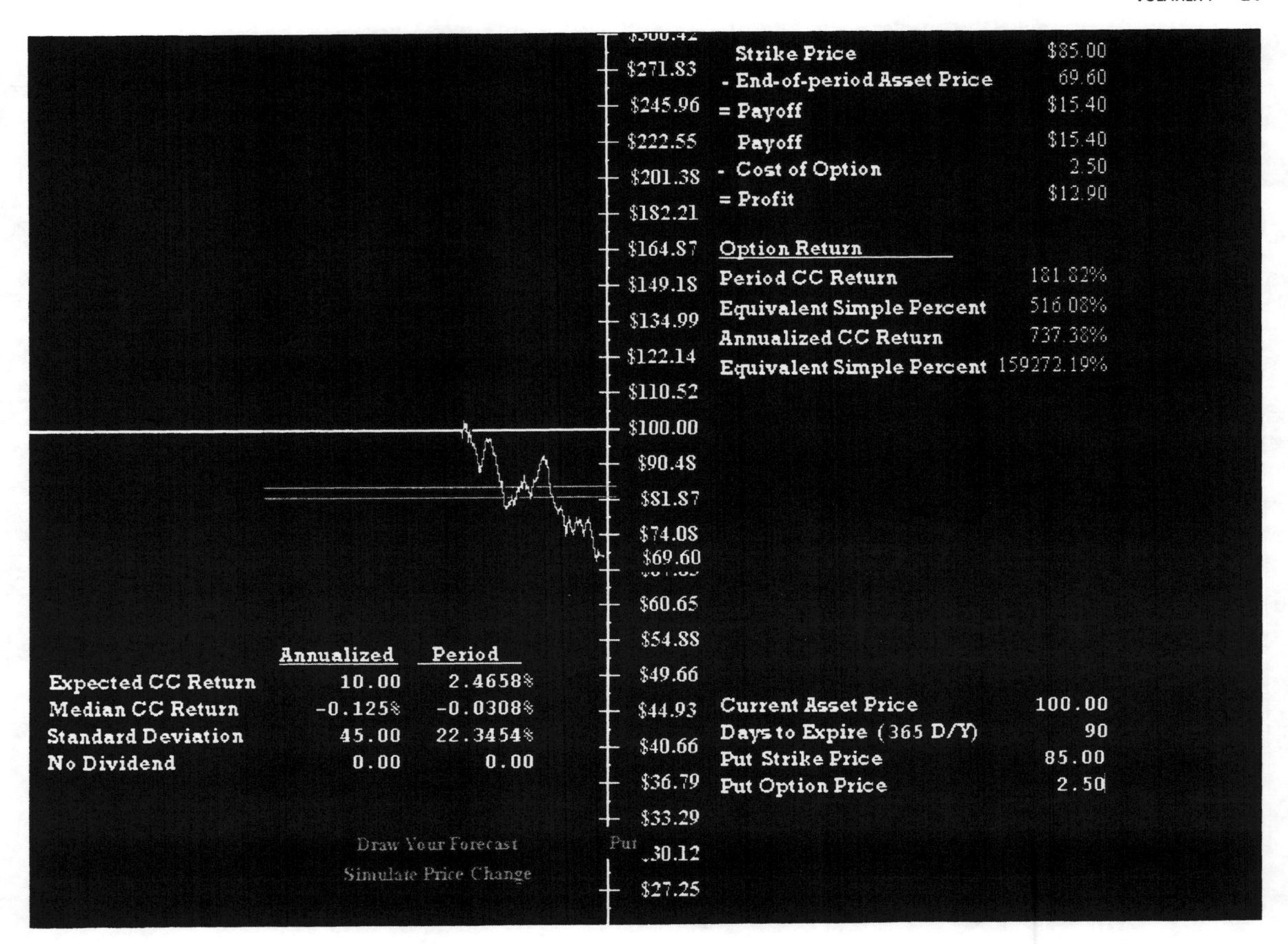

Strike Price		$85.00
- End-of-period Asset Price		69.60
= Payoff		$15.40
Payoff		$15.40
- Cost of Option		2.50
= Profit		$12.90

Option Return

Period CC Return	181.82%
Equivalent Simple Percent	516.08%
Annualized CC Return	737.38%
Equivalent Simple Percent	159272.19%

Price axis values:
$300.42
$271.83
$245.96
$222.55
$201.38
$182.21
$164.87
$149.18
$134.99
$122.14
$110.52
$100.00
$90.48
$81.87
$74.08
$69.60
$60.65
$54.88
$49.66
$44.93
$40.66
$36.79
$33.29
$30.12
$27.25

	Annualized	Period
Expected CC Return	10.00	2.4658%
Median CC Return	-0.125%	-0.0308%
Standard Deviation	45.00	22.3454%
No Dividend	0.00	0.00

Current Asset Price	100.00
Days to Expire (365 D/Y)	90
Put Strike Price	85.00
Put Option Price	2.50

Draw Your Forecast

Simulate Price Change

Put

Instead of buying a call, you might buy a put. A put gives you the right to sell a stock at a pre-set price.

Let's say you buy a put on this same stock. The forecast remains the same.

The put expires in 90 days. It has a strike price of $85.00. It sells for $2.50.

---

28. Click on Clear.

29. Click on Put.

30. For Put Strike Price, enter 85.00.

31. For Put Option Price, enter 2.50.

To be in the money on a put, the stock price has to go *below* the yellow line. To earn a profit from exercising the option, the stock price has to go below the green line.

---

32. Click on Simulate Price Change a few times. Each time, wait for the outcome. Keep clicking until you get a winner.

Chances are you'll see some breathtaking outcomes.

The option outcomes you've just simulated may suggest to you that options are nothing but risky gambles. They're not. Option prices and potential outcomes are completely rational. If they weren't, option sellers or buyers would have the opportunity to hedge their sales or purchases and earn riskless profits.

In *Black-Scholes Made Easy,* we go through a series of ideas and simulations that show the logic behind how options work. We keep the uncertainty of outcomes, but we show how it looks within a rational framework.

To understand European options, we use Black-Scholes. To understand American options, we add Black's approximation.

In the pages that follow, because it is easier to understand and to grasp intuitively, we begin by assuming that you, the investor, buy options and hold them until their maturity or expiration date. We look at potential outcomes of holding options until maturity. We look at their expected returns, probabilities of profit, and probabilities of being in the money. We look at alternative ways of valuing or pricing options held to maturity.

After building our knowledge by looking at options held to maturity, we look at a more advanced topic: the circumstances in which it might prove advantageous to exercise an option prior to maturity. We discuss the different components of an option's value. We show how, under certain circumstances, exercising an option sooner may give a higher present value and expected return than exercising it later or at maturity.

Options sold on exchanges are of two basic types: European style and American style. European-style options can be exercised only at maturity. Most of the options on market indices are European style.

American-style options can be exercised at any time—up to and at maturity. Most stock options are American style.

The terms *European* and *American* have nothing to do with geographic location. They merely designate different types of option structures.

With an American-style option, you have all the rights that come with a European-style option plus the right to exercise it prior to maturity. Under certain circumstances, the right of early exercise has value. Hence, under those circumstances, an otherwise identical American option is more valuable than a European option.

The Black-Scholes model was designed and developed to value only European-style options—options held to maturity. It does not automatically look at the potential value of the right to early exercise.

To value American-style options, Fischer Black developed an approach now called Black's approximation. The approach includes a look at the potential value of early exercise.

To understand and value options held to maturity, we use the Black-Scholes model and the Black-Scholes assumptions. To understand and value American options, we add Black's approximation.

When we look at circumstances under which you might gain an advantage through early exercise, you will see (among other things) that never can you gain an advantage from exercising early a call option on an underlying that pays no dividends. Hence, on call options written on underlyings that pay no dividends, there is no difference in value between a European call and an American call. To value them, you can use Black-Scholes without Black's approximation.

The model most commonly used to value American-style options is the binomial pricing model. It automatically takes into account the possibility of gaining advantage through early exercise.

If you find the Black-Scholes animation of value and would like for the author to develop an animated tutorial for the binomial pricing model, double-click on StayInTouch on the *Black-Scholes Made Easy* website and send him an e-mail.

Every Financial Forecast Is a Probability Distribution

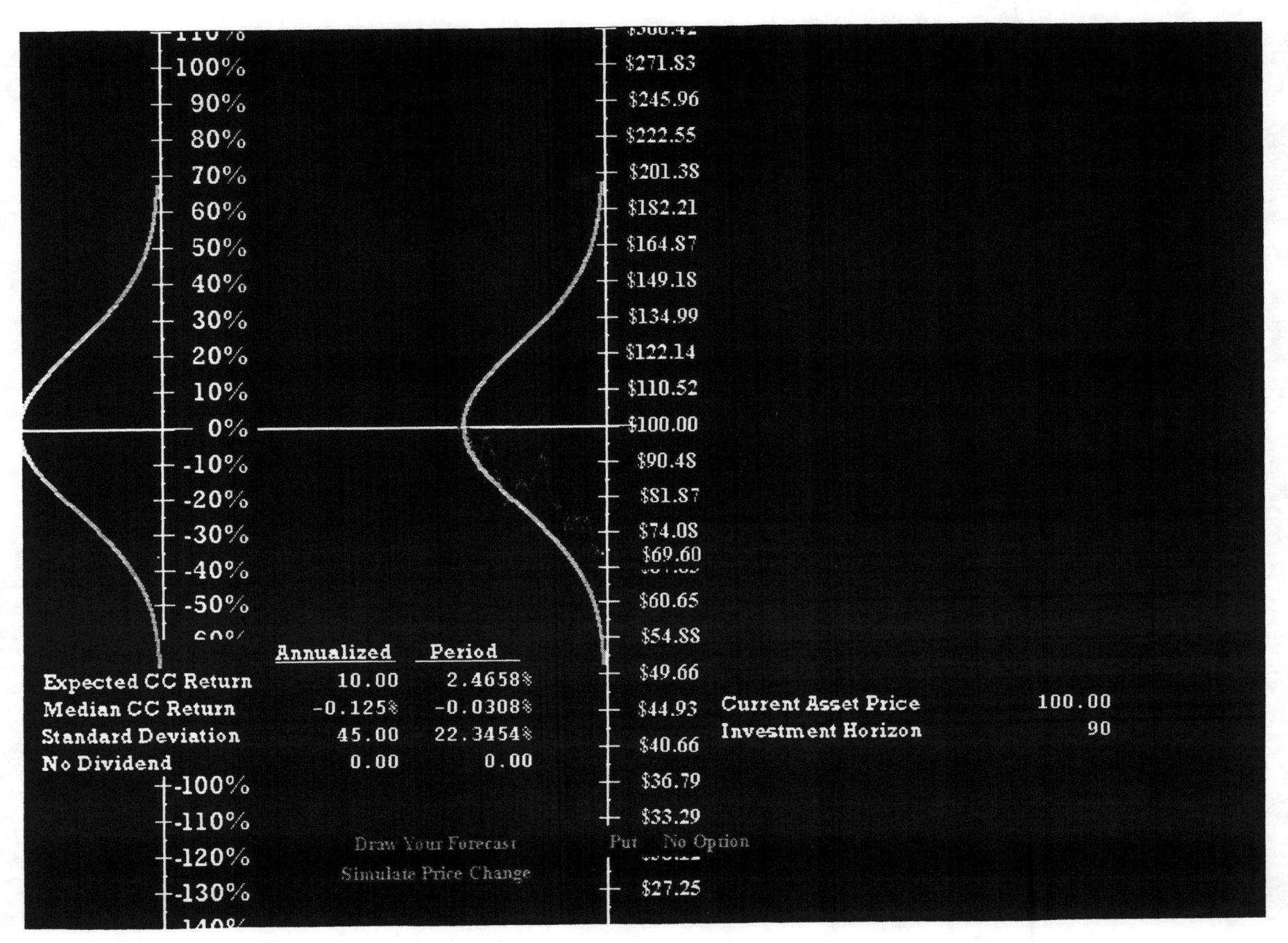

	Annualized	Period
Expected CC Return	10.00	2.4658%
Median CC Return	-0.125%	-0.0308%
Standard Deviation	45.00	22.3454%
No Dividend	0.00	0.00

Draw Your Forecast
Simulate Price Change

Put   No Option

Current Asset Price	100.00
Investment Horizon	90

A forecast for a stock is a bell-shaped curve.

Academics tell us, "Investing is about decision making under conditions of uncertainty." This statement is true. But it is not terribly useful. A more useful construct is that every financial forecast is a probability distribution.

The forecast that you've been using to draw the price path you have on-screen now is a probability distribution. You can draw it.

33. **Click on No Option.**

34. **Click twice on Draw Your Forecast.**

For the 90-day investment horizon, the animation draws a forecast of return and a price forecast. Under the Black-Scholes assumptions, this is what the forecast for a stock looks like. It is the familiar bell-shaped curve.

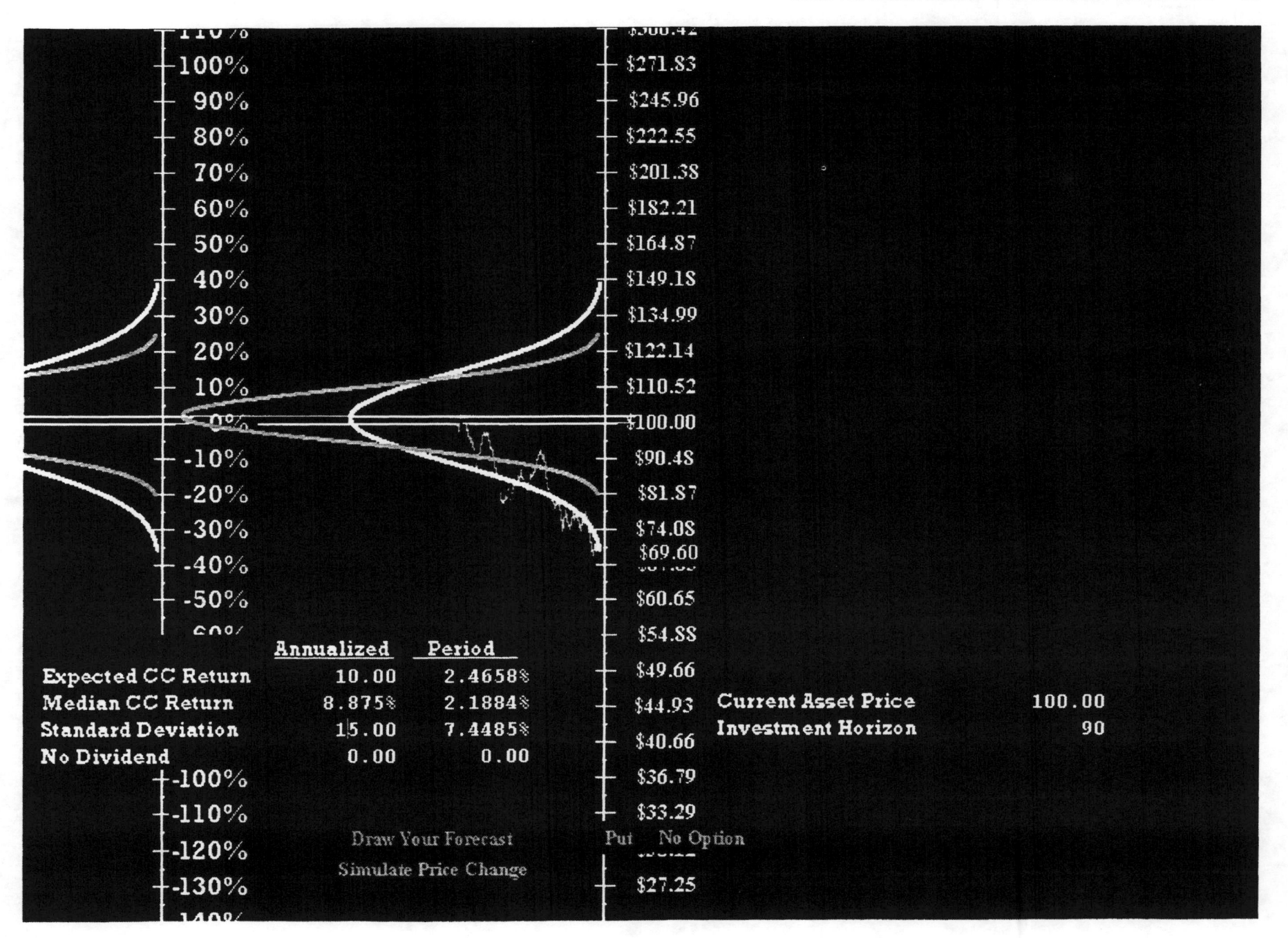

	Annualized	Period
Expected CC Return	10.00	2.4658%
Median CC Return	8.875%	2.1884%
Standard Deviation	15.00	7.4485%
No Dividend	0.00	0.00

Current Asset Price 100.00
Investment Horizon 90

Draw Your Forecast
Simulate Price Change

Put   No Option

Different forecasts look different.

Whenever you change a forecast's expected return or standard deviation, you get a different probability distribution.

---

35. For Standard Deviation, enter 10.00.

36. Click on Draw Your Forecast.

Notice the differences in placement and spread of the probability distributions.

---

37. For Standard Deviation, enter 30.00.

38. Click on Draw Your Forecast.

Most of what *Black-Scholes Made Easy* does is animate probability distributions. The animation combines the Black-Scholes assumptions, formulas, and ideas with what is known as structured Monte Carlo simulations.

Animations translate probability distributions into option prices and option prices into probability distributions. They translate probability distributions into potential price paths and price paths into illustrative payoffs.

The probability distributions we've been looking at are bell shaped. Later, we'll see that the probability distributions of options forecasts have a radically different shape.

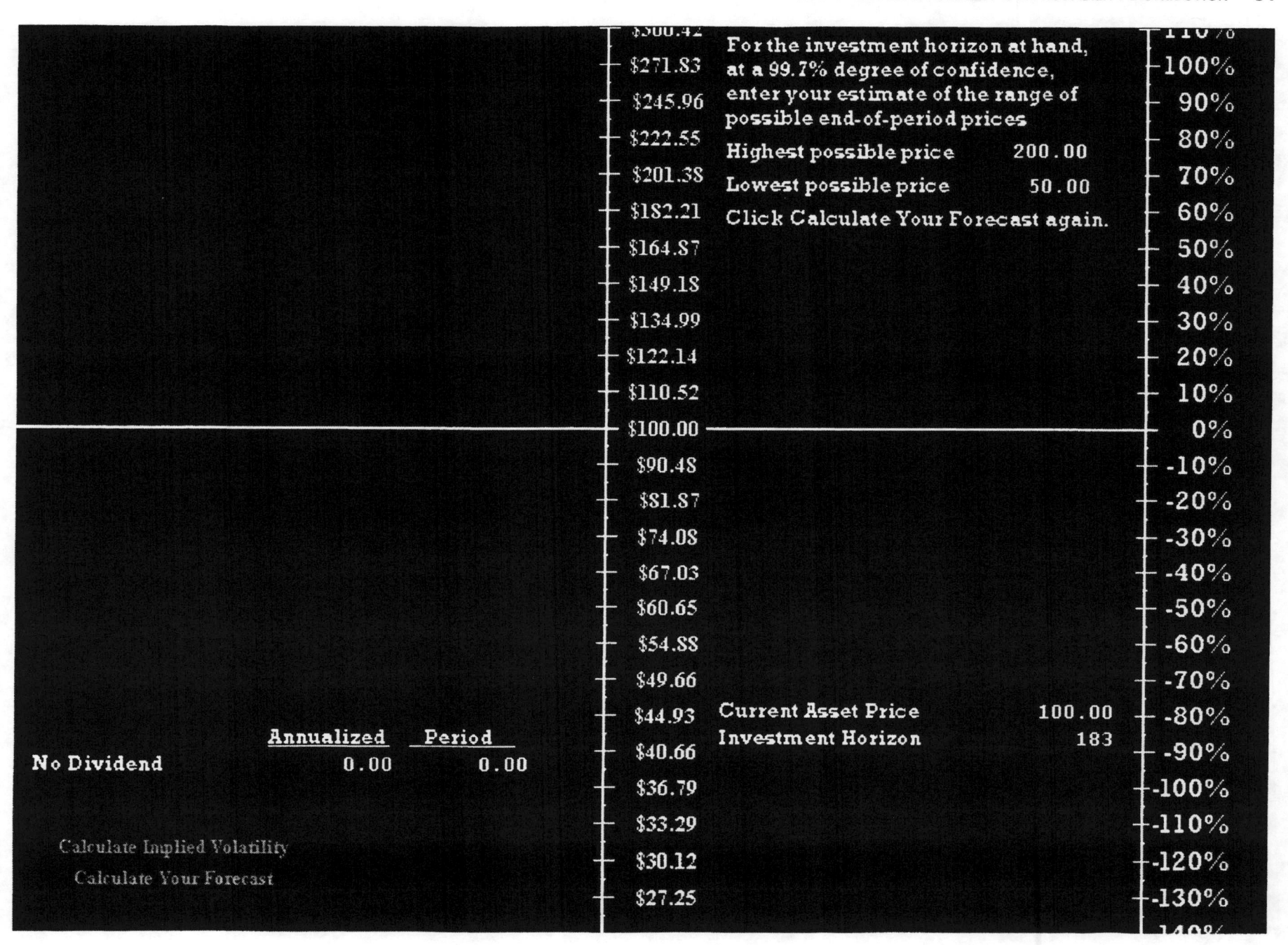

$300.42

$271.83

$245.96

$222.55

$201.38

$182.21

$164.87

$149.18

$134.99

$122.14

$110.52

$100.00

$90.48

$81.87

$74.08

$67.03

$60.65

$54.88

$49.66

$44.93

$40.66

$36.79

$33.29

$30.12

$27.25

110%

100%

90%

80%

70%

60%

50%

40%

30%

20%

10%

0%

-10%

-20%

-30%

-40%

-50%

-60%

-70%

-80%

-90%

-100%

-110%

-120%

-130%

140%

For the investment horizon at hand, at a 99.7% degree of confidence, enter your estimate of the range of possible end-of-period prices

Highest possible price   200.00

Lowest possible price   50.00

Click Calculate Your Forecast again.

Current Asset Price   100.00
Investment Horizon   183

Annualized   Period

No Dividend   0.00   0.00

Calculate Implied Volatility

Calculate Your Forecast

You can translate your estimate of possible end-of-period prices into a forecast of expected return and uncertainty.

Let's look at a crude way to translate your beliefs about a stock's future price performance into an elegant forecast of return and uncertainty.

Let's say you're interested in a stock that today is trading at $100. The stock pays no dividends.

With a 99.7% degree of confidence, you believe that, over the next six months, the trading price of the stock may reach as high as $200 or it may fall as low as $50.

What is the forecast of return and uncertainty implicit in your beliefs about the price of this stock?

Let's see.

1. To zero out all the data fields, click three times on Clear.

2. To make everything on-screen go away, click two or three times on Hide.

3. Click on Calculate Your Forecast.

4. Click in or tab to the field Current Asset Price.

5. Enter 100.00. (No $, please.)

6. For Investment Horizon, enter 183. That's 183 days for six months of a 365-day year.

7. For Highest possible price, enter 200.00. (No $, please.)

8. For Lowest possible price, enter 50.00.

9. Click Calculate Your Forecast.

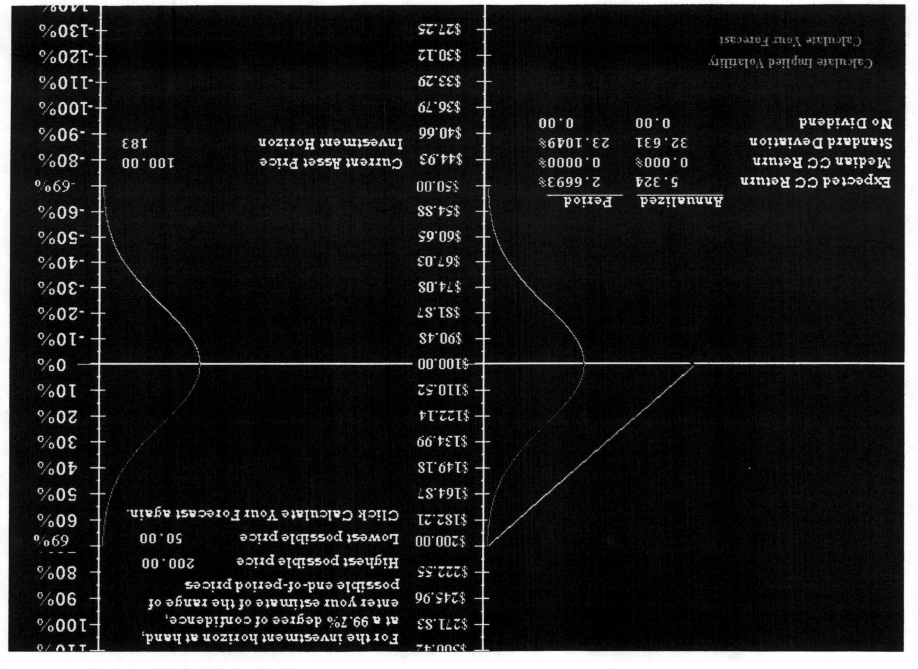

The bell-shaped curve tells us that you are 99.7% certain that the investment outcome will be within the curve.

The forecast the animation draws is a probability distribution—again the familiar bell-shaped curve.

To draw the forecast, the animation first calculates the continuously compounded rate of return (CCRR) that would be required for the current asset price of $100 to reach $200.

CCRR = ln(end-of-period price / starting price)
$$= \ln(\$200 / \$100)$$
$$= 69.3\%$$

The animation then calculates the continuously compounded rate of return that would be required for the current price of $100 to fall to $50.

CCRR = ln(end-of-period price / starting price)
$$= \ln(\$50 / \$100)$$
$$= -69.3\%$$

ln signifies taking the natural logarithm of a number. (In our discussion of geometric rates of return, we will review the meaning of the natural logarithm.)

The median or middle return of a normal, perfectly symmetrical probability distribution is equal to the average of the two extreme returns.

Median return = (69.3% + −69.3%)/2
$$= 0.0 / 2$$
$$= 0.0$$

Standard deviation is a measure of how much individual outcomes, on average, differ from a distribution's median outcome. At the 99.7% confidence level, a normal probability distribution spans six standard deviations. The range of this forecast for 183 days is from a return of 69.3% to a return of −69.3%. Therefore,

One standard deviation = (69.3% − −69.3%) / 6
$$= 138.6 / 6$$
$$= 23.1\%$$

You see on-screen that the period standard deviation is 23.1049%.

These two numbers, the median return and the standard deviation, are all the information you need to draw a normal probability distribution.

What this forecast with a median of 0.0% and a standard deviation of 23.1% says is that you are 99.7% confident that 183 days from today the price of the stock will be somewhere between $50 and $200. There is a 0.15% chance that the price will be greater than $200 and a 0.15% chance that the price will be less than $50.

You are 99.7% certain that the return will be somewhere between 69.3% and −69.3%. There is a 0.15% chance that the return will be greater than 69.3% and a 0.15% chance that the return will be less than −69.3%.

The bell shape of the probability distribution indicates that at the end of the 183 days prices are more likely to be near the middle of the distribution than they are to be at or near the extremes.

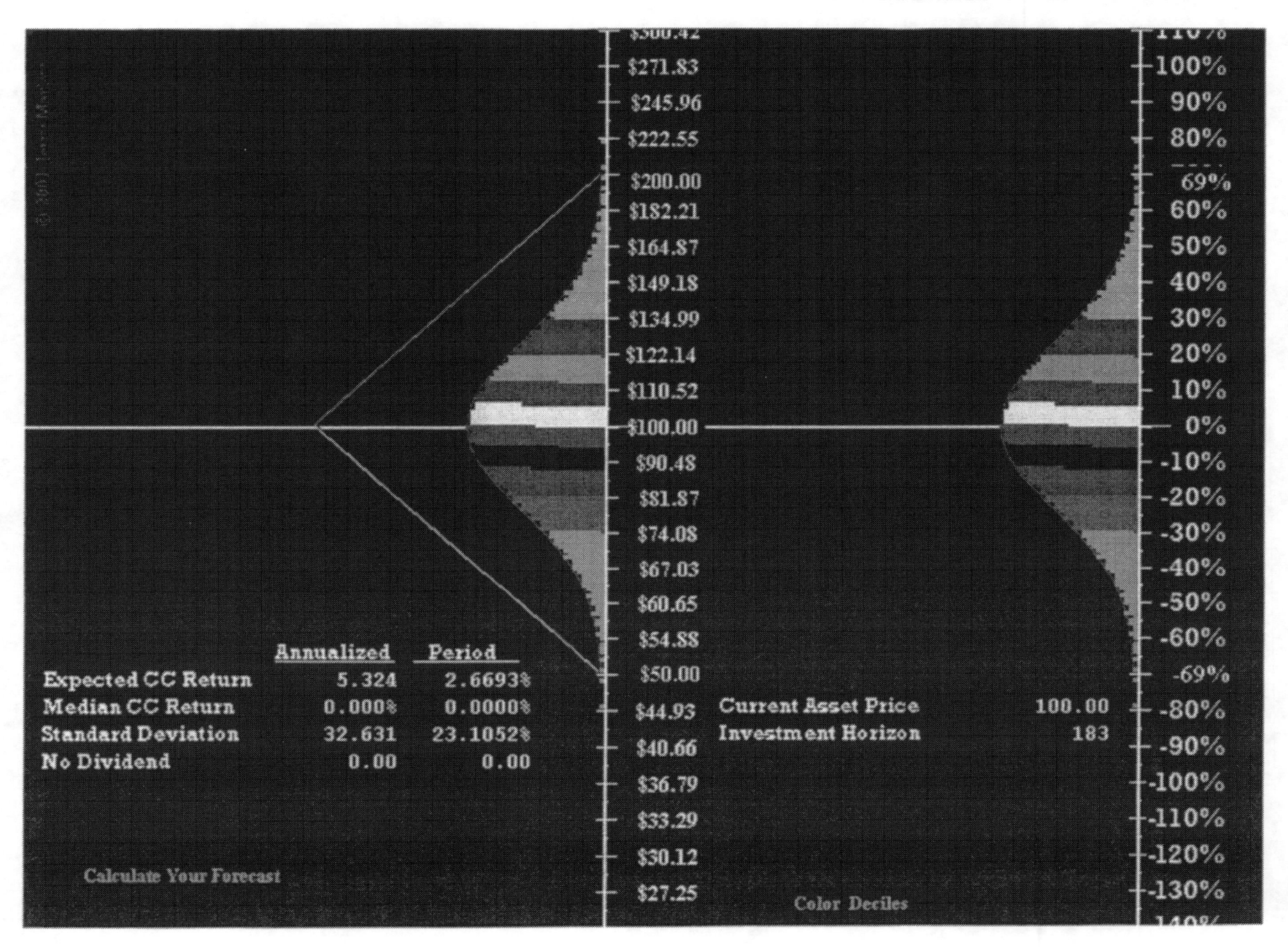

	Annualized	Period
Expected CC Return	5.324	2.6693%
Median CC Return	0.000%	0.0000%
Standard Deviation	32.631	23.1052%
No Dividend	0.00	0.00

Current Asset Price	100.00
Investment Horizon	183

Calculate Your Forecast

Color Deciles

At the end of the investment period, there's 1 chance in 10 that the price will be in any given decile of the probability distribution.

When you're working with normal probability distributions, on average 68.3% of the outcomes fall within one standard deviation of the median, 95.4% of the outcomes fall within two standard deviations of the median, and 99.7% of the outcomes fall within three standard deviations of the median.

(Later, we'll look at how you can calculate a stock's historical standard deviation from a history of its returns. We'll also discuss the relationship among median return, standard deviation, and expected return.)

In case you're not accustomed to working with standard deviations, the animation divides probability distributions into deciles.

10. Click on Color Deciles.

On average, 10% of the outcomes can be expected to fall within each decile or color band.

Or—to express the same idea a little differently—at the end of the investment period, there's 1 chance in 10 that the price will be in any given decile of the probability distribution.

Be kind to your brain.

The animations make the topics we're exploring seem simple and easy. They're not. By the end of the animations—which you could go through in a few hours—you will have explored ideas, principles, and concepts that graduate business schools sometimes take months or even years to cover.

To become familiar with the animation routines, at the end of each section, go back through the steps in the section and play around with numbers of your own. Get a feel for how changing one variable changes the animation outcomes.

Before beginning a new section, check if the numbering of the animation steps continues from the previous section. If it does, the new section picks up where the previous one left off. If you've been playing around with your own numbers, before continuing, step through the previous section and enter the numbers from this book.

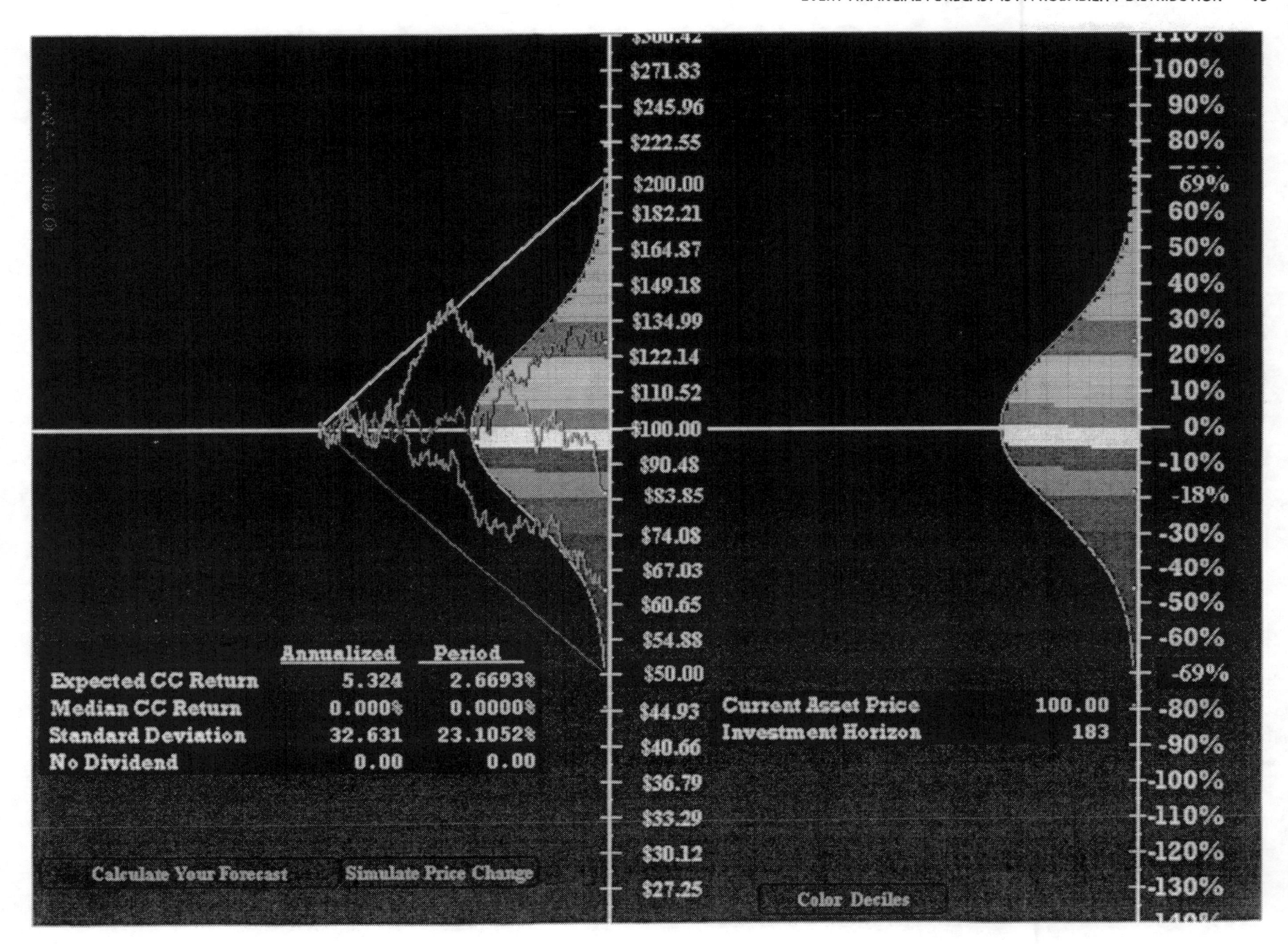

You can translate a forecast into potential price paths.

Using the median and standard deviation of a forecast, you can simulate potential price paths over the investment horizon.

Continuing with our example, we can simulate potential price paths over the investment horizon of 183 days.

11. Click on Simulate Price Change.

What you most likely see is a price path that moves around between the two extreme price paths and that ends up at a price somewhere in between $200 and $50.

12. Click on Simulate Price Change again.

Chances are you get a very different price path that ends up at a different end-of-period price.

13. Click on Simulate Price Change a few more times.

All of these potential price paths are being generated from the same forecast. You see that having a forecast does not necessarily give you much information about what the end-of-period price or end-of-period return is going to be. As the academics say, "Investing is about decision making under conditions of uncertainty."

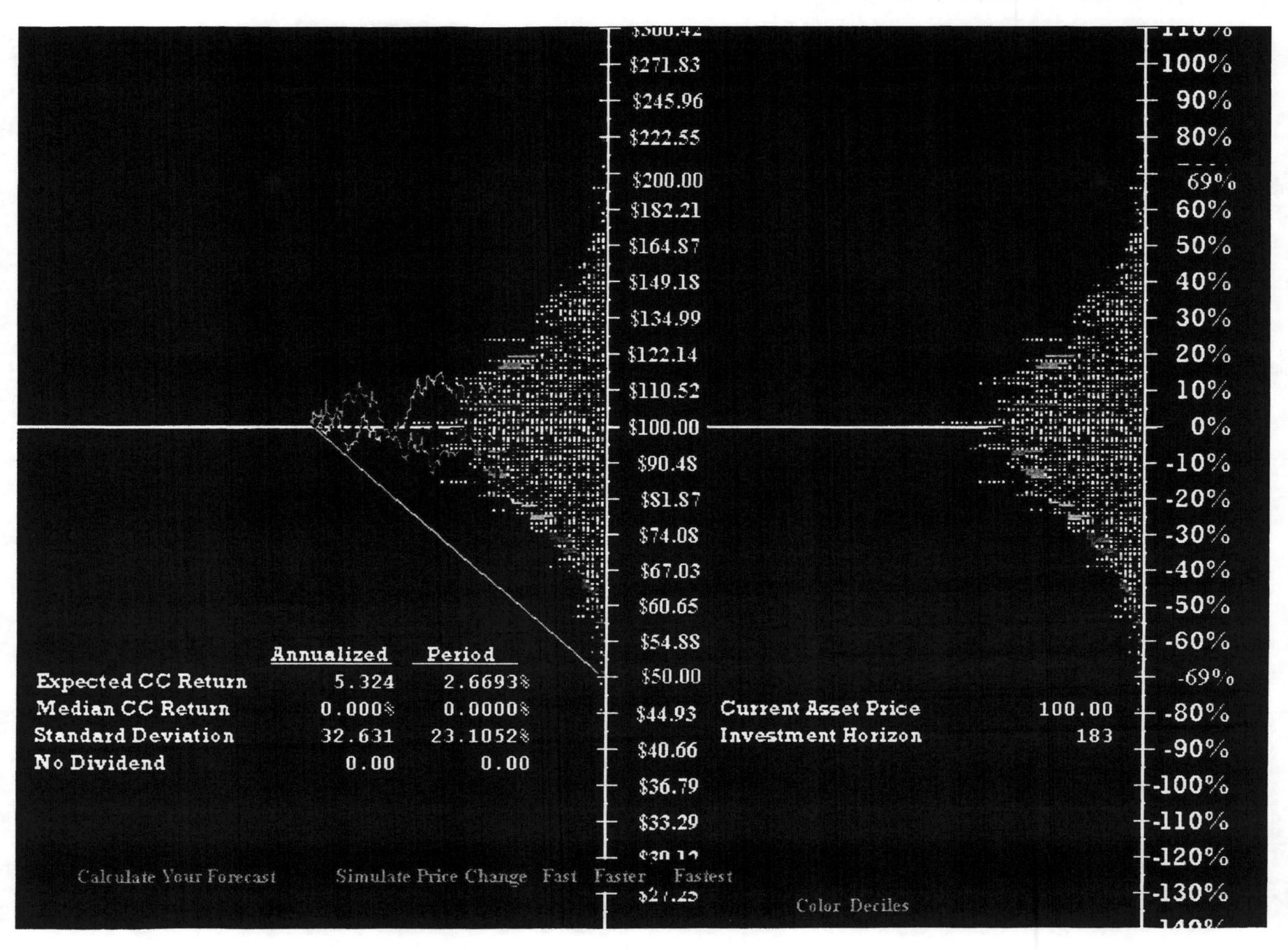

	Annualized	Period
Expected CC Return	5.324	2.6693%
Median CC Return	0.000%	0.0000%
Standard Deviation	32.631	23.1052%
No Dividend	0.00	0.00

Current Asset Price   100.00
Investment Horizon   183

Calculate Your Forecast   Simulate Price Change Fast Faster Fastest

Color Deciles

Structured Monte Carlo simulations show you the relationship between potential price paths and financial forecasts.

Notice that each time you generate a price path, the animation tabulates each end-of-period price and each end-of-period return with a little square.

Instead of drawing the potential price path, you can just simulate the end-of-period price and end-of-period return.

14. Click on Fast just to the right of Simulate Price Change.

You see that the animation skips the potential price path and jumps to the end-of-period price and return.

15. Click on Faster to the right of Simulate Price Change.

The animation keeps simulating end-of-period prices and returns. To tabulate each, it adds new squares at the heights of the end-of-period price and return.

16. Click on Fastest.

The animation simulates enough end-of-period prices and end-of-period returns to fill in the areas of the probability distributions. Each pattern of squares creates a histogram that approximates the shape of the probability distribution or forecast.

If you've never run a structured Monte Carlo simulation before, congratulations. You just did. That's what generating, accumulating, and tabulating outcomes in this way is called.

17. Click on Draw Your Forecast.

You see how closely the shape of the histogram matches that of your forecast.

Monte Carlo Simulations

Here we're using a Monte Carlo simulation to help depict some of the relationships among a probability distribution, potential price paths, and a histogram. Investment firms often use structured Monte Carlo simulations to price derivatives whose payoffs are based on the interactions of many different financial instruments.

Using the probability distribution of each instrument and the correlations among them, the firms simulate potential outcomes for each instrument and tabulate the combined outcomes. Even though the outcome for each instrument is uncertain, a histogram of the combined outcomes shows the range and pattern of potential interactions.

Later, we'll use structured Monte Carlo simulations as one way to price options.

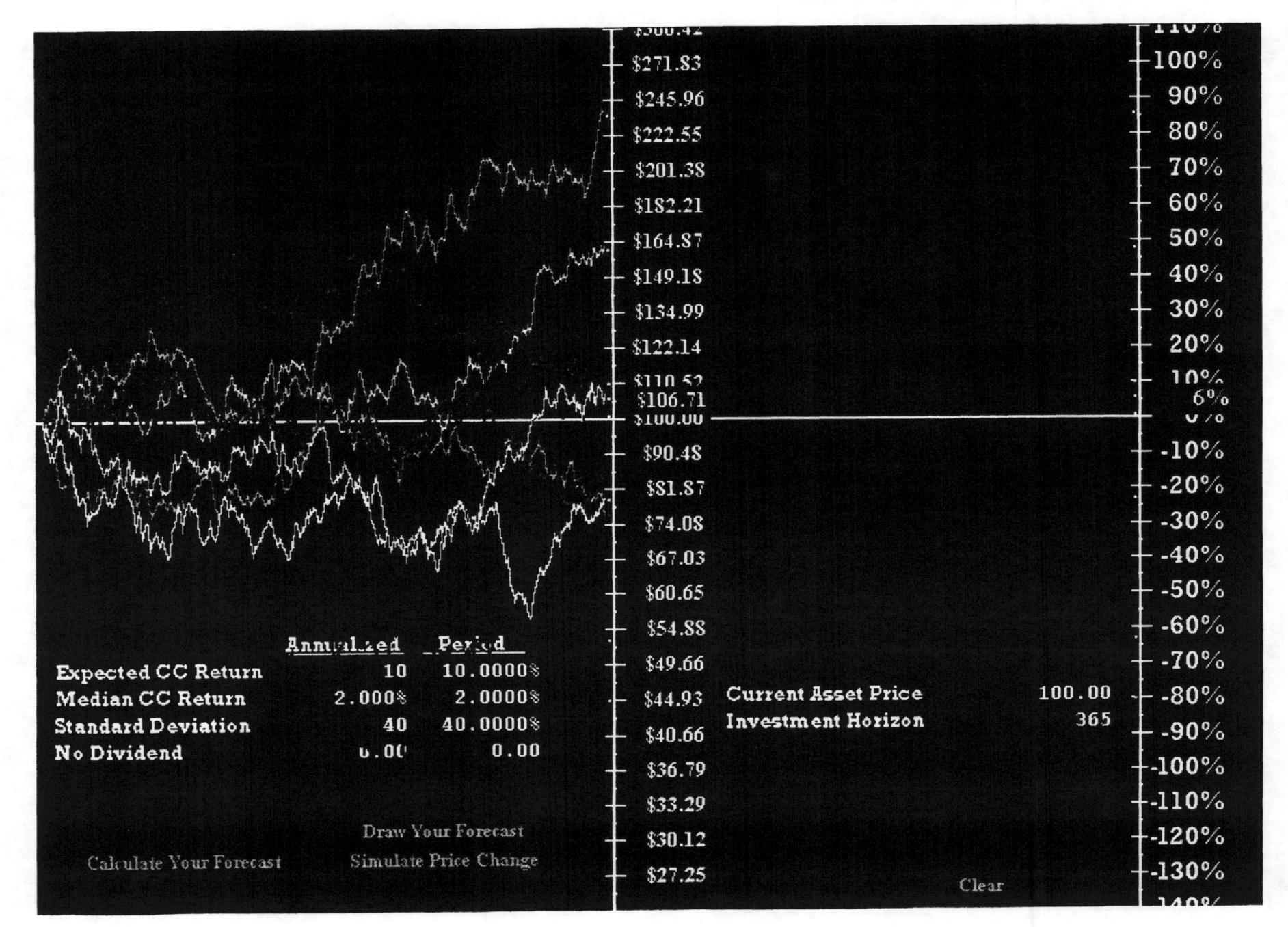

From its historical returns, you can calculate a stock's historical standard deviation.

Standard deviation is a measure of how much individual returns, on average, differ from a normal distribution's mean or median return. (In a normal distribution, the mean and median are the same.)

We've been using median returns and standard deviations to simulate potential future returns of stocks. From historical returns, you can calculate a stock's historical mean return and standard deviation.

To demonstrate, first we generate a hypothetical sample of historical returns; then we find the sample's mean and standard deviation.

> **18.** Click three times on Clear.
>
> **19.** Tab to Expected CC Return and enter 10.
>
> **20.** For Standard Deviation, enter 40.00.
>
> **21.** For Current Asset Price, enter 100.00.
>
> **22.** For Investment Horizon, enter 365.
>
> **23.** Click 10 times on Simulate Price Change. Each time, record the return.

The calculations that follow use the returns from the screen capture: −80%, 48%, 1%, −27%, −63%, −23%, 10%, 86%, −14%, and 6%. (With small samples like this one, the sample mean and standard deviation are likely to differ noticeably from those used to generate the returns.)

1. Record returns as decimals and sum.

$$
\begin{array}{r}
-0.800 \\
0.480 \\
0.010 \\
-0.270 \\
-0.630 \\
-0.230 \\
0.100 \\
0.860 \\
-0.140 \\
\underline{0.060} \\
-0.560
\end{array}
$$

2. Find the mean return.

$$\frac{-0.560}{10} = -0.056$$

3. Find the difference between each return and the mean.

$$
\begin{array}{rcr}
-0.800 - (-0.056) &=& -0.744 \\
0.480 - (-0.056) &=& 0.536 \\
0.010 - (-0.056) &=& 0.066 \\
-0.270 - (-0.056) &=& -0.214 \\
-0.630 - (-0.056) &=& -0.574 \\
-0.230 - (-0.056) &=& -0.174 \\
0.100 - (-0.056) &=& 0.156 \\
0.860 - (-0.056) &=& 0.916 \\
-0.140 - (-0.056) &=& -0.084 \\
0.060 - (-0.056) &=& 0.116
\end{array}
$$

4. Square the differences and sum the squares. (Squaring gets rid of the minus signs.)

$$
\begin{array}{rcl}
-0.744^2 &=& 0.553536 \\
0.536^2 &=& 0.287296 \\
0.066^2 &=& 0.004356 \\
-0.214^2 &=& 0.045796 \\
-0.574^2 &=& 0.329476 \\
-0.174^2 &=& 0.030276 \\
0.156^2 &=& 0.024336 \\
0.916^2 &=& 0.839056 \\
-0.084^2 &=& 0.007056 \\
0.116^2 &=& \underline{0.013456} \\
&& 2.134640
\end{array}
$$

5. Divide the sum by the number of returns minus one. The result of this operation is the variance.

$$\frac{2.134640}{(10-1)} = 0.237182$$

6. To get the standard deviation, take the square root of the variance.

$$\sqrt{0.237182} = 0.487014$$

Standard deviation = 48.70%

(In practice, it's much easier to use the STDEV function in spreadsheet software such as Excel.)

Black-Scholes Assumptions (Part I)

The animations you have drawn embody several of the Black-Scholes assumptions.

Black-Scholes Options-Pricing Theory makes a number of assumptions about investors and the behavior of the financial markets. The animations that you thus far have drawn embody several of these assumptions:

■ Stock returns expressed as geometric rates of return are normally distributed.

■ Price changes are lognormally distributed.

■ The potential price paths of a stock can be characterized by a geometric Brownian motion model.

■ The volatility of a stock's price path is constant over the investment horizon.

The next few pages explain what these assumptions mean, how they are incorporated into the animations, and how they may differ from your customary way of thinking.

Black-Scholes makes several other assumptions about investors and the behavior of the financial markets. We will draw your attention to those as they come into play in the animations.

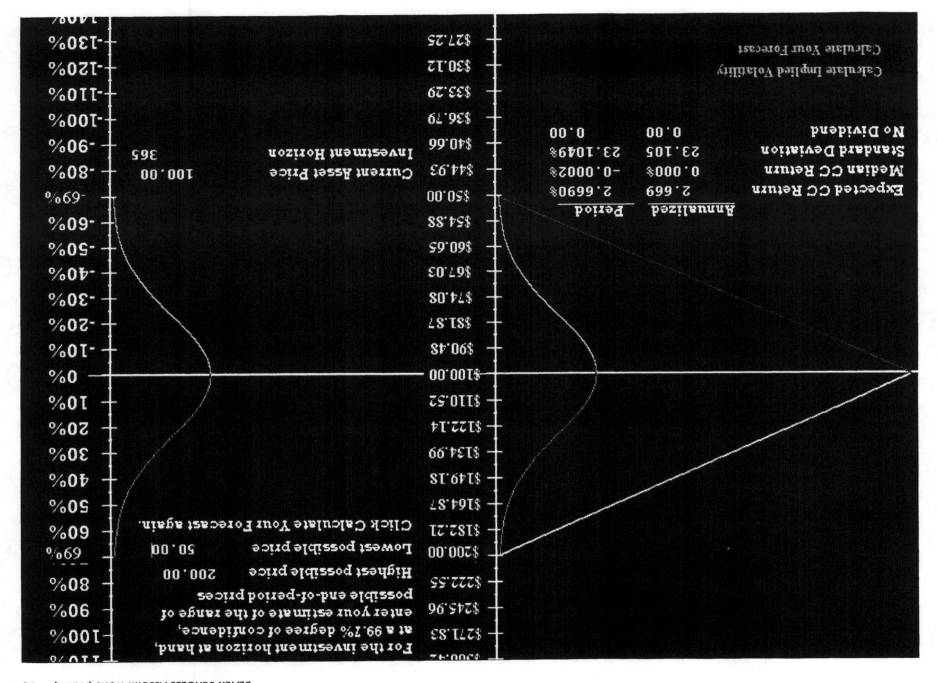

Assumption: Stock returns expressed as geometric or continuously compounded rates of return are normally distributed.

Black-Scholes Options-Pricing Theory assumes that stock returns expressed as geometric rates of return are normally distributed. Accordingly, the animations and simulations draw return forecasts as normal distributions on axes labeled with geometric rates of return.

To see how geometric rates of return correspond to price changes, let's take a look at a $100 stock whose one-year forecast ranges from doubling in value to losing half its value.

1. To zero out all the data fields, click twice on Clear.

2. To make everything on-screen go away, click two or three times on Hide.

3. Click on Calculate Your Forecast.

4. Click in or tab to the field Current Asset Price.

5. Enter 100.00.

6. For Investment Horizon, enter 365.

7. For Highest possible price, enter 200.00.

8. For Lowest possible price, enter 50.00.

9. Click Calculate Your Forecast.

You see that a doubling of the stock price corresponds to a geometric rate of return of 69%. A halving of the price corresponds to a geometric rate of return of −69%.

Geometric rates of return are the same as continuously compounded rates of return. The idea is that any percentage change in the stock price instantly creates a new base for future percentage changes. Consequently, when prices are going up, the base keeps getting bigger. When prices are going down, the base keeps getting smaller.

In general, the same principle is at work whenever you have compounding gains or losses.

For example, a 10% gain compounded seven times produces almost double the initial value:

$$(\$100.00)(110\%) = \$110.00$$
$$(\$110.00)(110\%) = \$121.00$$
$$(\$121.00)(110\%) = \$133.10$$
$$(\$133.10)(110\%) = \$146.41$$
$$(\$146.41)(110\%) = \$161.05$$
$$(\$161.05)(110\%) = \$177.16$$
$$(\$177.16)(110\%) = \$194.87$$

A 10% loss compounded seven times reduces the initial value by slightly more than half:

$$(\$100.00)(90\%) = \$90.00$$
$$(\$90.00)(90\%) = \$81.00$$
$$(\$81.00)(90\%) = \$72.90$$
$$(\$72.90)(90\%) = \$65.61$$
$$(\$65.61)(90\%) = \$59.05$$
$$(\$59.05)(90\%) = \$53.14$$
$$(\$53.14)(90\%) = \$47.83$$

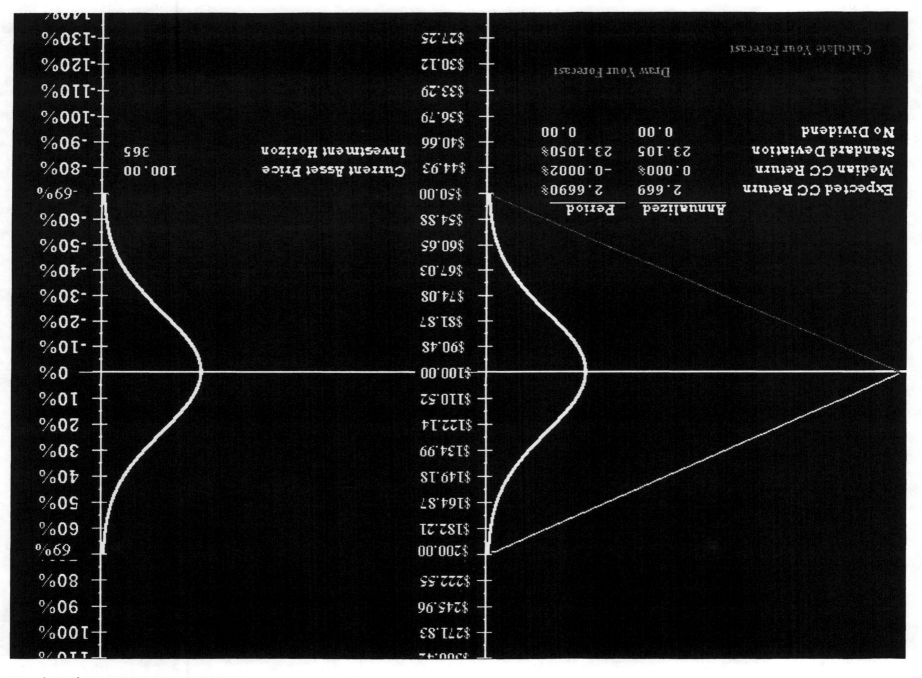

Assumption: Stock price changes are lognormally distributed.

The exponential e serves as the base for natural logarithms and is used to compute continuously compounded or geometric rates of return.

A more formal look at continuous compounding shows how one arrives at the value of the exponential e.

In general, if we let r represent a period, simple rate of return and n represent the number of times the rate of return is compounded during the period, then the growth factor for the period is equal to $(1 + r/n)^n$.

For example, for $100 with a period, simple rate of return of 70% compounded seven times,

$$(\$100)\left(1 + \frac{r}{n}\right)^n$$

gives:

$$(\$100)\left(1 + \frac{0.70}{7}\right)^7$$

$$= (\$100)(1.10)^7$$
$$= (\$100)(1.9487)$$
$$= \$194.87$$

To take another example, for $100 with a period, simple rate of return of 100% compounded a million times,

$$(\$100)\left(1 + \frac{r}{n}\right)^n$$

gives:

$$(\$100)\left(1 + \frac{1.00}{1,000,000}\right)^{1,000,000}$$

$$= (\$100)(1.000001)^{1,000,000}$$
$$= (\$100)(2.718280)$$
$$= \$271.83$$

While a million is a large number of times to compound a rate of return, with continuous compounding, n becomes infinitely large.

The exponential e is defined as the value of $(1 + r/n)^n$ with r equal to 100% and n infinitely large. The value of $(1 + 1.00/n)^n$ as n approaches infinity is approximately equal to 2.718281828459050. Hence, this number is the value of e, the base for natural logarithms.

Taking the natural log of an end-of-period price divided by the start-of-period price gives the continuously compounded rate of return:

$$\ln (\$200.00/\$100.00) = 69.315\%$$
$$\ln (\$271.83/\$100.00) = 100\%$$
$$\ln (\$50.00/\$100.00) = -69.315\%$$

Multiplying a start-of-period price by the exponential raised to the power of the continuously compounded rate of return gives the end-of-period value:

$$(\$100.00)(\exp(0.69315)) = \$200.00$$
$$(\$100.00)(\exp(1.00)) = \$271.83$$
$$(\$100.00)(\exp(-0.69315)) = \$50.00$$

In the animations, the prices on the price axis make up a logarithmic or log scale. They correspond to the continuously compounded rates of return on the return axis. When we draw a normal distribution on the logarithmic price scale, we model price changes as being lognormally distributed.

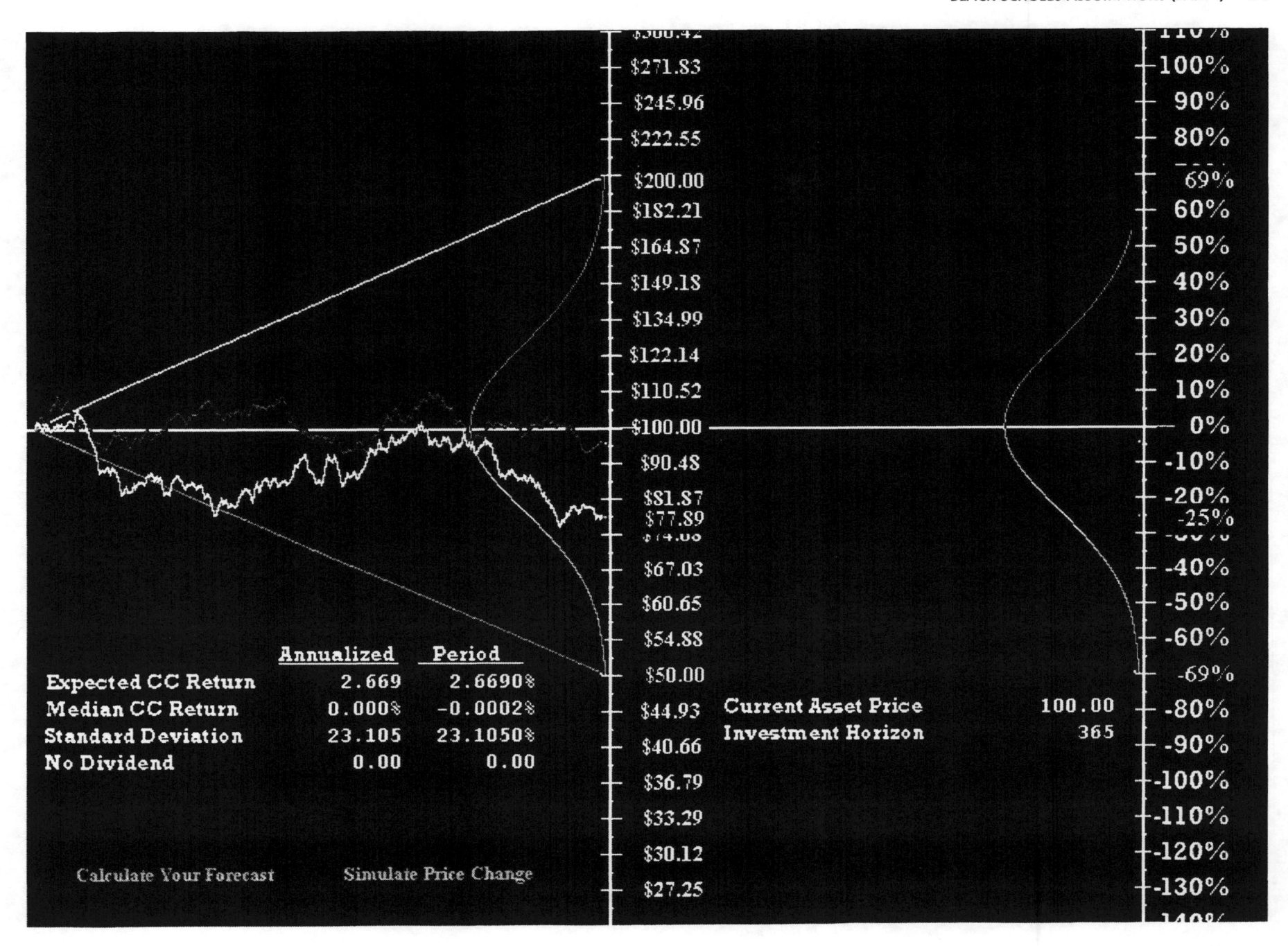

Assumption: The potential price paths of a stock can be characterized by a geometric Brownian motion model.

Under the Black-Scholes assumptions, stock price paths follow a pattern described as geometric Brownian motion. Brownian motion is named for Robert Brown, a Scottish botanist.

Under his microscope, Brown, in 1827, noticed a "rapid oscillatory motion" of pollen grains suspended in water.

In 1905, Albert Einstein explained the motion as resulting from random differences between the pressures of molecules bombarding opposite sides of each pollen grain. The differences cause a grain constantly to wobble back and forth. Over a period of time, a grain tends to drift from its starting point. The probability of a grain moving a certain distance is characterized by a normal distribution.

Scientists and mathematicians have found Brownian motion to be a good model for many phenomena.

In Black-Scholes modeling, stock prices correspond to Brown's pollen grains. Bids and offers correspond to the molecules of water. Trades correspond to the collisions of the water molecules with pollen grains. Bids and offers, in a random way, knock the price of a stock up and down around the median return.

> To take another look at potential price paths characterized by geometric Brownian motion,
>
> 10. Click a few times on Simulate Price Change.

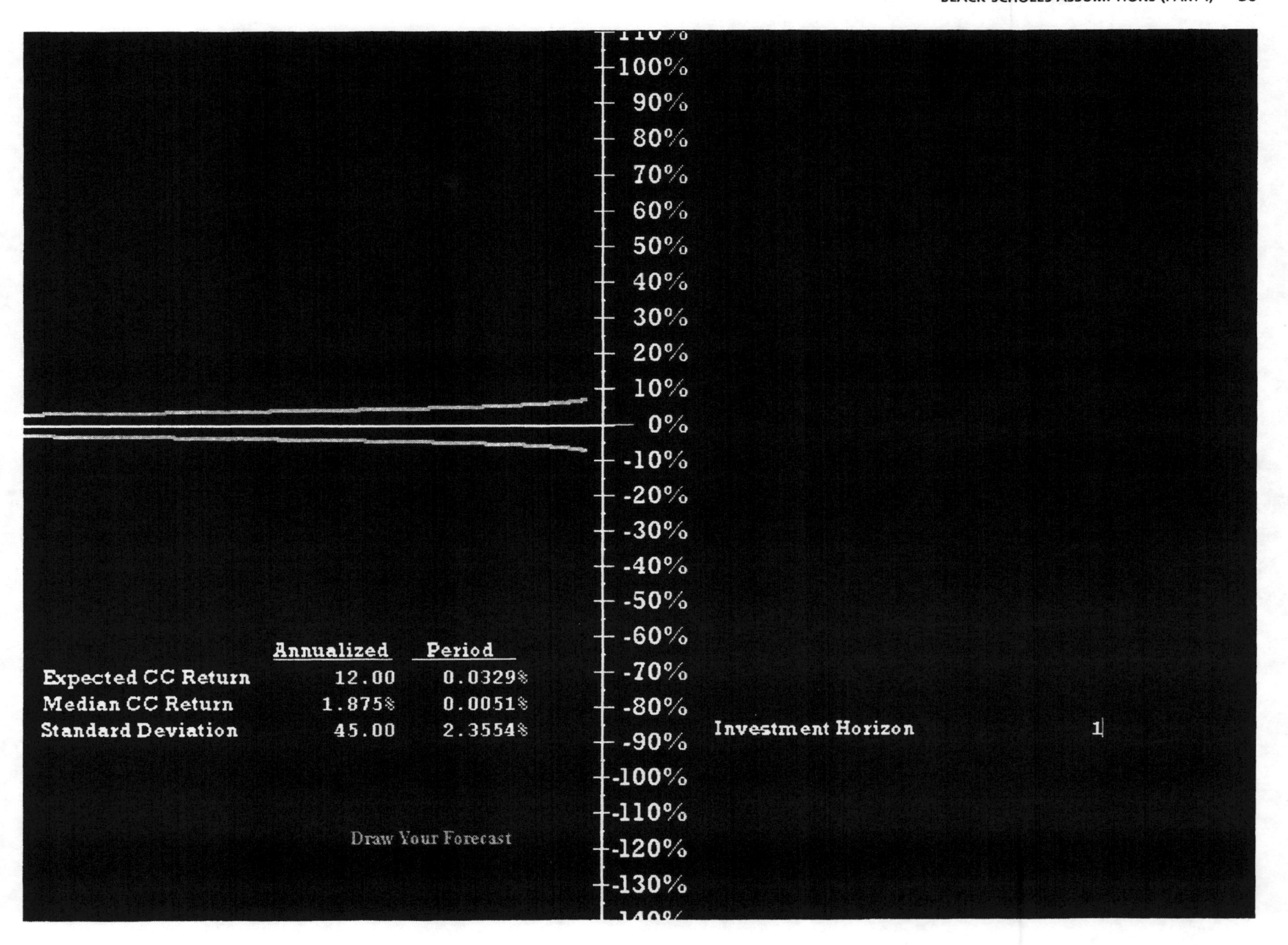

	Annualized	Period
Expected CC Return	12.00	0.0329%
Median CC Return	1.875%	0.0051%
Standard Deviation	45.00	2.3554%

Investment Horizon   1

Draw Your Forecast

Assumption: The volatility of a financial asset's price path is constant over the life of the option.

The characteristic volatilities of financial assets sometimes change. If the characteristic volatility changes during the life of an option, the value of the option changes.

The Black-Scholes model, however, does not allow for midlife volatility changes. It assumes that the underlying's volatility will be constant over the life of the option.

To model the potential price paths of financial assets, the animation:

■ Calculates the one-day distribution of possible returns

■ Takes a random sample of that distribution

■ Increases or decreases the start-of-day price by that amount

The animation repeats this cycle of calculations for however many days are in the investment horizon.

To see what the one-day distribution of an asset's returns might look like:

1. Click twice on Clear.

2. Click two or three times on Hide.

3. Click on Draw Your Forecast.

4. For Investment Horizon, enter 1.

5. For Annualized Expected CC Return, enter 12.00.

6. For Standard Deviation, enter 45.00.

7. Click on Draw Your Forecast.

Working with Geometric or Continuously Compounded Rates of Return

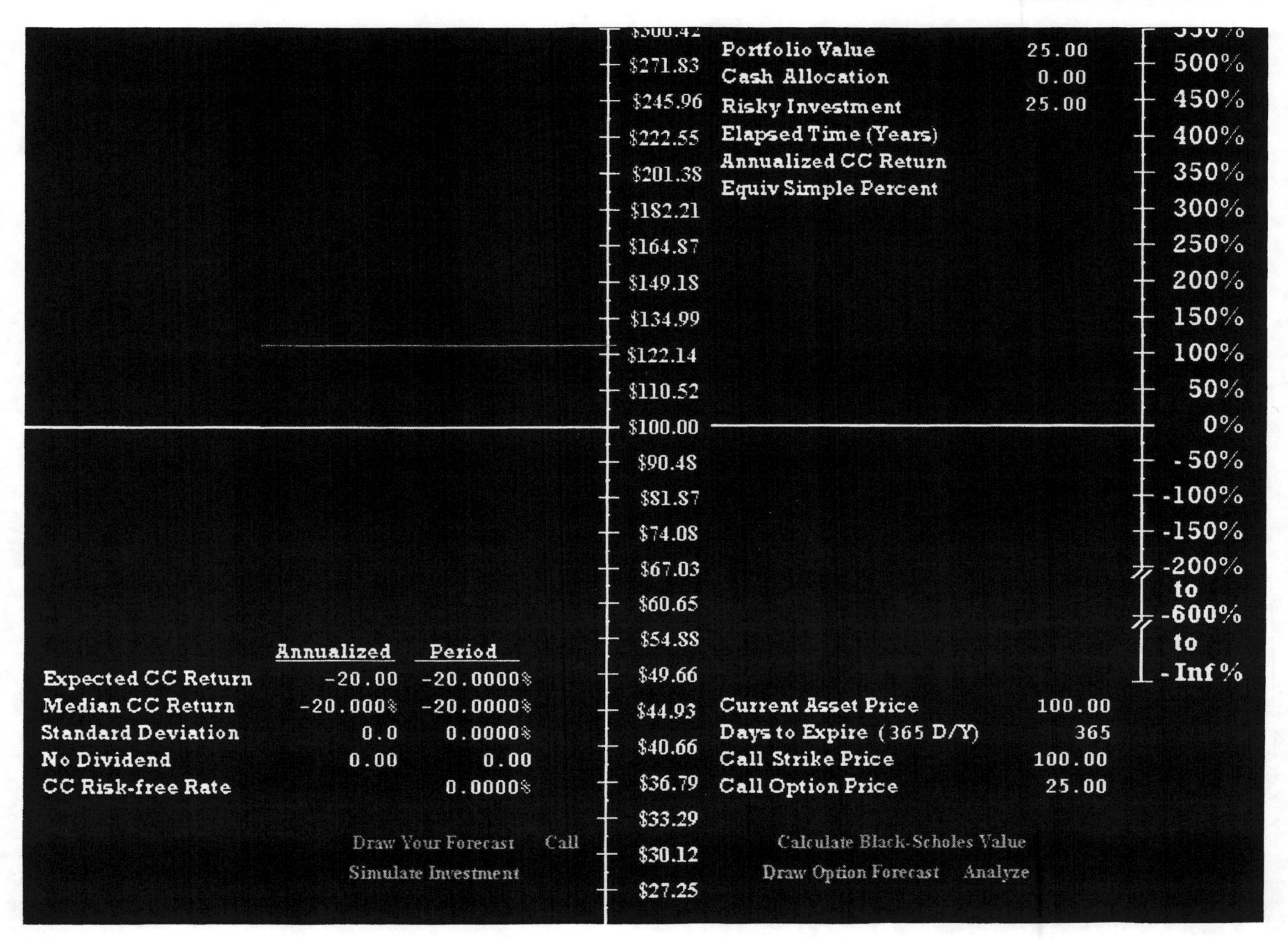

	$300.42	Portfolio Value	25.00	330%
	$271.83	Cash Allocation	0.00	500%
	$245.96	Risky Investment	25.00	450%
	$222.55	Elapsed Time (Years)		400%
	$201.38	Annualized CC Return		350%
		Equiv Simple Percent		
	$182.21			300%
	$164.87			250%
	$149.18			200%
	$134.99			150%
	$122.14			100%
	$110.52			50%
	$100.00			0%
	$90.48			-50%
	$81.87			-100%
	$74.08			-150%
	$67.03			-200%
	$60.65			to
	$54.88			-600%
				to
	$49.66			- Inf%

	Annualized	Period
Expected CC Return	-20.00	-20.0000%
Median CC Return	-20.000%	-20.0000%
Standard Deviation	0.0	0.0000%
No Dividend	0.00	0.00
CC Risk-free Rate		0.0000%

$44.93	Current Asset Price	100.00
$40.66	Days to Expire (365 D/Y)	365
	Call Strike Price	100.00
$36.79	Call Option Price	25.00
$33.29	
$30.12	
$27.25	

Draw Your Forecast   Call

Simulate Investment

Calculate Black-Scholes Value

Draw Option Forecast   Analyze

Geometric or continuously compounded rates of return may not be your customary way of thinking.

If you are accustomed to working with simple percentage, holding-period returns, you may find that continuously compounded rates of return give results at odds with your customary ways of thinking.

Let's look at a couple of examples of what some people find to be counterintuitive aspects of working with geometric rates of return.

Let's pose the first example as a question: If you lose all your money, what is your continuously compounded rate of return?

Let's say you invest in an at-the-money call option on a stock. The option ends the period out of the money (below the strike price). What is the return on your investment?

Let's see.

> 1. To zero out all the data fields, click three times on Clear.
>
> 2. To make everything on-screen go away, click twice on Hide.
>
> 3. Click on Simulate Price Change.

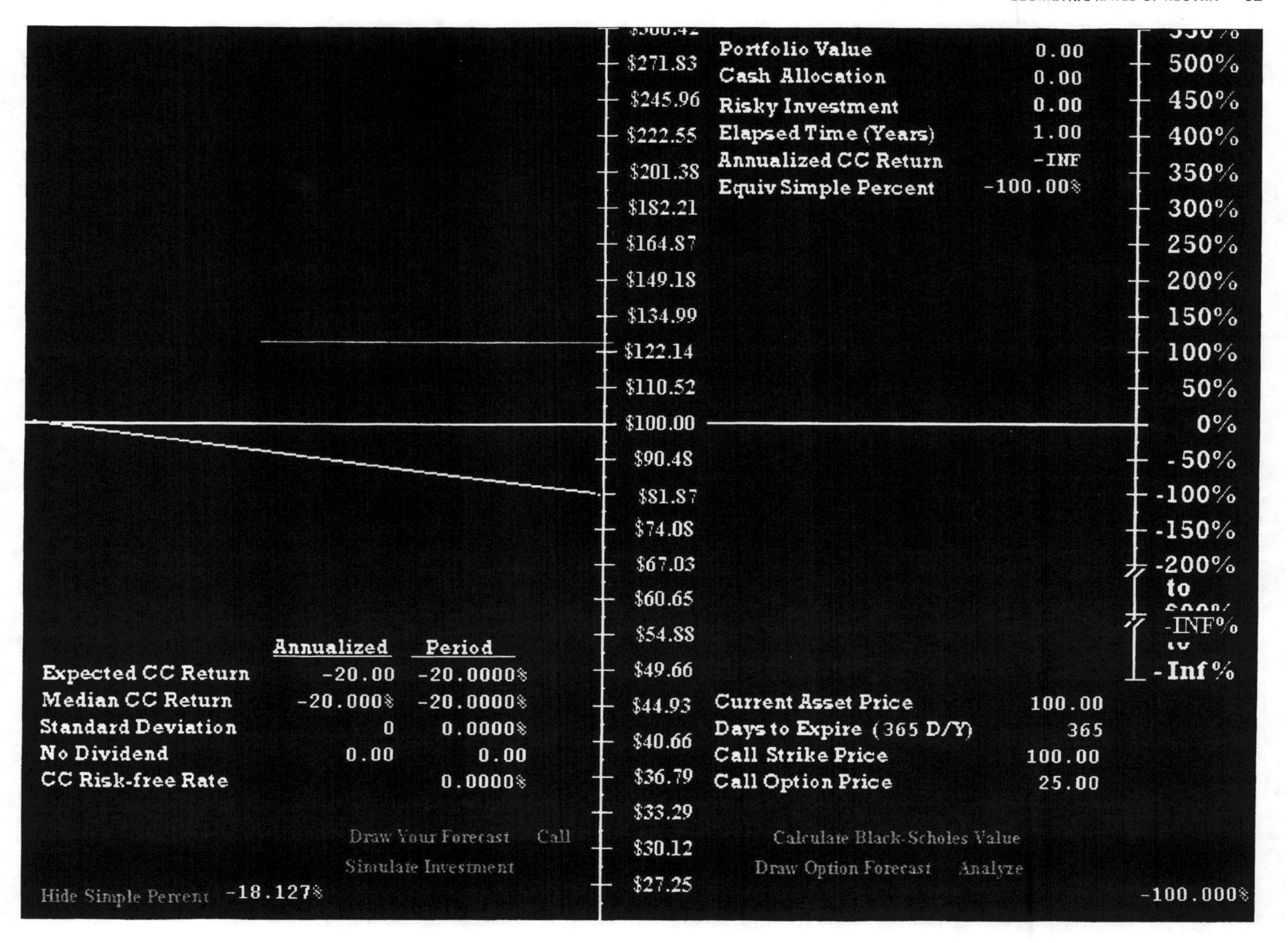

Portfolio Value		0.00
Cash Allocation		0.00
Risky Investment		0.00
Elapsed Time (Years)		1.00
Annualized CC Return		−INF
Equiv Simple Percent		−100.00%

	Annualized	Period
Expected CC Return	−20.00	−20.0000%
Median CC Return	−20.000%	−20.0000%
Standard Deviation	0	0.0000%
No Dividend	0.00	0.00
CC Risk-free Rate		0.0000%

Current Asset Price	100.00
Days to Expire (365 D/Y)	365
Call Strike Price	100.00
Call Option Price	25.00

Draw Your Forecast   Call

Simulate Investment

Hide Simple Percent   −18.127%

Calculate Black-Scholes Value

Draw Option Forecast   Analyze

−100.000%

When you lose all your money, you have a continuously compounded rate of return of negative infinity.

4. For Current Asset Price, enter 100.00. (No $, please.)

5. Click on Draw Option Forecast.

6. Click on Call.

7. For Days to Expire, enter 365.

8. For Call Strike Price, enter 100.00.

9. For Call Option Price, enter 25.00.

10. Click on Invest.

11. For Portfolio Value, enter 25.00.

12. For Risky Investment, enter 25.00. When you have an option on-screen, the risky allocation gets invested in the option.

13. For Expected CC Return, enter –20.00.

14. For Standard Deviation, enter 0.00.

15. Click on Simulate Investment.

The stock price goes to $81.87. The return on the stock is –20%.

The call option you bought finishes out of the money (below the strike price). You lose all your money. The value of your portfolio goes to $0.00. What is your continuously compounded rate of return?

$$CCRR = \ln(\text{end-of-period value} / \text{starting value})$$
$$= \ln(\$0.00 / \$100.00)$$
$$= \ln(0.00)$$
$$= -\text{Infinity}$$

When you lose all your money, you have a continuously compounded rate of return of negative infinity. As you will recall, when you're compounding negative returns, the base keeps getting smaller and smaller. With continuous compounding, to get to zero, the rate of return has to go to negative infinity.

To make it easier for you to keep straight the differences between holding-period returns and continuously compounded or geometric rates of return, the animation almost always displays results in both forms.

16. Click on Show Simple Percent.

The animation does its calculations using geometric rates of returns; then it translates those results into equivalent simple percents.

The little box on the bottom left of your screen displays as an equivalent simple percent the return on the underlying.

When you have an option on screen, the little box on the bottom right displays as an equivalent simple percent the return on the option.

In this example, you see that for the underlying's –20% return the equivalent simple percent is –18.127%. For the option's return of negative infinity, the equivalent simple percent is –100.00%.

Whenever you enter a new value into the field labeled Expected CC Return, the box on the bottom left displays the equivalent simple percent of the period expected continuously compounded rate of return.

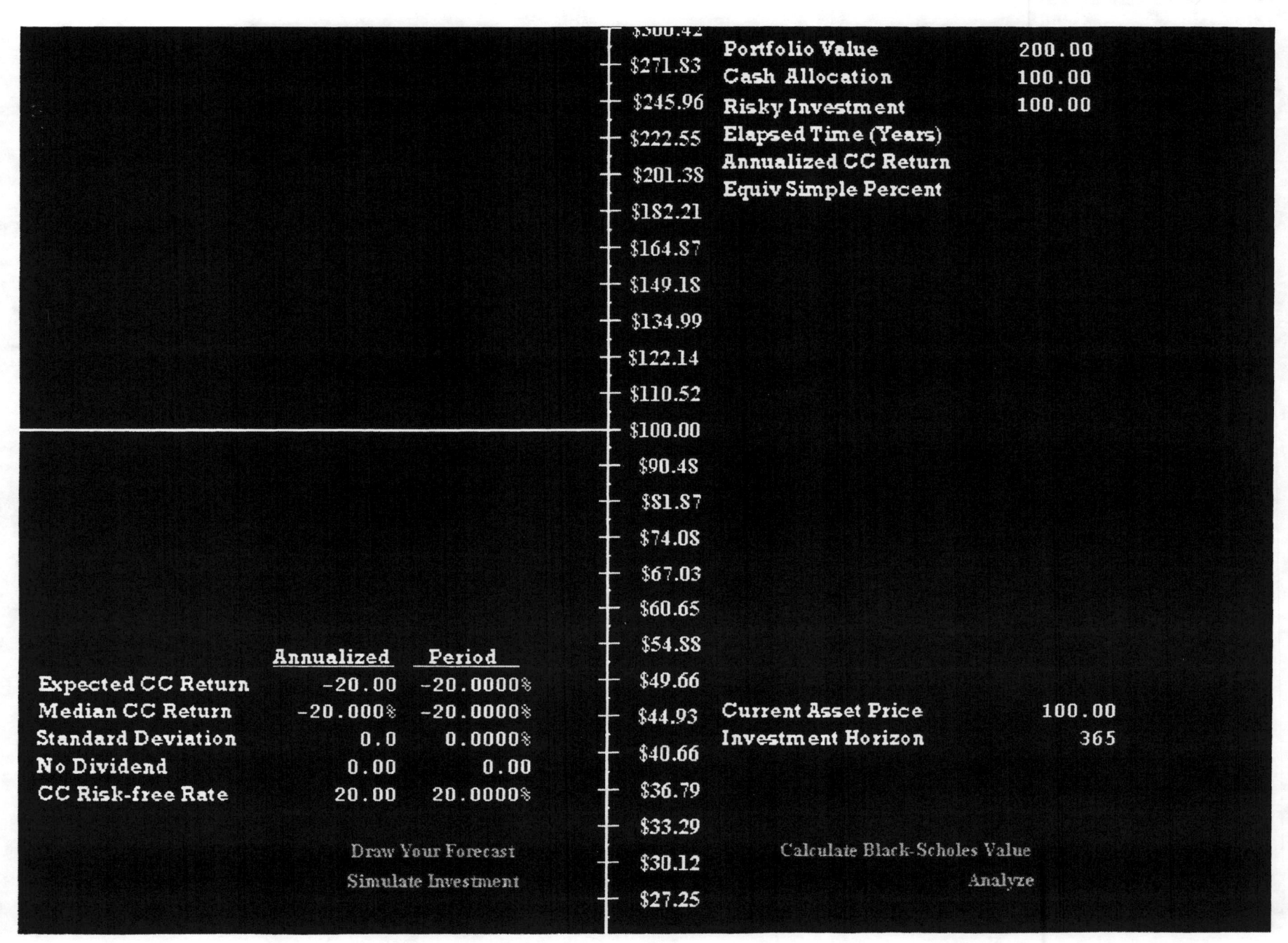

	Annualized	Period
Expected CC Return	-20.00	-20.0000%
Median CC Return	-20.000%	-20.0000%
Standard Deviation	0.0	0.0000%
No Dividend	0.00	0.00
CC Risk-free Rate	20.00	20.0000%

Draw Your Forecast

Simulate Investment

Portfolio Value	200.00
Cash Allocation	100.00
Risky Investment	100.00
Elapsed Time (Years)	
Annualized CC Return	
Equiv Simple Percent	

$300.42
$271.83
$245.96
$222.55
$201.38
$182.21
$164.87
$149.18
$134.99
$122.14
$110.52
$100.00
$90.48
$81.87
$74.08
$67.03
$60.65
$54.88
$49.66
$44.93
$40.66
$36.79
$33.29
$30.12
$27.25

Current Asset Price	100.00
Investment Horizon	365

Calculate Black-Scholes Value

Analyze

In your portfolio, you have two $100 investments. One earns a continuously compounded return of 20%. The other earns a continuously compounded return of -20%. What is the continuously compounded return on your portfolio?

Here's another example of how working with geometric or continuously compounded rates of return can give counterintuitive results.

Let's suppose that Jimmy Carter is president again. The continuously compounded risk-free rate of return is 20%. It's January 1. The value of your portfolio is $200. You're deciding how to allocate your portfolio between two investments: cash and a risky investment.

You allocate $100 to cash (meaning an instrument that will earn the risk-free rate of 20%).

You allocate $100 to a risky investment.

Over the course of the year, one investment earns a return of 20%. The other has a return of -20%.

At the end of the year, what is the return on your portfolio?

Jot down your answer here: _____

Let's see.

1. Click three times on Clear. (The third click clears the portfolio data fields.)
2. Click two or three times on Hide.
3. Click on Invest.
4. For Portfolio Value, enter 200.00. (No $, please.)
5. For Risky Investment, enter 100.00.
6. For CC Risk-free Rate, enter 20.00.
7. For Current Asset Price, enter 100.00.
8. For Investment Horizon, enter 365.
9. Click on Simulate Investment.
10. For Expected CC Return, enter -20.00.
11. For Standard Deviation, enter 0.00.
12. Click on Simulate Investment.

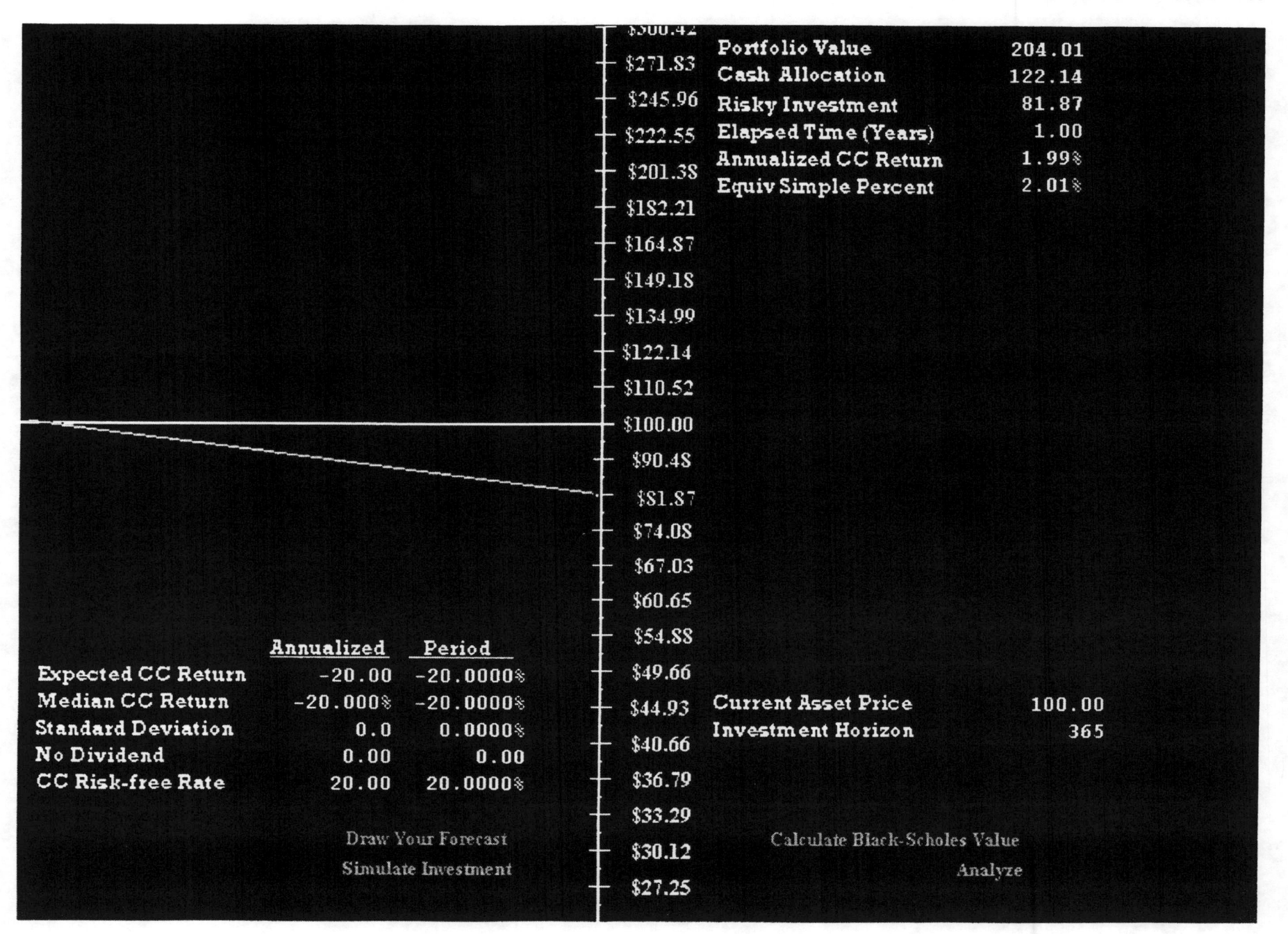

			Portfolio Value	204.01
			Cash Allocation	122.14
			Risky Investment	81.87
			Elapsed Time (Years)	1.00
			Annualized CC Return	1.99%
			Equiv Simple Percent	2.01%

$300.42
$271.83
$245.96
$222.55
$201.38
$182.21
$164.87
$149.18
$134.99
$122.14
$110.52
$100.00
$90.48
$81.87
$74.08
$67.03
$60.65
$54.88
$49.66
$44.93
$40.66
$36.79
$33.29
$30.12
$27.25

	Annualized	Period
Expected CC Return	-20.00	-20.0000%
Median CC Return	-20.000%	-20.0000%
Standard Deviation	0.0	0.0000%
No Dividend	0.00	0.00
CC Risk-free Rate	20.00	20.0000%

Current Asset Price   100.00
Investment Horizon   365

Draw Your Forecast
Simulate Investment

Calculate Black-Scholes Value
Analyze

The portfolio return is not zero, but 1.99%.

With a return of 20%, the cash allocation grows to $122.14.

End-of-period value of the cash allocation = ($100.00)(exp(0.20))
$$= (\$100.00)(1.2214)$$
$$= \$122.14$$

With a return of –20%, the value of the risky investment falls to $81.87.

End-of-period price of risky investment = ($100.00)(exp(–0.20))
$$= (\$100.00)(0.8187)$$
$$= \$81.87$$

The value of the portfolio goes from $200.00 to $204.01 for a return of 1.99%, which is equivalent to a simple or holding-period return of 2.01%.

Portfolio CCRR = ln(end-of-period value / starting value)
$$= \ln((\$122.14 + \$81.87) / \$200.00)$$
$$= \ln(\$204.01 / \$200.00)$$
$$= 1.99\%$$

Equivalent simple percent = exp(CCRR) – 1.00
$$= \exp(0.0199) - 1.00$$
$$= 1.0201 - 1.00$$
$$= 0.0201$$
$$= 2.01\%$$

When you have one investment that earns a return of 20% and another investment of equal initial value that has a return of –20%, the portfolio return is not zero, but 1.99%.

The average return is 1.99%.

When we compute an investment's expected return, you will see at work this same principle of the average return being greater than the middle return.

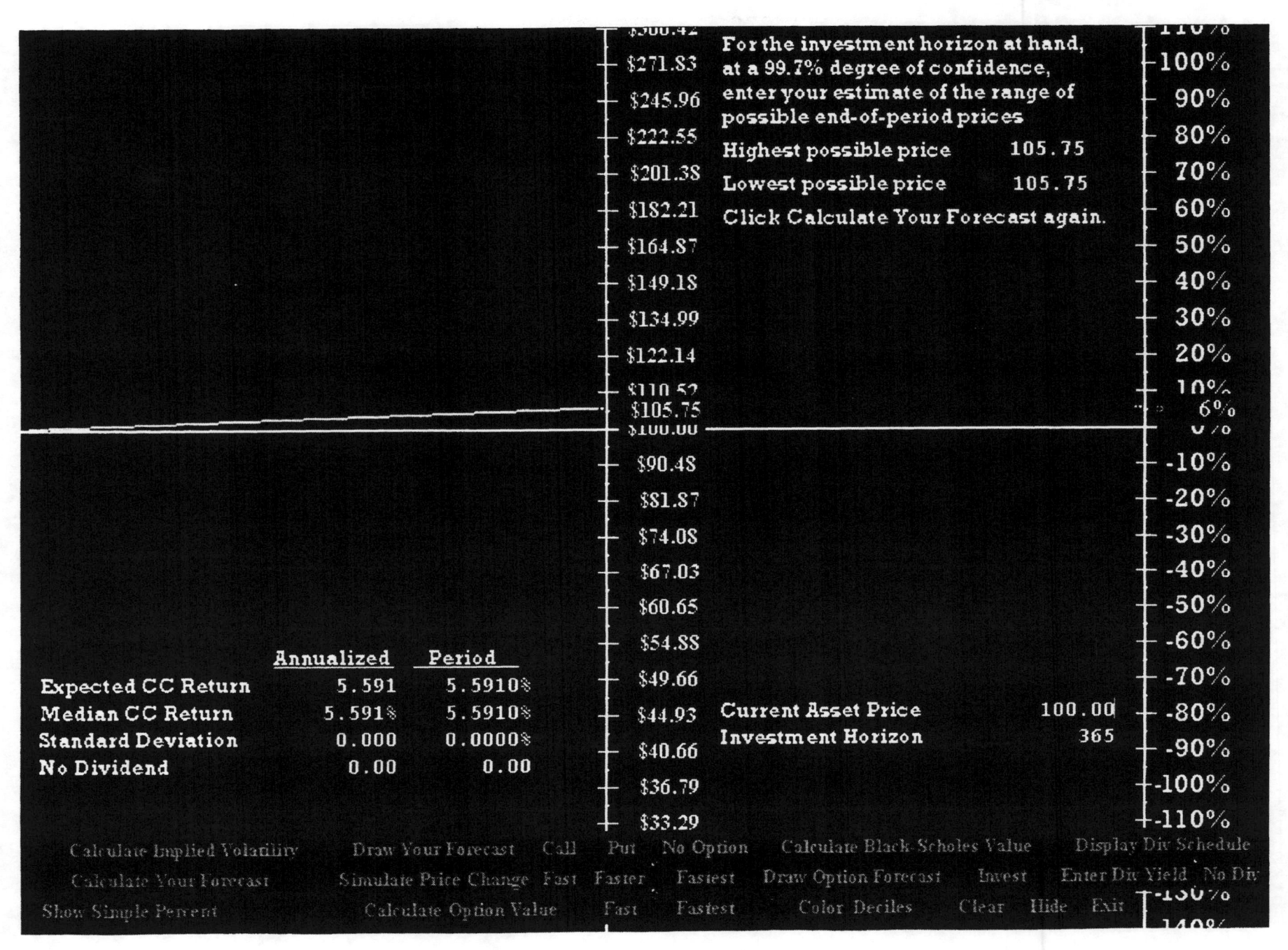

$300.42

$271.83

$245.96

$222.55

$201.38

$182.21

$164.87

$149.18

$134.99

$122.14

$110.52

$105.75

$100.00

$90.48

$81.87

$74.08

$67.03

$60.65

$54.88

$49.66

$44.93

$40.66

$36.79

$33.29

110%

100%

90%

80%

70%

60%

50%

40%

30%

20%

10%

6%

0%

-10%

-20%

-30%

-40%

-50%

-60%

-70%

-80%

-90%

-100%

-110%

For the investment horizon at hand,
at a 99.7% degree of confidence,
enter your estimate of the range of
possible end-of-period prices

Highest possible price   105.75

Lowest possible price   105.75

Click Calculate Your Forecast again.

	Annualized	Period
Expected CC Return	5.591	5.5910%
Median CC Return	5.591%	5.5910%
Standard Deviation	0.000	0.0000%
No Dividend	0.00	0.00

Current Asset Price   100.00

Investment Horizon   365

Calculate Implied Volatility   Draw Your Forecast   Call   Put   No Option   Calculate Black-Scholes Value   Display Div Schedule

Calculate Your Forecast   Simulate Price Change   Fast   Faster   Fastest   Draw Option Forecast   Invest   Enter Div Yield   No Div

Show Simple Percent   Calculate Option Value   Fast   Fastest   Color Deciles   Clear   Hide   Exit

To convert simple interest rates to continuously compounded rates of return, use Calculate Your Forecast.

As a practical matter, you may need to convert simple annual interest rates to continuously compounded rates of return. You can do so easily with Calculate Your Forecast.

Let's say that the annual risk-free interest rate is 5.75%. You want to know what that is as a continuously compounded rate of return.

1. Click three times on Clear.

2. Click twice on Hide.

3. Click on Calculate Your Forecast.

4. For Current Asset Price, enter 100.00.

5. For Investment Horizon, enter 365.

6. For Highest possible price, enter the value of $100.00 a year from today. In our example, that's 105.75.

7. For Lowest possible price, also enter the value of $100.00 a year from today. In our example, 105.75.

8. Click on Calculate Your Forecast.

The continuously compounded rate of return appears in the Expected CC Return box. In our example, it's 5.591%.

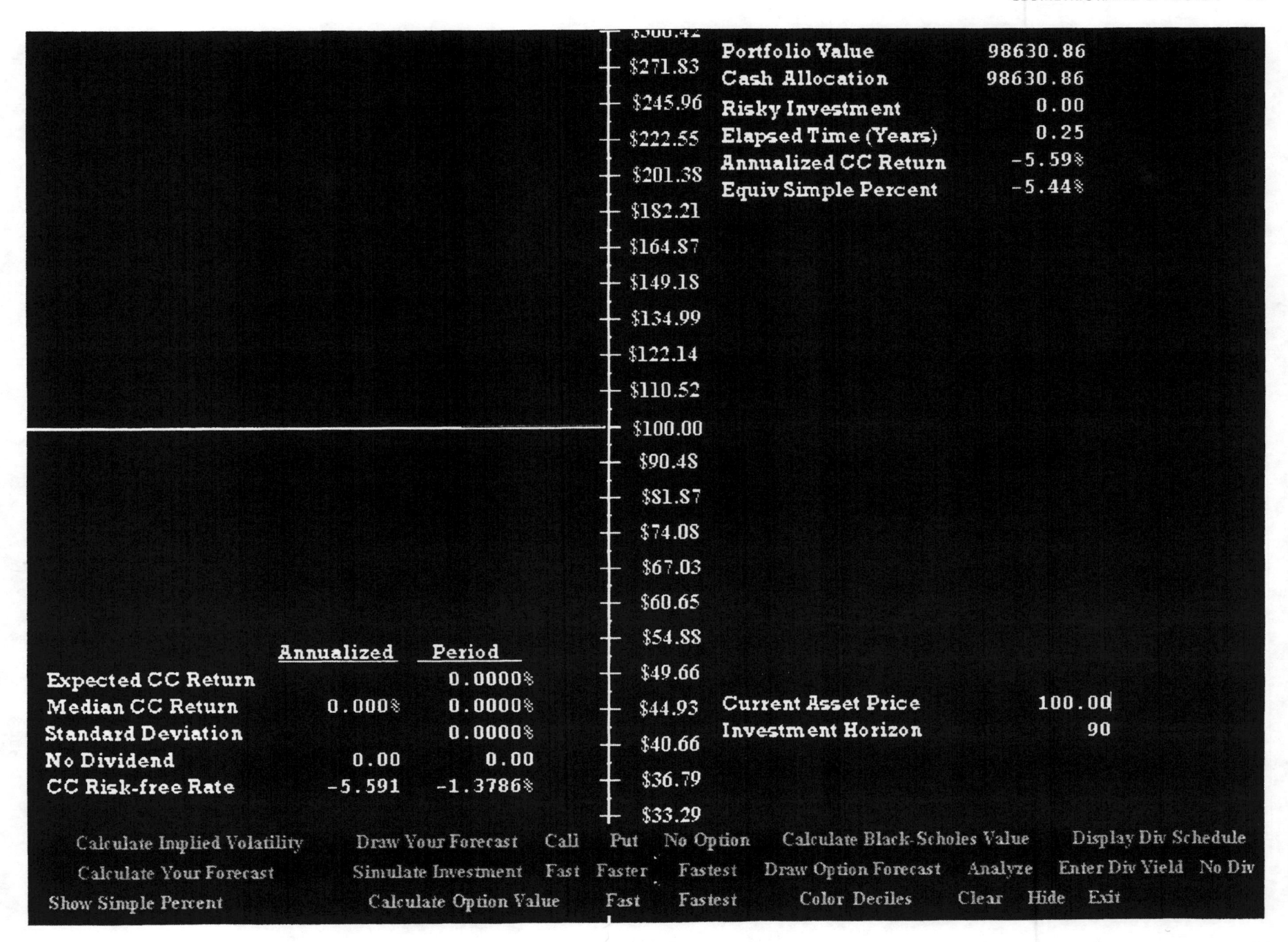

Portfolio Value	98630.86	
Cash Allocation	98630.86	
Risky Investment	0.00	
Elapsed Time (Years)	0.25	
Annualized CC Return	-5.59%	
Equiv Simple Percent	-5.44%	

$300.42
$271.83
$245.96
$222.55
$201.38
$182.21
$164.87
$149.18
$134.99
$122.14
$110.52
$100.00
$90.48
$81.87
$74.08
$67.03
$60.65
$54.88
$49.66
$44.93
$40.66
$36.79
$33.29

	Annualized	Period
Expected CC Return		0.0000%
Median CC Return	0.000%	0.0000%
Standard Deviation		0.0000%
No Dividend	0.00	0.00
CC Risk-free Rate	-5.591	-1.3786%

Current Asset Price   100.00
Investment Horizon   90

Calculate Implied Volatility   Draw Your Forecast   Call   Put   No Option   Calculate Black-Scholes Value   Display Div Schedule

Calculate Your Forecast   Simulate Investment   Fast Faster   Fastest   Draw Option Forecast   Analyze   Enter Div Yield   No Div

Show Simple Percent   Calculate Option Value   Fast   Fastest   Color Deciles   Clear   Hide   Exit

To find the present value of a future dollar amount, use Invest and Simulate Investment.

When you are figuring out your option strategies, you may want to know what amount of money you need to invest today at the risk-free rate of return to reach a target value on some future date. In other words, you may want to know the present value of a future value discounted at the risk-free rate.

The concepts of present value and future value occur in common, everyday financial transactions. You can multiply a present value by 1 plus the simple interest rate to get a future value.

For example, if you buy a certificate of deposit (CD) today for $100 and it pays 10% simple interest, its future value one year from today is $110.

$(\$100)(1.10) = \$110.00$

Or you can go the other way. To get a present value, you can divide the future value by 1 plus the simple interest rate.

If a CD will be worth $110 a year from today and it pays 10% simple interest, its present value is $100.

$\$110.00/1.10 = \$100.00$

Financial professionals would describe this operation as discounting the future value at the simple interest rate.

In the Black-Scholes world, you are more likely to want to discount a future value at the continuously compounded risk-free rate. Using the animation, the calculation is easy to make.

1. Click three times on Clear.
2. Click twice on Hide.
3. Click on Invest.
4. Click on Simulate Investment.
5. For Current Asset Price, enter 100.00.
6. For Investment Horizon, enter the number of days until the target date, for example, 90.
7. For CC Risk-Free Rate, enter the continuously compounded risk-free rate of return with a minus (–) sign. For example, if the relevant rate is 5.591%, enter –5.591.
8. For Portfolio Value, enter the amount you wish to have on your target date in the future. As an example, 100000. (No commas, please.)
9. Click on Simulate Investment.

In 90 days, $100,000 at a continuously compounded rate of return of –5.591% would decrease to $98,630.86. That means at a rate of 5.591%, in 90 days, $98,630.86 would grow to $100,000.

To verify,

10. In the CC Risk-free Rate field, delete the minus sign in front of –5.591.
11. Click on Simulate Investment.

Expected Return

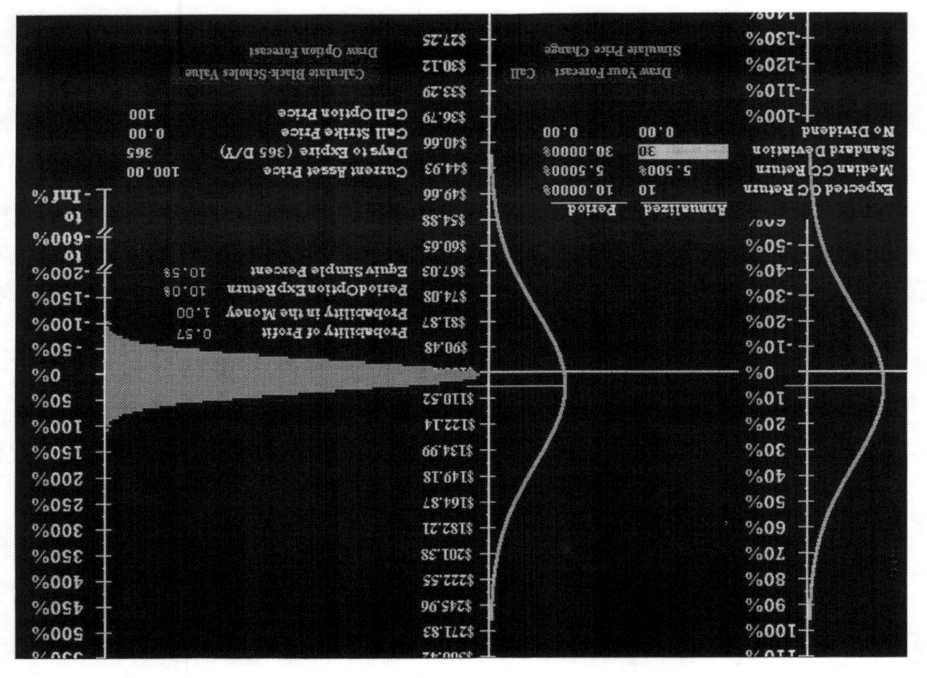

An investment's expected return is the average of all the returns in its probability distribution.

Many people casually assume that if you make an investment that has a certain expected return you can expect to earn that return. This is not the case. Expected return is a statistical concept that has a precise mathematical definition.

An investment's expected return is the average of all the returns in its probability distribution. What's more, when we assume that an investment's geometric rate of return is normally distributed, the average of the returns is not the same as the middle or median return.

In the simple portfolio example we looked at previously, we saw that the average of returns of 20% and −20% is not 0, but 1.99%. Similarly, the average of all the returns in a probability distribution is not the median. It's greater than the median.

The animation is designed to show how we can arrive at an expected return for an option. Nevertheless, we can torture the animation a bit and make it calculate the average or expected return for a stock forecast.

What we want to do is create an artificial call option that has the same probability distribution as the underlying stock. To create that probability distribution, we set the strike price of the call option equal to zero and set the option price equal to the trading price of the stock.

When we find the average return for this imaginary option's probability distribution, that is also the expected return for the stock forecast.

1. Click three times on Clear.
2. Click twice on Hide.
3. Click on Simulate Price Change.
4. For Current Asset Price, enter 100.00.
5. Click on Draw Your Forecast.
6. Click on Draw Option Forecast.
7. Click on Call.
8. For Days to Expire, enter 365.
9. For Call Strike Price, enter 0.00.
10. For Call Option Price, enter 100.00.
11. For Expected CC Return, enter 10.00.
12. For Standard Deviation, enter 30.00.
13. Click on Draw Your Forecast.

The animation first draws the return forecast for the underlying on the underlying return axes. It then draws the same probability distribution on the option return axes.

The scale on the option return axes is quite different, but the probability distribution is the same. If you look at it, you will see that both probability distributions extend from 95.5% to −84.5%.

Now, let's verify that the probability distribution for the option is the same as the probability distribution for the underlying.

14. Click on Draw Option Forecast.

The probability distributions are the same.

To calculate the "option's" expected return, the animation is going to sweep through the option's probability distribution and calculate a running average of all the returns in the probability distribution. You're running another structured Monte Carlo simulation.

When you see a return beyond the extremes of the probability distributions, remember that the outline probability distributions are drawn at the 97.7% confidence level. There is a 0.3% chance that an outcome will be above or below the probability distribution.

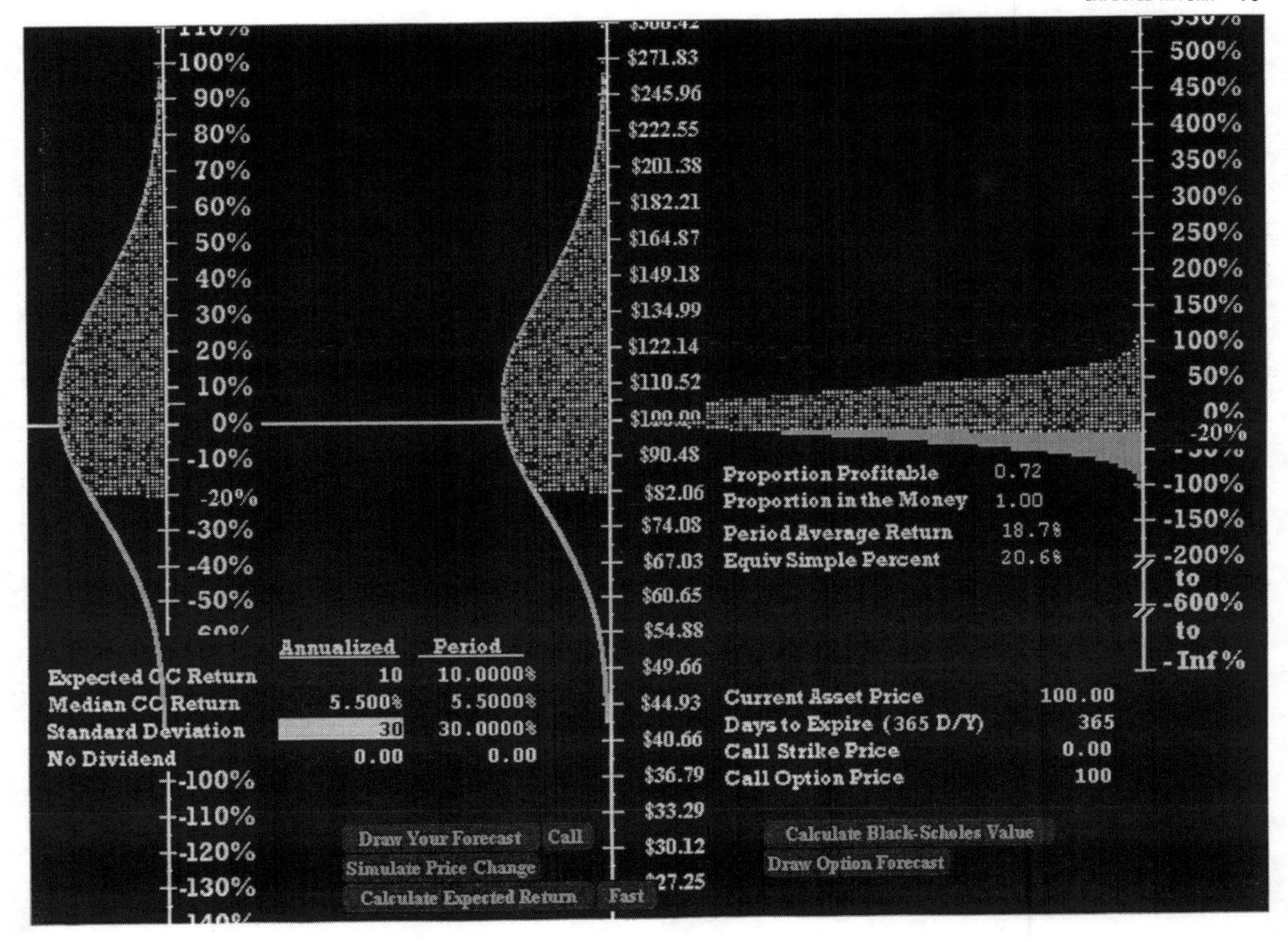

	110%	$388.42	350%
	100%	$271.83	500%
	90%	$245.96	450%
	80%	$222.55	400%
	70%	$201.38	350%
	60%	$182.21	300%
	50%	$164.87	250%
	40%	$149.18	200%
	30%	$134.99	150%
	20%	$122.14	100%
	10%	$110.52	50%
	0%	$100.00	0%
	-10%	$90.48	-20%

Proportion Profitable   0.72
$82.06   Proportion in the Money   1.00

Period Average Return   18.7%
Equiv Simple Percent   20.6%

	Annualized	Period
Expected CC Return	10	10.0000%
Median CC Return	5.500%	5.5000%
Standard Deviation	30	30.0000%
No Dividend	0.00	0.00

Current Asset Price   100.00
Days to Expire (365 D/Y)   365
Call Strike Price   0.00
Call Option Price   100

Draw Your Forecast   Call
Simulate Price Change
Calculate Expected Return   Fast

Calculate Black-Scholes Value
Draw Option Forecast

A stock's expected return is not the middle of its probability distribution. It's the middle plus half the standard deviation squared. With a high-volatility forecast, a stock's expected return may be positive, but its median return negative.

15. Click a few times on Calculate Expected Return.

Observe the results in the field labeled Period Average Return. This is the running average of the outcomes swept through thus far.

16. Click on Fast to the right of Calculate Expected Return.

The animation continues to calculate the average of the outcomes in the probability distribution.

17. To speed up the animation, click on Fastest.

The average of all the returns in the distribution is 10.0%. Hence, the expected return is 10.0%.

When you're working with probability distributions in which geometric rates of return are normally distributed, the expected return can be found by a simple formula:

Expected CC return = median CC return + 0.5(standard deviation)^2

In our example,

$$\begin{aligned} \text{Expected CC return} &= 0.0550 + (0.5)(0.30)^2 \\ &= 0.0550 + (0.5)(0.0900) \\ &= 0.0550 + 0.0450 \\ &= 0.1000 \\ &= 10\% \end{aligned}$$

When investment advisors give you a forecast for a stock, they usually quote an expected return and a standard deviation. Accordingly, the animation accepts the expected return as an input and calculates the forecast's median return.

The relationship among expected return, standard deviation, and median return means that for stocks with high-volatility forecasts, expected returns may be positive, but median returns negative. Consider a stock with an expected return of 6% and a standard deviation of 40%:

$$\begin{aligned} \text{Median CC return} &= \text{expected CC return} - 0.5\,(\text{standard deviation})^2 \\ &= 0.06 - (0.5)(0.40)^2 \\ &= 0.06 - (0.5)(0.16) \\ &= 0.06 - 0.08 \\ &= -0.02 \\ &= -2.00\% \end{aligned}$$

In other words, a high-volatility stock may have a positive expected return, but chances are better than even that you'll lose money.

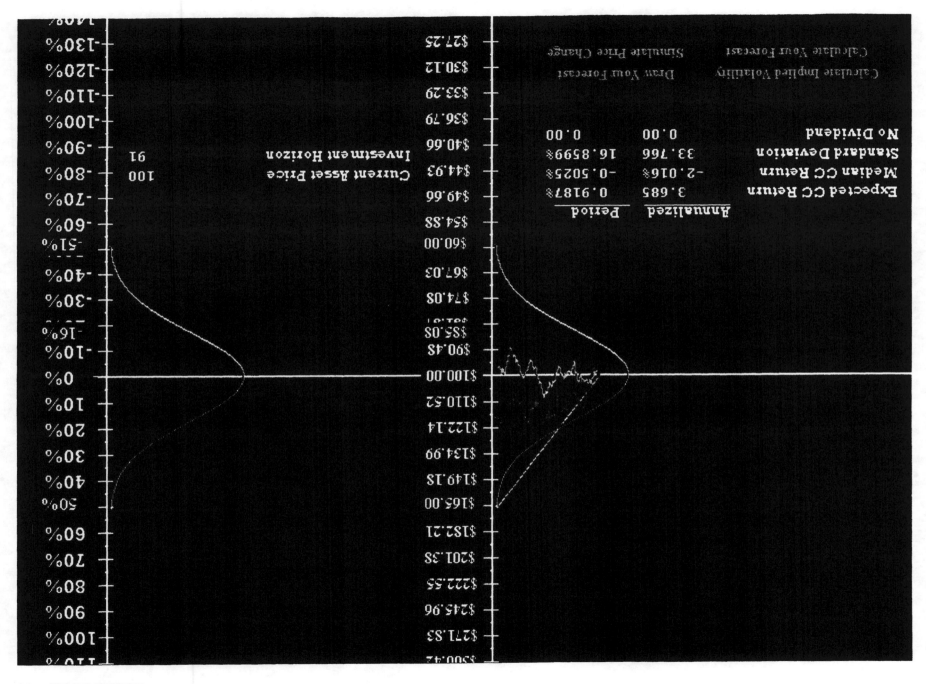

Expected return varies with time.

Let's look at how probability distributions change shape with the length of your investment horizon.

Let's say you're interested in a stock that is trading today at $100. It pays no dividends. You are 99.7% confident that three months from now the price will be somewhere between $60 and $165.

If we assume that the volatility of the stock's potential price path will not change and we extend this outlook to a year, what does the forecast look like?

First, we calculate your three-month forecast.

1. Click three times on Clear.

2. Click two or three times on Hide.

3. Click on Calculate Your Forecast.

4. For Current Asset Price, enter 100.00.

5. For Investment Horizon, enter 91.

6. For Highest possible price, enter 165.00.

7. For Lowest possible price, enter 60.00.

8. Click on Calculate Your Forecast.

The period expected return is 0.9187%. The period median continuously compounded rate of return is −0.5025. The period standard deviation is 16.8599.

Let's get a sense of what the volatility or uncertainty associated with this forecast looks like.

9. Click on Simulate Price Change a few times.

With this amount of volatility, in 91 days, the price path can deviate only so far from the median return.

When you calculate your forecast in this manner, from the period forecast, the animation calculates and displays the annualized forecast.

In our example, the annualized expected return is 3.685%.

The annualized median continuously compounded rate of return is −2.016%.

The annualized standard deviation is 33.766%.

Let's see what the annualized probability distribution looks like.

10. For Investment Horizon, enter 365.

11. Click on Draw Your Forecast.

Let's see what potential price paths for this forecast for one year look like.

12. Click on Simulate Price Change a few times.

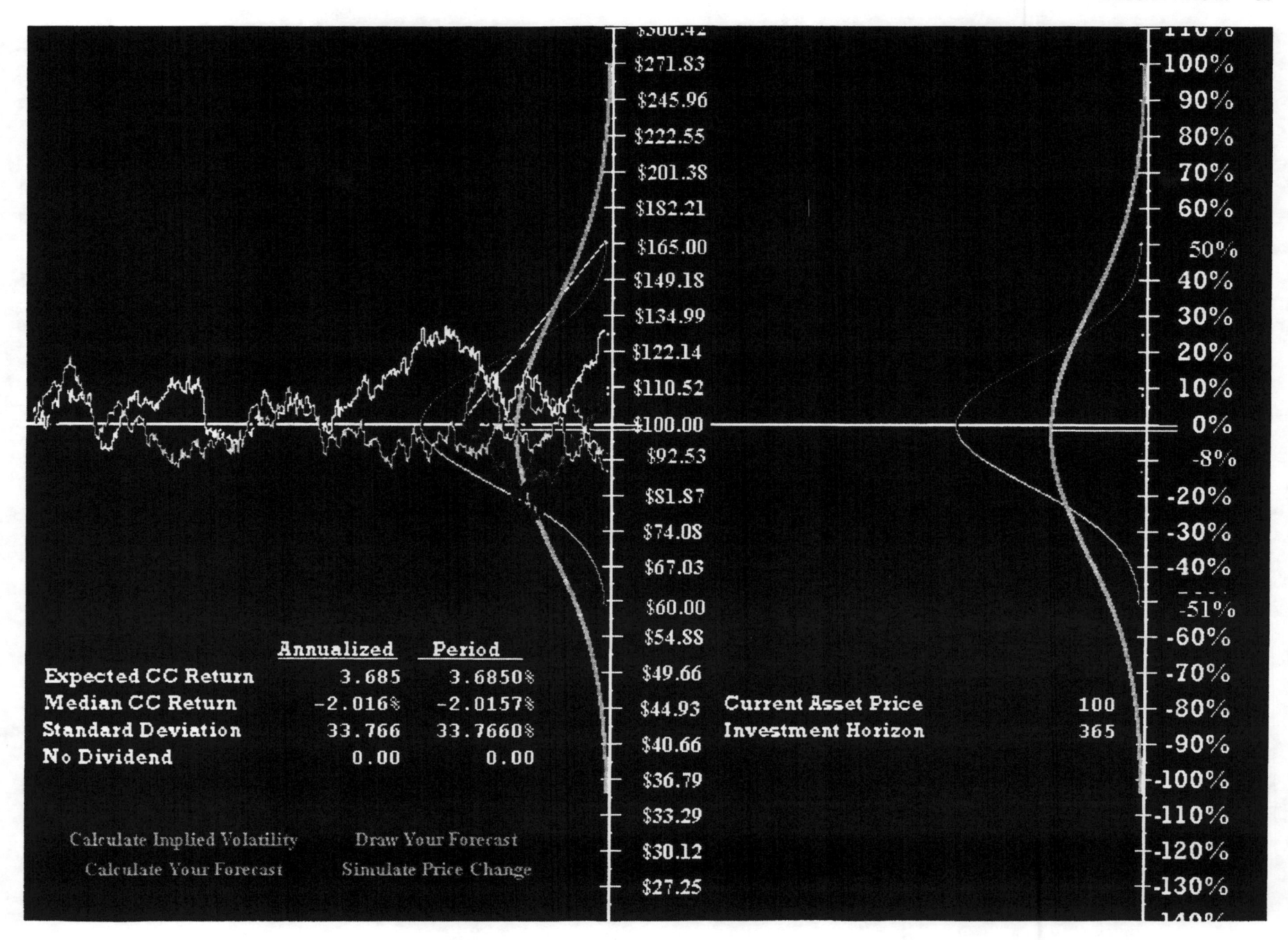

	Annualized	Period
Expected CC Return	3.685	3.6850%
Median CC Return	-2.016%	-2.0157%
Standard Deviation	33.766	33.7660%
No Dividend	0.00	0.00

Current Asset Price	100
Investment Horizon	365

Calculate Implied Volatility   Draw Your Forecast

Calculate Your Forecast   Simulate Price Change

Price axis (left): $300.42, $271.83, $245.96, $222.55, $201.38, $182.21, $165.00, $149.18, $134.99, $122.14, $110.52, $100.00, $92.53, $81.87, $74.08, $67.03, $60.00, $54.88, $49.66, $44.93, $40.66, $36.79, $33.29, $30.12, $27.25

Return axis (right): 110%, 100%, 90%, 80%, 70%, 60%, 50%, 40%, 30%, 20%, 10%, 0%, -8%, -20%, -30%, -40%, -51%, -60%, -70%, -80%, -90%, -100%, -110%, -120%, -130%, 140%

Uncertainty varies with the square root of time.

The day-to-day volatility is the same as it was for the 91-day period. Letting the simulation run for a year means that during that amount of time, the price path can deviate farther from the distribution's median return.

When you use geometric Brownian motion to model rates of return, the rules that govern how the expected return and standard deviation change over time are these:

■ The expected return varies with time. For example, if the expected return for one quarter is 3%, then the expected return for one year (four quarters) is 12%.

Expected CC return = (3%)(4)
= 12%

■ The standard deviation or uncertainty varies with the square root of time. For example, quadrupling the investment horizon doubles the uncertainty of the end-of-period price. If the standard deviation for one quarter is 30%, the standard deviation for one year (four quarters) is 60%.

Standard deviation = $(30\%)(\sqrt{4}\,)$
= (30%)(2)
= 60%

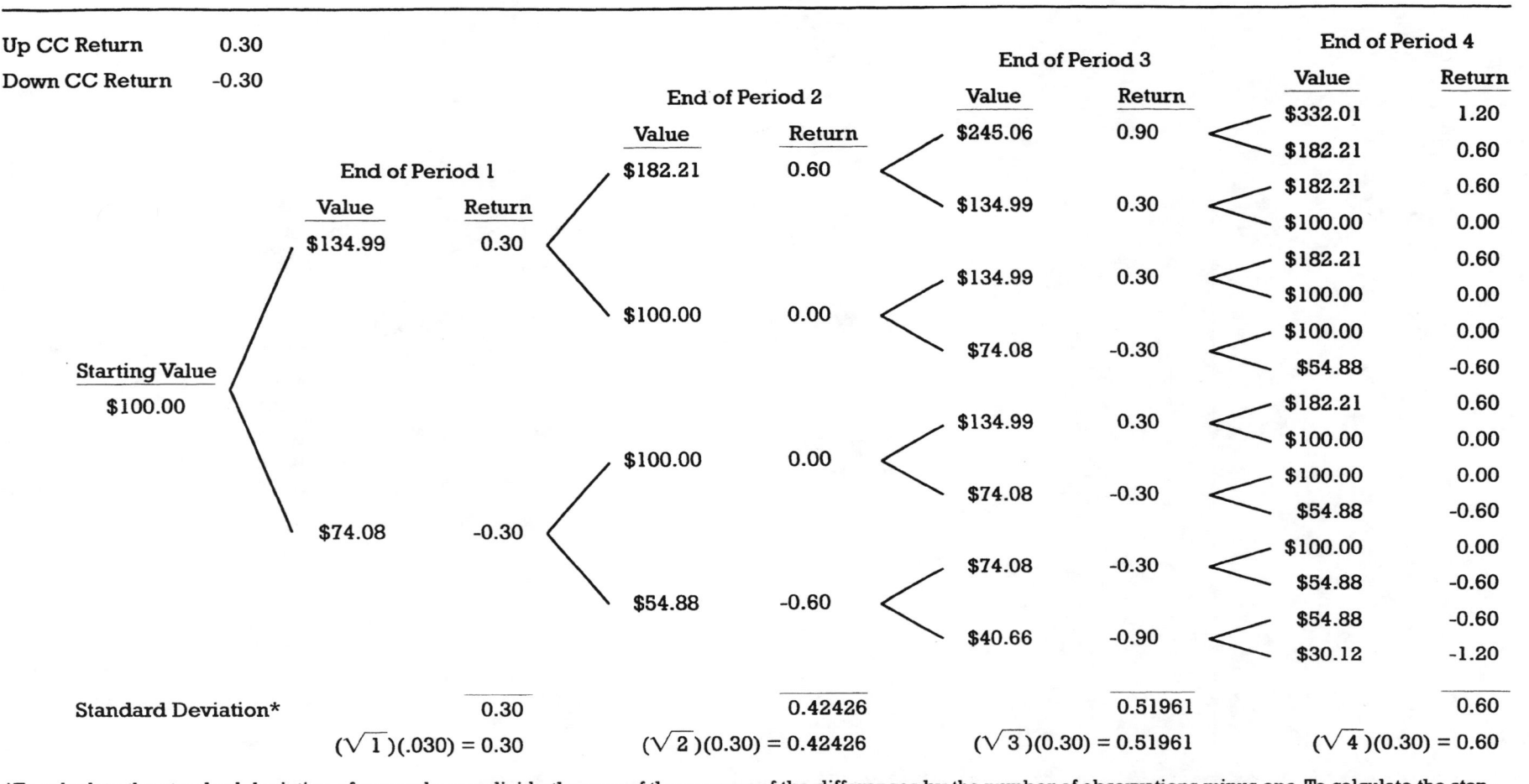

| Up CC Return | 0.30 |
| Down CC Return | -0.30 |

*To calculate the standard deviation of a sample, you divide the sum of the squares of the differences by the number of observations minus one. To calculate the standard deviation of an entire population, you divide by the number of observations. In the chart shown here, we are calculating standard deviations of entire populations. Accordingly, we divide sums of squares of differences by the number of observations. In Excel, you would use the function STDEVP.

Why does volatility vary not with time but with the square root of time? Because once prices get away from the median return, at every fork in the price-path tree, half the possible price paths lead back toward the median return.

If expected return varies with time, why, you might ask, does uncertainty or volatility vary with the square root of time?

To get a sense of why volatility varies with the square root of time, we can construct a simpler tree of possible price paths. We can take a look at the pattern of how end-of-period prices and returns differ from median prices and returns.

In the price-path tree shown here, we have very simple rules: At every fork in the tree, a price either goes up by a continuously compounded rate of 30% or it goes down by −30%. Up and down price movements are equally likely. The median return is 0.

You can begin at the starting value of $100 on the left and follow possible price paths across to the right. At the end of each period, you see the end-of-period value and the end-of-period cumulative return.

You'll notice several things: If you follow the extreme path at the top, you'll see that the cumulative return increases in proportion to time. At the end of period 1, the cumulative return is 0.30 or 30%; at the end of period 2, it's 0.60; at end of period 3, it's 0.90; at the end of period 4, it's 1.20.

If you follow the extreme path at the bottom, you see a similar pattern. The cumulative period return varies with time: −0.30, −0.60, −0.90, −1.20.

If the extreme price paths were the only available price paths, then the standard deviation would vary with time.

Standard deviation, however, measures the average difference between returns and the median return. In between the extreme paths, many of the potential price paths head back toward the median return. Those return outcomes differ from the median much less than do the returns on the outer extremes.

At the bottom of the chart, we've calculated the standard deviation of the cumulative returns at the end of each period.

To show what it means to say that standard deviation varies with the square root of time, we show that the period-2 standard deviation is equal to the period-1 standard deviation multiplied by the square root of 2. The period-3 standard deviation is equal to the period-1 standard deviation multiplied by the square root of 3. The period-4 standard deviation is equal to the period-1 standard deviation multiplied by the square root of 4.

A geometric Brownian motion price-path tree has many more potential price paths than the tree shown here, but the volatility pattern is essentially the same. Once prices get away from the median return, half the potential price paths lead back toward the median.

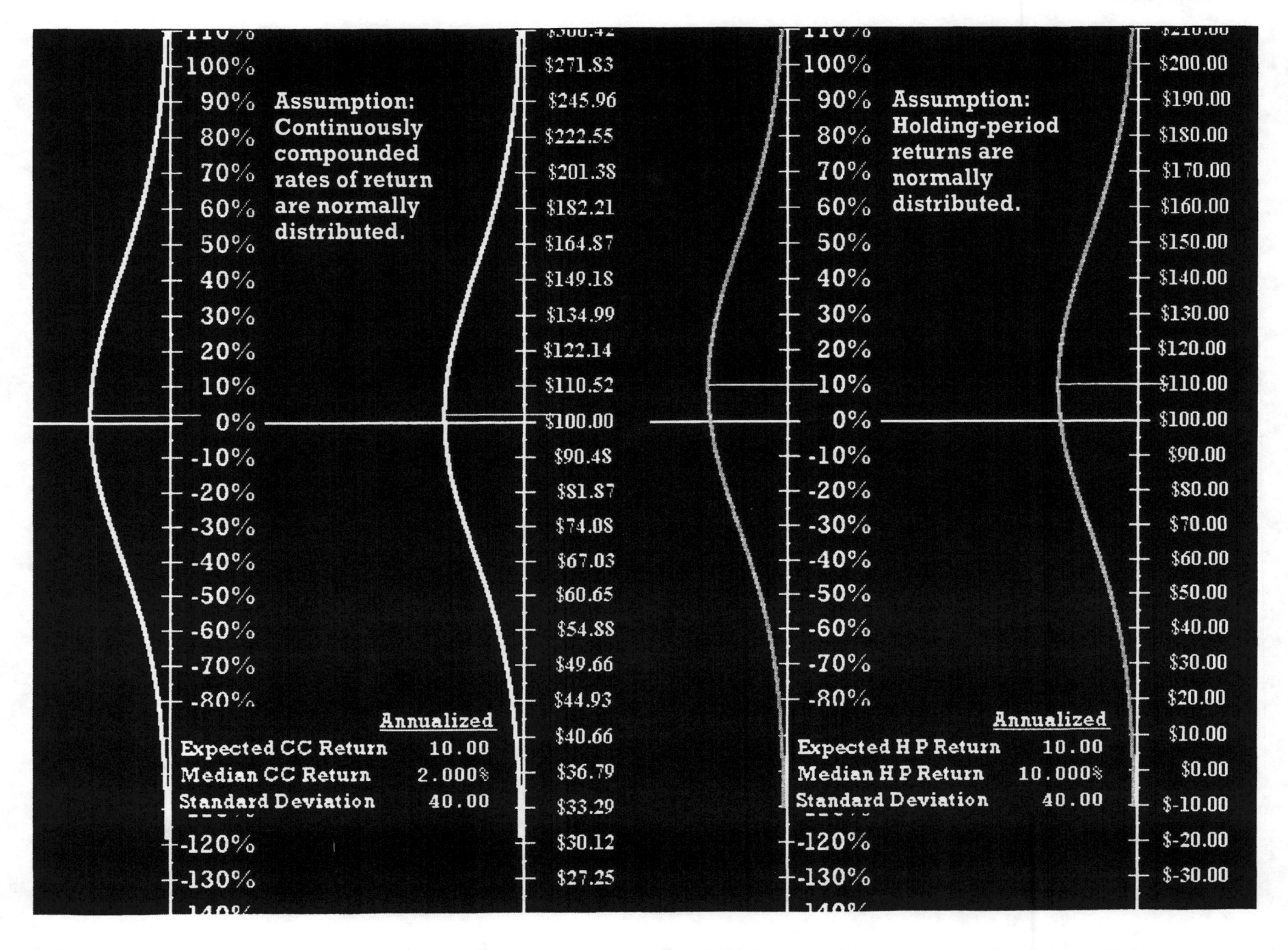

110% $300.42   110% $210.00
100% $271.83   100% $200.00
90%   Assumption: $245.96   90%   Assumption: $190.00
80%   Continuously $222.55   80%   Holding-period $180.00
      compounded   returns are
70%   rates of return $201.38   70%   normally $170.00
60%   are normally $182.21   60%   distributed. $160.00
      distributed.
50% $164.87   50% $150.00
40% $149.18   40% $140.00
30% $134.99   30% $130.00
20% $122.14   20% $120.00
10% $110.52   10% $110.00
0% $100.00   0% $100.00
-10% $90.48   -10% $90.00
-20% $81.87   -20% $80.00
-30% $74.08   -30% $70.00
-40% $67.03   -40% $60.00
-50% $60.65   -50% $50.00
-60% $54.88   -60% $40.00
-70% $49.66   -70% $30.00
-80% $44.93   -80% $20.00

                Annualized   Annualized
                             $40.66 $10.00
Expected CC Return   10.00   Expected H P Return   10.00
Median CC Return   2.000% $36.79   Median H P Return   10.000% $0.00
Standard Deviation 40.00   Standard Deviation   40.00
                             $33.29 $-10.00
-120% $30.12   -120% $-20.00
-130% $27.25   -130% $-30.00

When your portfolio manager or broker shows you a distribution of returns, ask whether he or she is talking continuously compounded or holding-period returns.

Oddly enough, portfolio-management theory ordinarily does not assume that stock returns expressed as geometric or continuously compounded rates of return are normally distributed. Rather, portfolio-management theory usually assumes that annual, holding-period returns are normally distributed.

What's the difference?

Let's say you're interested in a stock that today is trading at $100. Someone tells you that the stock has an expected return of 10% and a standard deviation of 40%. Depending on whether he or she is thinking and talking geometric or holding-period returns, the distribution of end-of-year prices being predicted is very different.

The return and price forecasts above left show forecasts under the assumption that continuously compounded rates of return are normally distributed. The return and price forecasts above right show forecasts under the assumption that holding-period returns are normally distributed. The table above highlights some of the differences.

How is an end-of-year price of –$10 possible? Ask someone who believes that holding-period returns are normally distributed.

	If Geometric Rate of Return	If Holding-Period Return
Maximum end-of-year value at 99.7% confidence level (+3 standard deviations)	$338.72	$230.00
Average end-of-year value	$110.52	$110.00
Median end-of-year value	$102.02	$110.00
Minimum end-of-year value at 99.7% confidence level (–3 standard deviations)	$30.72	–$10.00

When your portfolio manager or broker shows you a normal distribution of returns or gives you a forecast, clarify whether he or she is talking continuously compounded rates of return or holding-period returns. Be prepared for the possibility that your manager or broker may not know or— Heaven forbid!—may not know the difference.

If they do not know the difference, insist that they buy a copy of *Black-Scholes Made Easy* for everyone in their firm.

(Your animation is not programmed to draw any graphs in which holding-period returns are normally distributed.)

How Dividends Affect Price Paths and Forecasts

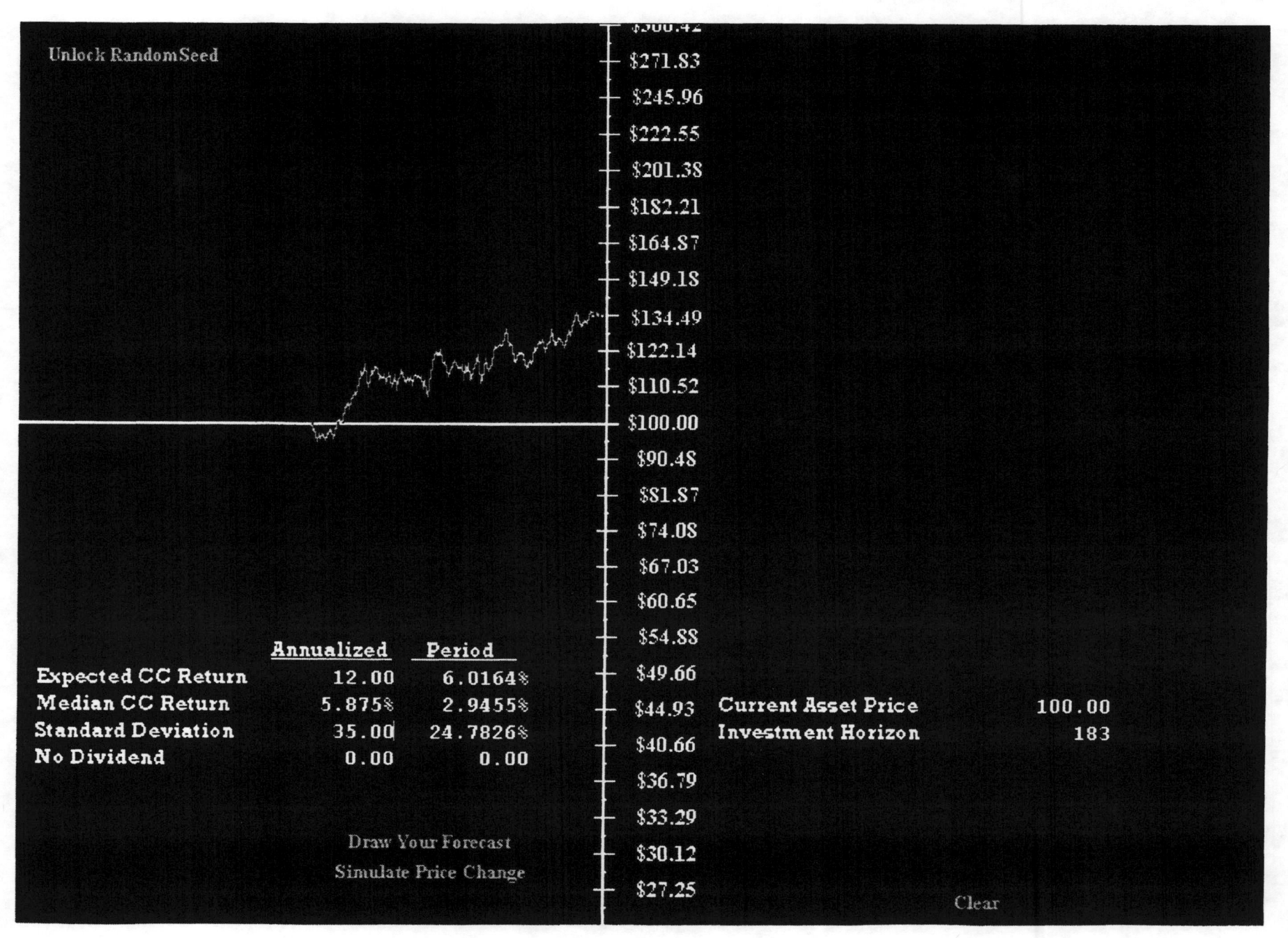

Unlock RandomSeed

$271.83
$245.96
$222.55
$201.38
$182.21
$164.87
$149.18
$134.49
$122.14
$110.52
$100.00
$90.48
$81.87
$74.08
$67.03
$60.65
$54.88
$49.66
$44.93
$40.66
$36.79
$33.29
$30.12
$27.25

	Annualized	Period
Expected CC Return	12.00	6.0164%
Median CC Return	5.875%	2.9455%
Standard Deviation	35.00	24.7826%
No Dividend	0.00	0.00

Draw Your Forecast

Simulate Price Change

Current Asset Price   100.00
Investment Horizon   183

Clear

Lock Random Seed lets you create the same price path with variations.

To see the effects that dividend payments and yields have on stock price paths and forecasts, we'll use the animation's Lock Random Seed capability. Lock Random Seed is kind of like the brake on a rigged roulette wheel. It causes Simulate Price Change to keep generating the same sequence of geometric Brownian motion perturbations and hence—if nothing else is changed—the same price path over and over again.

Let's see what that looks like.

> 1. Click three times on Clear.
>
> 2. Click twice on Hide.
>
> 3. Click on Simulate Price Change.
>
> 4. For Current Asset Price, enter 100.00.
>
> 5. For Investment Horizon, enter 183.
>
> 6. For Expected CC Return, enter 12.00.
>
> 7. For Standard Deviation, enter 35.00.
>
> 8. Click on Simulate Price Change.
>
> 9. To make the Lock Random Seed command button visible, mouse around at the top left of the screen.
>
> 10. Click on Lock Random Seed.

Watch the existing price path closely.

> 11. Click on Simulate Price Change.

Notice that the animation traces the same simulated price path again.

You can keep clicking on Simulate Price Change again and again and you'll get the same price path every time.

When you want to go back to random price paths, click on Unlock Random Seed.

How does Lock Random Seed work?

To simulate Brownian motion price paths, the animation generates a series of random numbers, finds the number in the stock's one-day probability distribution that corresponds to that random number, and increases or decreases the stock's price accordingly.

To generate random numbers, a computer starts with a number called the random seed and performs a sequence of operations on it. Whenever a computer starts with the same number as its random seed, it generates the same sequence of random numbers.

Lock Random Seed causes the computer to start with the same random seed next time that it used last time. It generates the same sequence of random numbers, which produces the same price path or—if you've changed anything—the same sequence of Brownian motion jolts to the price.

> 12. To see what the same sequence of perturbations look like with a different volatility, for Standard Deviation, enter 55.00.
>
> 13. Click on Simulate Price Change.

The so-called random numbers that computers generate aren't really random. Purists call them pseudorandom numbers. Numbers that are really random are trickier to generate.

> 14. Click on Unlock Random Seed.

(If ever the animation seems to be doing bizarre things, check to see if the random seed is locked.)

"Anyone who considers arithmetic methods of producing random digits is, of course, in a state of sin." — John von Neumann

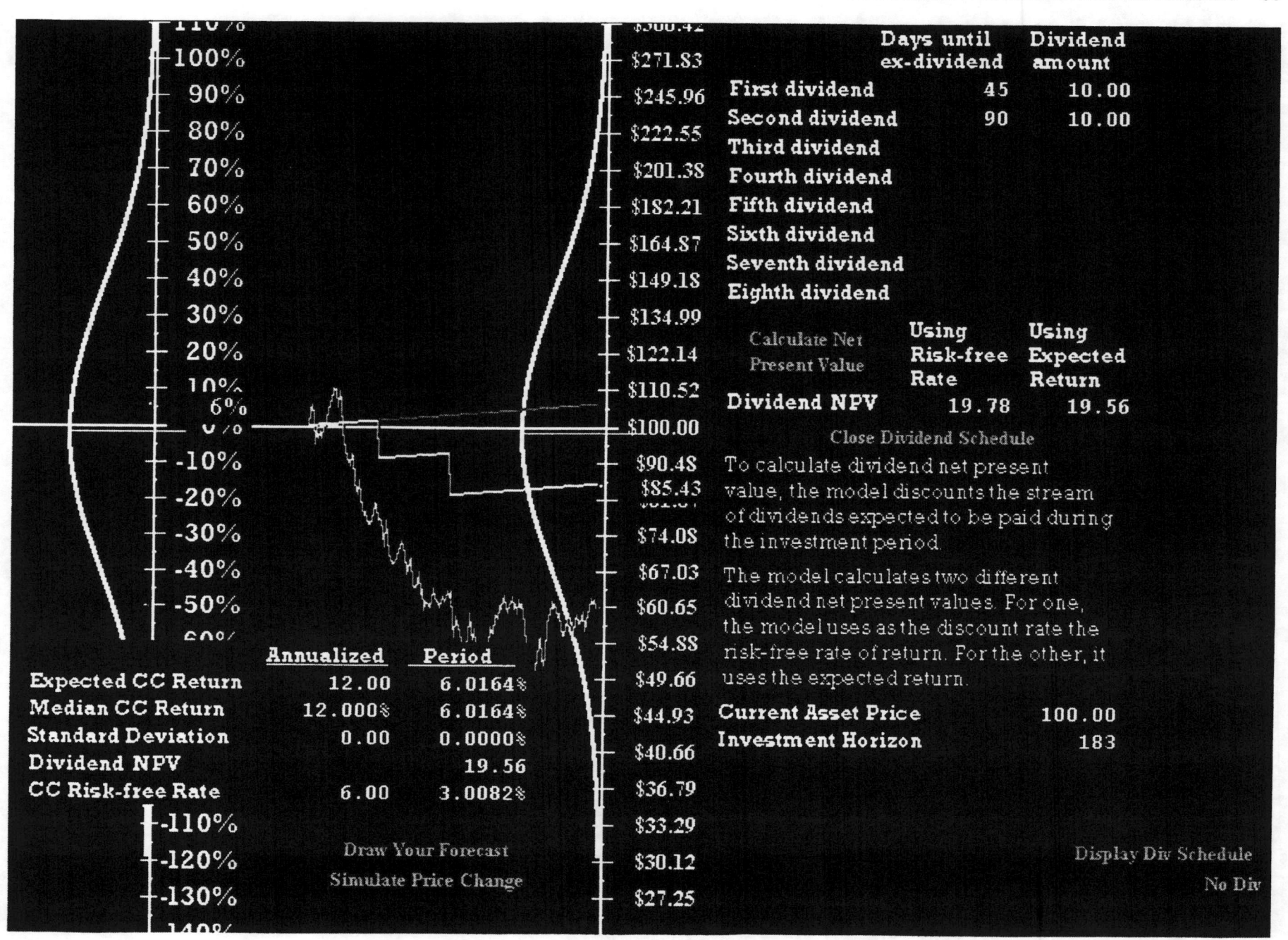

	110%
	100%
	90%
	80%
	70%
	60%
	50%
	40%
	30%
	20%
	10%
	6%
	0%
	-10%
	-20%
	-30%
	-40%
	-50%
	-60%

	Annualized	Period
Expected CC Return	12.00	6.0164%
Median CC Return	12.000%	6.0164%
Standard Deviation	0.00	0.0000%
Dividend NPV		19.56
CC Risk-free Rate	6.00	3.0082%

-110%
-120%
-130%
-140%

Draw Your Forecast
Simulate Price Change

$300.42
$271.83
$245.96
$222.55
$201.38
$182.21
$164.87
$149.18
$134.99
$122.14
$110.52
$100.00
$90.48
$85.43
$74.08
$67.03
$60.65
$54.88
$49.66
$44.93
$40.66
$36.79
$33.29
$30.12
$27.25

	Days until ex-dividend	Dividend amount
First dividend	45	10.00
Second dividend	90	10.00
Third dividend		
Fourth dividend		
Fifth dividend		
Sixth dividend		
Seventh dividend		
Eighth dividend		

Calculate Net Present Value	Using Risk-free Rate	Using Expected Return
Dividend NPV	19.78	19.56

Close Dividend Schedule

To calculate dividend net present value, the model discounts the stream of dividends expected to be paid during the investment period.

The model calculates two different dividend net present values. For one, the model uses as the discount rate the risk-free rate of return. For the other, it uses the expected return.

Current Asset Price	100.00
Investment Horizon	183

Display Div Schedule

No Div

You can expect a dividend payment to reduce the price of a stock by the amount of the dividend.

Thus far, we have been using as our examples stocks that pay no dividends.

15. Click once on Clear.

16. Click twice on Draw Your Forecast.

When a stock pays no dividends, price appreciation accounts for all of the stock's return. Consequently, the return probability distribution and the end-of-period price probability distribution sit at the same height.

17. Click on Simulate Price Change.

When a stock pays no dividends, in the model, geometric Brownian motion accounts for all the price changes.

When a stock pays dividends, in theory, the stock's price is reduced on the ex-dividend date by the amount of the dividend.

Accordingly, on the ex-dividend date the model reduces the price of the stock by the amount of the dividend.

To see in a stark way the effect that dividend payments have on a potential price path, we will remove all uncertainty from the forecast, generate a price path, introduce dividends, then generate a price path that shows the price drops that accompany dividend payments.

18. For Standard Deviation, enter 0.00.

19. Click on Simulate Price Change.

20. Click on Display Dividend Schedule.

21. For CC Risk-Free Rate, enter 6.00.

22. For the first dividend, under Days until ex-dividend, enter 45.

23. Under Dividend amount, enter an absurdly high dividend: 10.00.

24. For the second dividend, under Days until ex-dividend, enter 90.

25. Under Dividend amount, enter 10.00.

26. Click on Calculate Net Present Value.

27. Click on Simulate Price Change.

At days 45 and 90, you see the price drop by $10 because of the dividend payments.

Now we will look at the effect that dividend payments have on a volatile price path.

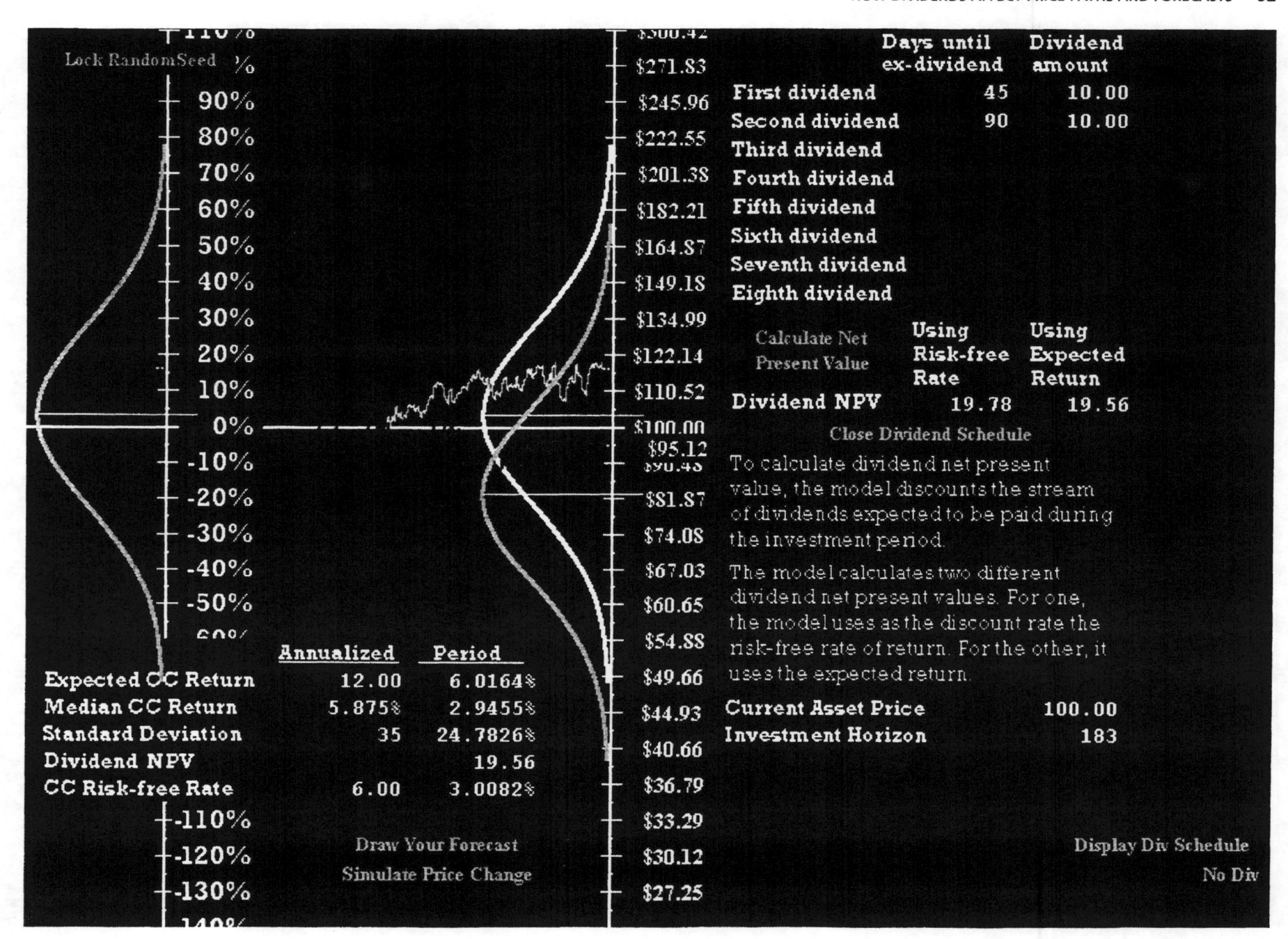

Lock RandomSeed %

110%
90%
80%
70%
60%
50%
40%
30%
20%
10%
0%
-10%
-20%
-30%
-40%
-50%

	Annualized	Period
Expected CC Return	12.00	6.0164%
Median CC Return	5.875%	2.9455%
Standard Deviation	35	24.7826%
Dividend NPV		19.56
CC Risk-free Rate	6.00	3.0082%

-110%
-120%
-130%

Draw Your Forecast
Simulate Price Change

$300.42
$271.83
$245.96
$222.55
$201.38
$182.21
$164.87
$149.18
$134.99
$122.14
$110.52
$100.00
$95.12
$90.43
$81.87
$74.08
$67.03
$60.65
$54.88
$49.66
$44.93
$40.66
$36.79
$33.29
$30.12
$27.25

	Days until ex-dividend	Dividend amount
First dividend	45	10.00
Second dividend	90	10.00
Third dividend		
Fourth dividend		
Fifth dividend		
Sixth dividend		
Seventh dividend		
Eighth dividend		

Calculate Net Present Value	Using Risk-free Rate	Using Expected Return
Dividend NPV	19.78	19.56

Close Dividend Schedule

To calculate dividend net present value, the model discounts the stream of dividends expected to be paid during the investment period.

The model calculates two different dividend net present values. For one, the model uses as the discount rate the risk-free rate of return. For the other, it uses the expected return.

Current Asset Price	100.00
Investment Horizon	183

Display Div Schedule

No Div

Dividends shift the price probability distribution below the return probability distribution.

To see the effect, we will use the animation's Lock Random Seed capability.

28. For Standard Deviation, enter 35.00.

29. Click once on Clear.

30. Click on No Div.

31. Click on Draw Your Forecast.

32. Click on Simulate Price Change.

33. Click on Lock Random Seed.

34. Click on Simulate Price Change again.

Notice that you get the same simulated price path.

Now we'll see what that price path looks like with dividend payments.

35. Click on Display Dividend Schedule.

36. For the first dividend, under Days until ex-dividend, enter 45.

37. Under Dividend amount, enter 10.00.

38. For the second dividend, under Days until ex-dividend, enter 90.

39. Under Dividend amount, enter 10.00.

40. Click on Calculate Net Present Value.

41. Click on Simulate Price Change.

You see that, on each ex-dividend day, the dividend payment lowers the price of the stock. The end-of-period price is lower. Similarly, dividend payments lower the entire probability distribution of the price forecast.

42. Click on Unlock Random Seed.

43. Click on Draw Your Forecast.

44. Click on Simulate Price Change a few more times.

45. Click on Simulate Price Change Fastest.

46. Click on Draw Your Forecast.

Dividend payments shift the price forecast lower than the return forecast. This shift makes sense because return is defined as price appreciation plus dividend income.

If you plan to invest in options, the difference between the return forecast and the price forecast is especially significant. Option payoffs are based on price performance, not return.

Later, when we look at circumstances under which it may be advantageous to exercise an option early, you will see that one of the most important considerations is the attempt to capture value from dividend payments.

To work with dividends, the animation requires that you first enter the investment horizon or time to expiration. If the time to expiration is blank or zero, the animation throws you an alert.

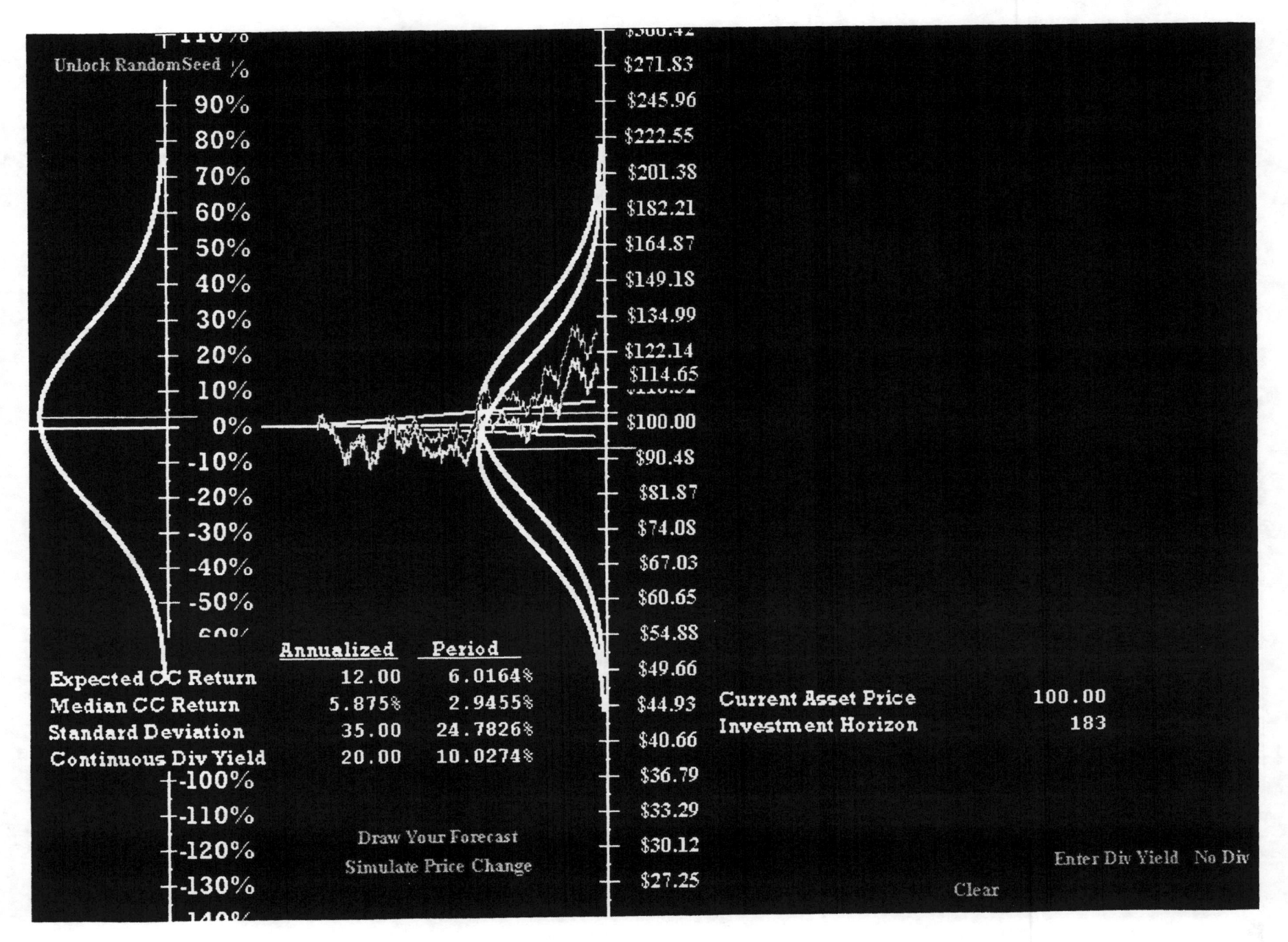

A dividend yield shifts the price probability distribution below the return probability distribution.

In addition to buying options on stocks, you also can buy options on market indices. Instead of being modeled as paying a schedule of cash dividends, indices often are modeled as paying a dividend yield.

You can enter a dividend yield into the animation. The effects are similar to those of entering a dividend schedule. A dividend yield shifts the price probability distribution below the return probability distribution.

First, we'll look at the effect of a dividend yield on a "stock" that has zero volatility.

47. Click on Clear.

48. Click on No Div.

49. For Standard Deviation, enter 0.00.

50. Click on Simulate Price Change.

51. Click on Enter Div Yield.

52. For Continuous Dividend Yield, enter 20.00.

53. Click on Simulate Price Change.

You see that both price paths are straight lines, but the path that pays the dividend yield diverges below the price path that pays no dividend yield.

Now we'll look at the effect of a dividend yield on volatile price paths and price forecasts.

54. Click on No Div.

55. For Standard Deviation, enter 35.00.

56. Click on Draw Your Forecast.

57. Click on Simulate Price Change.

You see that the return forecast and the price forecast are at the same height.

58. Click on Lock Random Seed at the top left of the screen.

59. Click on Enter Div Yield.

60. For Continuous Dividend Yield, enter 20.00.

61. Click on Simulate Price Change.

Notice that the volatile price path that pays a dividend yield diverges below the price path that pays no dividend yield.

62. Click on Unlock Random Seed.

63. Click on Draw Your Forecast.

Notice that the dividend yield shifts the price forecast below the return forecast.

If the stocks in an index pay a dividend yield, be sure to factor the yield into your calculations. Dividend yields affect the price paths upon which option payoffs are based.

Option Outcomes, Probability Distributions, and Expected Returns

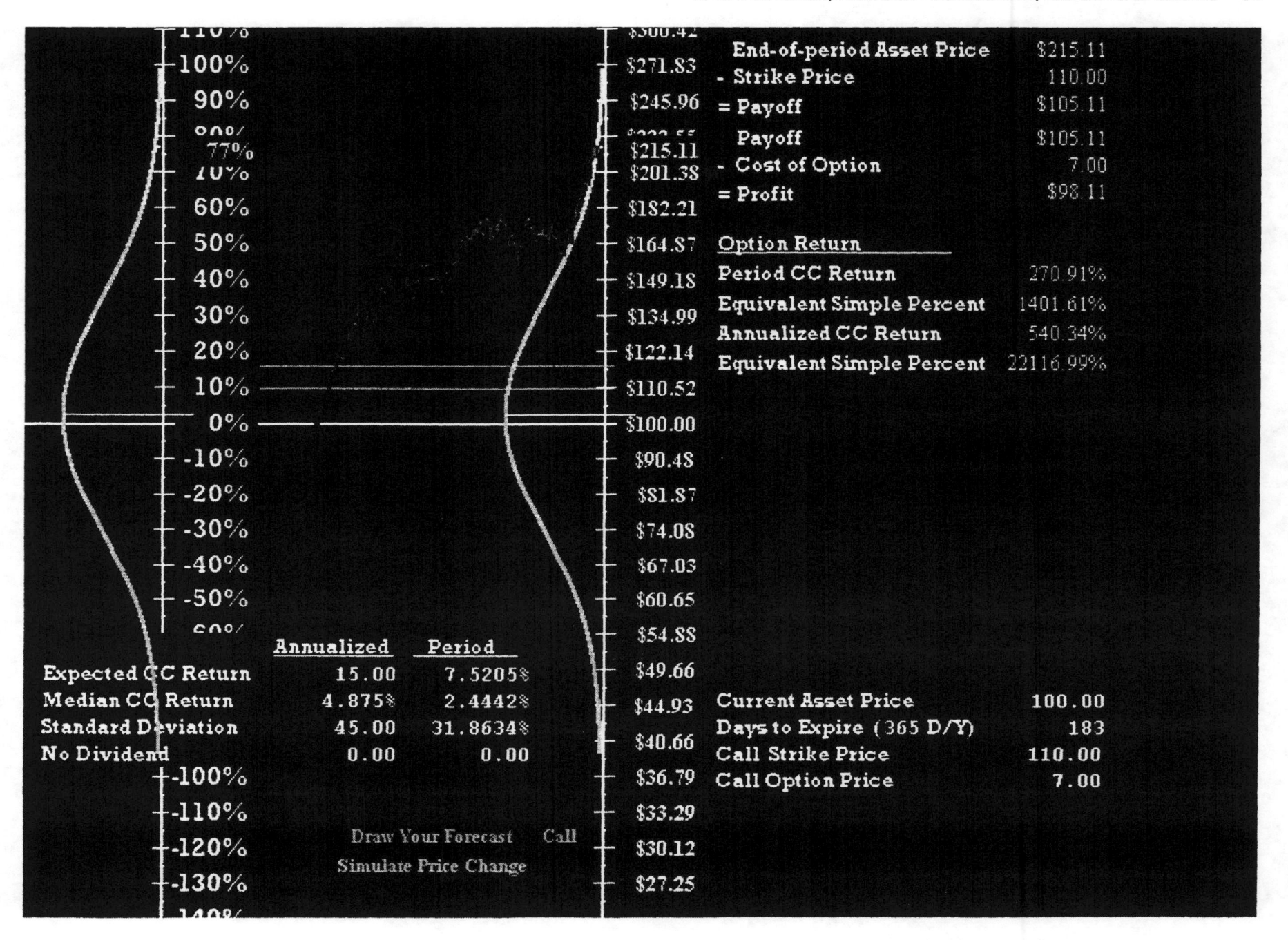

A call option gives you the right to buy a stock at a preset price.

When you buy a call option, you purchase the right to buy a stock at a pre-set price called the strike price. With American-style options, you can exercise this right at any time up until the option's expiration date. With European-style options, you can exercise the option only on the expiration date—that is, at maturity.

If the price of the stock is above the strike price or goes above the strike price and you exercise the option, you receive the difference between the stock price and the strike price at the time of exercise.

Given a stock forecast and an option, the animation simulates potential price paths for the stock and shows the option's corresponding end-of-period payoffs.

1. Click on No Div.

2. Click three times on Clear.

3. Click two or three times on Hide.

4. Click on Simulate Price Change.

5. For Expected CC Return, enter 15.00.

6. For Standard Deviation, enter 45.00.

7. For Current Asset Price, enter 100.00.

8. Click on Call.

9. For Days to Expire, enter 183.

10. For Call Strike Price, enter 110.00.

11. For Call Option Price, enter 7.00.

The yellow line on the price axis represents the option's strike price. For a call option to be in the money, the stock price must be above the yellow line.

The distance from the yellow line to the green line represents the option price or premium. For a call option to produce a profit, at the time of exercise the stock price must be above the green line.

12. Click twice on Draw Your Forecast.

The area of the probability distribution above the yellow line represents the probability that the option will finish in the money.

The area of the probability distribution above the green line represents the probability that the option will produce a profit.

13. Click on Simulate Price Change.

If the end-of-period price is below the strike price, you see that the payoff is zero, your "profit" is negative, and you lose all the money you invested in the option. You have a period continuously compounded rate of return of negative infinity and a holding-period return of −100%.

If the end-of-period price is above the strike price, you see that the payoff is equal to the end-of-period price minus the strike price.

14. Click on Simulate Price Change until you get a couple of winners.

Note the calculation of option payoffs for each simulated price path.

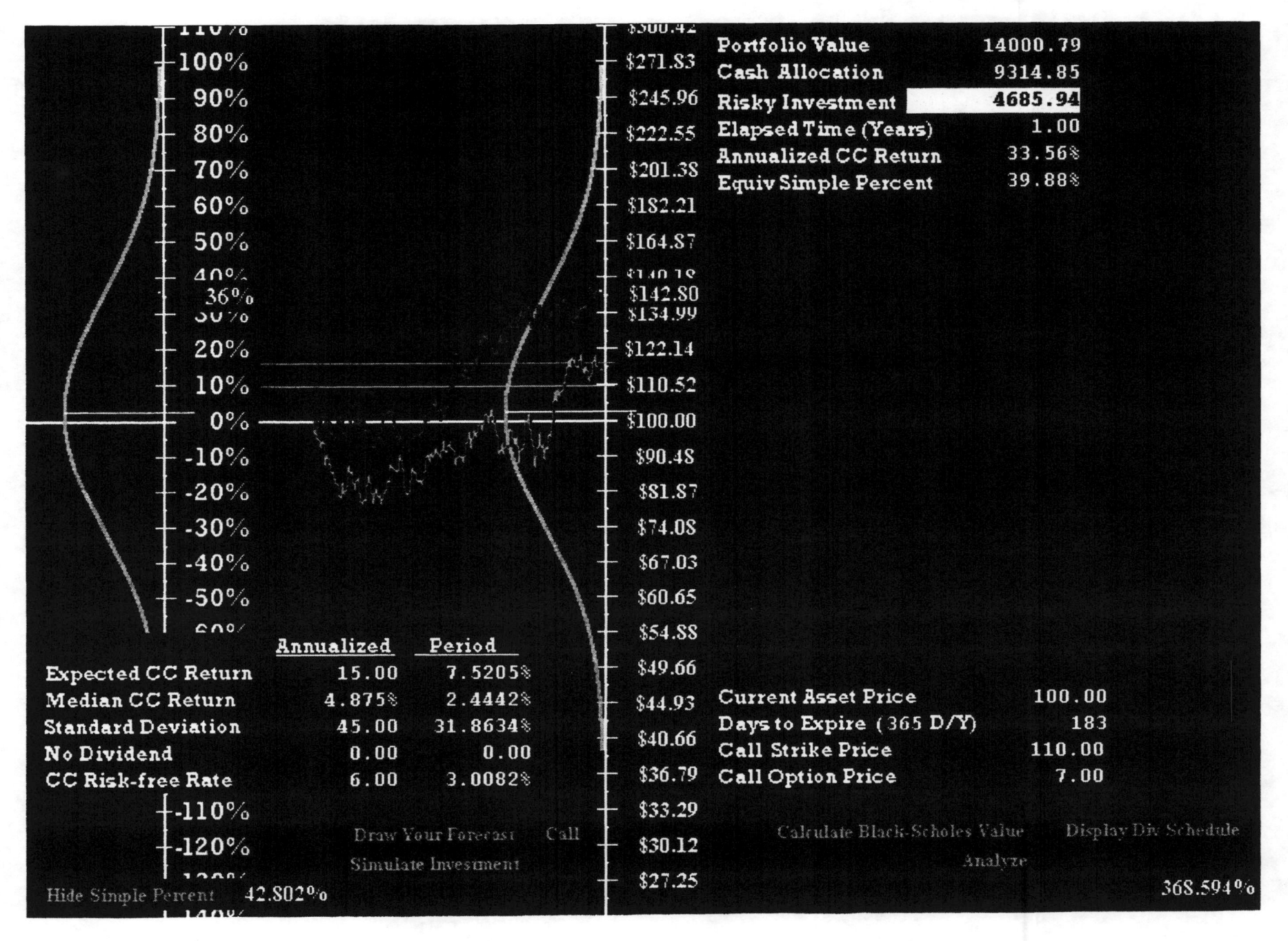

	Annualized	Period
Expected CC Return	15.00	7.5205%
Median CC Return	4.875%	2.4442%
Standard Deviation	45.00	31.8634%
No Dividend	0.00	0.00
CC Risk-free Rate	6.00	3.0082%

Portfolio Value	14000.79
Cash Allocation	9314.85
Risky Investment	**4685.94**
Elapsed Time (Years)	1.00
Annualized CC Return	33.56%
Equiv Simple Percent	39.88%

Current Asset Price	100.00
Days to Expire (365 D/Y)	183
Call Strike Price	110.00
Call Option Price	7.00

Draw Your Forecast   Call

Simulate Investment

Calculate Black-Scholes Value   Display Div Schedule

Analyze

Hide Simple Percent   42.802%

368.594%

Once you have your price forecast for a stock, you can simulate potential outcomes of investing in a call you hold until maturity.

Based on your forecast and the option structure, you can simulate potential outcomes of investing in the option and holding it until expiration.

Let's say you have $10,000 in your portfolio. You want to invest $1,000 in the option.

> 15. Click on Show Simple Percent.
>
> 16. Click on Invest.
>
> 17. For CC Risk-Free Rate, enter 6.00.
>
> 18. For Portfolio Value, enter 10000.00. (No $ or commas.)
>
> 19. For Risky Investment, enter 1000.00.
>
> 20. Click on Simulate Investment.

The simple percent box at the bottom right of the screen shows the equivalent simple percent of the continuously compounded rate of return on your investment in the option.

Regardless of how the option performs, the cash allocation earns the risk-free rate of return.

The animation displays the new value of the portfolio, the new value of the cash allocation, the proceeds of the investment in the option, the elapsed investment period in years, the annualized continuously compounded rate of return for the portfolio, and the equivalent simple percent.

To get a feel for how investing in call options can leverage your investment, make a few more investments of $1,000 in the option.

> 21. For Risky Investment, enter 1000.00.
>
> 22. Click on Simulate Investment.

If you wish to see only the effect on the portfolio of investing in the option, set the risk-free rate to zero.

> 23. For CC Risk-Free Rate, enter 0.0.
>
> 24. For Portfolio Value, enter 10000.00. (No $ or commas.)
>
> 25. For Risky Investment, enter 1000.00.
>
> 26. Click on Simulate Investment.

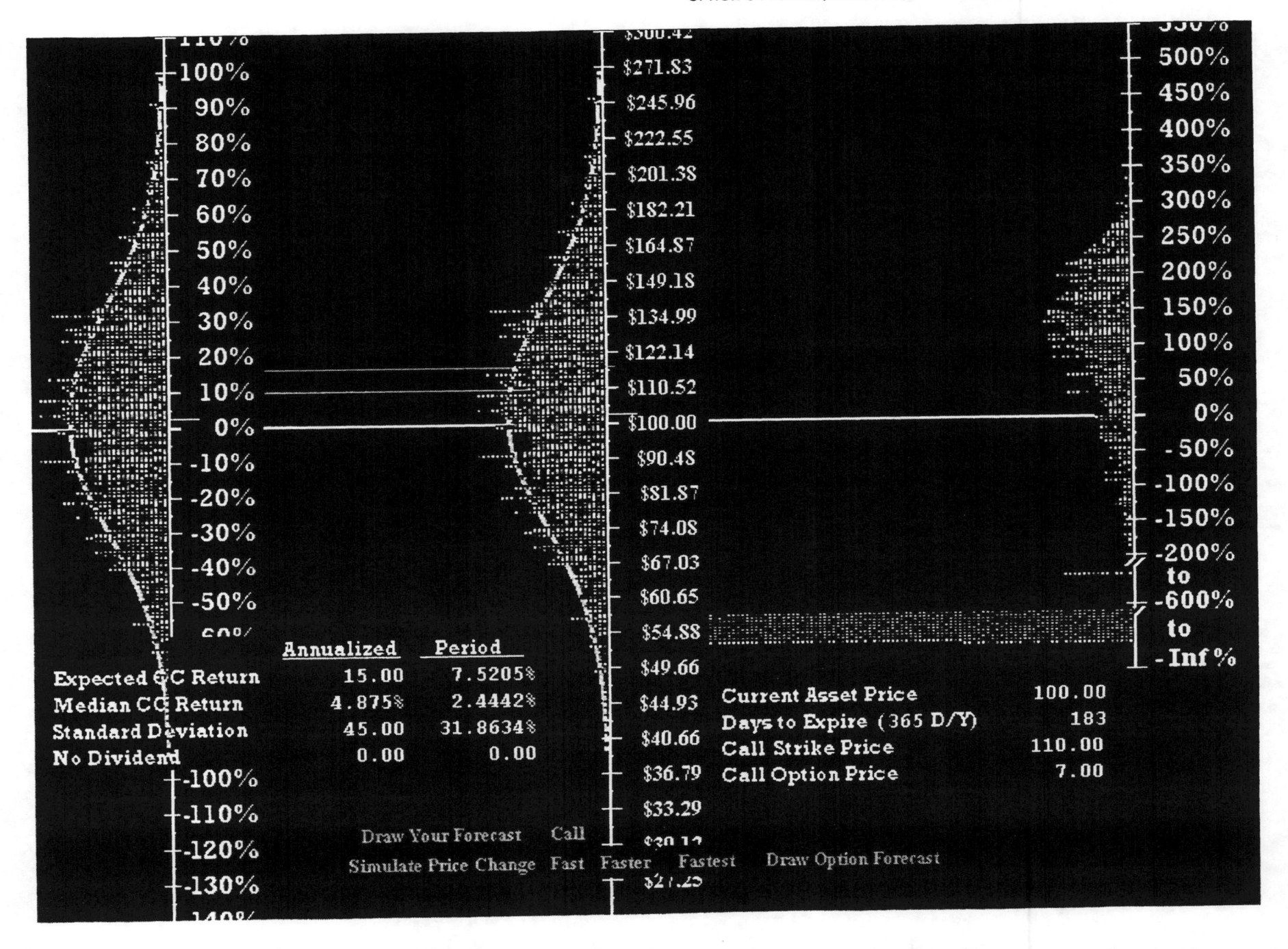

A histogram of option outcomes approximates a probability distribution or return forecast for the option.

Instead of displaying the option payoffs as numerical results, the animation can display option performance graphically as a return on your investment in the option.

---

27. To make the Invest data fields go away, click on Analyze.

28. To bring the option axes on-screen, click once on Draw Option Forecast.

29. Click on Simulate Price Change.

To tabulate each option return, the animation adds a little square to the option axes.

You can simulate a price change and option return without drawing the price path.

---

30. Click on Fast immediately to the right of Simulate Price Change.

You can speed up the simulation.

---

31. Click on Faster to the right of Simulate Price Change.

You can speed it up further.

---

32. Click on Fastest to the right of Simulate Price Change.

The histograms of squares on the left and in the middle of the screen approximate the probability distributions of the stock's return and price forecast.

Given this stock forecast and option structure, the histogram formed on the option axes approximates the probability distribution or forecast of the option return when the option is held to maturity. (For options, the words *expiration* and *maturity* mean the same thing.)

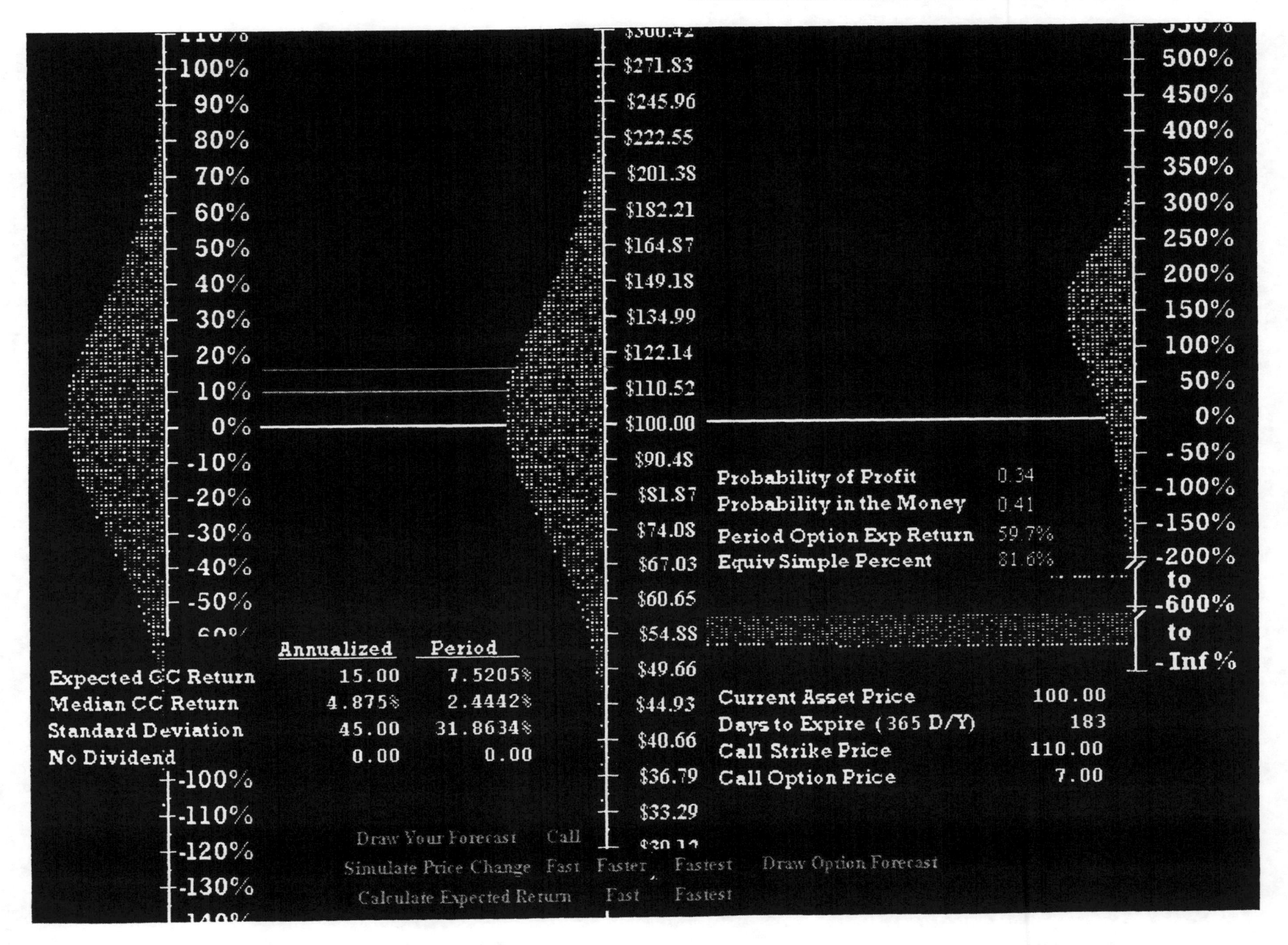

	Annualized	Period
Expected CC Return	15.00	7.5205%
Median CC Return	4.875%	2.4442%
Standard Deviation	45.00	31.8634%
No Dividend	0.00	0.00

Probability of Profit	0.34
Probability in the Money	0.41
Period Option Exp Return	59.7%
Equiv Simple Percent	81.6%

Current Asset Price	100.00
Days to Expire (365 D/Y)	183
Call Strike Price	110.00
Call Option Price	7.00

Draw Your Forecast   Call
Simulate Price Change   Fast   Faster   Fastest   Draw Option Forecast
Calculate Expected Return   Fast   Fastest

The expected return of an option held to maturity is the average of all the returns in its probability distribution.

Because we can translate each end-of-period stock price into an option return, we can sweep down through the stock forecast and simultaneously sweep down through the option forecast. Along the way, we can calculate several properties of the option forecast:

- The option's probability of profit
- The probability that the end-of-period stock price will be in the money
- The period expected return of the option
- The equivalent simple percent of the period option expected return

We continue with the example that you've entered into the animation already.

33. Click once on Clear.

34. Click a few times on Calculate Expected Return.

We begin to sweep down through the forecasts. Initially—for this stock forecast and option structure—all the option outcomes are profitable and in the money. Accordingly, the proportion profitable and proportion in the money is 1.00 or 100%. When the option outcomes begin to fall below the green line and then the yellow line, the proportion profitable and proportion in the money will fall below 1.00.

For period average return, the animation is simply calculating a running average of the option returns thus far swept through.

35. Click on Fast immediately to the right of Calculate Expected Return.

Automatically, the animation continues to sweep through the stock forecast, display the corresponding option outcomes, and tabulate the proportion of outcomes profitable and in the money.

36. Click on Fastest to the right of Calculate Expected Return.

The animation more quickly sweeps through the probability distributions. Once it finishes, the proportion of outcomes profitable becomes the probability of profit. The proportion of outcomes in the money becomes the probability of being in the money. The average return becomes the period expected return for the option.

When you click on Color Deciles, the animation uses the same techniques, performs the same calculations (though to greater precision), and divides each of the probability distributions into color-coded deciles.

37. Click on Color Deciles.

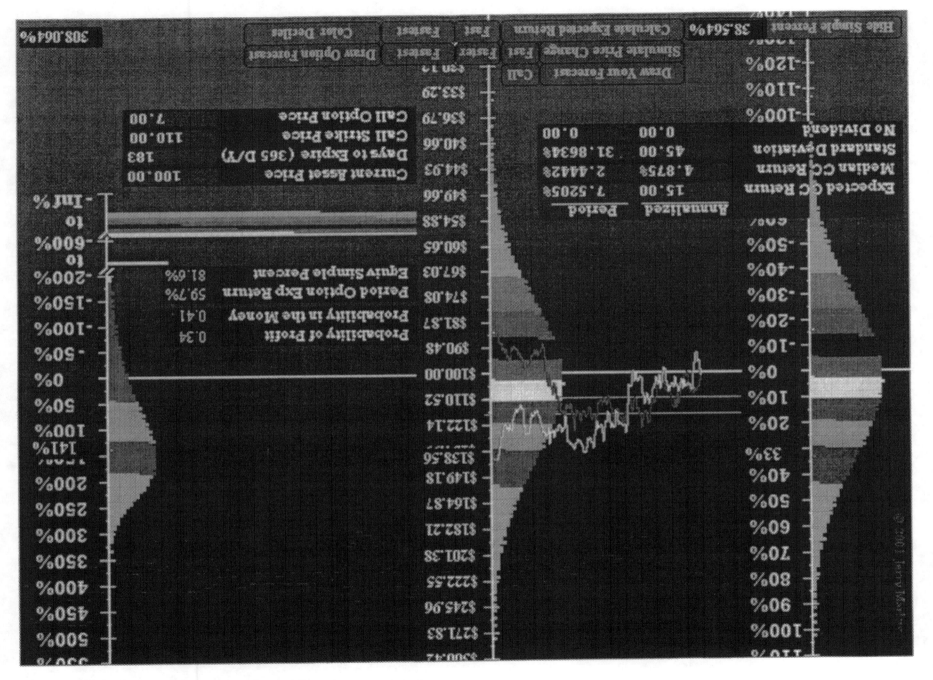

We can use color deciles to see how forecasts for stock return, stock price, and option return correspond to one another.

The outcomes of a given color in one probability distribution correspond to the outcomes of the same color in the other distributions.

> **38. Click on Simulate Price Change until you get a few winners.**

In general, the little squares that tabulate the outcomes appear in the same color in all three distributions.

The general statement is not precisely true for option returns that are below −200%.

The animation lumps together in one bucket all outcomes from −200% to −600%. A hit in this bucket means you've lost from 86.47% to 99.75% of your money. Because multiple deciles may show up in this bucket, the segregation of hits by color may not be maintained.

The animation lumps together in another bucket all outcomes between −600% and negative infinity. A hit in this bucket means you've lost between 99.75% and 100% of your money. Because multiple deciles usually show up in this bucket, the segregation of hits by color usually is not maintained.

Also, at the transition between any two deciles, the same bucket may contain two different colors. The tabulating square may end up in one color on one distribution and in a different color on another.

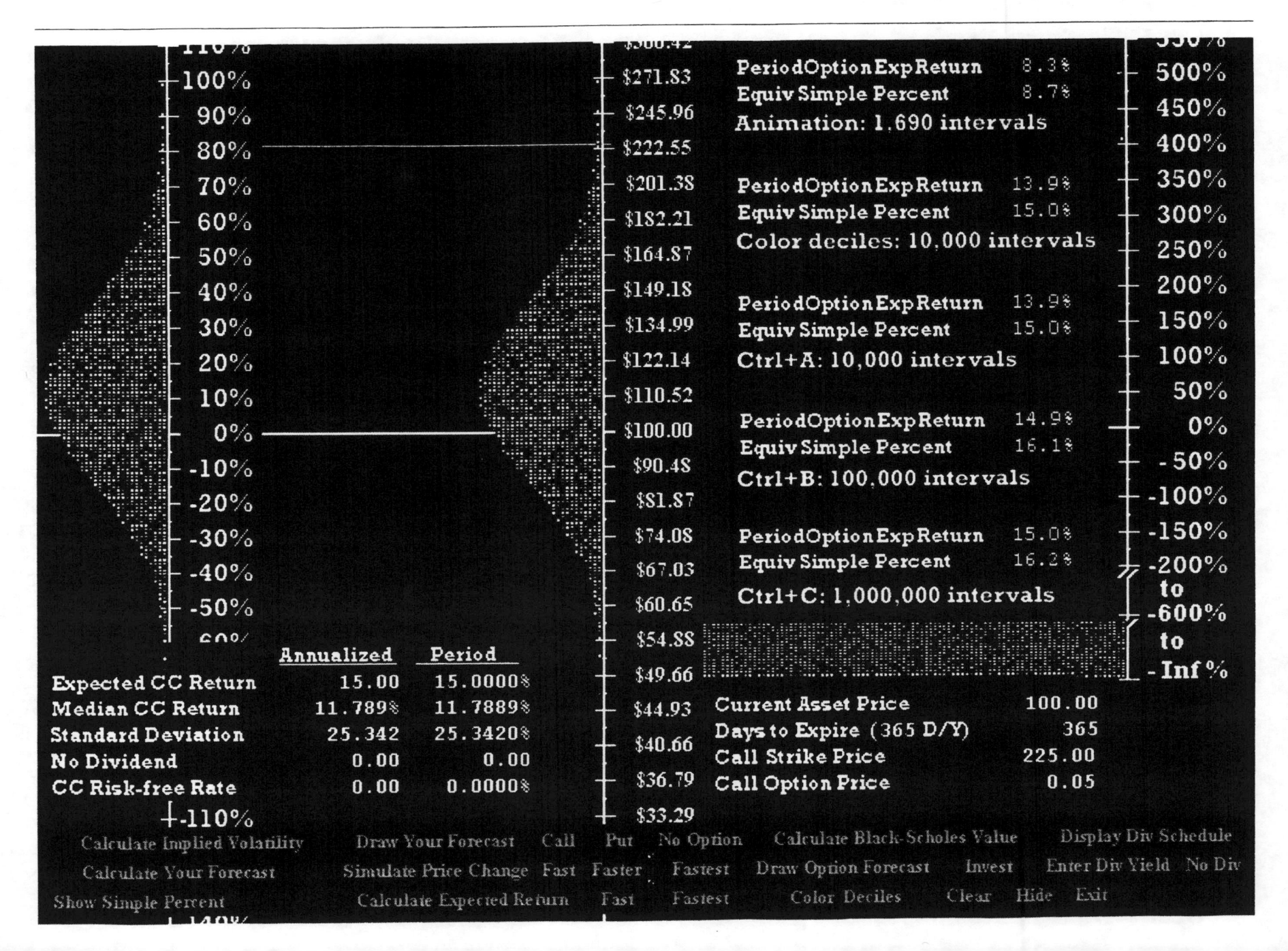

At extremes of probability distributions, Monte Carlo calculations are not very accurate. For greater accuracy, use Ctrl+A, B, or C.

When you click on Calculate Expected Return, Fast, or Fastest, the animation sweeps through the probability distribution, divides it into 1,690 intervals, and calculates an outcome for each one.

For strike prices that are well within a stock's probability distribution, the sweep gives reasonably accurate results. If, however, you are working with a strike price at the extreme of a probability distribution, the 1,690 intervals may not be enough to give accuracy sufficient for your purposes.

> **39. Click on Clear.**
>
> **40. For Days to Expire, enter 365.**
>
> **41. For Call Strike Price, enter 225.00.**
>
> **42. For Call Option Price, enter 0.05.**
>
> **43. For Standard Deviation, enter 25.342.**
>
> **44. Click on Calculate Expected Return Fastest.**

The Monte Carlo sweep through the probability distribution calculates the period option expected return to be 8.3%. By other methods, the expected return of this option can be shown to be 15%.

Why the error?

You see that there are only a few outcomes in the probability distribution above the strike price of $225. With only a small region above the strike price, the 1,690 intervals that the animation uses are not enough to achieve accuracy.

To achieve better accuracy at extremes, professional derivative-pricing software that runs Monte Carlo simulations divides probability distributions into 10,000, 100,000, or perhaps even a million intervals.

Dividing a probability distribution into that many intervals is not feasible for animations that must run on computers of many different speeds. The animation does, however, include calculation routines that divide the probability distribution into 10,000, 100,000, and 1 million intervals. These routines do not animate.

> **45. Click on Color Deciles.**

After drawing the color deciles, the routine divides the distribution into 10,000 intervals and calculates the expected return, in this case, 13.9%. Closer, but still not the right answer.

You also can divide the probability distribution into 10,000 intervals without drawing color deciles.

> **46. To have the Monte Carlo simulation divide the probability distribution into 10,000 intervals, hold down the Ctrl key on your keyboard and press the A key.**

The routine calculates the period option expected return to be 13.9%.

> **47. To divide the probability distribution into 100,000 intervals, hold down the Ctrl key and press the B key.**

The routine calculates the period option expected return to be 14.9%. Very close.

> **48. To divide the probability distribution into 1,000,000 intervals, hold down the Ctrl key and press the C key.**
>
> **49. Go have a sandwich.**

By dividing the probability distribution into a million intervals, the Monte Carlo routine calculates the period option expected return to be 15.0%.

> **50. If a calculation or animation is taking too long, to interrupt it, click long and hard on any of the empty areas on the screen.**

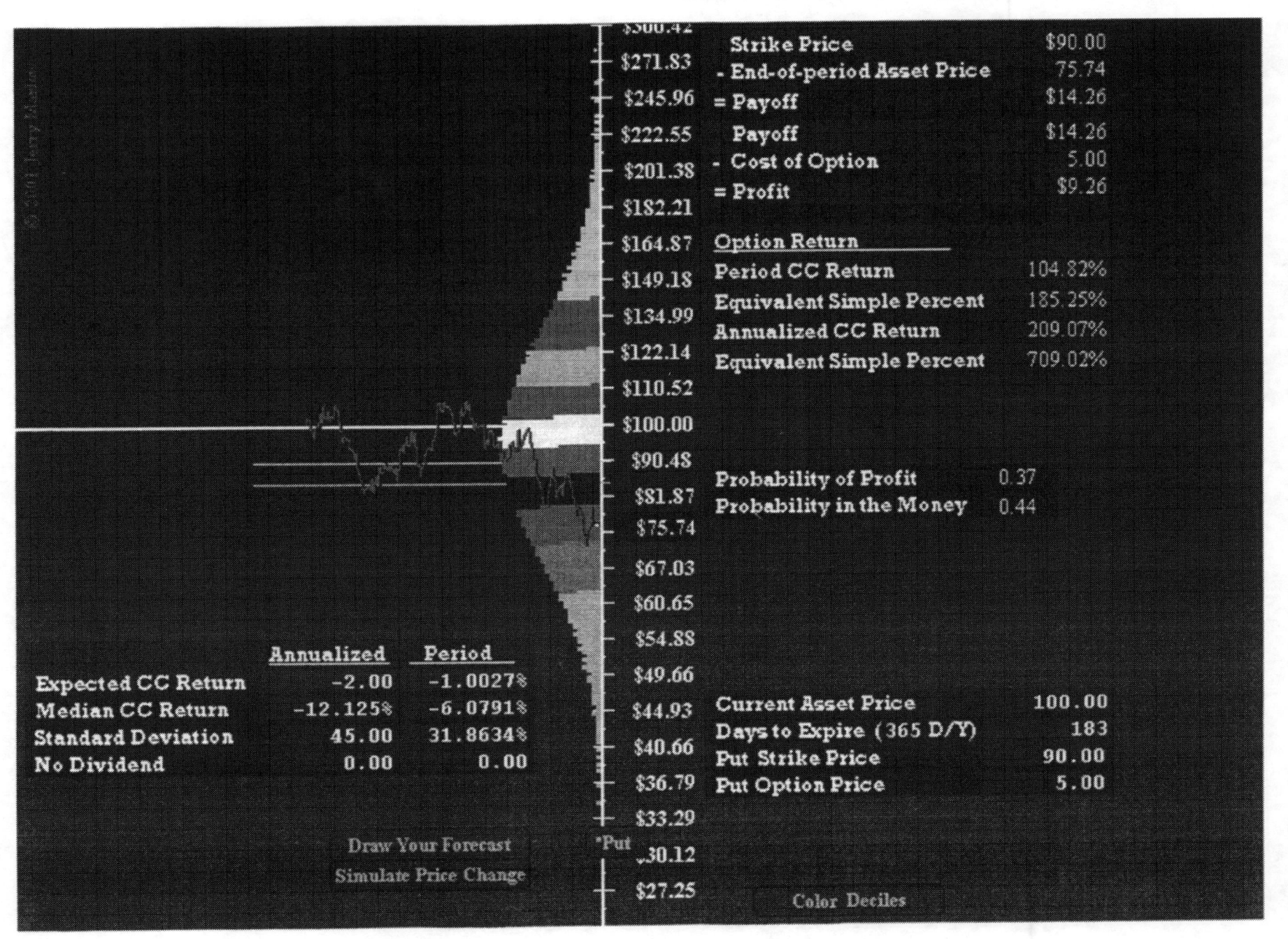

	$300.42	Strike Price	$90.00
	$271.83	- End-of-period Asset Price	75.74
	$245.96	= Payoff	$14.26
	$222.55	Payoff	$14.26
	$201.38	- Cost of Option	5.00
	$182.21	= Profit	$9.26
	$164.87	Option Return	
	$149.18	Period CC Return	104.82%
	$134.99	Equivalent Simple Percent	185.25%
	$122.14	Annualized CC Return	209.07%
	$110.52	Equivalent Simple Percent	709.02%
	$100.00		
	$90.48	Probability of Profit	0.37
	$81.87	Probability in the Money	0.44
	$75.74		
	$67.03		
	$60.65		
	$54.88		
	$49.66		
	$44.93	Current Asset Price	100.00
	$40.66	Days to Expire (365 D/Y)	183
	$36.79	Put Strike Price	90.00
	$33.29	Put Option Price	5.00
	$30.12	
	$27.25	Color Deciles

	Annualized	Period
Expected CC Return	-2.00	-1.0027%
Median CC Return	-12.125%	-6.0791%
Standard Deviation	45.00	31.8634%
No Dividend	0.00	0.00

Draw Your Forecast
Simulate Price Change

*Put

A put gives you the right to sell a stock at a preset price.

When you buy a put option, you purchase the right to sell a stock at a preset price called the strike price.

If the price of the stock is below the strike price or goes below the strike price and you exercise the option, you receive the difference between the strike price and the stock price at the time of exercise.

Given a stock forecast and a put, we can create the same types of animations that we created for call options.

We can simulate potential price paths for the stock and show the option's corresponding end-of-period payoffs.

---

1. Click three times on Clear.

2. Click twice on Hide.

3. Click on Simulate Price Change.

4. For Expected CC Return, enter –2.00.

5. For Standard Deviation, enter 45.00.

6. For Current Asset Price, enter 100.00.

7. Click on Put.

8. For Days to Expire, enter 183.

9. For Put Strike Price, enter 90.00.

10. For Put Option Price, enter 5.00.

The yellow line represents the option's strike price. For a put option to be in the money, the stock price must be below the yellow line.

The distance from the yellow line to the green line represents the option price or premium. For a put option to produce a profit at the time of exercise, the stock price must be below the green line.

---

11. Click on Color Deciles.

The area of the probability distribution below the yellow line represents the probability that the option will finish in the money.

The area of the probability distribution below the green line represents the probability that the option will produce a profit.

---

12. Click on Simulate Price Change. Keep clicking until you get a few winners.

When the end-of-period price is above the strike price, you see that the payoff is zero, your "profit" is negative, and you lose all the money you invested in the option. You have a period continuously compounded rate of return of negative infinity and a holding-period return of –100%.

When the end-of-period price is below the strike price, you see that the payoff is equal to the strike price minus the end-of-period price.

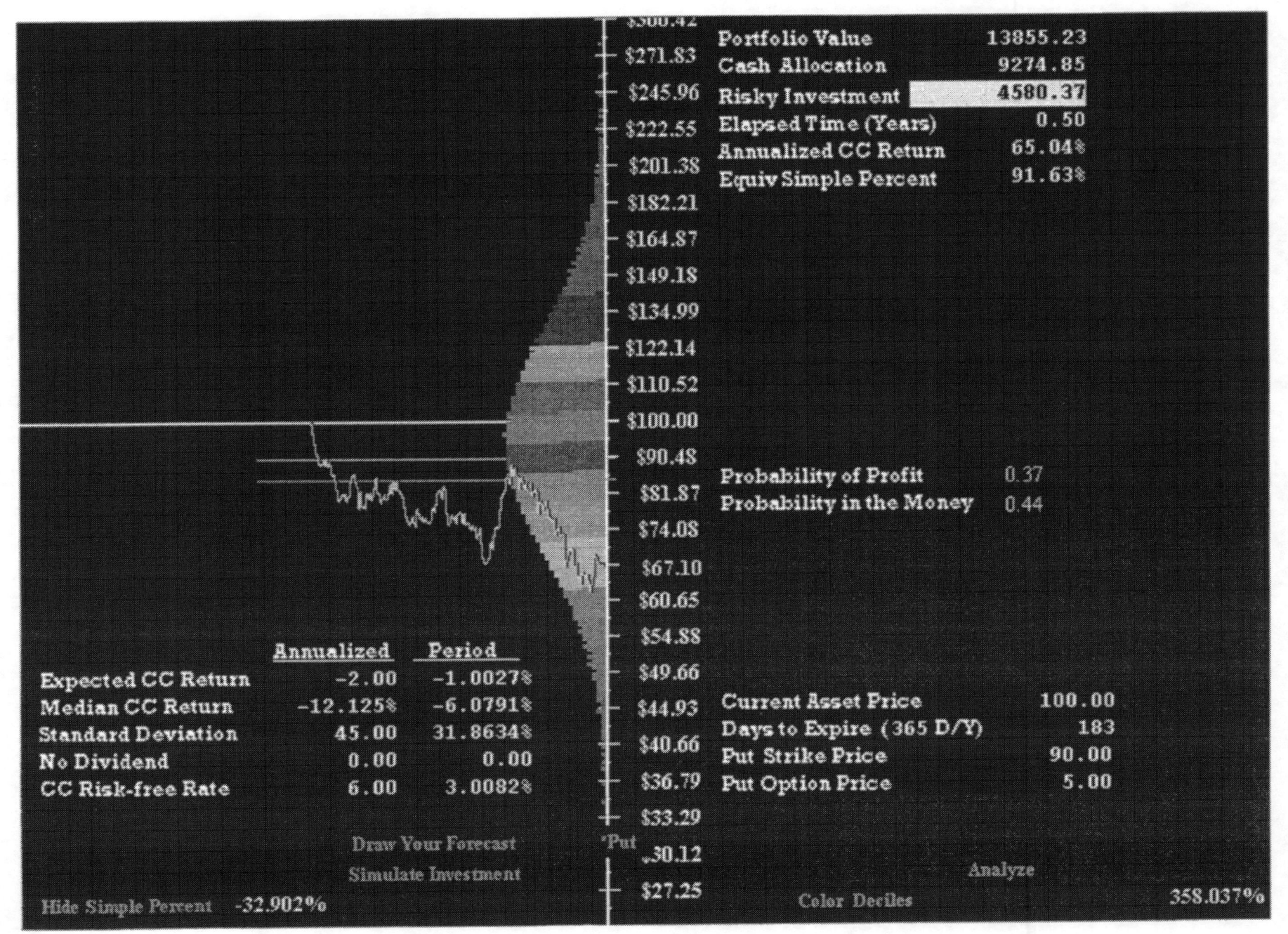

	$300.42	Portfolio Value	13855.23
	$271.83	Cash Allocation	9274.85
	$245.96	Risky Investment	**4580.37**
	$222.55	Elapsed Time (Years)	0.50
	$201.38	Annualized CC Return	65.04%
		Equiv Simple Percent	91.63%
	$182.21		
	$164.87		
	$149.18		
	$134.99		
	$122.14		
	$110.52		
	$100.00		
	$90.48		
		Probability of Profit	0.37
	$81.87	Probability in the Money	0.44
	$74.08		
	$67.10		
	$60.65		
	$54.88		
	$49.66		

	Annualized	Period
Expected CC Return	-2.00	-1.0027%
Median CC Return	-12.125%	-6.0791%
Standard Deviation	45.00	31.8634%
No Dividend	0.00	0.00
CC Risk-free Rate	6.00	3.0082%

$44.93	Current Asset Price	100.00
	Days to Expire (365 D/Y)	183
$40.66	Put Strike Price	90.00
$36.79	Put Option Price	5.00
$33.29		

Draw Your Forecast

Simulate Investment

Put $30.12   Analyze

$27.25   Color Deciles

Hide Simple Percent   -32.902%   358.037%

Once you have your price forecast for a stock, you can simulate potential outcomes of investing in a put you hold to maturity.

Let's say you have $10,000 in your portfolio. You want to invest $1,000 in the option.

13. Click on Show Simple Percent.

14. Click on Invest.

15. For CC Risk-Free Rate, enter 6.00.

16. For Portfolio Value, enter 10000.00. (No $ or commas.)

17. For Risky Investment, enter 1000.00.

18. Click on Simulate Investment.

The animation displays the new value of the portfolio, the new value of the cash allocation, the proceeds of the investment in the option, the elapsed investment period in years, the annualized continuously compounded rate of return for the portfolio, and the equivalent simple percent.

To get a feel for how investing in put options can leverage your investment, make a few more investments of $1,000 in the option.

19. For Risky Investment, enter 1000.00.

20. Click on Simulate Investment.

If you wish to see only the effect on the portfolio of investing in the option, set the risk-free rate to zero.

21. For CC Risk-Free Rate, enter 0.00.

22. For Portfolio Value, enter 10000.00. (No $ or commas.)

23. For Risky Investment, enter 1000.00.

24. Click on Simulate Investment.

Instead of displaying the option payoffs as numerical results, the animation can display option performance graphically as a return on your investment in the option.

25. To make the Invest data fields go away, click on Analyze.

26. To bring the option axes on-screen, click once on Draw Option Forecast.

27. Click on Simulate Price Change.

To tabulate each option return, the animation adds a little square to the option axes.

You can simulate a price change and option return without drawing the price path.

28. Click on Fast immediately to the right of Simulate Price Change.

You can speed up the simulation.

29. Click on Faster to the right of Simulate Price Change.

You can speed up the simulation further.

30. Click on Fastest to the right of Simulate Price Change.

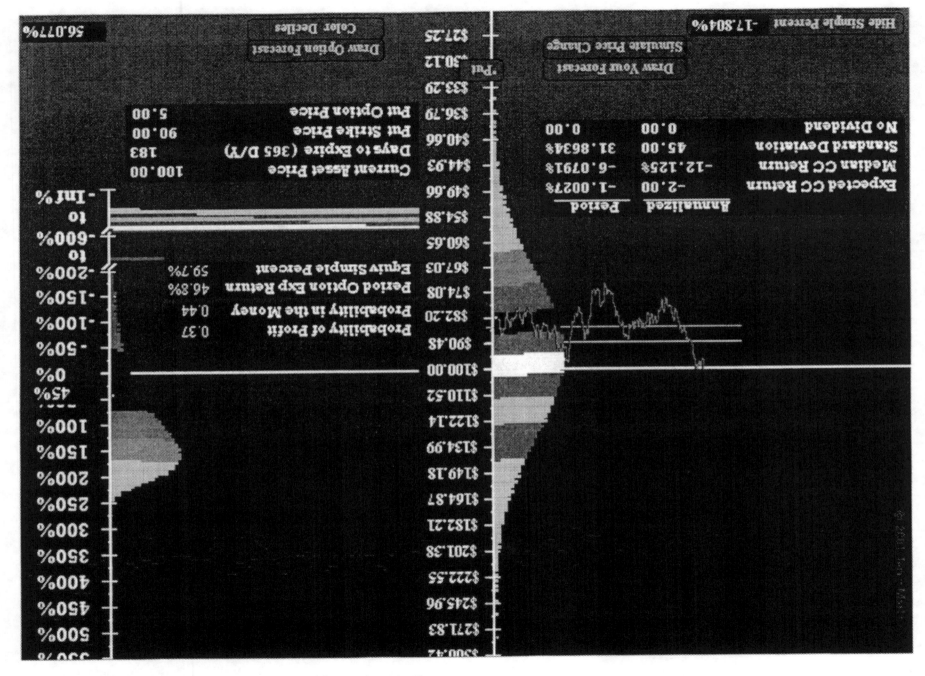

Given your price forecast for a stock, we can calculate a put's probability of profit and period expected return.

The histogram of squares on the left of the screen approximates the probability distributions of the stock's price forecast. Given this stock forecast and option structure, the histogram formed on the option axes approximates the probability distribution or forecast of the option return.

For the put, we can calculate:

■ The option's probability of profit

■ The probability that the end-of-period stock price will be in the money

■ The period expected return of the option

■ The equivalent simple percent of the period option expected return

> **31. Click once on Clear.**
>
> **32. Click a few times on Calculate Expected Return.**

For period average return, the animation is simply calculating a running average of the option returns thus far swept through.

> **33. Click on Fast immediately to the right of Calculate Expected Return.**

Automatically, the animation continues to sweep through the stock forecast, display the corresponding option outcomes, and tabulate the proportion of outcomes profitable and in the money.

> **34. Click on Fastest to the right of Calculate Expected Return.**

The animation more quickly sweeps through the probability distributions.

When you click on Color Deciles, the animation divides each of the probability distributions into color-coded deciles.

> **35. Click on Color Deciles.**

The outcomes of a given color in one probability distribution correspond to the outcomes of the same color in the other distributions.

After it draws the color deciles, the routine divides the probability distribution into 10,000 intervals and calculates the expected return and probability of profit.

> **36. Click on Simulate Price Change.**

In general, the little squares that tabulate the outcomes appear in the same color in all three distributions.

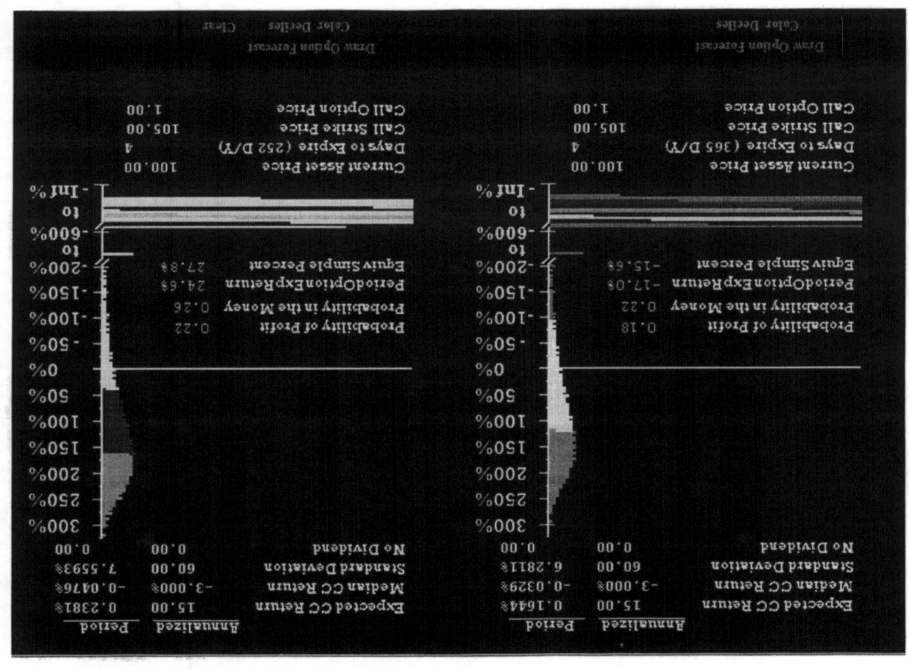

If you count days to expiration in trading days, set days per year to 252. Pay special heed if very few days are left until expiration.

One of the debates that people who trade options engage in is whether nontrading days account for some of a stock's volatility. People who believe nontrading days or events that occur on nontrading days account for some of a stock's volatility think of a year as having 365 days (366 in a leap year). They count days to expiration in calendar days.

People who believe only trading days matter think of a year as having 252 days. They count days to expiration in trading days.

The animation accommodates either belief. Whenever you have a call or put on-screen, you can enter any number you want for days per year.

Just click in or tab to the (___D/Y) field next to Days to Expire.

The animation uses the number in the days-per-year field and the number in the days-to-expire field to calculate the length of the current period as a fraction of a year. It then uses this fraction-of-a-year number to calculate period and annualized numbers from one another.

In particular, the animation uses the period length to calculate period numbers for expected return, median return, standard deviation, risk-free rate, and dividend yield. It then uses these numbers to do analysis and run simulations.

For long times to expiration, whether you use a 365- or 252-day year doesn't have much practical consequence. For example, 183 days of a 365-day year gets pretty much the same results as 126 days of a 252-day year. The important thing is to keep the way you count days to expiration consistent with the number of days you entered for days per year.

When you get down to short times to expiration, however, especially times in the vicinity of a week or less, the number in the days-per-year field and how you count days to expiration can make a big difference.

Let's say it's Monday. You're looking at an option that expires on Friday.

1. Click three times on Clear.

2. Click twice on Hide.

3. Click on Call.

4. Click on Draw Option Forecast.

5. For Current Asset Price, enter 100.00.

6. For (___D/Y), enter 365.

7. For Days to Expire, enter 4.

8. For Call Strike Price, enter 105.00.

9. For Call Option Price, enter 1.00.

10. For Expected CC Return, enter 15.00.

11. For Standard Deviation, enter 60.00.

Make note of the period figures for expected return, median return, and standard deviation.

12. Click on Color Deciles.

The animation calculates probability of profit as 0.18 and period option expected return as −17.0%.

13. For (___D/Y), enter 252.

You see that the period figures for expected return, median return, and standard deviation all increase.

14. Click on Color Deciles.

The animation calculates probability of profit as 0.22 and period option expected return as 24.6%. Big difference!

Figure out whether you believe in calendar days or trading days. For number of days per year, enter 365 or 252. Count days to expiration accordingly.

Draw Option Forecast   Color Deciles   Clear
Fast   Fastest

Simulate Price Change   Fast
Calculate Expected Return
Draw Your Forecast

	Annualized	Period
Expected CC Return	12.00	8.0548%
Median CC Return	1.875	1.2586%
Standard Deviation	45	36.8680%
No Dividend	0.00	0.00

Call Option Price   4.75
Call Strike Price   75.00
Days to Expire (365 D/Y)   245
Current Asset Price   60.00

Equiv Simple Percent   26.3%
PeriodOptionExpReturn   23.3%
Probability in the Money   0.28
Probability of Profit   0.23

$15.07
$19.97
$22.07
$24.39
$26.96
$29.50
$32.93
$36.39
$40.22
$44.45
$49.12
$54.29
$60.00
$66.31
$73.25
$80.99
$89.51
$98.92
$109.33
$120.83
$133.53
$147.55
$163.10

Right axis: 140% -130% -120% -110% -100% No Dividend ... -50% -40% -30% -20% -10% 0% 10% 20% 30% 40% 50% 60% 70% 80% 90% 100% 110%

Left axis: to -Inf% -600% to -200% -150% -100% -50% 0% 50% 100% 150% 200% 250% 300% 350% 400% 450% 500% 550%

Does the expression probability density function make your brain hurt?

Mathematicians often refer to probability distributions as probability density functions.

What the heck does that mean?

Then they start talking about the area under the curve.

What are they talking about?

Let's see.

1. Click three times on Clear.

2. Click twice on Hide.

3. Click on Simulate Price Change.

4. Click on Draw Your Forecast.

5. Click on Call.

6. Click on Draw Option Forecast.

7. For Current Asset Price, enter 60.00.

8. For Days to Expire, enter 245.

9. For Call Strike Price, enter 75.00.

10. For Call Option Price, enter 4.75.

11. If, in the previous exercise, you changed days per year, for (___D/Y), enter 365.

12. For Expected CC Return, enter 12.00.

13. For Standard Deviation, enter 45.00.

14. Click on Draw Your Forecast.

15. Click on Draw Option Forecast.

The idea of a probability density function is that the total area enclosed by a bell-shaped curve adds up to one. (Some like to say it adds up to unity.) Similarly, the total area defined by an option forecast adds up to one.

To make the idea of area under the curve more obvious, we've been sweeping through probability distributions with little squares.

16. Click on Calculate Expected Return Fastest.

We've used these little squares to build histograms and simulate outcomes.

The way we've been doing this may've given you the impression that we can calculate the probability of a particular outcome, say the probability of a stock return of 40% or an end-of-period price of $89.51.

In a formal sense, we cannot assign a probability to a particular outcome. We can only compute probabilities for intervals.

Hence, we cannot assign a probability to an outcome of 40%. We can only compute the probability of an outcome between, say, 39.5% and 40.5%.

Likewise, we cannot assign a probability to an outcome of $89.51. We can only compute the probability of an outcome between, say, $89.505 and $89.515.

So when you see a bunch of little squares stacked up next to 40%, keep in mind that they're really covering an interval between 39.5% and 40.5%. In the end-of-period price histograms shown in this example, the row of little squares adjacent to $89.51 covers the interval between $89.063 and $89.958.

The probability of outcomes in any one interval corresponds to the percentage of little squares that fall in that interval.

17. Click on Color Deciles.

If 10 percent of the little squares fall in the area between returns of 10% and 20%, then the probability of a return between 10% and 20% is 0.1. If 20 percent of the area under the curve falls above an end-of-period price of $81.87, then the probability of an end-of-period price above $81.87 is 0.2.

Now you understand probability density functions. Now you can make other peoples' brains hurt.

Option Pricing

Making options valuation intuitively accessible.

For the nonmathematician, the mathematics of options valuation can be daunting. To make options valuation intuitively accessible, we look at options valuation in four steps:

1. Using your forecast for a stock, calculate the probability-weighted net present value of an option on the stock when the option is held to maturity.

2. Examine the Black-Scholes methodology for calculating the value of a European.

3. Look at the assumptions that underlie the Black-Scholes methodology.

4. See how to make an option's probability-weighted net present value equal its Black-Scholes value.

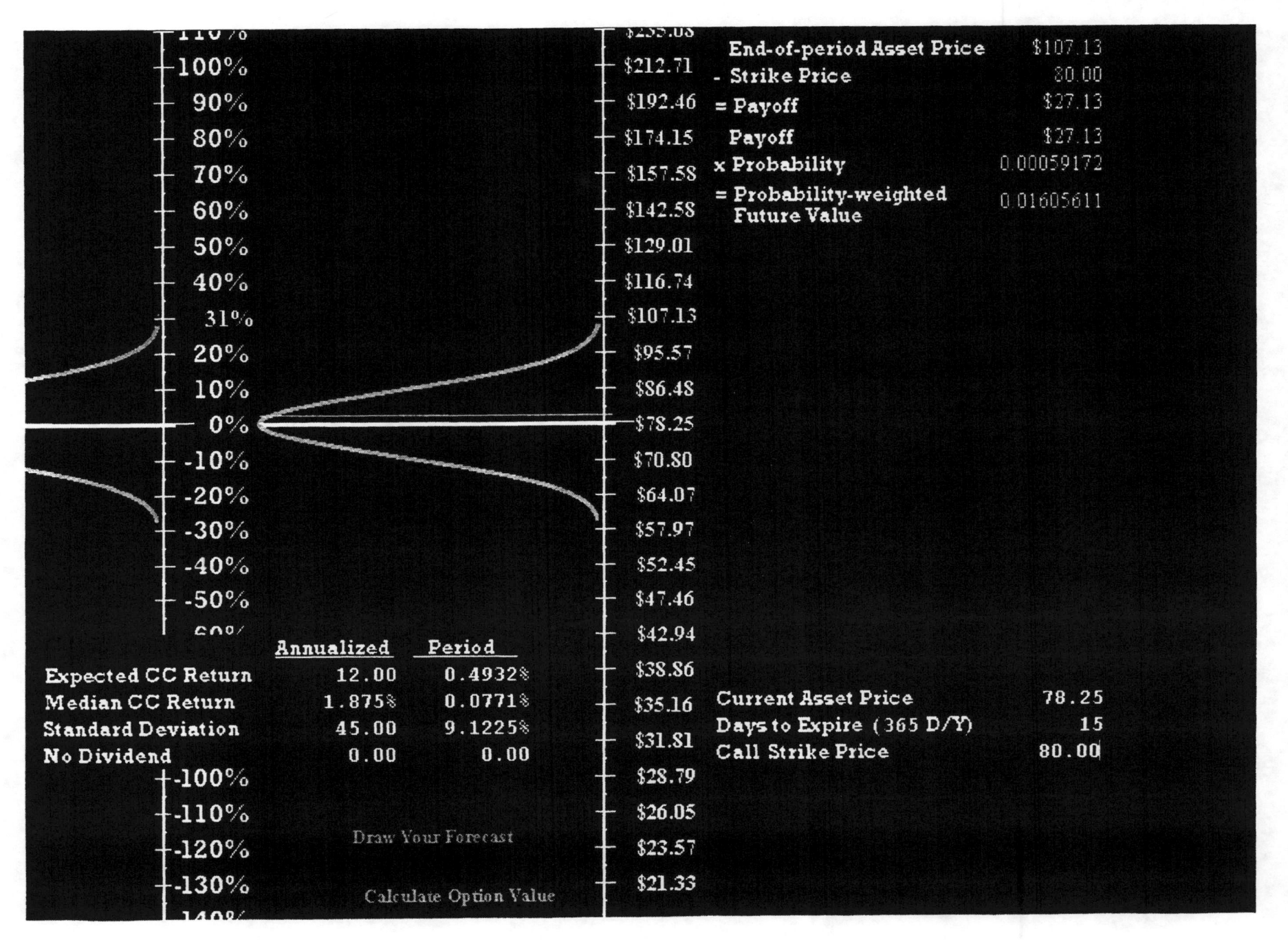

End-of-period Asset Price $107.13
- Strike Price 80.00
= Payoff $27.13

Payoff $27.13
x Probability 0.00059172
= Probability-weighted
  Future Value 0.01605611

	Annualized	Period
Expected CC Return	12.00	0.4932%
Median CC Return	1.875%	0.0771%
Standard Deviation	45.00	9.1225%
No Dividend	0.00	0.00

Current Asset Price 78.25
Days to Expire (365 D/Y) 15
Call Strike Price 80.00

Draw Your Forecast

Calculate Option Value

What's an option worth to you?
Its probability-weighted net present value.

Let's begin with a stock forecast and a call option. From these, we'll calculate the probability-weighted net present value of the option when it is held to maturity.

1. **Click three times on Clear.**

2. **Click twice on Hide.**

3. **Click on Calculate Option Value.**

4. **For expected CC Return, enter 12.00.**

5. **For Standard Deviation, enter 45.00.**

6. **For Current Asset Price, enter 78.25.**

7. **For Days to Expire, enter 15.**

8. **For Call Strike Price, enter 80.00.**

9. **Click on Draw Your Forecast.**

What we're going to do is sweep through the probability distribution of the stock forecast and calculate the probability-weighted net present value of all the option payoffs.

10. **Click on Calculate Option Value.**

The animation begins with the extreme high-price outcome for the stock forecast. From this outcome, it calculates the payoff.

If the stock price were to go to $107.13 and you exercised the option, your payoff would be $27.13.

11. **Click again on Calculate Option Value.**

Very often, financial calculations make use of the concept of probability-weighted value. If your brother-in-law owes you $500 and there's only 1 chance in 10 that he is going to pay you, the probability-weighted value of the obligation is ($500)($\frac{1}{10}$) or $50. If you believed that this was in fact the case, you might be willing to sell the obligation to a third party for $50.

Similarly, you might buy a raffle ticket. Let's say your local community organization is raffling off a new car. The car's fair market value is $39,375. The community organization will sell 100,000 tickets. The fair value of one ticket on the day of the raffle is $39,375 times 1/100,000 or $0.39.

We apply the same concept to find the probability-weighted future value of the stock-price outcome of $107.13.

Given the scale at which the animation draws probability distributions, it takes 1,690 little squares to fill in a probability distribution. Hence, the probability of any one representative outcome is 1/1,690 or 0.00059172.

When we multiply $107.13 times 0.00059172, we get $0.01605611—slightly more than 1.6 cents.

This is the fair value 15 days from now of this one outcome represented by the little square at $107.13. Hence, what we have calculated is the probability-weighted future value of this one outcome.

Next we want to calculate the probability-weighted present value of this one outcome.

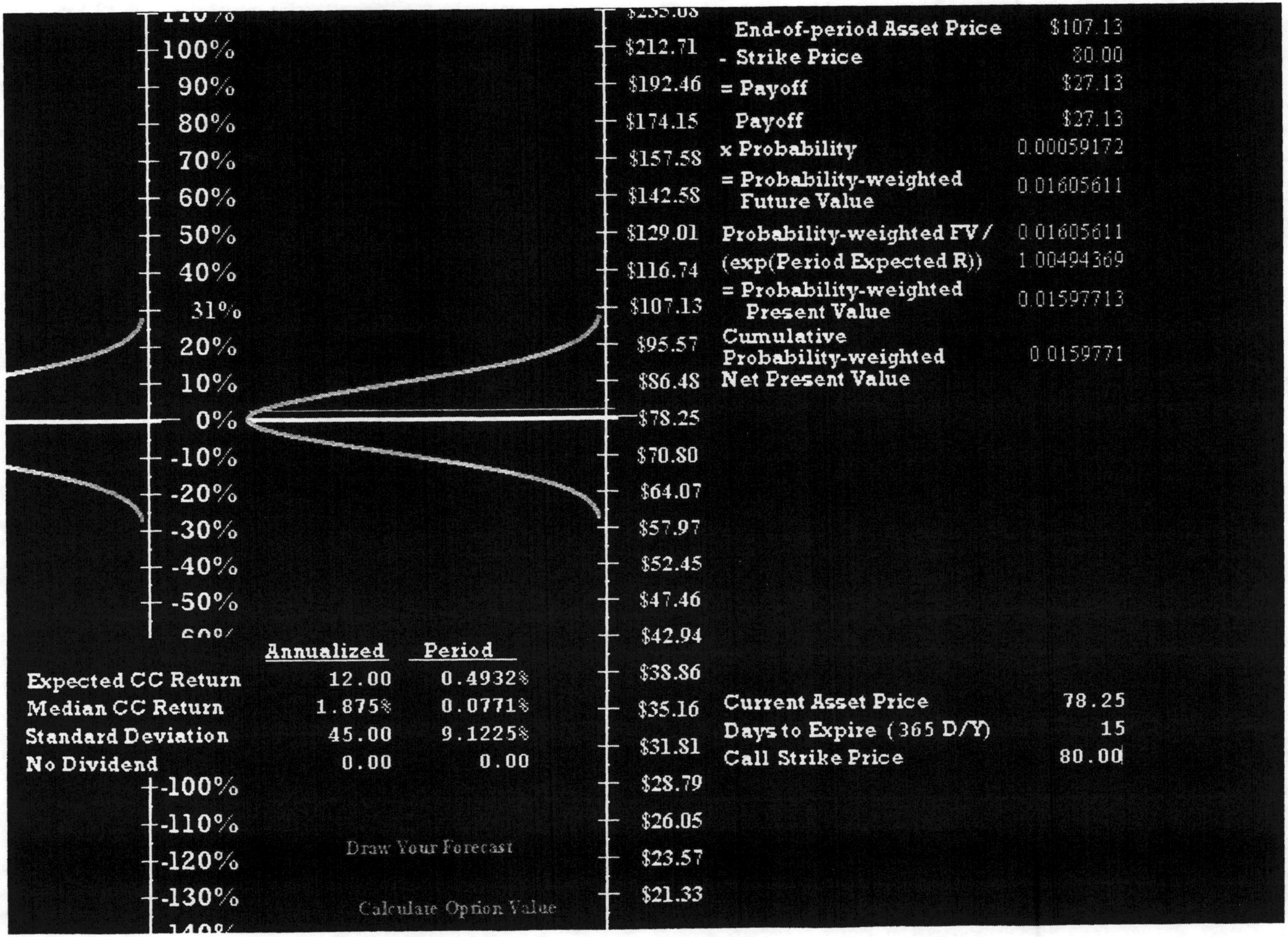
100%
90%
80%
70%
60%
50%
40%
31%
20%
10%
0%
-10%
-20%
-30%
-40%
-50%
$212.71
$192.46
$174.15
$157.58
$142.58
$129.01
$116.74
$107.13
$95.57
$86.48
$78.25
$70.80
$64.07
$57.97
$52.45
$47.46
$42.94
$38.86
$35.16
$31.81
$28.79
$26.05
$23.57
$21.33
End-of-period Asset Price $107.13
- Strike Price 80.00
= Payoff $27.13
Payoff $27.13
x Probability 0.00059172
= Probability-weighted Future Value 0.01605611
Probability-weighted FV / 0.01605611
(exp(Period Expected R)) 1.00494369
= Probability-weighted Present Value 0.01597713
Cumulative Probability-weighted Net Present Value 0.0159771
Annualized Period
Expected CC Return 12.00 0.4932%
Median CC Return 1.875% 0.0771%
Standard Deviation 45.00 9.1225%
No Dividend 0.00 0.00
Current Asset Price 78.25
Days to Expire (365 D/Y) 15
Call Strike Price 80.00
-100%
-110%
-120%
-130%
Draw Your Forecast
Calculate Option Value

Finding the probability-weighted net present value of an option's probability distribution is like doing discounted cash-flow analysis in corporate finance.

12. Click again on Calculate Option Value.

Earlier, we touched upon the concepts of present value and future value. You can multiply a present value by 1 plus the simple interest rate to get a future value.

If you buy a CD today for $100 and it pays 10% simple interest, its future value one year from today is $110.

($100.00)(1.10) = $110.00

Or you can go the other way. To get a present value, you discount the future value. You divide it by 1 plus the simple interest rate.

If a CD will be worth $110 a year from today and it pays 10% simple interest, its present value is $100.

$110.00/1.10 = $100.00

The relationship between continuously compounded rates of return and simple interest rates is:

1 + simple interest rate = exp (continuously compounded rate of return)

To discount the probability-weighted future value of an option outcome, we use the period expected continuously compounded rate of return.

In our example,

1 + simple interest rate = exp(0.004932)
= 1.00494369

Therefore, in our example, the probability-weighted net present value (PWNPV) of the one outcome of $107.13 is

PWNPV = probability weighted future value/exp (continuously compounded rate of return)
= $0.01605611/1.00494369
= $0.01597713

We have calculated the probability-weighted net present value of one outcome. If you were going to buy a raffle ticket on this one outcome, the raffle ticket's fair value would be $0.01597713 or slightly less than 1.6 cents.

13. Click again on Calculate Option Value.

Here we save the $0.01597713 as the first installment of the cumulative probability-weighted net present value for the entire probability distribution.

14. Click a few more times on Calculate Option Value.

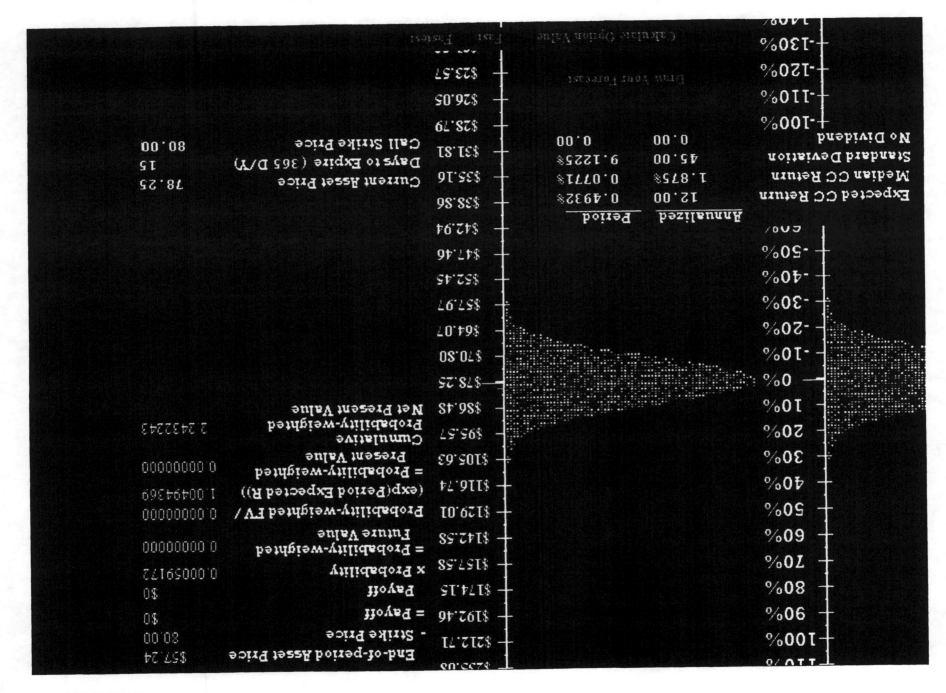

If you agree with the forecast and you do not require extra compensation for taking on the exposure to uncertainty, you might be willing to pay for an option its probability-weighted net present value.

The animation goes through the same series of calculations for each potential outcome and adds the probability-weighted net present value to the cumulative probability-weighted net present value.

> **15. Click on Fast immediately to the right of Calculate Option Value.**

The animation automatically continues to sweep through the stock forecasts and calculate the probability-weighted net present value for the potential outcomes.

> **16. Click on Fastest to the right of Calculate Option Value.**

The animation more quickly sweeps through the forecasts. When it finishes, it displays the cumulative probability-weighted net present value of the outcomes in the forecast.

If you agreed with the stock forecast and you did not require extra compensation for taking on the risk associated with an investment in the option, then you might reasonably accept that the probability-weighted net present value, $2.24, is fair value for this option.

The Black-Scholes value of an option is the expected cost of hedging the sale of the option.

In the previous section, we took a forecast for a stock and combined it with a call option. We calculated the probability-weighted net present value of the option held to maturity. Is this the price you would have to pay in the marketplace to buy this option?

No. Not if the risk-free rate is less than your expected return of 12%.

Why not?

If you were to pay $2.24 for the option in the previous example, an options trader could sell you the option and simultaneously hedge his exposure at a cost of less than $2.24. He would be able to perform arbitrage. He would be able to earn a risk-free profit.

Efficient financial markets quickly eliminate opportunities for arbitrage. Therefore, the fair price of an option is the cost to a trader of hedging the exposure he creates when he sells an option. The Black-Scholes formula for the value of an option gives the cost of hedging the sale of the option. The formulas rely on the Black-Scholes assumptions about the behavior of the financial markets.

In theory, after a trader sets up a hedge, delta hedging keeps his exposures in balance at no additional costs. Hence, the Black-Scholes value is the cost of setting up the hedge.

When a person hedges exposures, he balances his assets and liabilities in such a way that an increase in his assets offsets any increase in his liabilities. A decrease in his liabilities offsets any decrease in his assets. If he keeps himself perfectly hedged, his overall exposure remains neutral. He shouldn't care whether his assets and liabilities grow or shrink so long as they stay in synch.

The Black-Scholes formulas rely on a form of hedging known as delta hedging. An option's delta is the ratio of option-price change to stock-price change. In delta hedging, a trader sets up the hedge so that his assets and liabilities are in balance.

To hedge the sale of a call, the assets and liabilities a trader balances are these:

Assets

■ Delta shares of stock

Liabilities

■ A bond that grows or shrinks in value with the probability that the option is going to finish in the money

■ The value of the options that he has sold

As the number of days to expiration decreases and the stock price changes, the trader keeps his exposures in balance. Sometimes, he borrows more money and buys more stock. Sometimes, he sells stock and pays down some of the bond.

When the option expires, it is either in the money or out of it. If the trader has sold call options and the options expire in the money, at the time of expiration, he will own enough shares to satisfy the call. Receiving the strike price for the shares will enable him to pay off the bond.

If the call option expires out of the money, at the time of expiration, the trader will hold no shares. The value of the bond will have gone to zero, and he will owe no money on it.

Let's look at the delta hedging assets and liabilities in greater detail.

Number of options 10,000
Strike price $80.00
Standard deviation 45.0%
CC Risk-free rate 5.0%
Dividends $0.00

Daily Delta Hedging in Concept—Matching Assets to Liabilities

			Assets				
Days to Exp	Stock Price	Option Delta	Shares Required for Delta Hedge—Delta X Number of Options	Shares Purchased or Sold to Meet Requirement	Shares Held after Purchase or Sale	Cost of Shares Purchased or Sold	Total Assets—Market Value of Shares Held
15	$78.25	0.43081	4,308	4,308	4,308	$337,107	$337,107
14	$82.52	0.66193	6,619	2,311	6,619	$190,722	$546,225
13	$81.74	0.62430	6,243	−376	6,243	−$30,759	$510,303
12	$79.51	0.49427	4,943	−1,300	4,943	−$103,387	$392,994
11	$78.67	0.43792	4,379	−564	4,379	−$44,331	$344,512
10	$80.28	0.54084	5,408	1,029	5,408	$82,624	$434,186
9	$82.25	0.67195	6,720	1,311	6,720	$107,838	$552,679
8	$80.00	0.51984	5,198	−1,521	5,198	−$121,688	$415,872
7	$77.36	0.31138	3,114	−2,085	3,114	−$161,265	$240,884
6	$77.63	0.31628	3,163	49	3,163	$3,804	$245,528
5	$78.14	0.34189	3,419	256	3,419	$20,012	$267,153
4	$77.89	0.29729	2,973	−446	2,973	−$34,739	$231,559
3	$79.29	0.42542	4,254	1,281	4,254	$101,594	$337,316
2	$80.08	0.52189	5,219	965	5,219	$77,253	$417,930
1	$82.14	0.87251	8,725	3,506	8,725	$287,999	$716,680
0	$83.06	1.00000	10,000	1,275	10,000	$105,893	$830,600

Assets:
■ Delta shares of stock

An option's delta or hedge ratio is the ratio of a change in the option price to a change in the price of the underlying stock. For example, if a $1 change in the price of a stock will cause a $0.43081 change in the value of a call option, then the option's delta is 0.43081.

An option's delta remains the same only over a small price range for the stock. As the price of the stock changes, delta changes. Also, as the number of days to expiration changes, an option's delta changes.

A call option's delta always lies somewhere between 1.0 and 0. If a call is deep in the money and little time is left before it expires, the option's delta will be close to 1.0. A $1 change in the price of the stock will cause close to a $1 change in the value of the call.

If a call is deep out of the money and little time is left before the option expires, its delta will approach 0. A $1 change in the price of the stock will cause almost zero change in the value of the option.

To set up a delta hedge, a trader calculates the option's delta and buys delta shares of stock. Let's say the stock price is $78.25. The option's delta is 0.43081. The trader has sold 10,000 options.

To set up the hedge, the trader buys 4,308.1 shares of stock. He pays (4,308.1)($78.25) = $337,107.20 for the stock. At this point in time, his assets are 4,308.1 shares of stock with a market value of $337,107.20.

(To make the numbers come out right, we say the trader buys 4,308.1 shares of stock. In reality, the trader would buy 4,308 shares. Also 0.43081 is a rounded number. To perform the multiplication, we use the unrounded value and get the product $337,107.20. If you multiply 4,308.1 times $78.25, you get $337,108.825.)

To stay perfectly hedged, as the number of days to expiration and the stock price keep changing, a trader keeps recalculating the option's delta. When delta goes up, he borrows more money and buys more stock. When delta goes down, he sells off stock and pays down some of the bond.

At expiration, delta will be either one or zero. If a call option finishes in the money, delta will be one. The trader will own one share of stock for every option he has sold. He will hold the number of shares he needs to satisfy exercise of the call.

If the option finishes out of the money, delta will be zero. The trader will own no stock. The holder of the option will not exercise it.

The previous table shows daily price changes for a stock over 15 days. For each day and price, the table shows the delta for a call option on the stock and the shares purchased or sold to meet the requirements of a delta hedge.

Liabilities:

- **A bond that grows or shrinks in value with the probability that the option is going to finish in the money**
- **The value of the option**

To buy delta shares of stock, a trader raises money in two ways:

1. At the risk-free rate, he sells a bond short. That is, he borrows money.

2. He receives money from the sale of the options.

These actions create his liabilities.

How much money should he borrow?

Black-Scholes Options-Pricing Theory says the amount he should borrow is determined primarily by two factors: the probability that the option will finish in the money and the strike price.

Earlier we saw that, given a stock forecast and an option structure, the animation can calculate the probability that the option will finish in the money. As the days to expiration and the stock price change, the probability that an option will finish in the money changes.

The probability always lies somewhere between zero and one. If a call is deep in the money and little time is left before expiration, the probability that the option will finish in the money is close to one.

If an option is deep out of the money and little time is left before expiration, the probability is close to zero.

To set up a delta hedge for a call option, a trader calculates the probability that the option will finish in the money. He multiplies the probability times the option strike price. This calculation gives the probability-adjusted value of the bond at the time of the option's expiration.

Daily Delta Hedging in Concept—Matching Assets to Liabilities

Days to Exp	Stock Price	Value of Option	Probability Option Will Finish in the Money	Value of Bond at Expiry—Probability In-Money X Strike Price	Hedge Requirement—Bond Value Today	One-Day Interest on Previous Day's Total Bond	Money Borrowed or Repaid to Meet Hedge Requirement	Total Bond Obligation—Borrowing + Interest	Value of Options Sold	Total Liabilities—Borrowings + Interest due + Market Value of Options Sold
15	$78.25	$2.152	0.39530	$316,237	$315,588	$0.00	$315,588	$315,588	$21,520	$337,107
14	$82.52	$4.387	0.62915	$503,320	$502,356	$43.23	$186,725	$502,356	$43,868	$546,224
13	$81.74	$3.780	0.59168	$473,344	$472,502	$68.82	−$29,923	$472,502	$37,801	$510,303
12	$79.51	$2.418	0.46178	$369,425	$368,818	$64.73	−$103,748	$368,818	$24,179	$392,997
11	$78.67	$1.912	0.40735	$325,878	$325,387	$50.53	−$43,481	$325,387	$19,122	$344,509
10	$80.28	$2.579	0.51119	$408,953	$408,393	$44.58	$82,961	$408,393	$25,790	$434,183
9	$82.25	$3.649	0.64604	$516,829	$516,193	$55.95	$107,743	$516,193	$36,486	$552,679
8	$80.00	$2.169	0.49327	$394,619	$394,187	$70.72	−$122,077	$394,187	$21,688	$415,874
7	$77.36	$0.935	0.28971	$231,764	$231,542	$54.00	−$162,699	$231,542	$9,346	$240,887
6	$77.63	$0.889	0.29604	$236,829	$236,635	$31.72	$5,061	$236,635	$8,890	$245,525
5	$78.14	$0.912	0.32276	$258,211	$258,035	$32.42	$21,367	$258,035	$9,117	$267,152
4	$77.89	$0.673	0.28119	$224,949	$224,826	$35.35	−$33,244	$224,826	$6,733	$231,559
3	$79.29	$0.985	0.40950	$327,598	$327,463	$30.80	$102,607	$327,463	$9,854	$337,317
2	$80.08	$1.115	0.50861	$406,885	$406,774	$44.86	$79,265	$406,774	$11,152	$417,926
1	$82.14	$2.275	0.86753	$694,025	$693,930	$55.73	$287,101	$693,930	$22,752	$716,683
0	$83.06	$3.060	1.00000	$800,000	$800,000	$95.07	$105,975	$800,000	$30,600	$830,600

Liabilities

For example:

Probability finish in the Money	0.39530
X Strike price	$80.00
= Bond value at expiration	$31.6237

The trader calculates the present value of this amount.

Bond value at expiration	$31.6237
÷ exp(period risk-free rate)	1.00206
= Bond value today	$31.5588

For each option he sells, this is the amount the trader borrows. Had he sold 10,000 options, he would borrow (10,000) ($31.5588) = $315,588. This would be the amount of one of his liabilities when he sets up the hedge.

The trader's other liability is the value of the option. For now, let's just note that the value of the option at the time of setting up the hedge is $2.15197. Had he sold 10,000 options, the liability of the options would be $21,519.70.

Hence, at set up, for the sale of 10,000 options, we have:

Assets

Market value of delta shares of stock	$337,107.20

Liabilities

Present value of bond obligation	$315,587.50
Value of options sold	21,519.70
Total liabilities	$337,107.20

As the time to expiration and the stock price change, the probability that the option will finish in the money changes. To remain hedged, the trader recalculates the probability that the option will finish in the money and recalculates the present value of the hedge bond. The value of the options sold changes. The hedge stays in balance.

At expiration, the probability that the option will finish in the money is either one or zero. If a call option finishes in the money, the probability is one. The value of the bond will be equal to the strike price times the number of options sold.

When the option holder exercises the option, the trader receives the strike price times the number of options sold. He uses the proceeds to pay off the bond.

If a call option finishes out of the money, the final probability of finishing in the money is zero. The bond value is zero. The option holder does not exercise the option. The trader receives no money. The trader has no bond to pay off.

The table on page 134 shows the asset side of a delta hedge. The table above shows the liabilities side of the same hedge. For each day and price, the table shows the probability the option will finish in the money, the bond value, option value, and total liabilities.

Strike price $80.00
Days to expiration   15
Standard deviation 45.0%
CC risk-free rate   5.0%
Dividends $0.00

Black-Scholes value of an option equals the cost of setting up a self-financing hedge.

Setup costs = (Option delta × stock price) − present value of (probability finish in the money × strike price)

			Assets			Liabilities			
Days to Exp	Stock Price	Option Delta	Number of Shares Required for Delta Hedge— Delta X Number of Options	Cost of Shares Purchased— Number of Shares X Stock Price	Probability Option will Finish in the Money	Value of Bond at Expiry— Probability In-Money X Strike Price	Hedge Requirement— Bond Value Today	Value of Options— Cost of Shares Purchased - Bond Value Today	Black-Scholes Option Value
15	$78.25	0.43081	4,308	$337,107	0.39530	$316,237	$315,588	$21,520	$2.15197

In theory, once a trader sets up a delta hedge, it doesn't cost him any additional money to maintain it.

In the theory that underlies the Black-Scholes Option-Pricing Model, a trader rebalances his hedge continuously. Assets and liabilities stay perfectly in balance.

Once a trader sets up a delta hedge, any additional shares he needs to maintain the delta hedge he buys with money he borrows. In theory, to keep the hedge balanced, he requires no additional infusion of funds. The cost of a delta hedge is the cost of setting it up. Hence, an option's Black-Scholes value is the cost to a trader of setting up a delta hedge.

In our example earlier, we saw that at the setup of the delta hedge, the assets equal the liabilities.

Assets

Market value of delta shares of stock	$337,107.20

Liabilities

Present value of bond obligation	$315,587.50
Value of options sold	21,519.70
Total liabilities	$337,107.20

We did not say how the option value was derived.

The Black-Scholes value of an option is the cost of setting up the hedge. It is the difference between the value of delta shares of stock and the value of the bond.

Market value of delta shares of stock	$337,107.20
− Present value of bond obligation	315,587.50
Value of 10,000 options sold	$ 21,519.70
Value of one option	$ 2.15197

The table above shows the cost of setting up the hedge in our example.

	Annualized	Period
Standard Deviation	45.00	9.1225%
No Dividend	0.00	0.00
CC Risk-free Rate	5.00	0.2055%

Current Asset Price	
Current Asset Price	78.25
Days to Expire (365 D/Y)	15
Call Strike Price	80.00
Black-Scholes Value	2.15

Calculate Black-Scholes Value

To calculate the Black-Scholes value of an option, the animation calculates the cost of setting up the delta hedge.

To calculate the Black-Scholes value of a call, the animation goes through the same steps shown in the spreadsheet examples.

1. Click three times on Clear.

2. Click twice on Hide.

3. Click on Calculate Black-Scholes Value.

4. For Standard Deviation, enter 45.00.

5. For CC Risk-Free Rate, enter 5.00.

6. For Current Asset Price, enter 78.25.

7. For Days to Expire, enter 15.

8. For Call Strike Price, enter 80.00.

9. Click again on Calculate Black-Scholes Value.

	Option delta	0.43081
×	Current asset price	$78.25
=	Cost of delta shares	$33.71072
	Probability finish in the money	0.39530
×	Strike price	$80.00
=	Bond value at expiration	$-31.62367
	Bond value at expiration	$-31.62367
÷	exp(period risk-free rate)	1.00206
=	Bond value today	$-31.55875
	Cost of delta shares	$33.71072
+	Bond value today	$-31.55875
=	Black-Scholes value	$2.15197

Black-Scholes Assumptions (Part II)

Delta hedging brings into play several additional Black-Scholes assumptions.

Earlier, we reviewed some of the assumptions that underlie Black-Scholes Options-Pricing Theory:

- Stock returns expressed as geometric rates of return are normally distributed.

- Price changes are lognormally distributed.

- The potential price paths of a stock can be characterized by a geometric Brownian motion model.

- The volatility of a stock's price path is constant over the investment horizon.

Delta hedging brings into play several additional assumptions:

- Stock-price paths are continuous. There are no discontinuous jumps in price changes.

- A trader or investor can trade continuously.

- The financial markets are perfectly liquid. Hence, a trader's attempt to buy or sell will not move prices up or down.

- If he wishes to make a risk-free investment, a trader or investor can borrow at the risk-free rate.

- A trader or investor can sell stock short and have full use of the proceeds.

- The risk-free rate of interest will not change over the investment horizon.

- Traders and investors incur no transaction costs such as bid-ask spreads or brokerage fees and commissions.

- The price of an option is the cost of hedging a position in that option.

- The financial markets do not permit the existence of arbitrage opportunities.

- Investors are risk neutral. That is, they do not require greater expected returns as compensation for taking on greater exposures to uncertainty.

Number of options	10,000
Strike price	$80.00
Days to expiration	15
Standard deviation	45.0%
CC risk-free rate	5.0%
Dividends	$0.00

Daily Delta Hedging in Practice—Borrowing Enough Money to Cover Stock Purchases

						Liabilities				
Days to Exp	Stock Price	Value of Option	Probability Option Will Finish in the Money	Value of Bond at Expiry— Probability In-Money X Strike Price	Hedge Require-ment— Bond Value Today	One-Day Interest on Previous Day's Total Bond	Money Borrowed for or Repaid from Stock Transaction	Total Bond Obligation— Borrowing + Interest	Value of Options Sold	Total Liabilities— Borrowings + Interest due + Market Value of Options Sold
15	$78.25	$2.152	0.39530	$316,237	$315,588	$0.00	$315,588	$315,588	$21,520	$337,107
14	$82.52	$4.387				$43.23	$190,765	$506,396	$43,868	$550,264
13	$81.74	$3.780				$69.37	-$30,689	$475,776	$37,801	$513,577
12	$79.51	$2.418				$65.18	-$103,322	$372,519	$24,179	$396,698
11	$78.67	$1.912				$51.03	-$44,280	$328,291	$19,122	$347,413
10	$80.28	$2.579				$44.97	$82,669	$411,005	$25,790	$436,795
9	$82.25	$3.649				$56.31	$107,894	$518,956	$36,486	$555,442
8	$80.00	$2.169				$71.09	-$121,617	$397,410	$21,688	$419,097
7	$77.36	$0.935				$54.44	-$161,210	$236,254	$9,346	$245,600
6	$77.63	$0.889				$32.37	$3,836	$240,123	$8,890	$249,013
5	$78.14	$0.912				$32.90	$20,045	$260,200	$9,117	$269,317
4	$77.89	$0.673				$35.65	-$34,703	$225,532	$6,733	$232,265
3	$79.29	$0.985				$30.90	$101,625	$327,188	$9,854	$337,042
2	$80.08	$1.115				$44.82	$77,298	$404,531	$11,152	$415,683
1	$82.14	$2.275				$55.42	$288,055	$692,641	$22,752	$715,394
0	$83.06	$3.060				$94.89	$105,988	$798,724	$30,600	$829,324

Delta hedging in practice is different from delta hedging in theory.

In actuality, the examples in the spread-sheet tables did not satisfy the Black-Scholes assumptions. We did not rebalance the hedge continuously. We didn't even rebalance it whenever there was a small change in delta. Instead, we rebalanced once a day. With daily rebalancing, the amount of money borrowed was not always sufficient to cover the cost of the shares purchased.

In practice, a trader simply may borrow the amount of money necessary to cover the purchase of the shares required to maintain the delta hedge. The table above shows this practice.

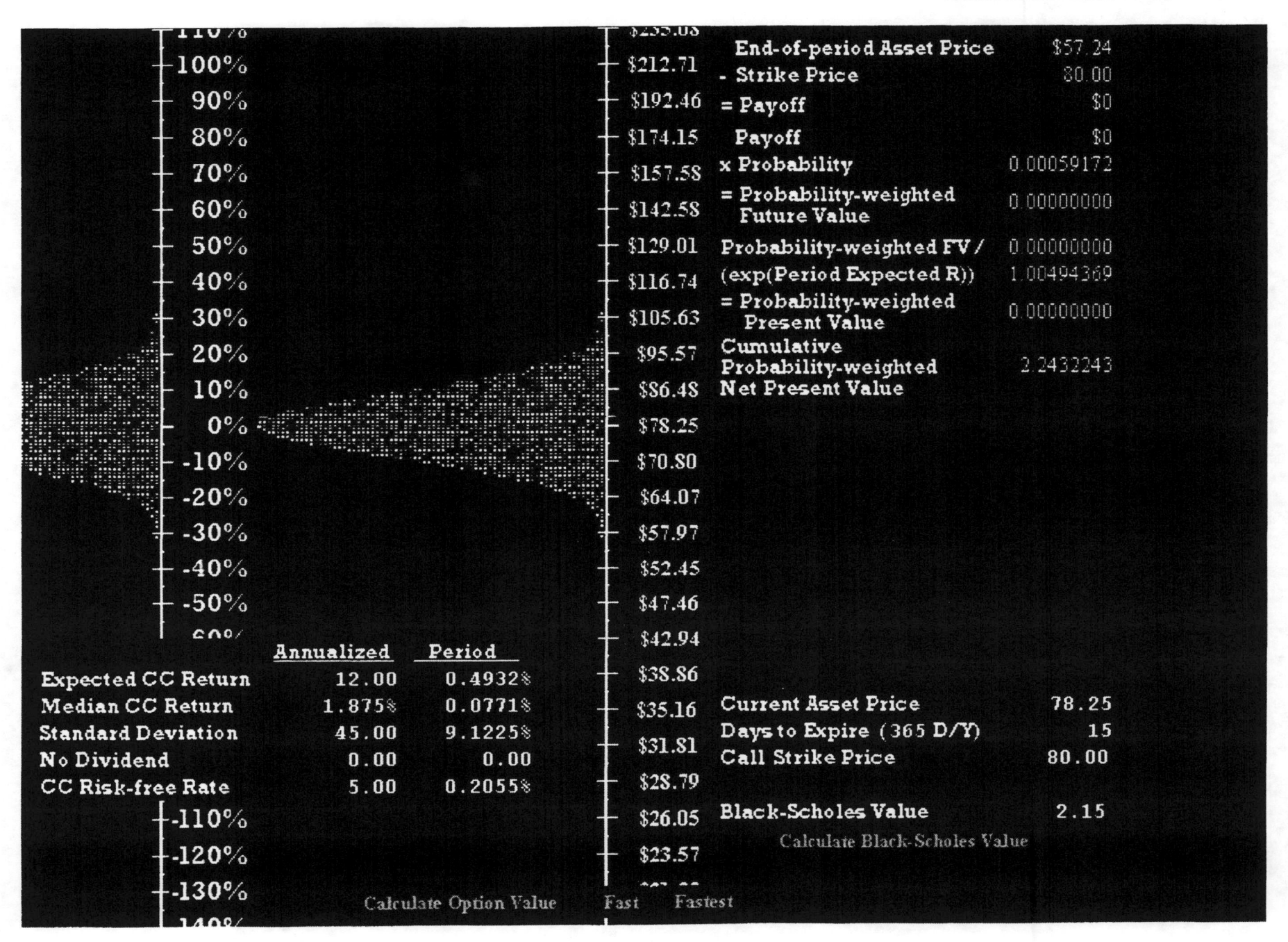

The Black-Scholes assumptions envision a risk-neutral world— a world in which every asset's expected return is equal to the risk-free rate of return.

Earlier, to calculate an option's probability-weighted net present value, we used a forecast of the stock's expected return.

1. Click three times on Clear.

2. Click two or three times on Hide.

3. Click on Calculate Option Value.

4. For Expected CC Return, enter 12.00.

5. For Standard Deviation, enter 45.00.

6. For Current Asset Price, enter 78.25.

7. For Days to Expire, enter 15.

8. For Call Strike Price, enter 80.00.

9. Click on Fastest to the right of Calculate Option Value.

In our example, for an expected return of 12%, we got a probability-weighted net present value of $2.24.

When we calculated the Black-Scholes value of the option, we got a value of $2.15.

10. Click on Calculate Black-Scholes Value.

11. For CC Risk-free Rate, enter 5.00.

12. Click on Calculate Black-Scholes Value.

If you were willing to pay $2.24 for this option, a trader could hedge the sale for $2.15 and turn a risk-free profit. He could perform arbitrage.

Why the difference in the two valuations?

The Black-Scholes value is the cost of hedging the sale of the option. Nowhere in the Black-Scholes formulas does the expected return of the underlying stock appear.

The Black-Scholes formulas assume that the financial markets do not allow arbitrage opportunities to exist. They assume or imply that investors do not require higher expected returns for taking on an exposure to uncertainty. The formulas assume or imply a risk-neutral world— a world in which every asset's average return is equal to the risk-free rate of return.

As we've seen earlier, an investment's expected return is the average of all the returns in its probability distribution. In the risk-neutral world of Black-Scholes, the expected return of every investment is the risk-free rate.

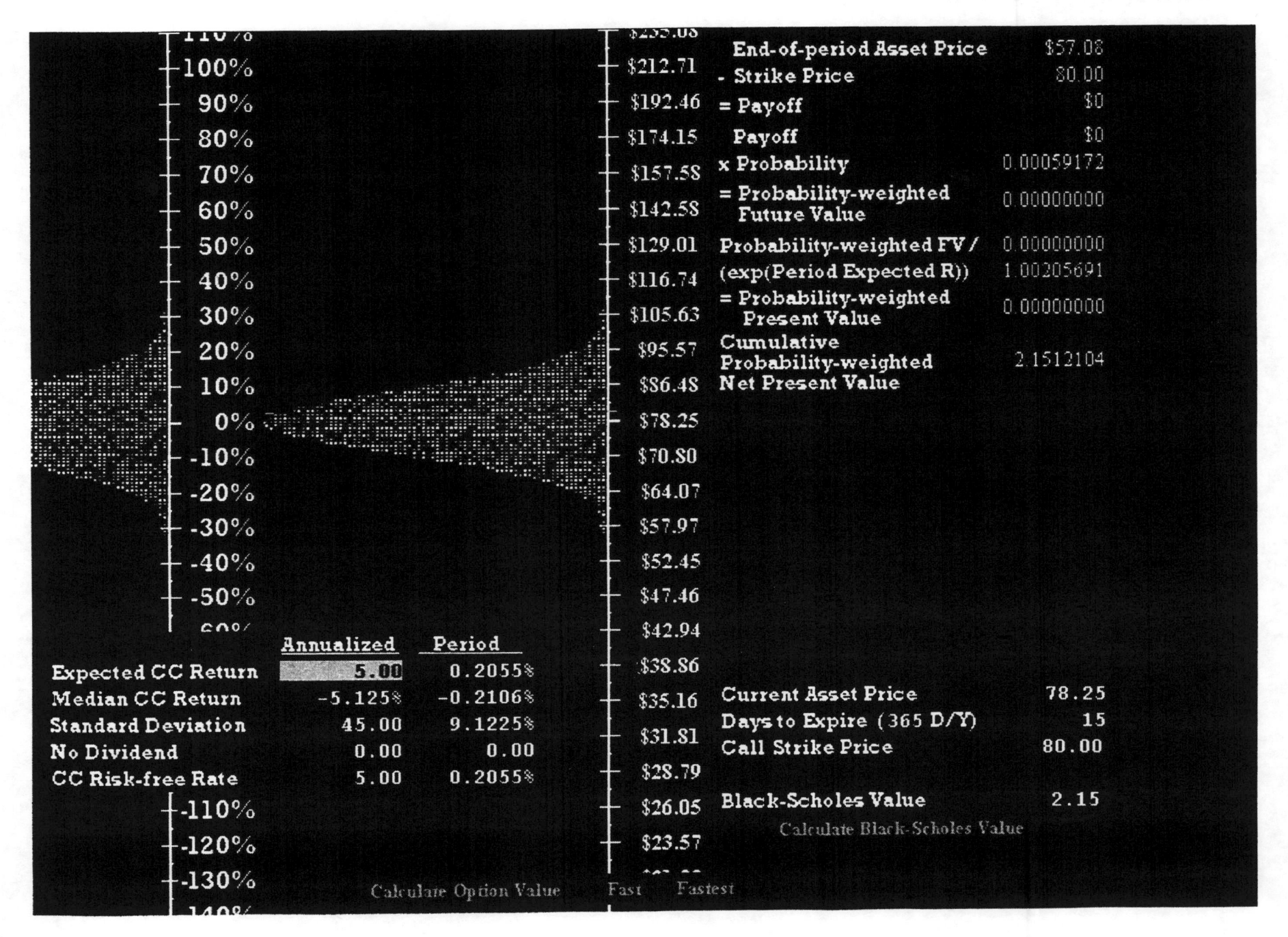

	Annualized	Period
Expected CC Return	5.00	0.2055%
Median CC Return	-5.125%	-0.2106%
Standard Deviation	45.00	9.1225%
No Dividend	0.00	0.00
CC Risk-free Rate	5.00	0.2055%

End-of-period Asset Price	$57.08
- Strike Price	80.00
= Payoff	$0
Payoff	$0
x Probability	0.00059172
= Probability-weighted Future Value	0.00000000
Probability-weighted FV /	0.00000000
(exp(Period Expected R))	1.00205691
= Probability-weighted Present Value	0.00000000
Cumulative Probability-weighted Net Present Value	2.1512104

Current Asset Price	78.25
Days to Expire (365 D/Y)	15
Call Strike Price	80.00
Black-Scholes Value	2.15

Calculate Black-Scholes Value

Calculate Option Value   Fast   Fastest

To bring an option's probability-weighted net present value into line with its Black-Scholes value, set the stock's expected return equal to the risk-free rate.

If you accept Black-Scholes's no-arbitrage, risk-neutral assumptions, then you can bring an option's probability-weighted net present value into line with its Black-Scholes value. All you have to do is set the expected return of your forecast equal to the risk-free rate.

> 13. Click on Clear.
>
> 14. For Expected CC Return, enter the risk-free rate of 5.00.
>
> 15. Click on Calculate Option Value Fastest.

With the expected return equal to the risk-free rate, the option's probability-weighted net present value is equal to or extremely close to the Black-Scholes value.

In the opinion of many, the great brilliance of Fischer Black and Myron Scholes was not that they figured out how to value stock options. We have seen that we can find the same value by setting the expected return equal to the risk-free rate and calculating the option's probability-weighted net present value. As my Uncle Glenn used to say at the dinner table whenever his son-in-law Charles would give voice to his insights into life's most profound mysteries, "Hell! Ev'r'body knows that!"

The great brilliance of Black and Scholes was that they figured out how a market-maker can use delta hedging to sell options risk free.

Is it coincidence that—when you use the same expected returns—an option's Black-Scholes value and its probability-weighted net present value are the same? Or do the laws of markets and mathematics require that they be the same? On your next Zen retreat, let that question be your koan.

	Annualized	Period
Expected C Return	6.00	6.0000%
Median Return	-51.986%	-51.9859%
Standard Deviation	**107.6902**	107.6902%
No Dividend	0.00	0.00
CC Risk-free Rate	6.00	6.0000%

110%
100%
90%
80%
70%
60%
50%
40%
30%
20%
10%
0%
-10%
-20%
-30%
-40%
-50%
-60%

-110%
-120%
-130%
-140%

Calculate Option Value

$135.91
$122.98
$111.28
$100.69
$91.11
$82.44
$74.59
$67.49
$61.07
$55.26
$50.00
$45.24
$40.94
$37.04
$33.52
$30.33
$27.44
$24.83
$22.47
$20.33
$18.39
$16.64
$15.06

Fast   Fastest

End-of-period Asset Price	$0.74
- Strike Price	500.00
= Payoff	$0
Payoff	$0
x Probability	0.00059172
= Probability-weighted Future Value	0.00000000
Probability-weighted FV /	0.00000000
(exp(Period Expected R))	1.06183655
= Probability-weighted Present Value	0.00000000
Cumulative Probability-weighted Net Present Value	0.9057153

Animation: 1,690 intervals: 0.9057153

Ctrl+A: 10,000 intervals: 0.9781469

Ctrl+B: 100,000 intervals: 0.9974290

Ctrl+C: 1,000,000 intervals: 1.0004003

Current Asset Price	50.00
Days to Expire (365 D/Y)	365
Call Strike Price	500.00

Black-Scholes Value   1.00

Calculate Black-Scholes Value

For strike prices at extremes of widely spread probability distributions, Monte Carlo simulations do not calculate option values very accurately. Use Ctrl+A, B, or C.

Earlier, we saw that when a strike price is at an extreme of a stock's probability distribution Monte Carlo simulations do not calculate the option's expected return very accurately. It has too few in-the-money outcomes to work with. To improve the accuracy, we increased the number of intervals into which the simulation divided the probability distribution.

Similarly, when a strike price is at either extreme of a widely spread probability distribution, Monte Carlo simulations do not calculate very accurately an option's probability-weighted net present value.

For a probability distribution with a large standard deviation, let's compare the Black-Scholes value and the probability-weighted net present value when expected return and risk-free rate are the same. The values should be the same.

> 16. Click three times on Clear.
>
> 17. For Expected CC Return, enter 6.00.
>
> 18. For Standard Deviation, enter 107.6902.
>
> 19. For CC Risk-Free Rate, enter 6.00.
>
> 20. For Current Asset Price, enter 50.00.
>
> 21. For Days to Expire, enter 365.
>
> 22. For Call Strike Price, enter 500.00.
>
> 23. Click on Calculate Black-Scholes Value.

The Black-Scholes value is $1.00.

> 24. Click on Calculate Option Value Fast or Fastest.

The animation calculates the probability-weighted net present value to be 0.9057153 or roughly $0.91. Not very close.

To improve the accuracy, we can increase the number of intervals into which the simulation divides the probability distribution.

> 25. To have the Monte Carlo simulation divide the probability distribution into 10,000 intervals, hold down the Ctrl key on your keyboard and press the A key.

The routine calculates the probability-weighted net present value to be 0.9781469. Closer, but still not the right answer.

> 26. To divide the probability distribution into 100,000 intervals, hold down the Ctrl key and press the B key.

The routine calculates the probability-weighted net present value to be 0.9974290. Very close. To the nearest penny, it would round up to $1.00.

> 27. To divide the probability distribution into 1,000,000 intervals, hold down the Ctrl key and press the C key.
>
> 28. Go have a latte.

By dividing the probability distribution into a million intervals, the Monte Carlo routine calculates the probability-weighted net present value to be 1.0004003.

> 29. If a calculation or animation is taking too long, to interrupt it, click long and hard on any of the empty areas on the screen.

The Black-Scholes value of a put is the amount of money a trader has to charge for it to set up a delta hedge with her assets and liabilities in balance.

If a put finishes in the money, the trader has to buy from the option holder the underlying at the strike price. To be perfectly hedged for this outcome, at the time of expiration the trader wants to be short all the shares she has to buy. To pay for the stock she has to buy, she wants to liquidate a loan she has made.

If a put finishes out of the money, the holder of the option will not exercise it. For this outcome, the trader does not want to be short any stock. She does not want to be owed any money.

To set up a hedge for the sale of a put, a trader sells short some of the stock. The proceeds of the short sale and the money she receives for the option the trader lends at the risk-free rate.

The amount of stock the trader sells short is determined by the option's delta. The delta of a put is negative. As the value of the underlying stock goes up, the value of the put goes down. If we preserve the minus sign in front of the delta, we can say—as with setting up a hedge for a call option—that the trader "buys" delta shares of stock. A negative "buy" is a sell.

For example:

Option delta	−0.5691
× Current asset price	$78.2500
= Cost of delta shares	$−44.5392

A negative "cost" means the trader receives money.

The amount of money the trader lends out is determined by the probability that the option will finish in the money and the strike price. The trader lends out the present value of the probability the option will finish in the money times the strike price.

Probability finish in the money	0.60470
× Strike price	$80.00000
= Bond value at expiration	$48.376333
Bond value at expiration	$48.37633
÷ exp(period risk-free rate)	1.00206
= Bond value today	$48.27703

When the trader sets up the hedge, she wants her assets and liabilities to be in balance. The missing number is the amount of money she charges for the option. The Black-Scholes value of the option is the amount of money she has to charge for it for the delta-hedge assets and liabilities to be in balance.

Cost of delta shares	$-44.53928
+ Bond value today	$48.27703
Black-Scholes value	$3.73775

Upon setting up the hedge, the hedge's assets and liabilities look like this:

Assets

Bond value	$48.27703

Liabilities

Value of delta shares	$44.53928
Value of options sold	$3.73775
Total liabilities	$48.27703

	Annualized	Period
Standard Deviation	45.00	9.1225%
No Dividend	0.00	0.00
CC Risk-free Rate	5.00	0.2055%

Current Asset Price	78.25
Days to Expire (365 D/Y)	15
Put Strike Price	80.00
Put Option Price	
Black-Scholes Value	3.74

Put   Calculate Black-Scholes Value

To calculate the Black-Scholes value of a put, the animation calculates the cost of setting up a delta hedge.

1. Click three times on Clear.

2. Click twice on Hide.

3. Click on Calculate Black-Scholes Value.

4. Click on Put.

5. For Standard Deviation, enter 45.00.

6. For CC Risk-Free Rate, enter 5.00.

7. For Current Asset Price, enter 78.25.

8. For Days to Expire, enter 15.

9. For Put Strike Price, enter 80.00.

10. Click again on Calculate Black-Scholes Value.

The Black-Scholes value of a put is

	Option delta	−0.56919
×	Current asset price	$78.25000
=	Cost of delta shares	$−44.53928
	Probability finish in the money	0.60470
×	Strike price	$80.00000
=	Bond value at expiration	$48.376333
	Bond value at expiration	$48.37633
÷	exp(period risk-free rate)	1.00206
=	Bond value today	$48.27703
	Cost of delta shares	$−44.53928
+	Bond value today	$48.27703
	Black-Scholes value	$3.73775

What to remember about hedging: The value of an option to you is its probability-weighted net present value. The price of an option is the cost to a market maker of hedging the sale plus a profit margin.

If you plan on making a market in options and selling them to investors, you'll need the ability to hedge complex positions in many different options with different expiration dates and strike prices. To hedge those complex positions, you'll need a more thorough understanding of hedging than is offered here. You'll need software with a different focus than *Black-Scholes Made Easy*.

The intention here is to show that the Black-Scholes value of an option is the cost to the trader or market maker of hedging the sale of the option. If we apply the Black-Scholes assumptions to the calculations, then an option's probability-weighted net present value is equal to or very nearly equal to the Black-Scholes value.

These are principles that apply generally in the financial markets. The value of an asset is its probability-weighted net present value. The price of synthetic financial instruments like options and other derivatives is the cost to the market maker of hedging the sale plus a profit margin.

To price synthetic financial instruments, financial institutions often use Monte Carlo simulations to calculate their probability-weighted net present values. To avoid risk in their sales of synthetic instruments, financial institutions hedge their positions. They make money on bid-ask spreads and on transaction fees and commissions. If they stay perfectly hedged, they earn profits whether the value of an asset goes up, down, or remains the same.

If you buy derivatives and you don't comprehend the pricing methodology and know the forecasts for the underlyings, then you don't know how big a profit margin you're forking over. You may be the one who gets forked.

When and Why You Can Gain an Advantage from Early Exercise of Some American Options and Black's Approximation for Valuing American Options

Under some circumstances, you can gain an advantage if you exercise an American option prior to maturity. The right of early exercise gives some American options greater value than otherwise identical European options. Accordingly, they command a higher price in the marketplace.

Up until now, we've been looking at potential outcomes of investing in options and holding them until maturity. Implicitly, we've been assuming that all options are European options—that they can be exercised only at maturity.

Most stock options, however, are American. They give you all the rights that European options give plus the right of early exercise.

Under certain circumstances, exercising some types of options prior to maturity gives you an advantage. The probability-weighted net present value and expected return of early or immediate exercise is greater than that of later exercise.

Insofar as early exercise gives you a potential advantage, American options have greater value than otherwise identical European options. In the marketplace, they command a higher price.

Now we look at the types of options and the circumstances under which early exercise can give you an advantage. First we establish criteria for how we tell whether early exercise is advantageous.

	Strike Price	$70.00
$176.69	- End-of-period Asset Price	190.26
$159.87	= Payoff	$0
$144.66	Payoff	$0
$130.89	x Probability	0.00059172
$118.44	= Probability-weighted Future Value	0.00000000
$107.17	Probability-weighted FV /	0.00000000
$96.97	(exp(Period Expected R))	1.03053923
$87.74	= Probability-weighted Present Value	0.00000000
$79.39	Cumulative Probability-weighted	9.9542587
$71.84	Net Present Value	

Put's strike price	$70.00
–Spot price	65.00
Exercise-today value	$ 5.00
PW net present value	$9.95
–Exercise-today value	5.00
Time value	$ 4.95

Asset price levels (left axis): 110%, 100%, 90%, 80%, 70%, 60%, 50%, 40%, 30%, 20%, 10%, 0%, -10%, -20%, -30%, -40%, -50%, 60%

Strike price
Spot price

	Annualized	Period
Expected CC Return	6.00	3.0082%
Median CC Return	-4.125%	-2.0682%
Standard Deviation	45.00	31.8634%
No Dividend	0.00	0.00

-100%, -110%, -120%, -130%, -140%

Asset price column: $193.21, $176.69, $159.87, $144.66, $130.89, $118.44, $107.17, $96.97, $87.74, $79.39, $71.84, $65.00, $58.81, $53.22, $48.15, $43.57, $39.42, $35.67, $32.28, $29.21, $26.43, $23.91, $21.64, $19.58

Current Asset Price	65.00
Days to Expire (365 D/Y)	183
Put Strike Price	70.00
Put Option Price	

Calculate Option Value   Fast   Fastest

If an option's probability-weighted net present value of future exercise is greater than its exercise-today value, the option has time value. It makes sense to hold onto it.

One of the ways that we've been using to find the value today of an option that we plan to hold to maturity has been to sweep through the underlying's probability distribution of possible end-of-period outcomes, from the outcomes compute the option payoffs, and discount the payoffs to an interest-adjusted value for today. We call this adjusted value the option's probability-weighted net present value of end-of-period exercise.

1. Click three times on Clear.

2. Click twice on Hide.

3. Click on Put.

4. Click on Calculate Option Value.

5. For Expected CC Return, enter 6.00.

6. For Standard Deviation, enter 45.00.

7. For Current Asset Price, enter 65.00.

8. For Days to Expire, enter 183.

9. For Put Strike Price, enter 70.00.

10. Click on Calculate Option Value Fast or Fastest. (You can jump back and forth.)

In working with options, it's easy to get pulled out of today and start thinking about what might happen some time in the future. Instead of trying to work with hopes and fears that tend to run wild, we can work with probability-weighted net present values. They are not future values. They do not in any way depend on what you might have paid for an option. They are values today of all those outcomes you think possibly might happen in the future. They are values we can compare and use to make decisions today.

In our example, rounded to the nearest penny, the option's probability-weighted net present value is $9.95.

The easiest number to compare to an option's probability-weighted net present value is its exercise-today value—the payoff you would get if you exercised the option today. (You even can think of the exercise-today value as a probability-weighted net present value. There's only one outcome. It's 100% certain. The time of discount is zero.)

A put's exercise-today value is the difference between the option's strike price and the current market price or spot price of the underlying.

In our example, the option is in the money. Its exercise-today value is $70.00 − $65.00 = $5.00.

The probability-weighted net present value of holding the option until maturity is greater than the exercise-today value. It's $4.95 greater.

When the probability-weighted net present value of holding onto an option is greater than its exercise-today value, we say that the option has time value. On average, you expect it to have a greater exercise payoff in the future than it has today.

An option's time value is the difference between its probability-weighted net present value of future exercise and its exercise-today value. Here the option's time value is

$9.95 − $5.00 = $4.95

If you owned this option, it would not make sense to exercise it today. You would lose value. You would lose the option's time value.

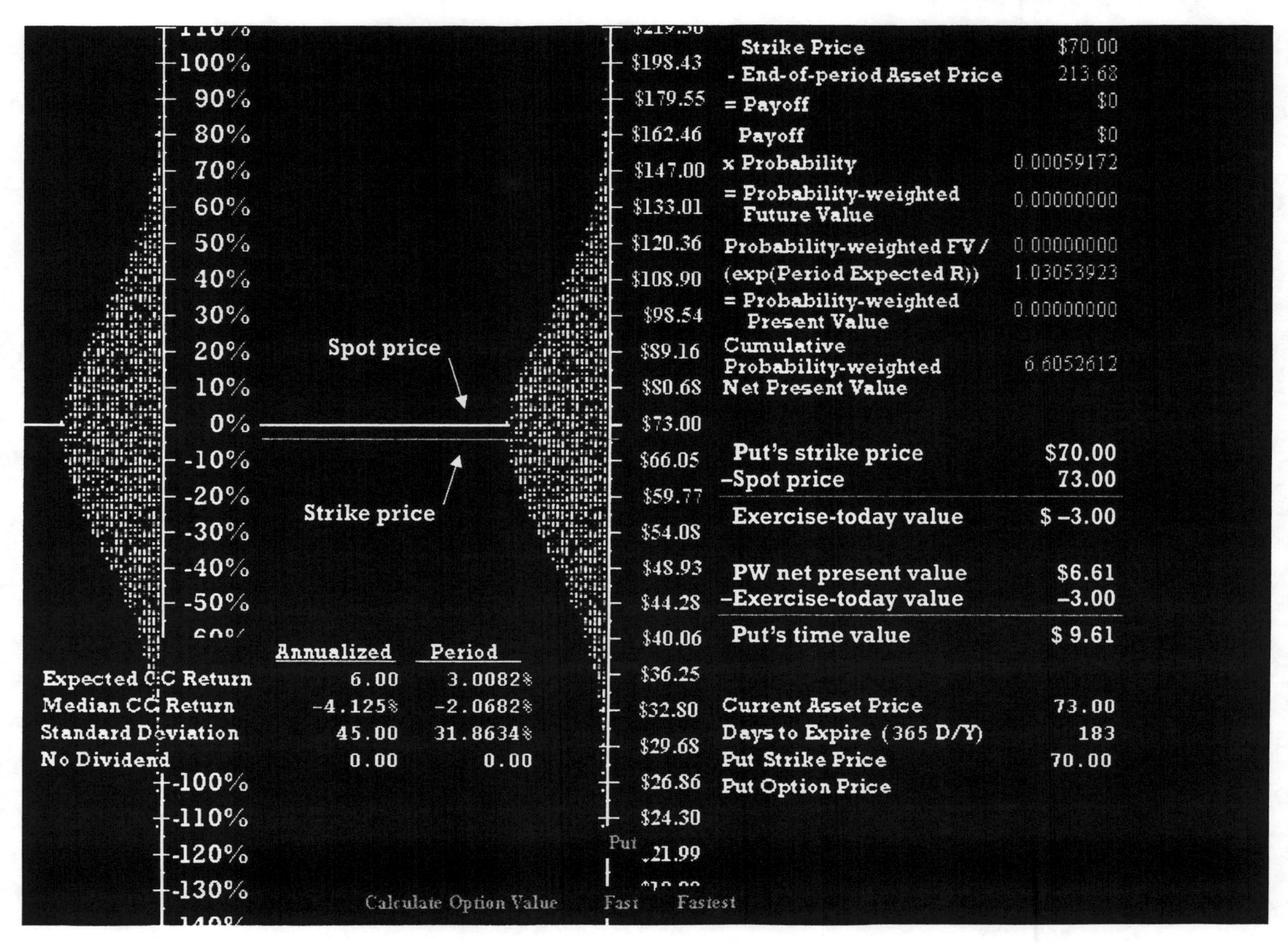

	Strike Price	$70.00
$198.43	- End-of-period Asset Price	213.68
$179.55	= Payoff	$0
$162.46	Payoff	$0
$147.00	x Probability	0.00059172
$133.01	= Probability-weighted Future Value	0.00000000
$120.36	Probability-weighted FV /	0.00000000
$108.90	(exp(Period Expected R))	1.03053923
$98.54	= Probability-weighted Present Value	0.00000000
$89.16	Cumulative Probability-weighted	6.6052612
$80.68	Net Present Value	
$73.00		
$66.05	Put's strike price	$70.00
$59.77	–Spot price	73.00
	Exercise-today value	$ –3.00
$54.08		
$48.93	PW net present value	$6.61
$44.28	–Exercise-today value	–3.00
$40.06	Put's time value	$ 9.61
$36.25		
$32.80	Current Asset Price	73.00
$29.68	Days to Expire (365 D/Y)	183
	Put Strike Price	70.00
$26.86	Put Option Price	
$24.30		
$21.99		

	Annualized	Period
Expected CC Return	6.00	3.0082%
Median CC Return	-4.125%	-2.0682%
Standard Deviation	45.00	31.8634%
No Dividend	0.00	0.00

Spot price

Strike price

Put

Calculate Option Value   Fast   Fastest

If an option is out of the money, it has no exercise-today value. It has only time value. It would make no sense to exercise it today.

Now let's compare probability-weighted net present value of end-of-period exercise, exercise-today value, and time value for a put that is out of the money.

> 11. For Current Asset Price, enter 73.00.
>
> 12. Click on Calculate Option Value Fast or Fastest.

Rounded to the nearest penny, the option's probability-weighted net present value of end-of-period exercise is $6.61.

The spot price is greater than the strike price. Hence, the put is out of the money.

If you exercised the put today, you would compel someone to buy from you for $70 a stock with a market price of $73. You would lose money. You would lose $3.

The option's only value is its time value—the difference between its probability-weighted net present value and its exercise-today value. In this example, the time value is $6.61 minus –$3.00 = $9.61. You definitely would not want to exercise this option today.

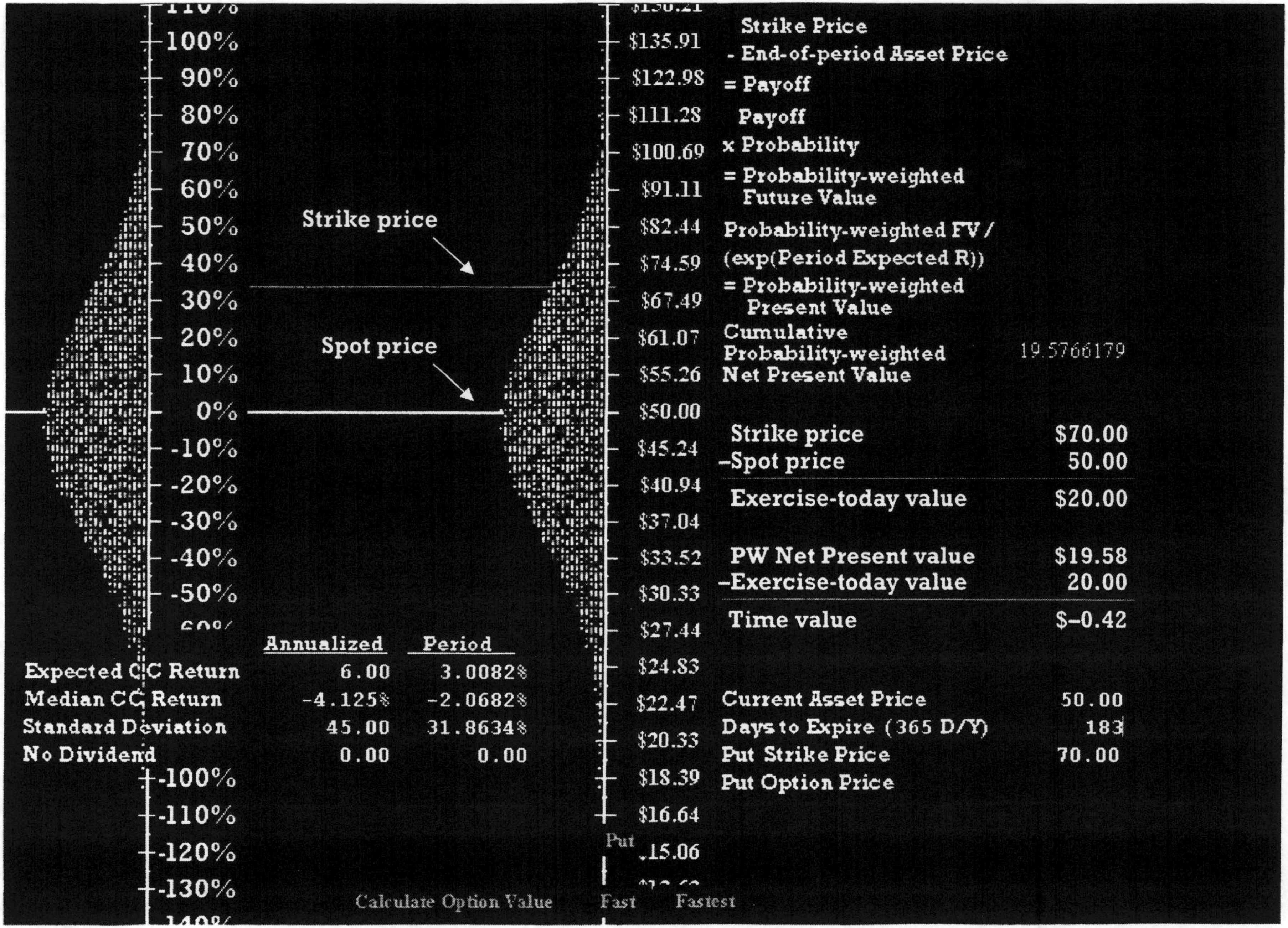

	110%	
	100%	
	90%	
	80%	
	70%	
	60%	
	50%	Strike price
	40%	
	30%	
	20%	Spot price
	10%	
	0%	
	-10%	
	-20%	
	-30%	
	-40%	
	-50%	
	-60%	

	Annualized	Period
Expected CC Return	6.00	3.0082%
Median CC Return	-4.125%	-2.0682%
Standard Deviation	45.00	31.8634%
No Dividend	0.00	0.00

	-100%
	-110%
	-120%
	-130%
	-140%

Calculate Option Value   Fast   Fastest

Right column values:

$130.21
$135.91 Strike Price
$122.98 - End-of-period Asset Price
$111.28 = Payoff
$100.69 Payoff
$91.11   x Probability
$82.44   = Probability-weighted Future Value
$74.59   Probability-weighted FV /
$67.49   (exp(Period Expected R))
$61.07   = Probability-weighted Present Value
$55.26   Cumulative Probability-weighted Net Present Value   19.5766179
$50.00
$45.24
$40.94
$37.04
$33.52
$30.33
$27.44
$24.83
$22.47
$20.33
$18.39
$16.64
$15.06

Strike price	$70.00
–Spot price	50.00
Exercise-today value	$20.00
PW Net Present value	$19.58
–Exercise-today value	20.00
Time value	$-0.42
Current Asset Price	50.00
Days to Expire (365 D/Y)	183
Put Strike Price	70.00
Put Option Price	

As a put goes deep into the money, it may be advantageous to exercise the option as soon as its exercise-today value becomes equal to the probability-weighted net present value of holding onto it until maturity.

Now let's compare values for a put that has gone deep in the money.

> **13. For Current Asset Price, enter 50.00.**
>
> **14. Click on Calculate Option Value Fast or Fastest.**

Rounded to the nearest penny, the option's probability-weighted net present value of end-of-period exercise is $19.58.

The option's exercise-today value is $70.00 − $50.00 = $20.00.

The option's exercise-today value is greater than its probability-weighted net present value of end-of-period exercise. It's $0.42 greater.

The option has negative time value. On average, you can expect the option to have a lower exercise payoff in the future than it has today.

If you owned this option, the logical thing to do would be to exercise it today. In fact—except under weird assumptions—it becomes logical to exercise an option as soon as its exercise-today value becomes equal to the probability-weighted net present value of future exercise.

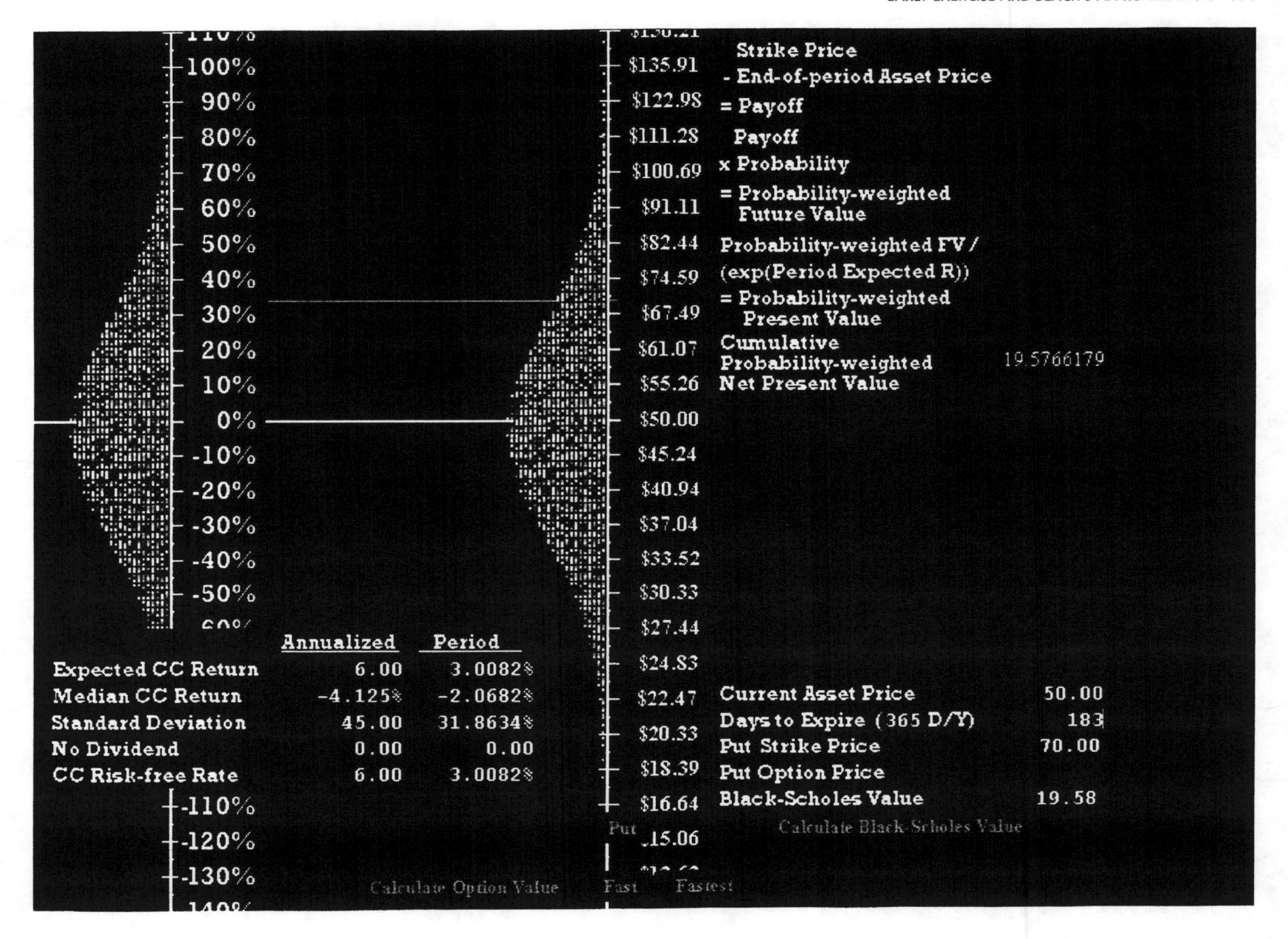

	Strike Price
	- End-of-period Asset Price
$135.91	
$122.98	= Payoff
$111.28	Payoff
$100.69	x Probability
$91.11	= Probability-weighted Future Value
$82.44	Probability-weighted FV /
$74.59	(exp(Period Expected R))
$67.49	= Probability-weighted Present Value
$61.07	Cumulative
$55.26	Probability-weighted 19.5766179
$50.00	Net Present Value

	Annualized	Period
Expected CC Return	6.00	3.0082%
Median CC Return	-4.125%	-2.0682%
Standard Deviation	45.00	31.8634%
No Dividend	0.00	0.00
CC Risk-free Rate	6.00	3.0082%

Current Asset Price	50.00
Days to Expire (365 D/Y)	183
Put Strike Price	70.00
Put Option Price	
Black-Scholes Value	19.58

Calculate Black-Scholes Value

Put

Calculate Option Value   Fast   Fastest

An option's value is the greater of its Black-Scholes value and its early-exercise value—Black's approximation.

What is the value of this option?

We calculated its probability-weighted net present value of end-of-period exercise to be $19.58. Earlier, we saw that when an option's expected return is equal to the risk-free rate its Black-Scholes value is equal to its probability-weighted net present value of end-of-period exercise.

> 15. Click on Calculate Black-Scholes Value.
>
> 16. For CC Risk-Free Rate, enter 6.00.
>
> 17. Click on Calculate Black-Scholes Value.

We see that with a risk-free rate of 6% the option's Black-Scholes value is also $19.58.

Clearly, the market price of the option cannot be $19.58. If it was, it would be a perpetual-money machine. You could keep buying the option for $19.58 and exercising it to get $20.00.

To adapt the Black-Scholes model to valuing American options, Fischer Black observed that the value of an American option is the greater of its Black-Scholes value or its early-exercise value. This method of valuing American options is now called Black's approximation.

Exercising today is one form of early exercise. In this example, according to Black's approximation, the value of this American option is $20.00.

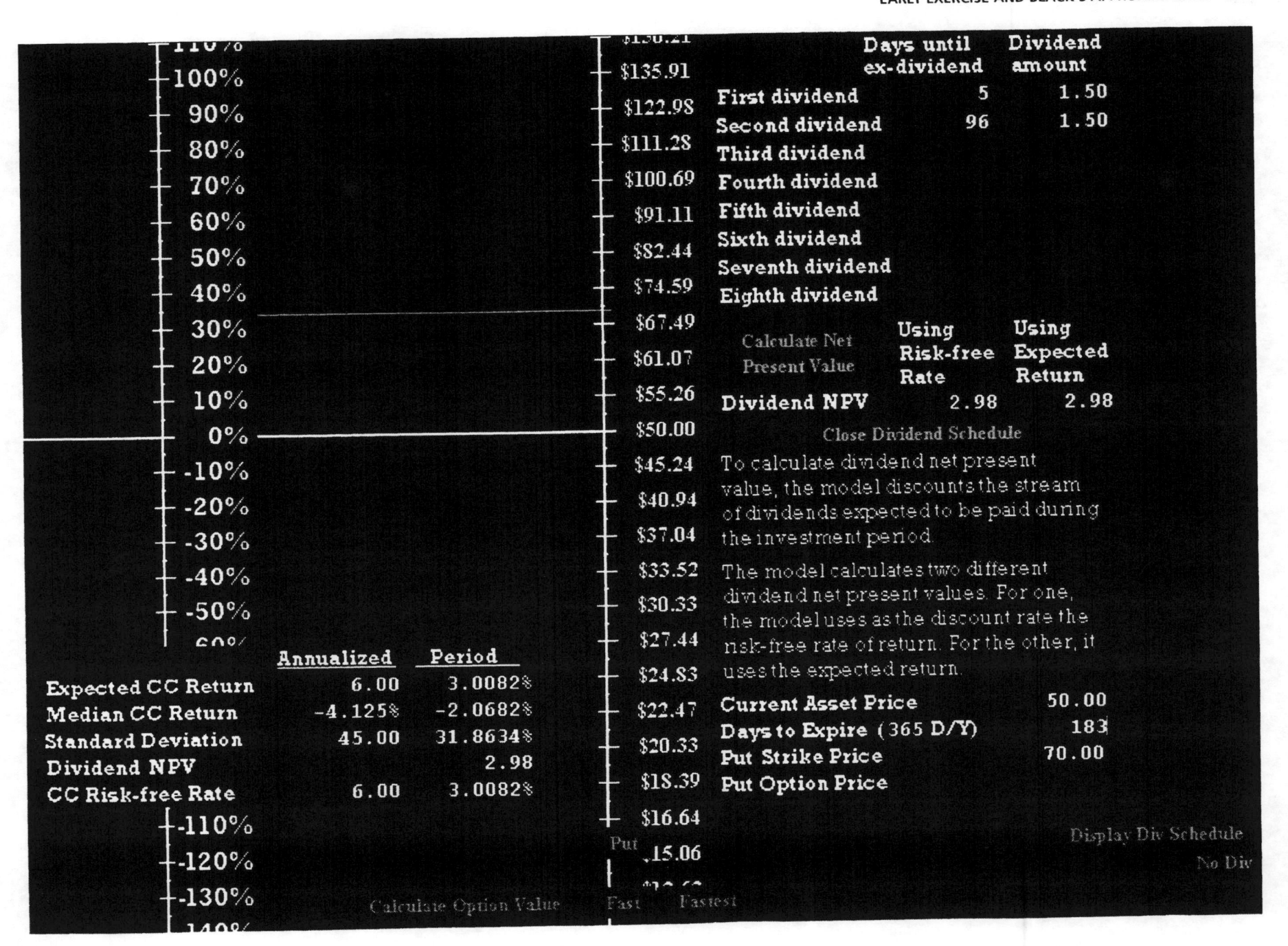

	Annualized	Period
Expected CC Return	6.00	3.0082%
Median CC Return	-4.125%	-2.0682%
Standard Deviation	45.00	31.8634%
Dividend NPV		2.98
CC Risk-free Rate	6.00	3.0082%

Vertical axis labels (left): 110%, 100%, 90%, 80%, 70%, 60%, 50%, 40%, 30%, 20%, 10%, 0%, -10%, -20%, -30%, -40%, -50%, 60%, -110%, -120%, -130%, 140%

Price axis labels (center): $130.21, $135.91, $122.98, $111.28, $100.69, $91.11, $82.44, $74.59, $67.49, $61.07, $55.26, $50.00, $45.24, $40.94, $37.04, $33.52, $30.33, $27.44, $24.83, $22.47, $20.33, $18.39, $16.64, Put $15.06

	Days until ex-dividend	Dividend amount
First dividend	5	1.50
Second dividend	96	1.50
Third dividend		
Fourth dividend		
Fifth dividend		
Sixth dividend		
Seventh dividend		
Eighth dividend		

Calculate Net Present Value	Using Risk-free Rate	Using Expected Return
Dividend NPV	2.98	2.98

Close Dividend Schedule

To calculate dividend net present value, the model discounts the stream of dividends expected to be paid during the investment period.

The model calculates two different dividend net present values. For one, the model uses as the discount rate the risk-free rate of return. For the other, it uses the expected return.

Current Asset Price	50.00
Days to Expire (365 D/Y)	183
Put Strike Price	70.00
Put Option Price	

Display Div Schedule

No Div

Calculate Option Value   Fast   Fastest

What if a put's underlying pays lumpy dividends? Under what circumstances is it logical to exercise the put early?

What if, in our example, we add dividends to the put's underlying? Dividend payments lower a stock's price, which drives puts farther into the money.

Will it still be optimal to exercise the put today?

Let's see.

18. Click once on Clear.

19. Click on Display Div Schedule.

20. For First dividend, Days until ex-dividend, enter 5.

21. For First dividend, Dividend amount, enter 1.50.

22. For Second dividend, Days until ex-dividend, enter 96.

23. For Second dividend, Dividend amount, enter 1.50.

24. Click on Calculate Net Present Value.

25. Click on Close Dividend Schedule.

26. Click on Calculate Option Value Fast or Fastest.

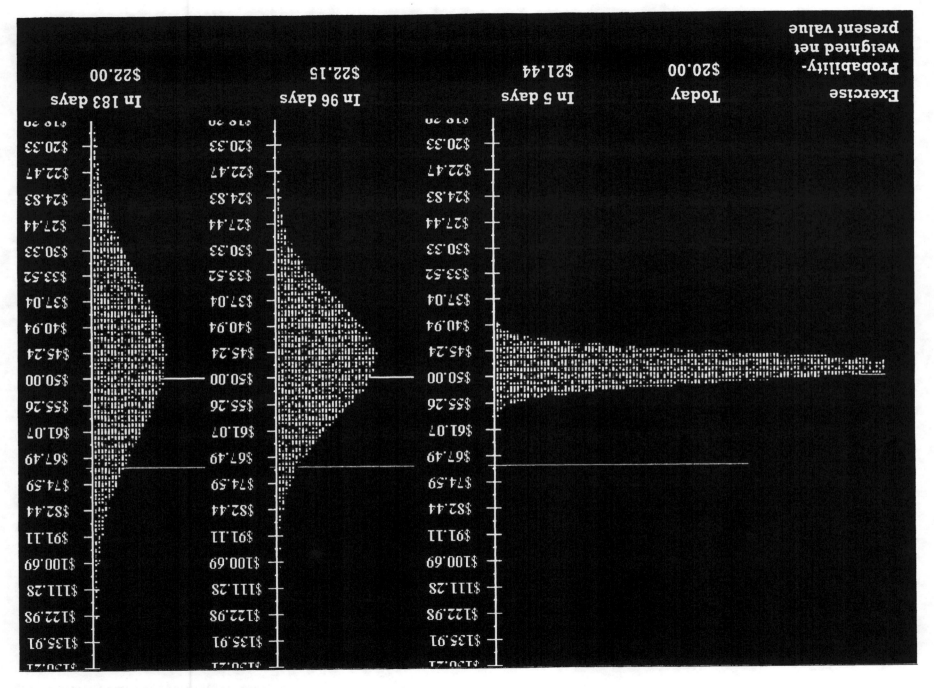

If a put goes deep in the money and the underlying pays dividends, it may be optimal to exercise the option on the last ex-dividend date.

With two dividends of $1.50 being paid before expiration and with ex-dividend dates 5 and 96 days in the future, the probability-weighted net present value of holding the option until maturity is $22.00.

The exercise-today value is still $20.00. With the addition of dividends to the underlying, we no longer gain an advantage from exercising the option today.

Does holding the option until maturity offer the highest probability-weighted net present value?

Let's look at possible exercise on the two ex-dividend dates 5 and 96 days into the future.

> **27. For Days to Expire, enter 96.**
>
> **28. Click on Calculate Option Value Fast or Fastest.**

Exercise on the second ex-dividend date gives a probability-weighted net present value of $22.15—a higher value than for either exercising the option today or holding it until maturity.

Let's look at a possible exercise on the first dividend's ex-dividend date.

> **29. For Days to Expire, enter 5.**
>
> **30. Click on Calculate Option Value Fast or Fastest.**

Exercise on the first ex-dividend date gives a probability-weighted net present value of $21.44—more than for exercise today but less than for holding the option until maturity or for exercising it on the second ex-dividend date.

If a put is deep in the money and the underlying pays dividends, often it will be optimal to exercise the option on the underlying's last ex-dividend date.

What is the value of this option?

Since we've had the underlying's expected return set to the risk-free rate, the Black-Scholes value for each of the exercise dates is the same as the probability-weighted net present value.

Using Black's approximation, the option's value is the highest of the values for the four exercise dates—$22.15.

(To create the exhibit above and others like it, the author used Print Scrn to capture animation screens and pasted them into image-editing software. There he chopped up the captures and assembled them into exhibits. You can do the same.)

	$135.91		$135.91		$135.91
$122.98		$122.98		$122.98
$111.28		$111.28		$111.28
$100.69		$100.69		$100.69
$91.11		$91.11		$91.11
$82.44		$82.44		$82.44
$74.59		$74.59		$74.59
$67.49		$67.49		$67.49
$61.07		$61.07		$61.07
$55.26		$55.26		$55.26
$50.00		$50.00		$50.00
$45.24		$45.24		$45.24
$40.94		$40.94		$40.94
$37.04		$37.04		$37.04
$33.52		$33.52		$33.52
$30.33		$30.33		$30.33
$27.44		$27.44		$27.44
$24.83		$24.83		$24.83
$22.47		$22.47		$22.47
$20.33		$20.33		$20.33

Exercise	Today	On first ex-div day	On last ex-div day	At maturity
Probability-weighted net present value	$20.00	$21.44	$22.15	$22.00

What's going on here? As the probability distribution shifts down relative to the strike price and changes shape, the payoff of each little square keeps changing.

If you stare long enough at the three probability distributions above, you will have an important insight: An option's probability-weighted net present value depends on a dynamic combination of factors. The probability-weighted net present value is determined both by how high or low the probability distribution is relative to the strike price and by how spread out it is.

You probably didn't notice, but when we set up this underlying, the annualized expected return of 6% and standard deviation of 45% gave us a median return of −4.125%. A negative median return means that, as we increase our investment horizon, the end-of-period probability distribution creeps down the price and return axes.

Little Squares on First Ex-div Date
In our example, when we look ahead just five days, the median return hasn't had enough time to sink the distribution very much.

We see a narrow probability distribution. There's not much uncertainty. The dividend payment has shifted the distribution down some.

The entire probability distribution is below the strike price. Every little square is in the money (as each would be even without the dividend payment).

The downward shift makes prospective payoffs at exercise in five days greater for all the little squares.

Looking just five days into the future, however, none of the squares are super deep into the money. There's almost no chance of the stock price going really low and generating a really big payoff.

Little Squares on Last Ex-div Date
When we look 96 days into the future at the second ex-dividend date, the negative median return has shifted the probability distribution down a tad. The dividend payment also has acted to shift it down. More of the little squares are below the strike price than there would be without the dividend payment.

We see substantially more uncertainty than we saw at five days. The distribution is much more spread out than at five days. Some of the little squares are out of the money. Others are very deep in the money.

Little Squares at Maturity
When we look 183 days into the future, the negative median return has sunk the probability distribution slightly farther. There have been no more dividends.

We see more uncertainty. The distribution is more spread out. More of the little squares are out of the money. Some are deeper into the money.

Strike price leverages value of each little square
For all three horizons, we're looking at probability distributions for the underlying. Option structures leverage the outcome for every little square. Options magnify the effect of lifting, falling, and changes in shape of the underlying's probability distribution.

How much an option leverages the outcome of each little square depends on where that little square is in relation to the strike price.

As you peer different distances into the future, the option's probability-weighted net present value tells you the net effect on all the little squares of the rises, falls, and changes in shape.

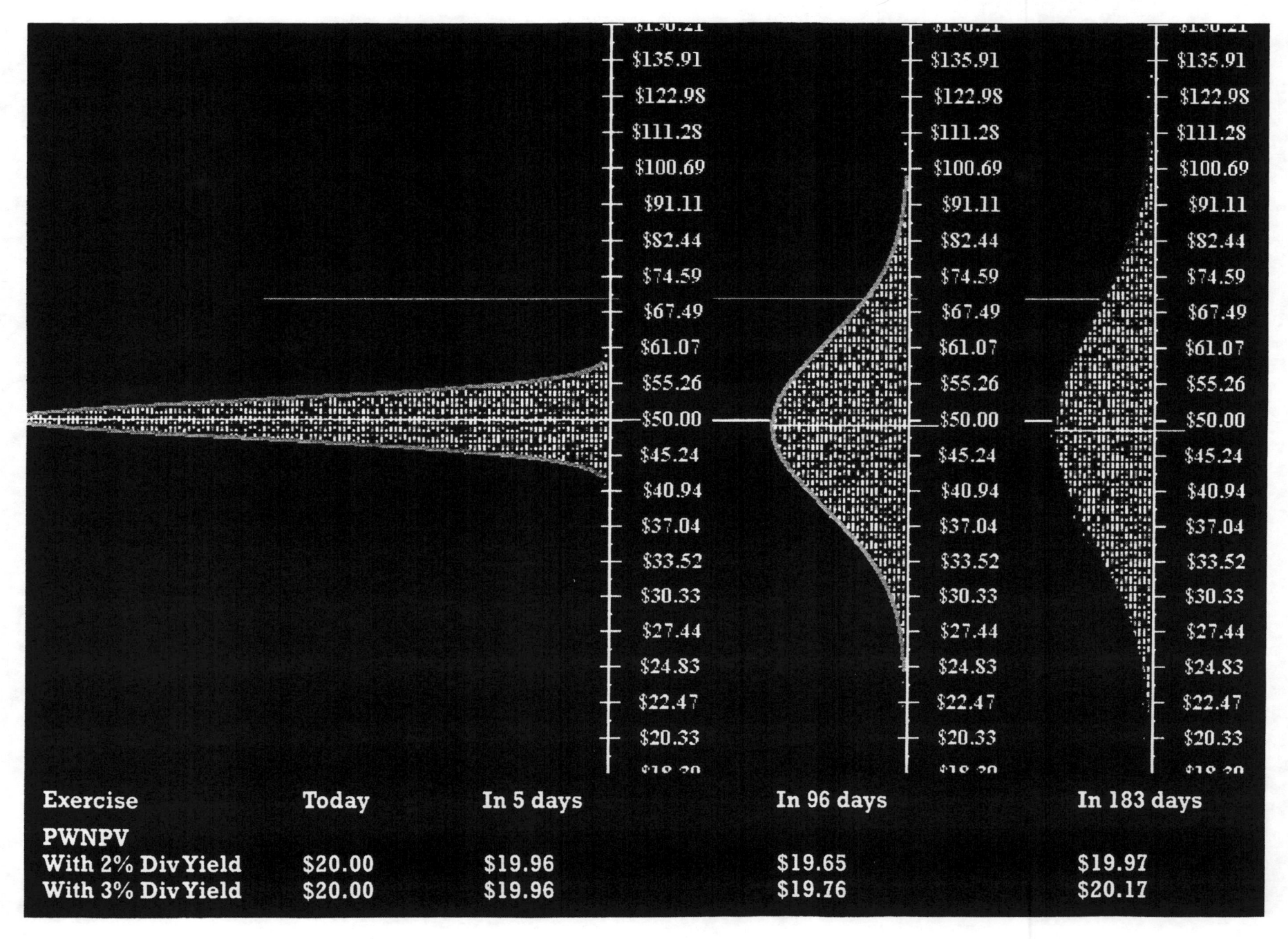

			$135.91				$135.91				$135.91
			$122.98				$122.98				$122.98
			$111.28				$111.28				$111.28
			$100.69				$100.69				$100.69
			$91.11				$91.11				$91.11
			$82.44				$82.44				$82.44
			$74.59				$74.59				$74.59
			$67.49				$67.49				$67.49
			$61.07				$61.07				$61.07
			$55.26				$55.26				$55.26
			$50.00				$50.00				$50.00
			$45.24				$45.24				$45.24
			$40.94				$40.94				$40.94
			$37.04				$37.04				$37.04
			$33.52				$33.52				$33.52
			$30.33				$30.33				$30.33
			$27.44				$27.44				$27.44
			$24.83				$24.83				$24.83
			$22.47				$22.47				$22.47
			$20.33				$20.33				$20.33

Exercise	Today	In 5 days	In 96 days	In 183 days
PWNPV				
With 2% Div Yield	$20.00	$19.96	$19.65	$19.97
With 3% Div Yield	$20.00	$19.96	$19.76	$20.17

If a put goes deep in the money and the underlying pays a dividend yield, the effect on the option's probability-weighted net present value is complex. You're on your own!

Instead of paying lumpy dividends, let's say an underlying pays a dividend yield. What are the early-exercise implications for deep-in-the-money puts?

In our example, we'll keep everything else the same and look at two different yields: 2% and 3%.

> 31. Click on Clear.
>
> 32. Click on Enter Div Yield.
>
> 33. For Continuous Div Yield, enter 3.00.
>
> 34. For Days to Expire, enter 5.
>
> 35. Click on Calculate Option Value Fastest.

Note the option's probability-weighted net present value.

> 36. For Continuous Div Yield, enter 2.00.
>
> 37. Click on Draw Your Forecast.
>
> 38. Click on Calculate Black-Scholes Value.

(Because the expected return equals the risk-free rate, calculating the Black-Scholes value is the same as calculating the probability-weighted net present value.)

The probability distributions are so similar as to be indistinguishable. At five days, we get the same probability-weighted net present value for both dividend yields: $19.96.

So far, you're better off if you exercise the put today.

We do the same thing for 96 days.

> 39. Click on Clear.
>
> 40. For Continuous Div Yield, enter 3.00.
>
> 41. For Days to Expire, enter 96.
>
> 42. Click on Calculate Option Value Fastest.

Note the option's value.

> 43. For Continuous Div Yield, enter 2.00.
>
> 44. Click on Draw Your Forecast.
>
> 45. Click on Calculate Black-Scholes Value.

At 96 days, the probability-weighted net present values are $19.65 for the 2% yield and $19.76 for the 3%.

For both puts, you're better off if you exercise today.

We do the same thing for 183 days, which we've taken to be the put's expiration date.

> 46. Click on Clear.
>
> 47. For Continuous Div Yield, enter 3.00.

> 48. For Days to Expire, enter 183.
>
> 49. Click on Calculate Option Value Fastest.

Note the option's value.

> 50. For Continuous Div Yield, enter 2.00.
>
> 51. Click on Draw Your Forecast.
>
> 52. Click on Calculate Black-Scholes Value.

At 183 days, the probability-weighted net present value for the 2% yield is $19.97. Exercising today would still give you a higher present value.

For the 3% yield, however, the probability-weighted net present value has gone to $20.17—more than the exercise-today payoff.

The probability distributions diverge in subtle ways. The values of both puts have gone down and then back up. After 183 days, the values of both puts would continue to grow. Were you to hold the put for the 2% yield seven more days, its value would go to $20.00.

What's the right thing to do under these circumstances?

Most authors duck the issue.

Me too.

110%		$103.23	Days until ex-dividend	Dividend amount
100%		$149.51		
90%		$135.28	First dividend	12	.75
			Second dividend	102	.75
80%		$122.40	Third dividend		
70%		$110.76	Fourth dividend		
60%		$100.22	Fifth dividend		
50%		$90.68	Sixth dividend		
			Seventh dividend		
40%		$82.05	Eighth dividend		
30%		$74.24			

(Scale values continue on the left and right axes.)

Calculate Net Present Value	Using Risk-free Rate	Using Expected Return
Dividend NPV	1.49	1.49

Close Dividend Schedule

To calculate dividend net present value, the model discounts the stream of dividends expected to be paid during the investment period.

The model calculates two different dividend net present values. For one, the model uses as the discount rate the risk-free rate of return. For the other, it uses the expected return.

	Annualized	Period
Expected CC Return	5.00	1.8356%
Median CC Return	-3.000%	-1.1014%
Standard Deviation	40.00	24.2363%
Dividend NPV		1.49
CC Risk-free Rate	5.00	1.8356%

Current Asset Price	55.00
Days to Expire (365 D/Y)	134
Call Strike Price	45.00
Call Option Price	

Right axis values: $149.51, $135.28, $122.40, $110.76, $100.22, $90.68, $82.05, $74.24, $67.18, $60.78, $55.00, $49.77, $45.03, $40.75, $36.87, $33.36, $30.18, $27.31, $24.71, $22.36, $20.23, $18.31, $16.57

Left axis values: 110%, 100%, 90%, 80%, 70%, 60%, 50%, 40%, 30%, 20%, 10%, 0%, -10%, -20%, -30%, -40%, -50%, -110%, -120%, -130%

Call

Display Div Schedule

No Div

Calculate Option Value   Fast   Fastest

If its underlying pays lumpy dividends and a call goes deep into the money, when should you exercise it?

In the case of a deep-in-the-money put on an underlying that pays dividends, we saw that the put value increased whenever a dividend payment pushed the underlying's probability distribution down. In our example, we saw that the best time to exercise the put was immediately *after* the dividend.

For a call option, when an underlying's dividend payments push the probability distribution down, it pushes more little squares out of the money. When might the time of optimal exercise be?

Let's see.

1. Click three times on Clear.

2. Click twice on Hide.

3. Click on Call.

4. Click on Calculate Option Value.

To simplify things a little, we're going to make the underlying expected return and the risk-free rate the same.

5. For Expected CC Return, enter 5.00.

6. For Standard Deviation, enter 40.00.

This combination of expected return and standard deviation gives us a negative median return. Over time, the negative return will push the middle of the underlying's probability distribution down.

7. For Current Asset Price, enter 55.00.

8. For Days to Expire, enter 134.

9. For Call Strike Price, enter 45.00.

10. Click on Display Div Schedule.

11. For CC Risk-Free Rate, enter 5.00.

12. For First dividend, Days until ex-dividend, enter 12.

13. For First dividend, Dividend amount, enter 0.75.

14. For Second dividend, Days until ex-dividend, enter 102.

15. For Second dividend, Dividend amount, enter 0.75.

16. Click on Calculate Net Present Value.

17. Click on Close Dividend Schedule.

18. Click on Calculate Option Value Fastest.

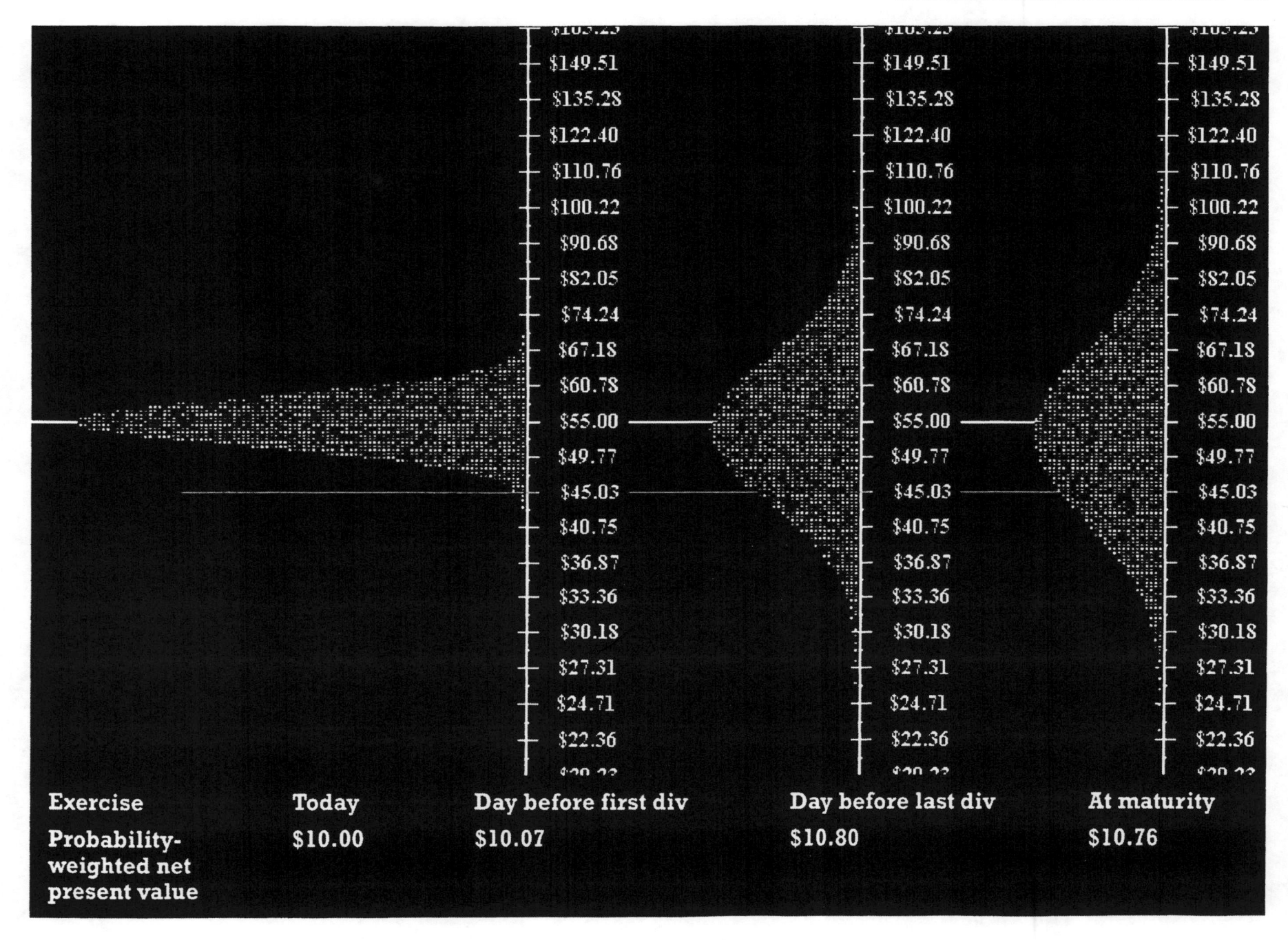

	$103.25		$103.25		$103.25
	$149.51		$149.51		$149.51
	$135.28		$135.28		$135.28
	$122.40		$122.40		$122.40
	$110.76		$110.76		$110.76
	$100.22		$100.22		$100.22
	$90.68		$90.68		$90.68
	$82.05		$82.05		$82.05
	$74.24		$74.24		$74.24
	$67.18		$67.18		$67.18
	$60.78		$60.78		$60.78
	$55.00		$55.00		$55.00
	$49.77		$49.77		$49.77
	$45.03		$45.03		$45.03
	$40.75		$40.75		$40.75
	$36.87		$36.87		$36.87
	$33.36		$33.36		$33.36
	$30.18		$30.18		$30.18
	$27.31		$27.31		$27.31
	$24.71		$24.71		$24.71
	$22.36		$22.36		$22.36

Exercise	Today	Day before first div	Day before last div	At maturity
Probability-weighted net present value	$10.00	$10.07	$10.80	$10.76

If a call goes deep into the money and the underlying pays lumpy dividends, it may be optimal to exercise the option on the last day before the underlying goes ex-dividend for the last time.

The probability-weighted net present value of the option's possible payoffs at maturity is $10.76.

If you were to exercise the option today, your payoff from early exercise would be $10.00. The option has time value. On average, it promises to be worth more when held to maturity than when exercised today.

Let's look at the probability-weighted net present value on the day before the first ex-dividend date, day 11.

> **19. Tab to the Days to Expire field. Enter 11.**
>
> **20. Click on Calculate Option Value Fastest.**

The probability-weighted net present value is $10.07—more than the exercise-today value, less than the value for exercise at maturity.

The underlying's last ex-dividend date is 102 days away. On that day, the dividend will push the underlying's probability distribution down. Let's look at the probability-weighted net present value of the underlying's probability distribution on the day before, on day 101.

> **21. For Days to Expire, enter 101.**
>
> **22. Click on Calculate Option Value Fastest.**

The probability-weighted net present value is $10.80—four cents more than for holding the option until maturity.

Looking into the future, right now it looks like the optimal time to exercise this option is on the last day before the underlying goes ex-dividend for the last time.

Using Black's approximation, we would value this option at $10.80—the highest Black-Scholes value of its possible exercise times.

Often when a call goes deep into the money and the underlying pays lumpy dividends, it is optimal to exercise the option on the last day before the underlying goes ex-dividend for the last time.

What we've seen is a common pattern but not a rule on which you can depend. You have to do the analysis.

The outcomes vary with your forecast for the underlying's expected return—or with the risk-free rate if you use it as the expected return. Outcomes vary with your forecast for the underlying's volatility and with the size of the predicted dividend payments.

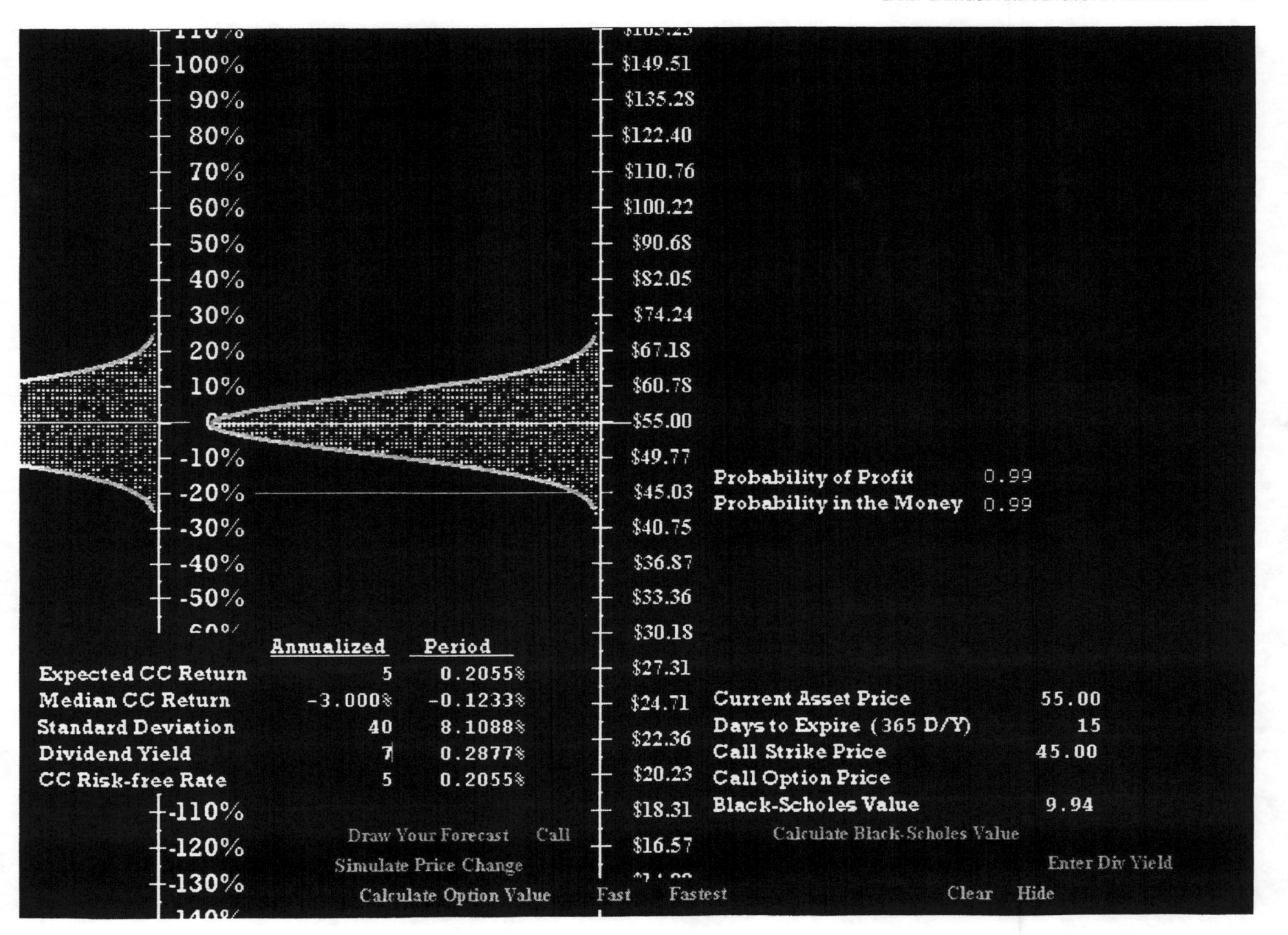

If the underlying pays a dividend yield and a call goes deep into the money, what determines the best time to exercise the option?

Let's look at how a dividend yield might affect a call's probability-weighted net present values for different times to exercise. As examples, we'll look at dividend yields of 5% and 7% for times to exercise of 0, 15, 30, 60, and 120 days.

Except for the times to exercise and a dividend yield instead of lumpy dividends, we keep the setting from the previous example. The spot price of $55 and strike price of $45 give us an exercise-today payoff of $10.

23. Click once on Clear.

24. Click on Enter Div Yield.

25. For Days to Expire, enter 15.

26. For Continuous Div Yield, enter 5.00.

27. Click on Calculate Option Value Fastest.

Note the probability-weighted net present value.

28. For Continuous Div Yield, enter 7.00.

29. Click on Draw Your Forecast.

30. Click on Calculate Black-Scholes Value.

The probability distributions are so similar as to be indistinguishable.

Looking ahead to exercise in 15 days, a dividend yield of 5% gives us a value of $9.99. A dividend yield of 7% gives us a value of $9.94. Both values are below the exercise-today value of $10.00.

31. Click once on Clear.

32. For Days to Expire, enter 30.

33. For Continuous Div Yield, enter 5.00.

34. Click on Calculate Option Value Fastest.

Note the value.

35. For Continuous Div Yield, enter 7.00.

36. Click on Draw Your Forecast.

37. Click on Calculate Black-Scholes Value.

At 30 days, a 5% dividend yield gives us a value of $10.05. We're above the exercise-today value.

A 7% yield gives us a value of $9.96.

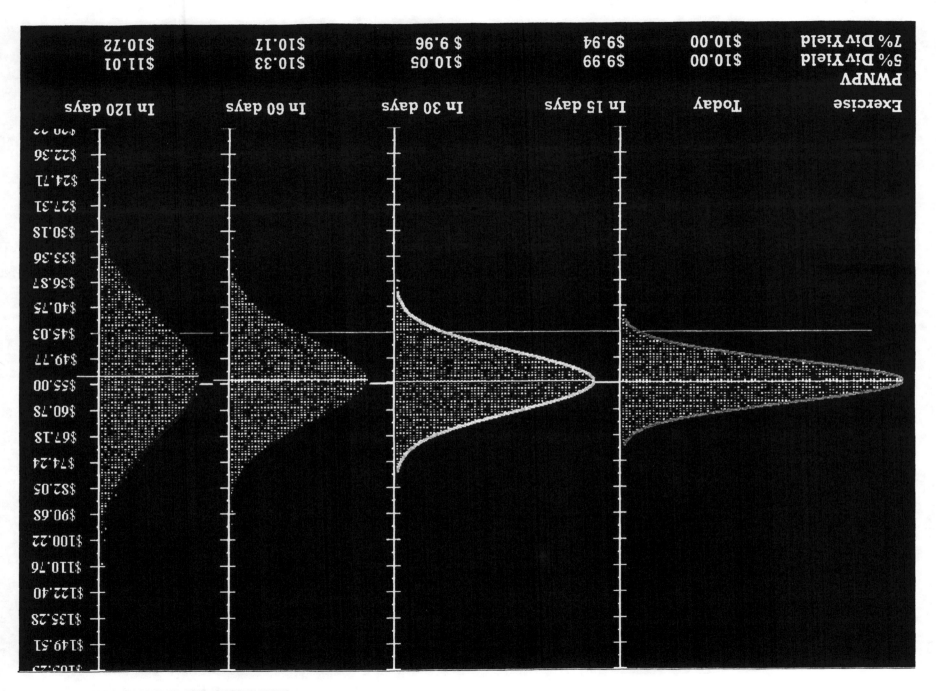

Exercise	Today	In 15 days	In 30 days	In 60 days	In 120 days
PWNPV					
5% Div Yield	$10.00	$9.99	$10.05	$10.33	$11.01
7% Div Yield	$10.00	$9.94	$9.96	$10.17	$10.72

If a call goes deep into the money and the underlying pays a dividend yield, the time of optimal exercise depends on the size of the yield, the option's remaining time value, the underlying's volatility, and its expected return and/or the risk-free rate.

38. Click once on clear.

39. For Days to Expire, enter 60.

40. For Continuous Div Yield, enter 5.00.

41. Click on Calculate Option Value Fastest.

Note the value.

42. For Continuous Div Yield, enter 7.00.

43. Click on Draw Your Forecast.

44. Click on Calculate Black-Scholes Value.

At 60 days, a 5% dividend yield gives us a value of $10.33. A 7% yield gives us a value of $10.17. For both yields, we're above the exercise-today value.

45. Click once on Clear.

46. For Days to Expire, enter 120.

47. For Continuous Div Yield, enter 5.00.

48. Click on Calculate Option Value Fastest.

Note the value.

49. For Continuous Div Yield, enter 7.00.

50. Click on Draw Your Forecast.

51. Click on Calculate Black-Scholes Value.

At 120 days, a 5% dividend yield gives us a value of $11.01. A 7% yield gives us a value of $10.72.

In the progression from exercise today to exercise in 120 days, the probability distributions for 5% and 7% are visually indistinguishable.

Over time, the negative median returns and dividend yields push the underlying's probability distributions down the price axis.

From the calculated values, we see that the higher the dividend yield is, the lower the value of the call.

Early on, the tails of the probability distributions below the strike price drag the averages of the little squares' payoffs below the exercise-today values.

Later, the higher and higher payoffs from the outcomes at the tops of the probability distributions more than compensate for the absence of payoffs from little squares below the strike price.

With days to expiration of 120 days, if you don't mind the intervening dip in value, it makes sense to hold on to both options. Had the options only 15 days until expiration, it would be logical to exercise both of them today.

The examples show the complexity of finding the right time to exercise calls on underlyings that pay dividend yields.

Using Black's approximation and times to expiration of 120 days, the value of the call on the underlying with the 5% dividend yield is $11.01. For the 7% dividend yield, it is $10.72.

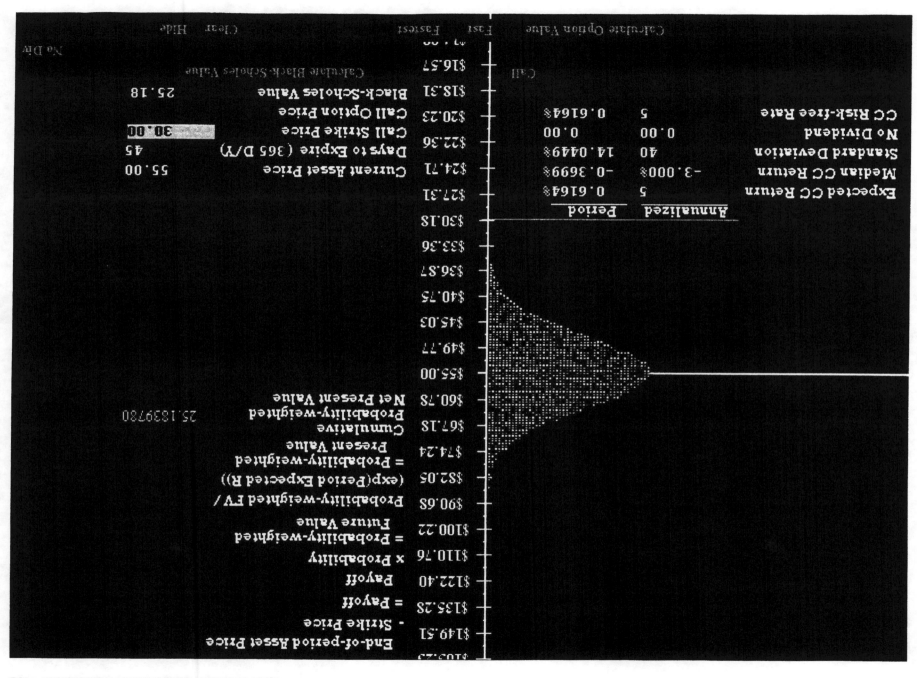

If you own a call on an underlying that pays no dividends, when does exercising it early give you an advantage? Never!

Now let's do something that's a lot easier—look at a call on an underlying that pays no dividends. The call is super deep into the money.

52. Click once on Clear.

53. Click on No Div.

54. For Days to Expire, enter 45.

55. For Call Strike Price, enter 30.00.

56. Click on Calculate Option Value Fastest.

57. Click on Calculate Black-Scholes Value.

You cannot get much deeper into the money. The entire probability distribution is above the strike price.

Still, the probability-weighted net present value is 18 cents higher than the exercise-today value.

Under ordinary conditions, on an underlying that pays no dividends, you can never have a call option that has no time value. To see for yourself, try different numbers of days to expiration, different strike prices, and different risk-free rates.

If you're calculating the option's Black-Scholes value, the only way to get the time value to be zero or negative is to set the risk-free rate to zero or below.

If you're using expected return to calculate the option's probability-weighted net present value, if you set the expected return below zero, the time value will go negative. If you set the strike price equal to zero, the option value will equal the exercise-today value, which will be equal to the spot price of the underlying.

On underlyings that pay no dividends, European calls and American calls have the same value. You can use Black-Scholes to value them without using Black's approximation.

Some American options have more value than otherwise identical European options because of the potential value of early exercise. Since the right to early exercise has no value for a call written on an underlying that pays no dividends, the right of early exercise has no value.

On these underlyings, European and American calls have the same value.

Instead of looking at possible early-exercise points and using Black's approximation, you can use Black-Scholes to value them. You can do other types of analyses that rely on the Black-Scholes assumptions.

Sensitivity of Option Values to Changes in Volatility, Spot Price of Underlying, Time to Expiration, and Risk-Free Rate

Factors that change an option's value change how many little squares are above or below the strike price and how far they are above it or below it.

The value of an option is determined by where all those little squares in the probability distribution of the underlying fall relative to the option's strike price. Factors that change where they fall change the option's value.

Changes in the spot price of the underlying, the option's time to expiration, the underlying's expected volatility, and the risk-free rate all change the underlying's probability distribution. When these factors change, the probability distribution of the underlying may go up or down, spread out or contract. The number of little squares above or below the strike price increases or decreases accordingly. The distance of the little squares from the strike price—and, hence, the size of their payoffs—increase or decrease. The value of the option changes accordingly.

Many books and tutorials on options quickly launch into a discussion of the Greeks—the symbols for how much an option's value changes with changes in the spot price of the underlying, the option's time to expiration, the underlying's volatility, and the risk-free rate. They give you a calculator or formula for calculating the Greeks and act as if they've given you something of great value.

We're not going to do that.

Once you're an experienced options trader, you'll understand the Greeks and they will be of value to you. You'll use them to set up and manage hedges for options you sell. You'll use them to help manage your risk exposures.

If you're just learning about options, a more useful approach, which we will follow here, is to look at how changes in different factors change where the little squares fall relative to the option's strike price.

Calculation of the Greeks under the Black-Scholes assumptions assumes that all options are European style. We'll follow that assumption.

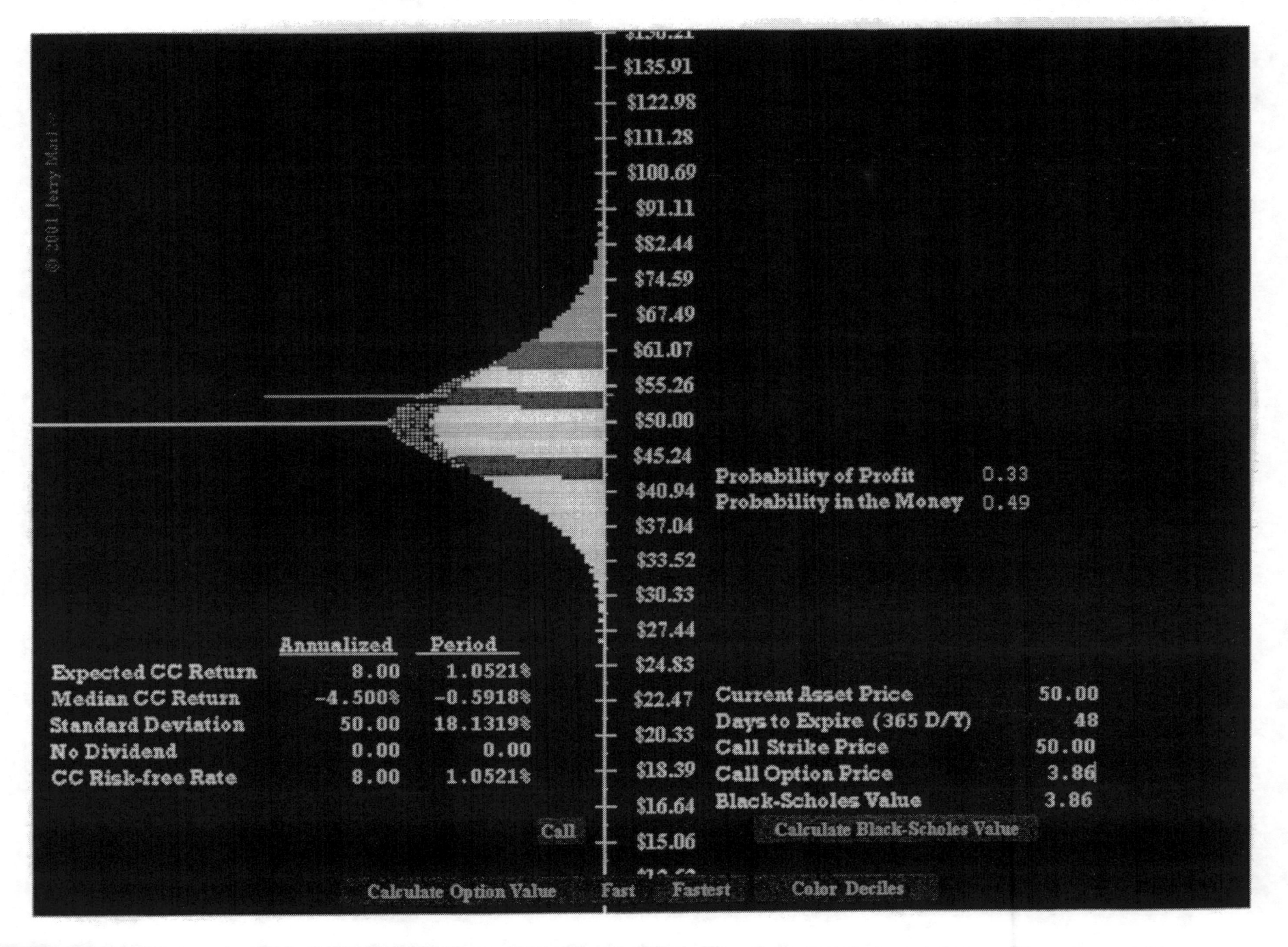

The deeper an option goes into the money, the less sensitive it is to changes in the factors that determine its value.

How much a change in spot price, time to expiration, volatility, or the risk-free rate changes an option's value depends on how much it alters the position of the little squares in the underlying's probability distribution relative to the strike price.

If an option is deep in the money or at the money, a change in one of the factors does not change very much the proportion of squares above and below the strike price. The percentage change in option value is relatively small.

If, for instance, the volatility of an at-the-money call option increases by 25%, the proportion of squares above and below the strike price changes very little.

1. Click three times on Clear.

2. Click twice on Hide.

3. Click on Call.

4. Click on Calculate Option Value Fast.

5. Click on Calculate Black-Scholes Value.

6. For Expected CC Return, enter 8.00.

7. For Standard Deviation, enter 40.00.

8. For CC Risk-Free Rate, enter 8.00.

9. For Current Asset Price, enter 50.00.

10. For Days to Expire, enter 48.

11. For Call Strike Price, enter 50.00.

This is an at-the-money option. The strike price is equal to the spot price.

We've set it up so that the expected return equals the risk-free rate and the median return is zero.

12. Click on Calculate Black-Scholes Value.

The option's Black-Scholes value is $3.14.

13. For Call Option Price, enter 3.14.

14. Click on Color Deciles.

The probability of being in the money is .50. That means 50% of the little squares are above the strike price; 50%, below.

Let's see how much the proportion of little squares above the strike price changes when we increase the standard deviation by 25%.

15. Click on Calculate Option Value Fastest.

16. For Standard Deviation, enter 50.00.

(Increasing a standard deviation of 40.00 by 10.00 is a 25% change: 10/40 = 25%.)

17. Click on Calculate Black-Scholes Value.

The option's Black-Scholes value is $3.86.

18. For Call Option Price, enter 3.86.

19. Click on Color Deciles.

We've gone from a .50 probability of being in the money to .49. That's a change of

$$(.49 - .50)/.50 = -2\%$$

Let's see the percentage change in the option's value:

$$(\$3.86 - \$3.14)/\$3.14 = 23\%$$

Thus, in this instance, a 25% change in expected volatility gives us a 23% increase in option value.

Let's compare these sensitivities to those of an option that is otherwise identical but that is far out of the money.

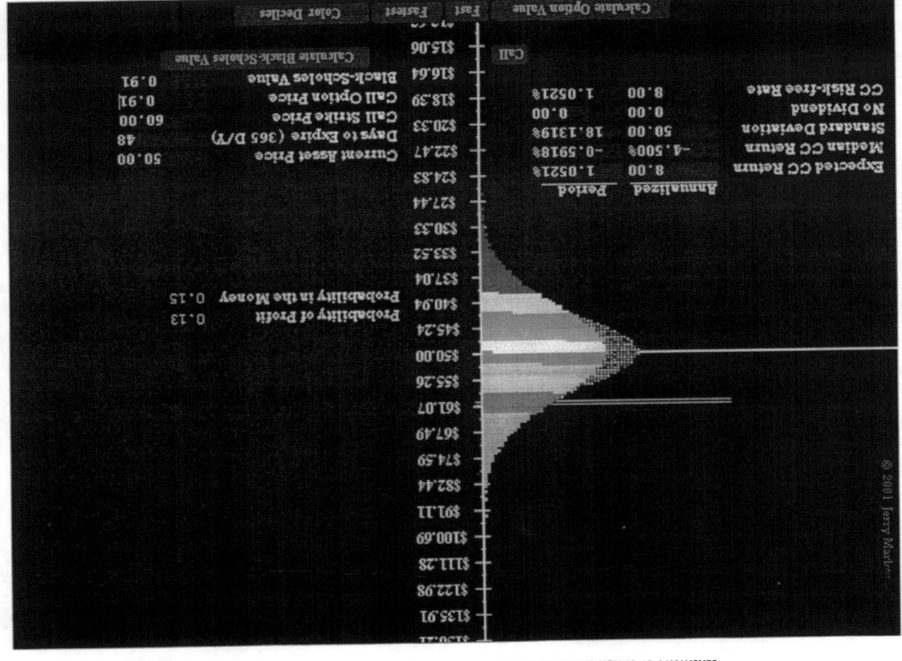

The farther an option is out of the money, the more sensitive it is to changes in the factors that affect its value.

Now we look at the sensitivities of an option that is otherwise the same but far out of the money. Instead of starting with 50% of the little squares above the strike price, we start with 10% above.

> 20. Click on Clear.
> 21. For Standard Deviation, enter 40.00.
> 22. For Call Strike Price, enter 60.00.
> 23. Click on Calculate Black-Scholes Value.

The option's Black-Scholes value is $0.46.

> 24. For Call Option Price, enter 0.46.
> 25. Click on Color Deciles.

The probability of being in the money is .10. That means 10% of the little squares are above the strike price; 90%, below.

Let's see how much the proportion of little squares above the strike price changes this time when we increase the standard deviation by 25%.

> 26. Click on Calculate Option Value Fastest.
> 27. For Standard Deviation, enter 50.00.
> 28. Click on Calculate Black-Scholes Value.

The option's Black-Scholes value is $0.91.

> 29. For Call Option Price, enter 0.91.
> 30. Click on Color Deciles.

We've gone from a .10 probability of being in the money to .15. That's a change of

$$(.15 - .10)/.10 = 50\%$$

Let's see the percentage change in the option's value:

$$(\$0.91 - \$0.46)/\$0.46 = 98\%$$

Thus, we see changes in the factors that affect option value have their greatest effects on options that are far out of the money.

V, vega—If volatility increases, more little squares are above the strike price. Little squares are farther above the strike price. The value of a call option goes up.

One of the Black-Scholes assumptions is that the expected volatility of the underlying is constant over the life of an option. However, the expected volatility may change.

V, vega, is the measure of how sensitive an option's price is to changes in the volatility of the underlying.

In our examples above, when we increased the volatility of the underlying, the probability distribution spread out. More of the little squares went above the strike price. Those already above went farther above. The value of the options went up.

What we saw holds as a general rule: When all else stays the same, an increase in volatility increases the value of a call option.

Keep in mind that an increase in volatility lowers the underlying's median return. In our examples, the increase changed the median return from zero to −4.50%.

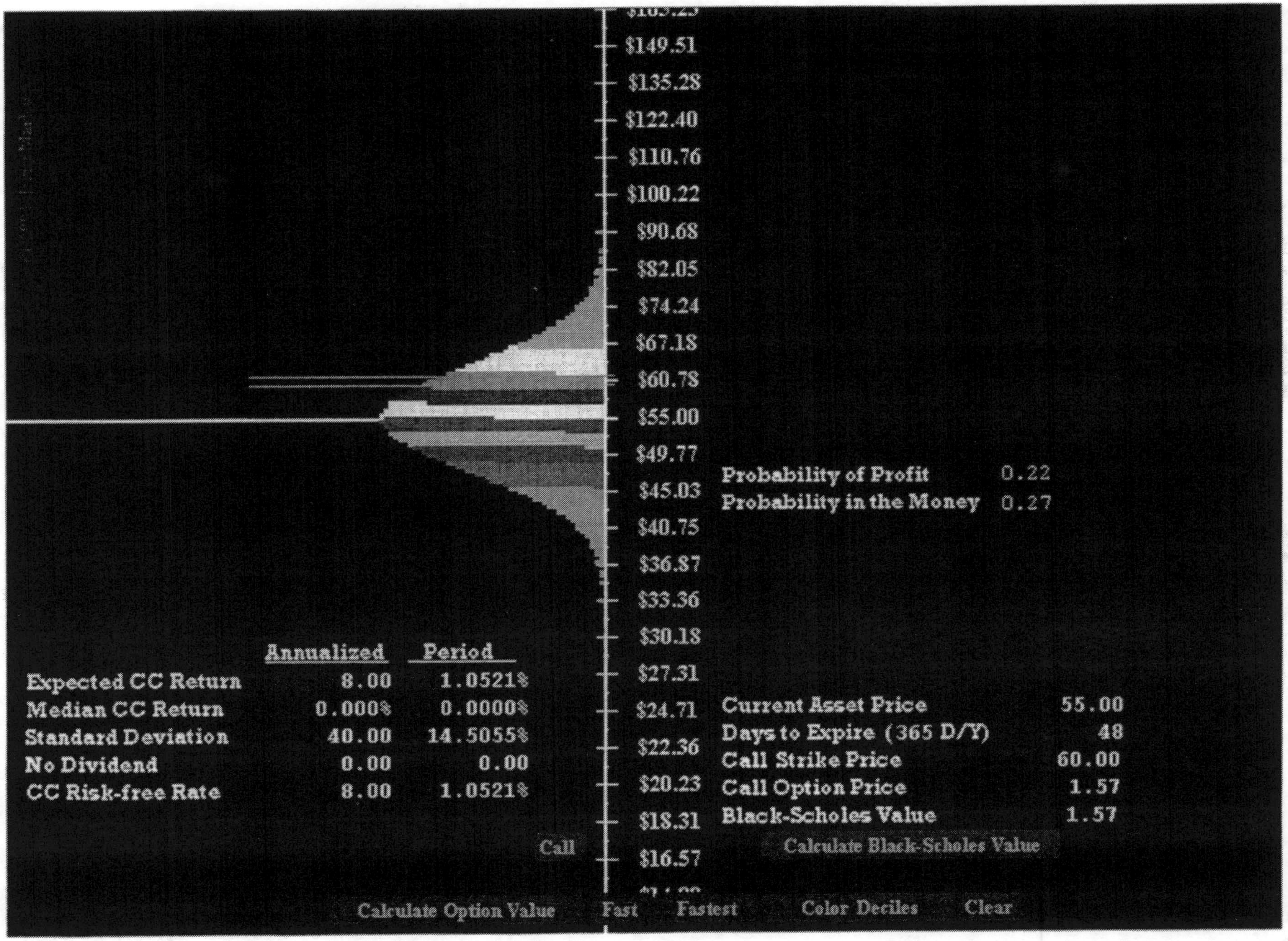

$149.51

$135.28

$122.40

$110.76

$100.22

$90.68

$82.05

$74.24

$67.18

$60.78

$55.00

$49.77

Probability of Profit   0.22
Probability in the Money   0.27

$45.03

$40.75

$36.87

$33.36

$30.18

	Annualized	Period
Expected CC Return	8.00	1.0521%
Median CC Return	0.000%	0.0000%
Standard Deviation	40.00	14.5055%
No Dividend	0.00	0.00
CC Risk-free Rate	8.00	1.0521%

$27.31

$24.71   Current Asset Price   55.00
         Days to Expire (365 D/Y)   48
$22.36   Call Strike Price   60.00
$20.23   Call Option Price   1.57
         Black-Scholes Value   1.57
$18.31
Call   Calculate Black-Scholes Value
$16.57

Calculate Option Value   Fast   Fastest   Color Deciles   Clear

Δ, delta—When the spot price of the underlying increases, more little squares are above the strike price. Little squares are farther above it. The value of a call goes up.

Delta is the rate of change of the option price with respect to the price of the underlying asset. Let's see how a change in the underlying's spot price changes where the little squares fall relative to a call option's strike price.

First we redraw our baseline call option.

1. Click three times on Clear.
2. Click twice on Hide.
3. Click on Call.
4. Click on Calculate Option Value Fast.
5. Click on Calculate Black-Scholes Value.
6. Tab to Expected CC Return. Enter 8.00.
7. Tab to Standard Deviation. Enter 40.00.
8. For CC Risk-free Rate, enter 8.0.
9. For Current Asset Price, enter 50.00.
10. For Days to Expire, enter 48.
11. For Call Strike Price, enter 60.00.
12. Click on Calculate Black-Scholes Value.

The option's Black-Scholes value is $0.46.

13. For Call Option Price, enter 0.46.
14. Click on Color Deciles.

Ten percent of the little squares are above the strike price.

Let's see how a change in the underlying's spot price changes the value of the call. We'll increase the asset price by 10%.

15. For Current Asset Price, enter 55.00.
16. Click on Calculate Black-Scholes Value.

The option value is $1.57.

17. For Call Option Price, enter 1.57.
18. Click on Color Deciles.

The shape of the probability distribution remains the same.

Now 27% of the little squares are above the strike price. That's an increase of

$(.27 - .10)/.10 = 170\%$

The option's value increased by

$(\$1.57 - \$0.46)/\$0.46 = 241\%$

In this case, a 10% increase in spot price gives a 241% increase in option value.

When the spot price of the underlying increases, the value of a call goes up.

To calculate an approximation of delta, you could follow these steps:

1. Reestablish the baseline call.
2. Increase the spot price by 1%.
3. Find the percentage change in Black-Scholes value.
4. Divide the percentage change in value by 1%.

To get a display of the Black-Scholes value to more decimal places, use the sweep method of calculating its value.

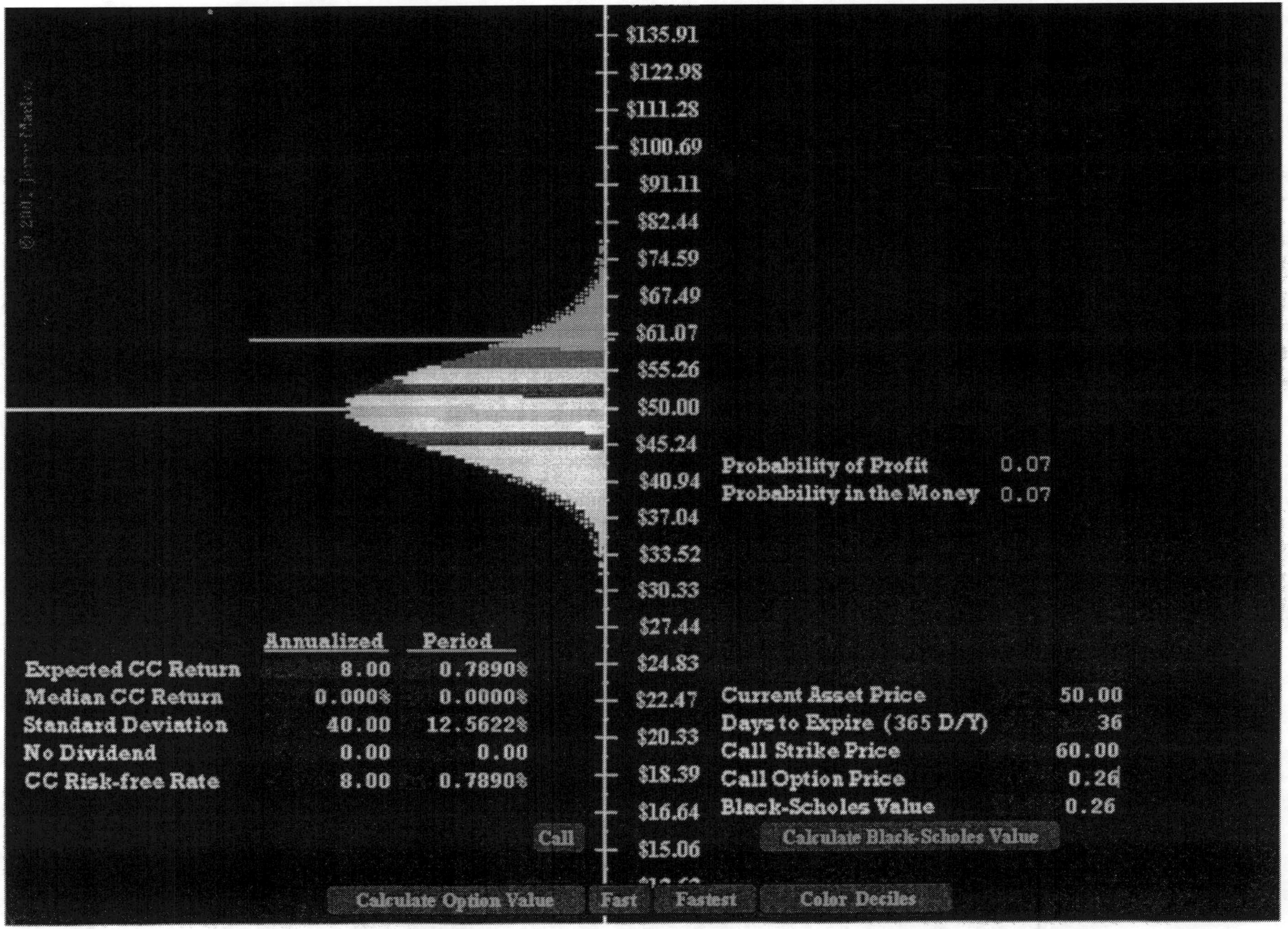

$135.91

$122.98

$111.28

$100.69

$91.11

$82.44

$74.59

$67.49

$61.07

$55.26

$50.00

$45.24

$40.94   Probability of Profit   0.07
          Probability in the Money 0.07

$37.04

$33.52

$30.33

$27.44

	Annualized	Period
Expected CC Return	8.00	0.7890%
Median CC Return	0.000%	0.0000%
Standard Deviation	40.00	12.5622%
No Dividend	0.00	0.00
CC Risk-free Rate	8.00	0.7890%

$24.83

$22.47   Current Asset Price   50.00
          Days to Expire (365 D/Y)   36
$20.33   Call Strike Price   60.00
          Call Option Price   0.26
$18.39   Black-Scholes Value   0.26
$16.64
Call $15.06   Calculate Black-Scholes Value

Calculate Option Value   Fast   Fastest   Color Deciles

Θ, theta—If the underlying pays no dividends, as a call option's time to expiration grows shorter, fewer little squares are above the strike price. The ones above are not as far above. The option's value goes down.

Θ, theta, is the rate of change of an option's value with changes in its time to maturity. Let's see how a change in the option's time to maturity changes where the little squares fall relative to the option's strike price.

We redraw our baseline call option.

1. Click three times on Clear.

2. Tab to Expected CC Return. Enter 8.00.

3. For Standard Deviation, enter 40.00.

4. For CC Risk-free Rate, enter 8.0.

5. For Current Asset Price, enter 50.00.

6. For Days to Expire, enter 48.

7. For Call Strike Price, enter 60.00.

8. Click on Calculate Black-Scholes Value.

The option's Black-Scholes value is $0.46.

9. For Call Option Price, enter 0.46.

10. Click on Color Deciles.

Ten percent of the little squares are above the strike price.

So that we can make a visual comparison, we draw our baseline forecast with little squares.

11. Click on Calculate Option Value Fastest.

Let's see how a shortening of the option's time to maturity changes the value of the call. We'll decrease the time to maturity by 25%, from 48 days to 36.

12. For Days to Expire, enter 36.

13. Click on Calculate Black-Scholes Value.

The option value is $0.26.

14. For Call Option Price, enter 0.26.

15. Click on Color Deciles.

Volatility, as measured by the standard deviation of the probability distribution, changes with the square root of time. In this example, the period standard deviation decreases from 14.5055% to 12.5622%.

$$(14.5055\%)\left(\sqrt{\frac{36}{48}}\right) = 12.5622\%$$

The probability distribution narrows. Fewer little squares are above the strike line. Those that are above don't go up as far. Now 7% of the little squares are above the strike price. That's a change of

$$(.07 - .10)/.10 = -30\%$$

The option's value changes by

$$(\$0.26 - \$0.46)/\$0.46 = -43\%$$

When you hold all other factors the same, if the underlying pays no dividends, as a call's time to maturity shortens, its Black-Scholes value goes down.

Sometimes people refer to an option's decline in value with the passage of time as its time decay.

To calculate an approximation of theta, you could follow these steps:

1. Reestablish the baseline call.

2. Decrease the time to expiration by one day.

3. Find the percentage change in time to expiration.

4. Find the percentage change in Black-Scholes value.

5. Divide the percentage change in Black-Scholes value by the percentage change in time to expiration.

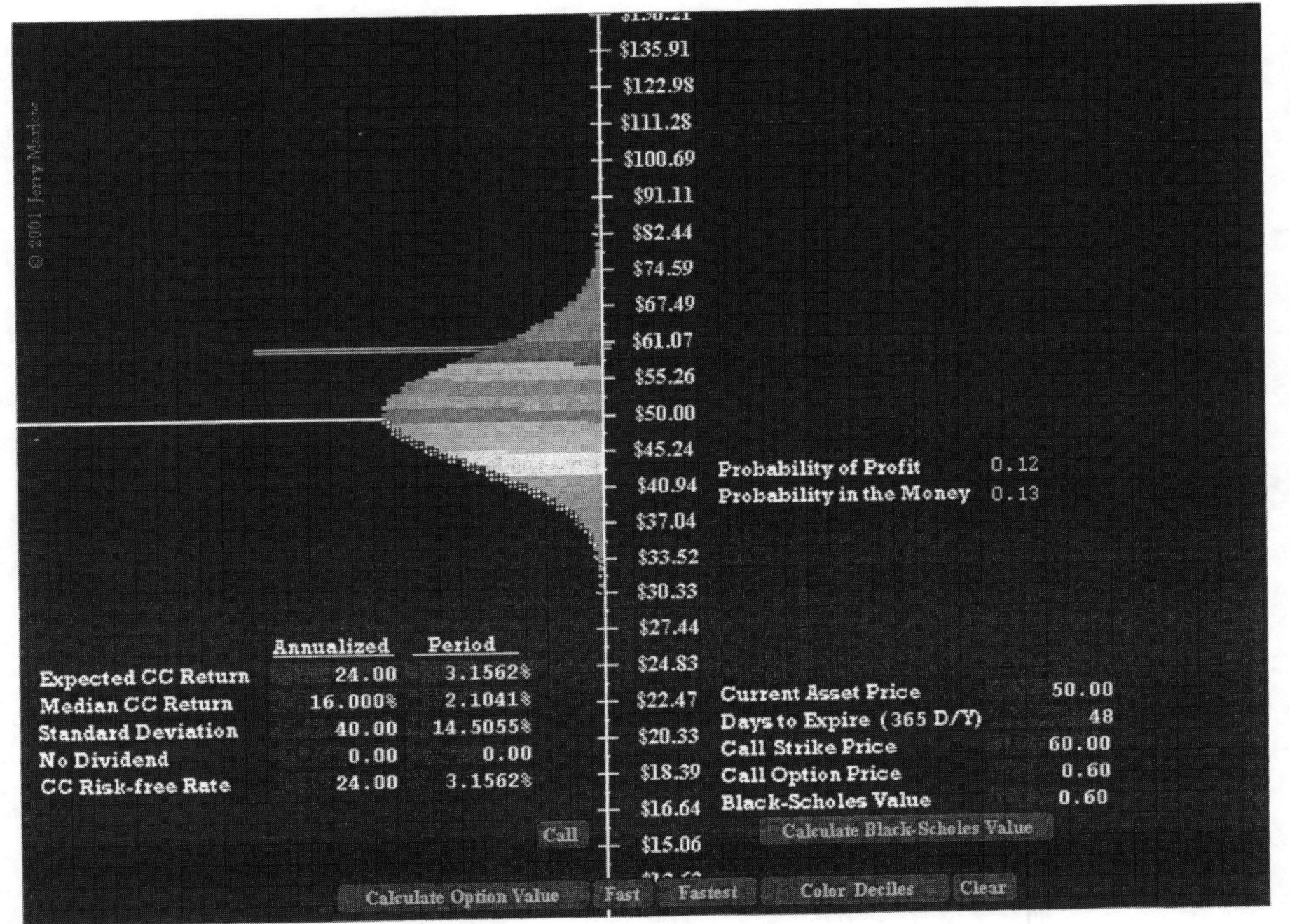

P, rho—An increase in the risk-free rate increases the underlying's median return. The number of little squares above the strike price increases. The squares above are higher above. The Black-Scholes value of a call goes up.

Rho is the rate of change of the Black-Scholes value of an option as the risk-free rate changes.

To see the effect, let's redraw our baseline call.

1. Click three times on Clear.
2. Click twice on Hide.
3. Click on Call.
4. Click on Calculate Option Value Fast.
5. Click on Calculate Black-Scholes Value.
6. Tab to Expected CC Return. Enter 8.00.
7. Tab to Standard Deviation. Enter 40.00.
8. For CC Risk-free Rate, enter 8.0.
9. For Current Asset Price, enter 50.00.
10. For Days to Expire, enter 48.
11. For Call Strike Price, enter 60.00.
12. Click on Calculate Black-Scholes Value.

The option's Black-Scholes value is $0.46.

13. For Call Option Price, enter 0.46.
14. Click on Color Deciles.

Ten percent of the little squares are above the strike price.

So that we can make a visual comparison, we draw our baseline forecast with little squares.

15. Click on Calculate Option Value Fastest.

To be able to see the effect of an increase in the risk-free rate on the little squares, we have to change the interest rate a lot. We'll increase it by 200%.

16. For Expected CC Return, enter 24.00.
17. For CC Risk-Free Rate, enter 24.00.
18. Click on Calculate Black-Scholes Value.

The option value is $0.60.

19. For Call Option Price, enter 0.60.
20. Click on Color Deciles.

Black-Scholes uses the risk-free rate as the option's expected return. An increase in the risk-free rate increases the underlying's median return. Here it increases the annualized median return from 0% to 16%. The increase in the median return lifts the probability distribution.

The number of little squares above the strike price increases. Here it goes up by

$(.13 - .10)/.10 = 30\%$

The option's value increases. It goes up by

$(\$0.60 - \$0.46)/\$0.46 = 30\%$

Holding all other factors the same, under the Black-Scholes assumptions, the higher the risk-free rate, the greater a call's value.

To calculate an approximation of rho, you could:

1. Reestablish the baseline call.
2. Increase the risk-free rate by 1%.
3. Find the percentage change in Black-Scholes value.
4. Divide the percentage change by 1%.

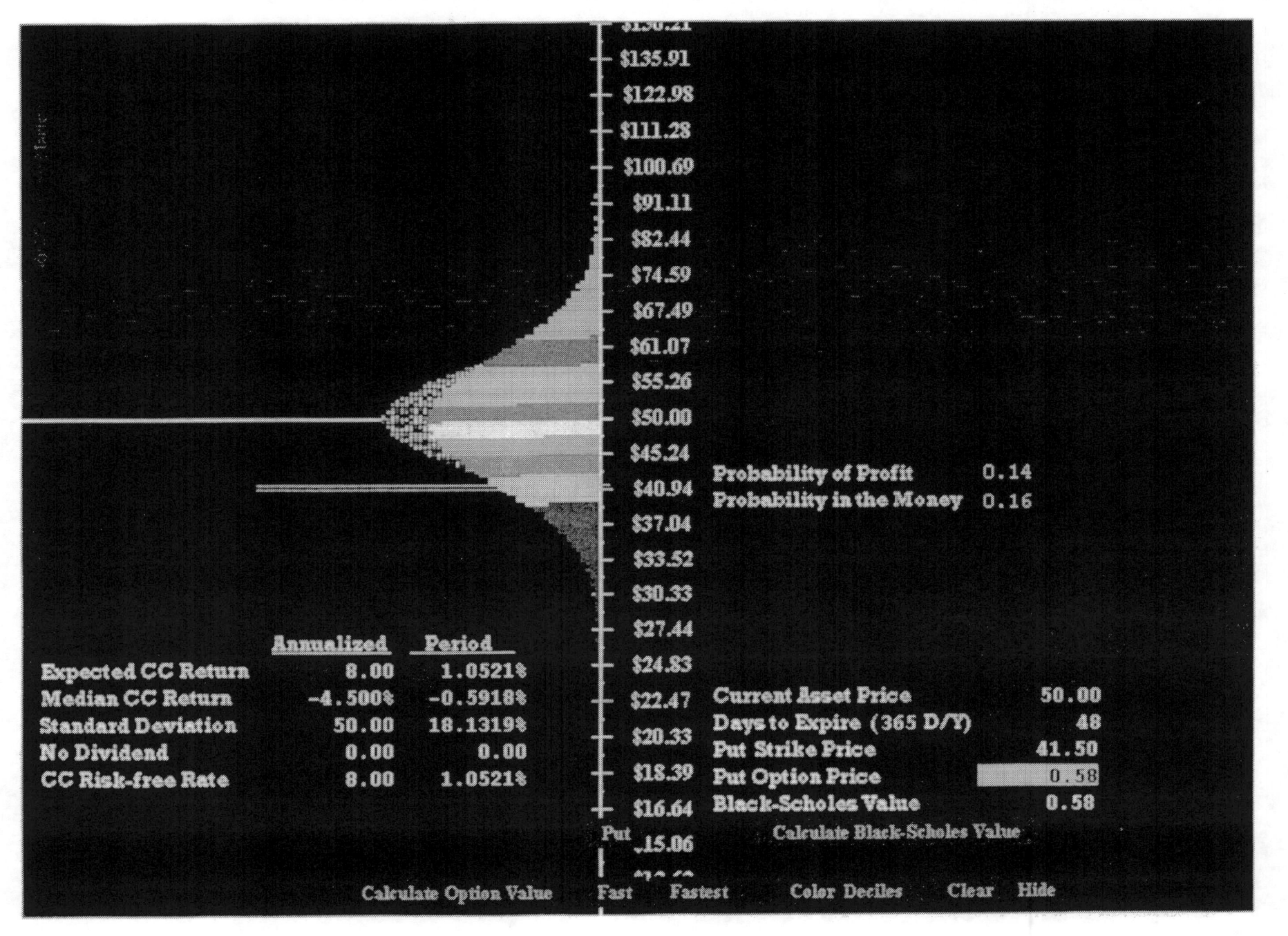

V, vega—If volatility increases, the underlying's probability distribution spreads and drops down. The value of a put goes up.

Now we look at the sensitivity of the Black-Scholes value of puts to changes in the underlying's volatility, spot price, the option's time to expiration, and the risk-free rate.

First we establish a baseline put.

1. Click three times on Clear.

2. Click twice on Hide.

3. Click on Put.

4. Click on Calculate Option Value Fastest.

5. Click on Calculate Black-Scholes Value.

6. For Expected CC Return, enter 8.00.

7. Tab to Standard Deviation. Enter 40.00.

8. Tab to CC Risk-Free Rate. Enter 8.00.

9. For Current Asset Price, enter 50.00.

10. For Days to Expire, enter 48.

11. For Put Strike Price, enter 41.50.

12. Click on Calculate Black-Scholes Value.

The value of the put is $0.26.

13. For Put Option Price, enter 0.26.

14. Click on Color Deciles.

Ten percent of the little squares are below the strike price. Ninety percent are above.

15. Click on Calculate Option Value Fast or Fastest.

Let's see how much the proportion of little squares below the strike price changes when we increase the standard deviation by 25%.

16. For Standard Deviation, enter 50.00.

17. Click on Calculate Black-Scholes Value.

The option's Black-Scholes value is $0.58.

18. For Put Option Price, enter 0.58.

19. Click on Color Deciles.

Once again, an increase in volatility has lowered the underlying's median return. The probability distribution is both more spread out and a tiny bit lower. The greater spread means that some of the little squares are farther away from the strike price—and, thereby, worth more.

We've gone from 10% of the little squares below the strike price to 16%. That's a change of

$$(.16 - .10)/.10 = 60\%$$

Let's see the percentage change in the option's value:

$$(\$0.58 - \$0.26)/\$0.26 = 123\%$$

When all else stays the same, an increase in volatility increases the value of a put.

To calculate an approximation of vega, you could:

1. Reestablish the baseline put.

2. Increase the standard deviation by 1%.

3. Find the percentage change in Black-Scholes value.

4. Divide the percentage change by 1%.

To get a display of the Black-Scholes value to more decimal places, use the sweep method of calculating its value.

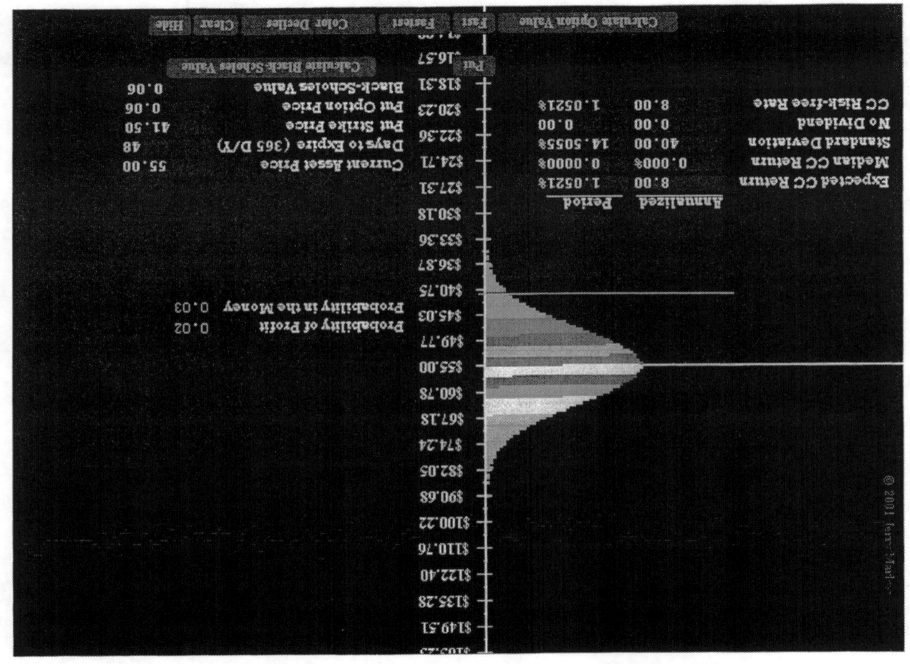

Δ, delta—When the spot price of the underlying increases, the value of a put goes down.

We look at how a change in the underlying's spot price changes the value of a put.

First we reestablish our baseline put.

1. Click three times on Clear.
2. For Expected CC Return, enter 8.00.
3. Tab to Standard Deviation. Enter 40.00.
4. Tab to CC Risk-free Rate. Enter 8.00.
5. Tab to Current Asset Price. Enter 50.00.
6. For Days to Expire, enter 48.
7. For Put Strike Price, enter 41.50.
8. Click on Calculate Black-Scholes Value.

The value of the baseline put is $0.26.

9. For Put Option Price, enter 0.26.
10. Click on Color Deciles.

Ten percent of the little squares are below the strike price.

11. Click on Calculate Option Value Fastest.

Let's see how much the proportion of little squares below the strike price changes when we increase the spot price by 10%.

12. For Current Asset Price, enter 55.00.
13. Click on Calculate Black-Scholes Value.

The option's Black-Scholes value is $0.06.

14. For Put Option Price, enter 0.06.
15. Click on Color Deciles.

An increase in the spot price of the underlying lifts the probability distribution. It stays the same shape.

Fewer of the little squares are below the strike price. The value of the option goes down.

We've gone from 10% of the little squares below the strike price to 3%. That's a change of

$(.03 - .10)/.10 = -70\%$

Let's see the percentage change in the option's value:

$(\$0.06 - \$0.26)/\$0.26 = -77\%$

When all else stays the same, an increase in the spot price decrease the value of a put.

To calculate an approximation of delta, you could:

1. Reestablish the baseline put.
2. Increase the spot price by 1%.
3. Find the percentage change in Black-Scholes value.
4. Divide the percentage change by 1%.

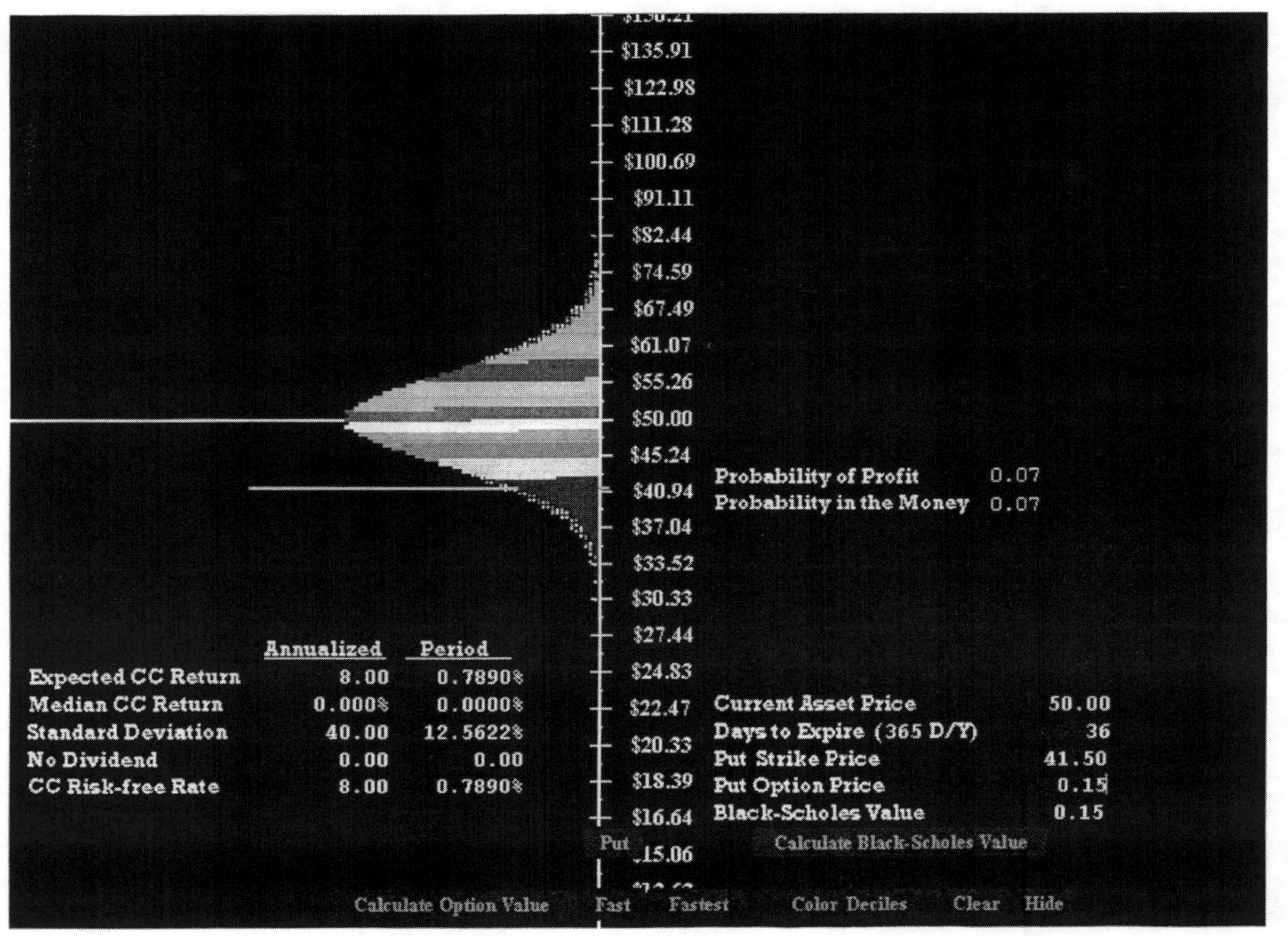

Θ, theta—As a put's time to expiration grows shorter, its value goes down. Usually!

Let's look at how a shortening of time to maturity affects a put's Black–Scholes value.

We reestablish our baseline put.

1. **Click three times on Clear.**
2. **For Expected CC Return, enter 8.00.**
3. **Tab to Standard Deviation. Enter 40.00.**
4. **Tab to CC Risk-free Rate. Enter 8.00.**
5. **Tab to Current Asset Price. Enter 50.00.**
6. **For Days to Expire, enter 48.**
7. **For Put Strike Price, enter 41.50.**
8. **Click on Calculate Black-Scholes Value.**

The option's value is $0.26.

9. **For Put Option Price, enter 0.26.**
10. **Click on Color Deciles.**

Ten percent of the little squares are below the strike price.

11. **Click on Calculate Option Value Fastest.**

Let's see how a change in the option's time to maturity changes the distribution of little squares. We decrease the time to maturity by 25%, from 48 days to 36 days.

12. **For Days to Expire, enter 36.**
13. **Click on Calculate Black-Scholes Value.**

The option value is $0.15.

14. **For Put Option Price, enter 0.15.**
15. **Click on Color Deciles.**

Volatility, as measured by the standard deviation of the probability distribution, changes with the square root of time. In this example, the period standard deviation decreases from 14.5055% to 12.5622%.

$$(14.5055\%)\left(\sqrt{\frac{36}{48}}\right) = 12.5622\%$$

The probability distribution narrows.

The median return remains zero. The middle of the probability distribution stays at the same height.

Now 7% of the little squares are below the strike price. That's a change of

$$(.07 - .10)/.10 = -30\%$$

The option's value changes by

$$(\$0.15 - \$0.26)/\$0.15 = -42\%$$

Holding all other factors the same, as a European put's time to expiration shortens, its value usually goes down. When we looked at when it is optimal to exercise American puts early, we saw that the put's value does not always go down.

To calculate an approximation of theta, you could:

1. Reestablish the baseline put.
2. Decrease the time to expiration by one day.
3. Find the percentage change in time to expiration.
4. Find the percentage change in Black-Scholes value.
5. Divide the percentage change in Black-Scholes value by the percentage change in time to expiration.

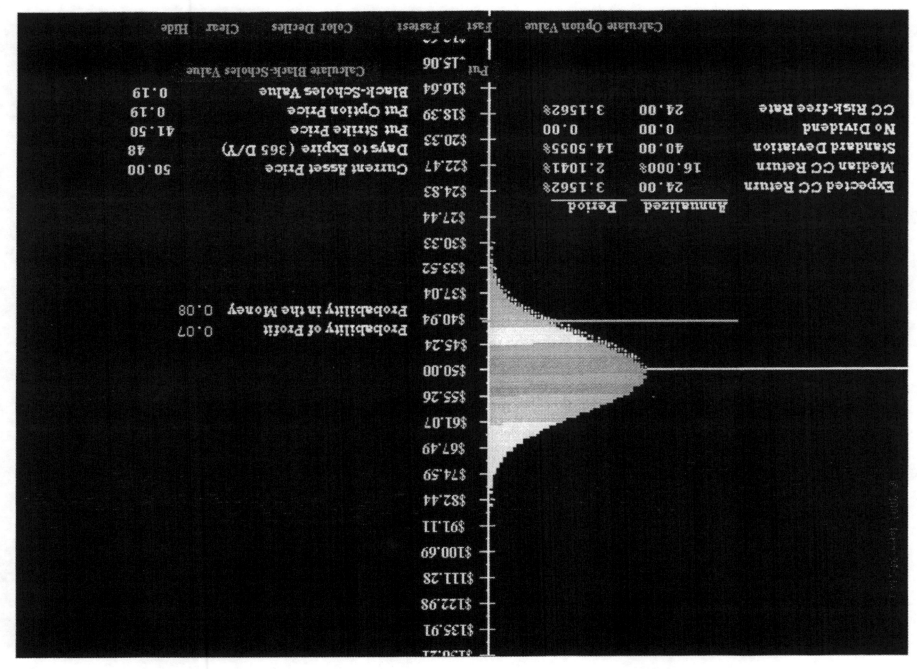

P, rho—An increase in the risk-free rate increases the underlying's median return. The Black-Scholes value of a put goes down.

Let's look at how an increase in the risk-free rate affects a put's Black-Scholes value.

We reestablish our baseline put.

1. Click three times on Clear.
2. For Expected CC Return, enter 8.00.
3. Tab to Standard Deviation. Enter 40.00.
4. Tab to CC Risk-free Rate. Enter 8.00.
5. Tab to Current Asset Price. Enter 50.00.
6. For Days to Expire, enter 48.
7. For Put Strike Price, enter 41.50.
8. Click on Calculate Black-Scholes Value.

The option's value is $0.26.

9. For Put Option Price, enter 0.26.
10. Click on Color Deciles.

Ten percent of the little squares are below the strike price.

11. Click on Calculate Option Value Fastest.

To be able to see the effect on the little squares, we increase the risk-free rate by 200%.

12. For Expected CC Return, enter 24.00.
13. For CC Risk-Free Rate, enter 24.00.
14. Click on Calculate Black-Scholes Value.

The option value is $0.19.

15. For Put Option Price, enter 0.19.
16. Click on Color Deciles.

Black-Scholes uses the risk-free rate as the option's expected return. An increase in the risk-free rate increases the underlying's median return. The increase in the median return lifts the probability distribution.

The shape of the probability distribution stays the same.

The number of little squares below the strike price decreases. Here it changes by

$(.08 - .10)/.10 = -20\%$

The option's value goes down. Here it changes by

$(\$0.19 - \$0.26)/\$0.26 = -27\%$

Holding all other factors the same, the higher the risk-free rate, the less a put's value.

To calculate an approximation of rho, you could:

1. Reestablish the baseline put.
2. Increase the risk-free rate by 1%.
3. Find the percentage change in Black-Scholes value.
4. Divide the percentage change by 1%.

Using Options to Leverage Your Expected Return

	Annualized	Period
No Dividend	0.00	0.00
CC Risk-free Rate	6.00	3.0082%
Implied Volatility	40.048%	28.3568%

Draw Market-Equilibrium Forecast

Simulate Implied Volatility

Current Asset Price	34.00
Days to Expire (365 D/Y)	183
Call Strike Price	35.00
Call Option Price	3.85

Given a European option's Black-Scholes value or the value of an American call on an underlying that pays no dividends, we can extract the implied volatility of the underlying.

Earlier, we saw that given a volatility estimate for an underlying we can calculate a Black-Scholes value for an option on that underlying.

1. Click three times on Clear.

2. Click twice on Hide.

3. Click on Calculate Black-Scholes Value.

4. For Standard Deviation, enter 40.00.

5. For CC Risk-Free Rate, enter 6.00.

6. For Current Asset Price, enter 34.00.

7. For Days to Expire, enter 183.

8. For Call Strike Price, enter 35.00.

9. Click again on Calculate Black-Scholes Value.

The Black-Scholes value for this call is $3.85.

We can go the other way as well. Given a price on a European option, we can extract the volatility estimate that the option price implies.

10. Click on Hide.

11. Click on Calculate Implied Volatility.

12. For Call Option Price, enter 3.85.

13. Click again on Calculate Implied Volatility.

The animation extracts from the price an annualized volatility estimate of 40.048%, which is reasonably close to the 40.00% we originally used to calculate the Black-Scholes value. (If you were to calculate the Black-Scholes value for a volatility of 40.048%, you would get $3.85.)

Because European and American calls on underlyings that pay no dividends have the same value, we also can use the Black-Scholes methodology to extract implied volatilities from those American calls.

We can think of implied volatility as the market-equilibrium estimate of the uncertainty associated with the underlying's future price movements.

As we've seen, the prime determinant of an option price is the uncertainty associated with the underlying's future price movements.

The financial markets are auctions. In stock markets, the expected future value of stocks is auctioned off. In options markets, the expected future volatility of underlyings is auctioned off.

If market participants thought that the volatility estimate implicit in an option's price was out of line, they could perform arbitrage on the option. Arbitrage would force the option price into line with the market's consensus estimate of the underlying's volatility.

Hence, we can think of implied volatility as a market consensus or market-equilibrium view of the uncertainty associated with the underlying's future price movements.

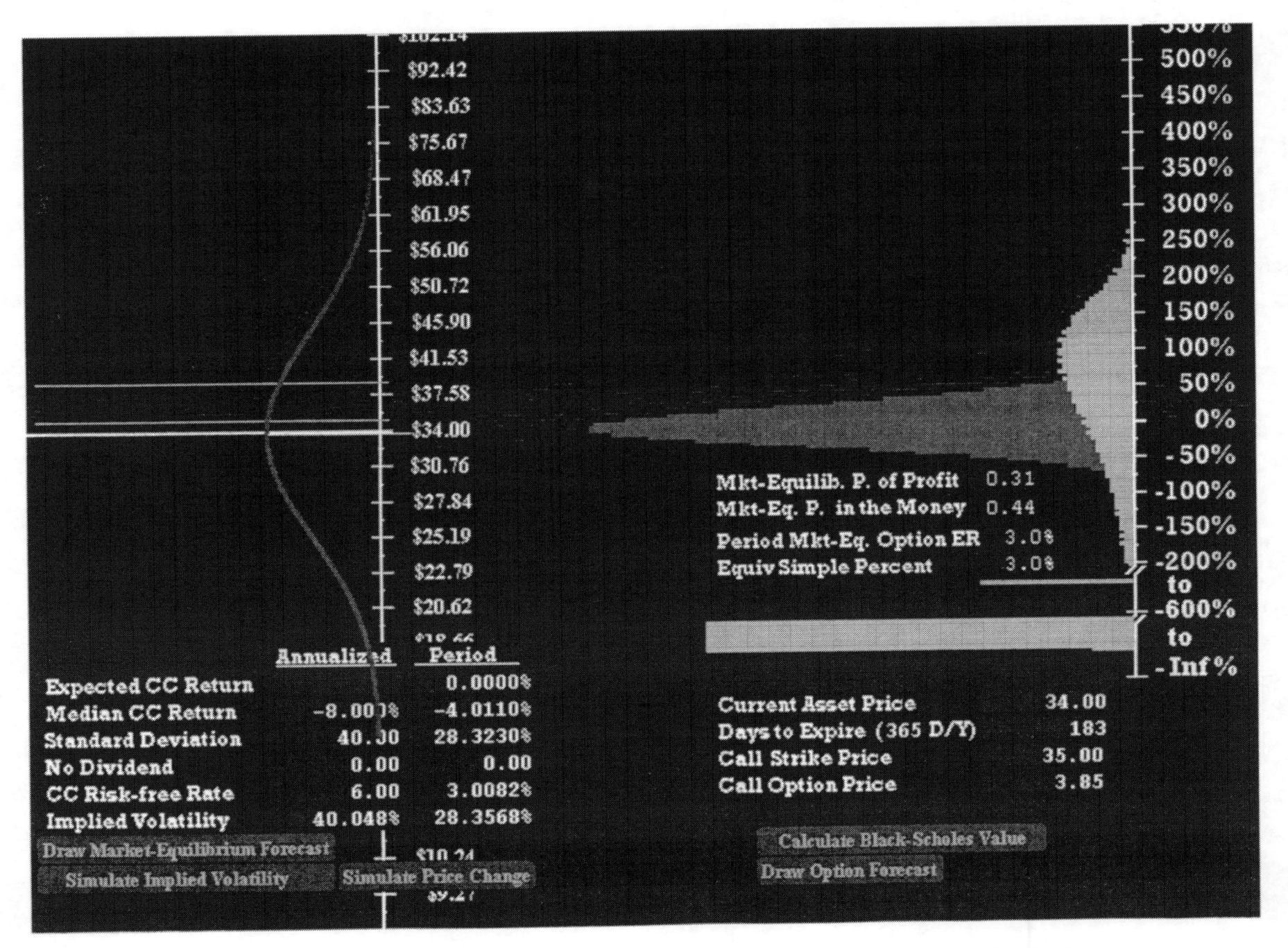

If we extract from an option price the implied volatility of a stock and we use the assumption that the expected return of every asset is the risk-free rate, we can draw a risk-neutralized, market-equilibrium forecast for the stock.

As you will recall, one of the assumptions of Black-Scholes Options-Pricing Theory is that the investment world is risk neutral. The expected return of every asset is the risk-free rate of return.

We also have seen that we can think of implied volatility as the market-equilibrium estimate of the uncertainty associated with a stock's future price movements.

If we combine the risk-free rate of return with a stock's implied volatility, we have what we might call a risk-neutralized, market-equilibrium forecast for the stock. We can draw this forecast.

> 14. Click on Draw Option Forecast.
>
> 15. Click on Simulate Price Change.
>
> 16. Click on Draw Market-Equilibrium Forecast.

The animation first draws on the option axes the risk-neutralized, implied forecast for the stock.

It then draws the implied forecast for the stock on the price axes.

Finally, the animation draws on the option axes the implied forecast for the option.

For the implied option forecast, the animation calculates the probability of profit, the probability of being in the money, and the period expected return.

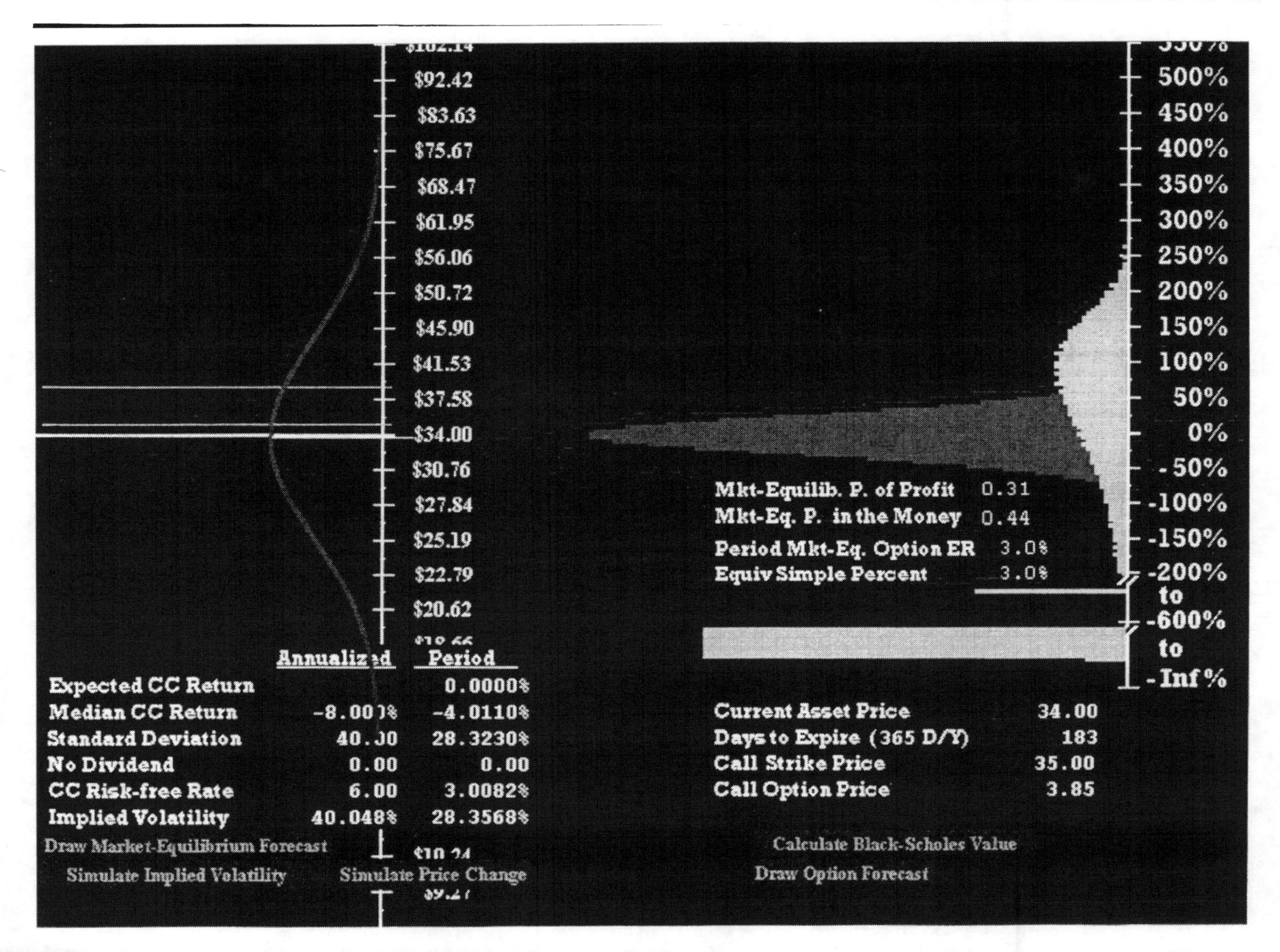

$102.14
$92.42
$83.63
$75.67
$68.47
$61.95
$56.06
$50.72
$45.90
$41.53
$37.58
$34.00
$30.76
$27.84
$25.19
$22.79
$20.62

550%
500%
450%
400%
350%
300%
250%
200%
150%
100%
50%
0%
-50%
-100%
-150%
-200%
to
-600%
to
-Inf%

Mkt-Equilib. P. of Profit   0.31
Mkt-Eq. P. in the Money   0.44
Period Mkt-Eq. Option ER   3.0%
Equiv Simple Percent   3.0%

	Annualized	Period
Expected CC Return		0.0000%
Median CC Return	-8.00%	-4.0110%
Standard Deviation	40.00	28.3230%
No Dividend	0.00	0.00
CC Risk-free Rate	6.00	3.0082%
Implied Volatility	40.048%	28.3568%

Current Asset Price   34.00
Days to Expire (365 D/Y)   183
Call Strike Price   35.00
Call Option Price   3.85

Draw Market-Equilibrium Forecast

Simulate Implied Volatility   Simulate Price Change

Calculate Black-Scholes Value

Draw Option Forecast

If you agree with the stock forecast that an option price implies, then the stock and the option have the same expected return.

When we calculate the period expected return for the risk-neutralized, market-equilibrium forecast, we get the period risk-free rate of return—in this case 3%. The period expected return for the option is the same as the period expected return for the stock.

This is as it should be. Remember, one of the Black-Scholes assumptions is that all assets have the same expected return—the risk-free rate.

The two probability distributions drawn on the options axes are very different. Nevertheless, their average returns are the same.

If you agreed with this forecast and you invested in the stock, you would expect your return to be somewhere between roughly 85% and −85%.

If you agreed with this forecast and you invested in the option, you would expect your return to be somewhere between 250% and negative infinity.

Whether you invested in the stock or in the option, your expected return would be 3%.

Investing in the option and investing in the stock are equally fair bets. The average outcomes are the same.

If you agreed with the implied forecast, you would have little or no incentive to invest in the option instead of in the stock. You would be taking on a greater exposure to uncertainty with no increase in your expected return.

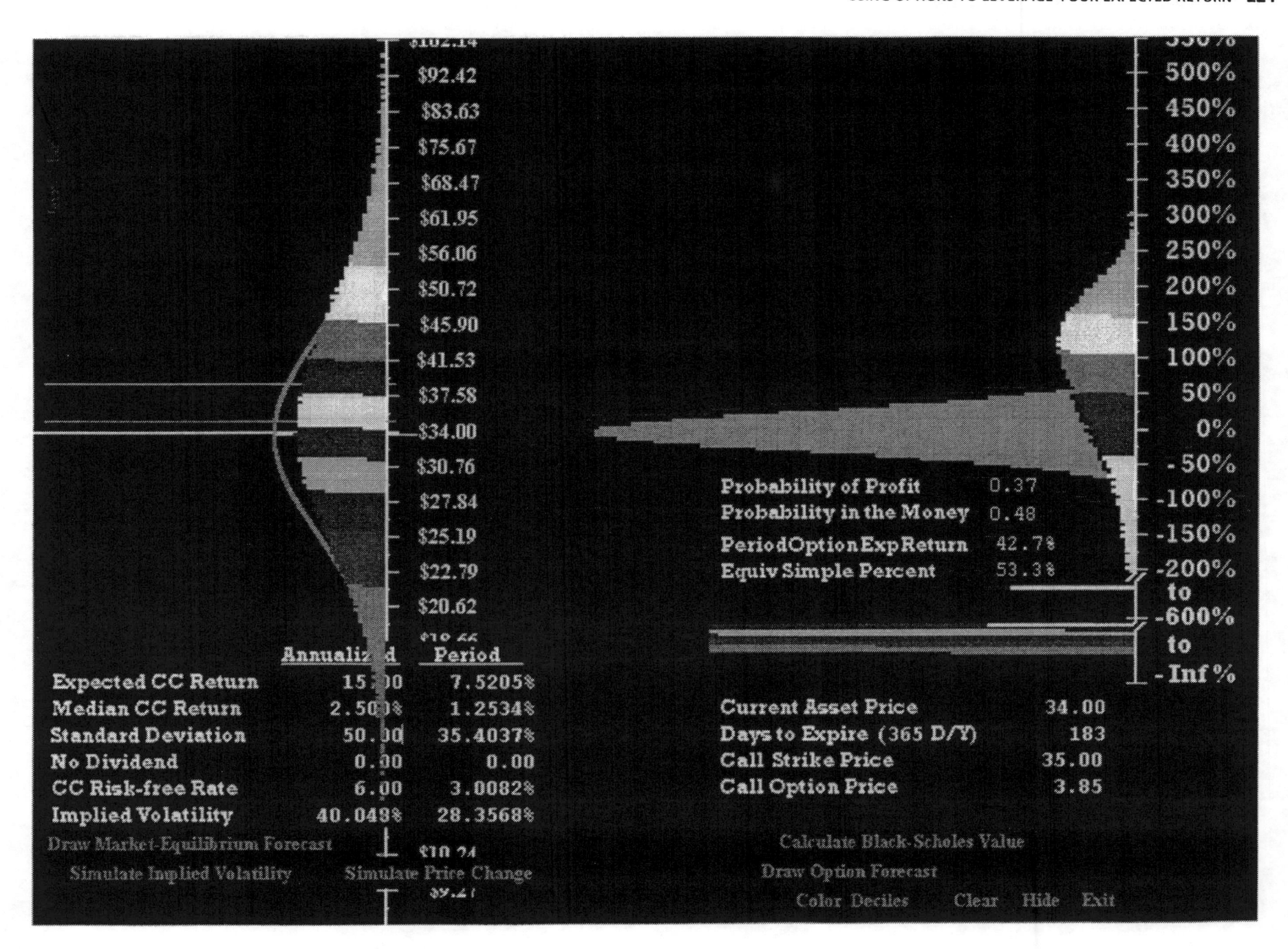

	$102.14		550%
	$92.42		500%
	$83.63		450%
	$75.67		400%
	$68.47		350%
	$61.95		300%
	$56.06		250%
	$50.72		200%
	$45.90		150%
	$41.53		100%
	$37.58		50%
	$34.00		0%
	$30.76		-50%
	$27.84		-100%
	$25.19		-150%
	$22.79		-200%
	$20.62		to
			-600%

Probability of Profit   0.37
Probability in the Money   0.48
Period Option Exp Return   42.7%
Equiv Simple Percent   53.3%

	Annualized	Period
Expected CC Return	15.00	7.5205%
Median CC Return	2.500%	1.2534%
Standard Deviation	50.00	35.4037%
No Dividend	0.00	0.00
CC Risk-free Rate	6.00	3.0082%
Implied Volatility	40.049%	28.3568%

Current Asset Price	34.00
Days to Expire (365 D/Y)	183
Call Strike Price	35.00
Call Option Price	3.85

Draw Market-Equilibrium Forecast

Simulate Implied Volatility   Simulate Price Change

Calculate Black-Scholes Value

Draw Option Forecast

Color Deciles   Clear   Hide   Exit

If you disagree with the stock forecast that an option price implies, then you can use the option to leverage your expected return.

Let's say you do not agree with the risk-neutralized, market-equilibrium forecast. You think that instead of having an expected return of 6% and a standard deviation of 40.048% this stock has an annualized expected return of 15% and a standard deviation of 50%.

Given your forecast, will the option also have an expected return of 15%?

Let's see.

17. For Expected CC Return, enter 15.00.

18. For Standard Deviation, enter 50.00.

19. Click on Color Deciles.

The animation draws your forecast for the stock and your forecast for the option.

The difference in the stock forecasts is not enormous. However, given your forecast for the stock, the period expected return for the option is not 15%, but 42.7%.

The option's structure leverages the difference between the implied forecast and your forecast.

When you disagree with the risk-neutralized, market-equilibrium forecast, you can use options to leverage your expected return.

Black-Scholes Assumptions (Part III)

Nasdaq-100® Index Options
Current Price: 1731.16
Annualized Nasdaq-100® Index Dividend Yield: 0.11%

NDX
European

Mar 19

Calls	Bid	Ask	Mid
Jun 1100. (NDV FB-E)	643.1	665.1	654.1
Jun 1400. (NDV FH-E)	396.0	418.0	407.0
Jun 1600. (NDV FL-E)	262.2	284.2	273.2
Jun 1700. (NDV FN-E)	206.9	228.9	217.9
Jun 1800. (NDV FP-E)	161.8	179.8	170.8
Jun 1900. (NDV FR-E)	122.6	140.6	131.6
Jun 2050. (NDX FA-E)	80.1	92.1	86.1
Jun 2100. (NDX FB-E)	68.1	80.1	74.1
Jun 2200. (NDX FD-E)	48.3	60.3	54.3
Jun 2300. (NDX FF-E)	36.3	42.3	39.3
Jun 2400. (NDX FH-E)	25.2	31.2	28.2

Calls	Bid	Ask	Mid
Sep 1100. (NDV IB-E)	679.6	701.6	690.6
Sep 1400. (NDV IH-E)	456.7	478.7	467.7
Sep 1600. (NDV IL-E)	335.3	357.3	346.3
Sep 1700. (NDV IN-E)	283.4	305.4	294.4
Sep 1800. (NDV IP-E)	237.4	259.4	248.4
Sep 1900. (NDV IR-E)	199.1	217.1	208.1
Sep 2050. (NDX IA-E)	148.3	166.3	157.3
Sep 2100. (NDX IB-E)	133.7	151.7	142.7
Sep 2200. (NDX ID-E)	107.9	125.9	116.9
Sep 2300. (NDX IF-E)	86.1	104.1	95.1
Sep 2400. (NDX IH-E)	70.9	82.9	76.9

Does the behavior of the financial markets conform to the Black-Scholes assumptions?

Thus far, blithely we have been assuming that the behavior of the financial markets conforms to the Black-Scholes assumptions.

But does it?

We've already noted that the Black-Scholes model is designed to value and analyze European options. While many index options are European, most stock options are American.

Before you rely too heavily on the Black-Scholes methodologies, you may want to consider how well the behavior of the financial markets conforms to each of the assumptions.

We now look at some of the discrepancies between the Black-Scholes assumptions and market behavior.

As you will recall, one of the assumptions is:

■ Traders and investors incur no transaction costs such as bid-ask spreads or brokerage fees and commissions.

In reality, traders and investors face bid-ask spreads and incur transaction costs.

For a given option, the implied volatility of the bid price differs from the implied volatility of the ask price.

Using data from the table above, we can extract and compare implied volatilities for bid and ask prices. We'll use the data for the Nasdaq-100® Index Options call option Jun 1600, which has a bid price of 262.2 and an ask price of 284.2. This is a European option. The index pays a dividend yield of 0.11%. Such a tiny dividend yield has no practical impact. Even so, we shall include it in our calculations.

1. Click three times on Clear.

2. Click twice on Hide.

3. Click on Simulate Price Change.

4. Click on Draw Your Forecast.

5. Click once on Hide.

6. Click on Call.

7. Click on Calculate Implied Volatility.

8. For CC Risk-Free Rate, enter 6.00.

9. For Current Asset Price, enter 1731.16.

10. For Days to Expire, enter 74.

11. For Call Strike Price, enter 1600.00.

12. For Call Option Price, enter the bid price of 262.20.

13. Click on Enter Div Yield.

14. For Continuous Div Yield, enter 0.11.

15. Click on Calculate Implied Volatility.

Using the bid price as the Black-Scholes value gives us an annualized implied volatility of 59.770%.

16. Click on Draw Market-Equilibrium Forecast.

The animation draws the period forecast implicit in the bid price.

17. For Call Option Price, enter the ask price of 284.20.

18. Click on Calculate Implied Volatility.

Using the ask price as the Black-Scholes value gives us an annualized implied volatility of 67.637%.

19. Click on Draw Market-Equilibrium Forecast.

The animation draws the forecast implicit in the ask price.

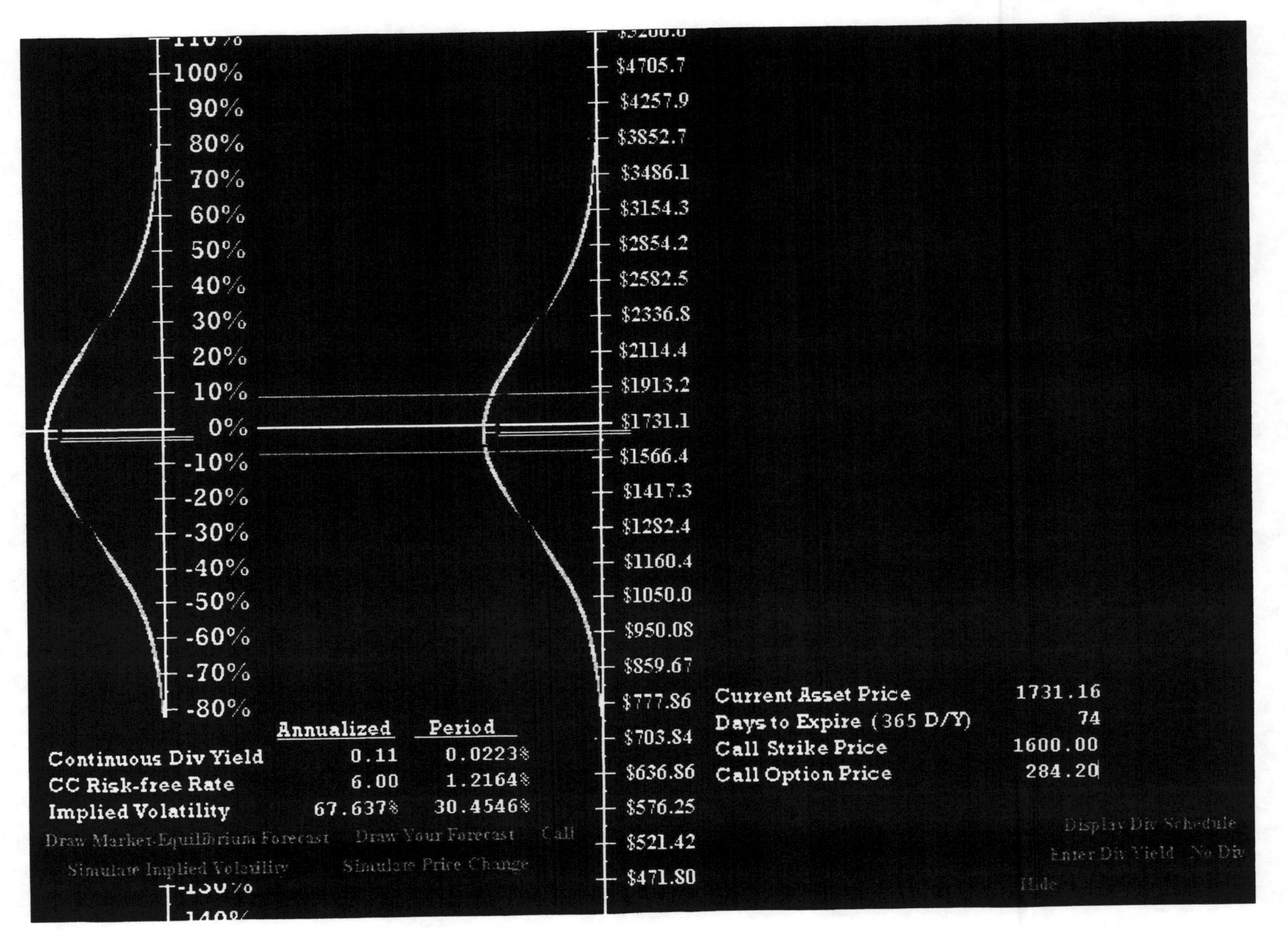

	Annualized	Period
Continuous Div Yield	0.11	0.0223%
CC Risk-free Rate	6.00	1.2164%
Implied Volatility	67.637%	30.4546%

Draw Market-Equilibrium Forecast   Draw Your Forecast   Call

Simulate Implied Volatility   Simulate Price Change

Current Asset Price	1731.16
Days to Expire (365 D/Y)	74
Call Strike Price	1600.00
Call Option Price	284.20

Display Div Schedule

Enter Div Yield   No Div

Hide

The bid price and the ask price give us different implied volatilities. To get an advantage from buying an option, you have to beat the forecast implicit in the ask price.

An option's bid and ask prices give us different implied volatilities. To calculate an underlying's implied volatility, which price do you use?

It depends on your purpose. If you want to see the risk-neutralized, market-equilibrium forecast implicit in an option price, you may want to use the midpoint of the bid and ask prices.

If you want to consider whether to buy an option because you disagree with the risk-neutralized, market-equilibrium forecast, you may want to look at the forecast implicit in the ask price. To get an advantage from buying the option, this is the forecast you have to beat.

Nasdaq-100® Index Options
Current Price: 1731.16
Annualized Nasdaq-100® Index Dividend Yield: 0.11%

NDX
European   Mar 19

Calls	Bid	Ask	Mid
Jun 1100. (NDV FB-E)	643.1	665.1	654.1
Jun 1400. (NDV FH-E)	396.0	418.0	407.0
Jun 1600. (NDV FL-E)	262.2	284.2	273.2
Jun 1700. (NDV FN-E)	206.9	228.9	217.9
Jun 1800. (NDV FP-E)	161.8	179.8	170.8
Jun 1900. (NDV FR-E)	122.6	140.6	131.6
Jun 2050. (NDX FA-E)	80.1	92.1	86.1
Jun 2100. (NDX FB-E)	68.1	80.1	74.1
Jun 2200. (NDX FD-E)	48.3	60.3	54.3
Jun 2300. (NDX FF-E)	36.3	42.3	39.3
Jun 2400. (NDX FH-E)	25.2	31.2	28.2
Jun 2500. (NDX FJ-E)	18.6	21.6	20.1
Jun 2600. (NDX FL-E)	12.8	15.8	14.3
Jun 2700. (NDX FN-E)	9.0	10.5	9.8
Jun 2800. (NDX FP-E)	6.3	7.8	7.1
Jun 2900. (NDX FR-E)	4.7	5.7	5.2
Jun 3050. (NDY FA-E)	2.9	3.9	3.4
Jun 3100. (NDY FB-E)	2.5	3.5	3.0
Jun 3200. (NDY FD-E)	2.0	2.7	2.4
Jun 3300. (NDY FF-E)	1.5	2.3	1.9
Jun 3400. (NDY FH-E)	1.0	1.7	1.4
Jun 3500. (NDY FJ-E)	0.5	1.2	0.9

Calls	Bid	Ask	Mid
Sep 1100. (NDV IB-E)	679.6	701.6	690.6
Sep 1400. (NDV IH-E)	456.7	478.7	467.7
Sep 1600. (NDV IL-E)	335.3	357.3	346.3
Sep 1700. (NDV IN-E)	283.4	305.4	294.4
Sep 1800. (NDV IP-E)	237.4	259.4	248.4
Sep 1900. (NDV IR-E)	199.1	217.1	208.1
Sep 2050. (NDX IA-E)	148.3	166.3	157.3
Sep 2100. (NDX IB-E)	133.7	151.7	142.7
Sep 2200. (NDX ID-E)	107.9	125.9	116.9
Sep 2300. (NDX IF-E)	86.1	104.1	95.1
Sep 2400. (NDX IH-E)	70.9	82.9	76.9

Do option prices imply that a stock's volatility will be constant over a given investment horizon?

Black-Scholes Options-Pricing Theory also makes the following assumption:

■ The volatility of a stock's price path is constant over the investment horizon.

If the market's behavior conformed to this assumption, then to calculate option prices for a given stock at different strike prices, an options trader would always enter into the Black-Scholes formula the same volatility estimate.

We would come along to extract the implied volatility from the option prices. From different option prices at different strike prices, we would always get the same implied volatility.

In reality, do we get the same implied volatilities?

No. It doesn't matter whether we use the bid prices, the ask prices, or the midpoints. We get different implied volatilities at different strike prices.

Continuing to use data from the table above, we extract implied volatilities for options at different strike prices. We'll use the June 1 call data.

> 20. Click once on Clear.
>
> For each option:
>
> A. Enter the Call Strike Price.
>
> B. For Call Option Price, enter the midpoint Price.
>
> C. Click on Calculate Implied Volatility.
>
> D. Click on Draw Market-Equilibrium Forecast.

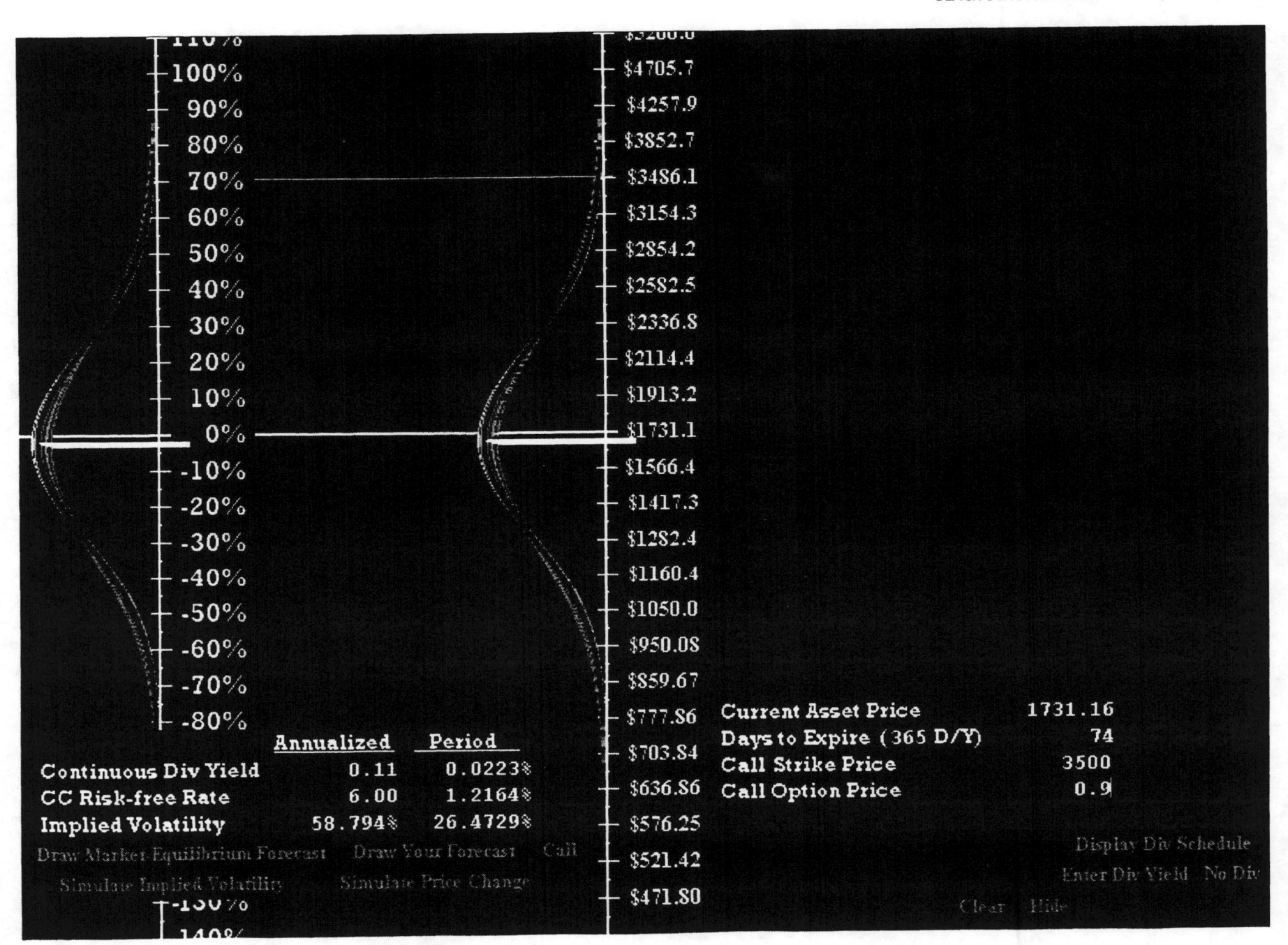

110%
100% — $4705.7
90% — $4257.9
80% — $3852.7
70% — $3486.1
60% — $3154.3
50% — $2854.2
40% — $2582.5
30% — $2336.8
20% — $2114.4
10% — $1913.2
0% — $1731.1
-10% — $1566.4
-20% — $1417.3
-30% — $1282.4
-40% — $1160.4
-50% — $1050.0
-60% — $950.08
-70% — $859.67
-80% — $777.86
— $703.84
— $636.86
— $576.25
— $521.42
— $471.80
-130%
140%

	Annualized	Period
Continuous Div Yield	0.11	0.0223%
CC Risk-free Rate	6.00	1.2164%
Implied Volatility	58.794%	26.4729%

Draw Market-Equilibrium Forecast   Draw Your Forecast   Call

Simulate Implied Volatility   Simulate Price Change

Current Asset Price	1731.16
Days to Expire (365 D/Y)	74
Call Strike Price	3500
Call Option Price	0.9

Display Div Schedule

Enter Div Yield   No Div

Clear   Hide

Different strike prices give us different implied volatilities for the same underlying. This is the so-called volatility smile.

What we get is a range of implied volatilities. The implied volatility is generally the lowest for strike prices near the spot or current market price of the underlying. (Though that's not happening here with the volatile March 19 Nasdaq 100 Index.)

For strike prices above and below the spot price, the implied volatilities generally go up. When you graph implied volatility against strike price, the graph looks like a smile—hence the volatility smile. (Maybe a crooked smirk here?)

Why does the volatility smile exist?

The most common explanation is that market participants do not agree with the Black-Scholes assumption of constant volatility. Instead, they believe that if the spot price changes much the option's volatility will go up. The option will become more valuable.

Some market gurus put forth the idea that market participants who fear a crash bid up the price of deep out-of-the-money puts. Those relatively higher prices translate into higher implied volatilities for those options.

Given the smile, when we use an option price to calculate a stock's implied volatility, the volatility estimate applies only for that particular strike price and time to expiration. It does not hold for different strike prices or for different expiration dates.

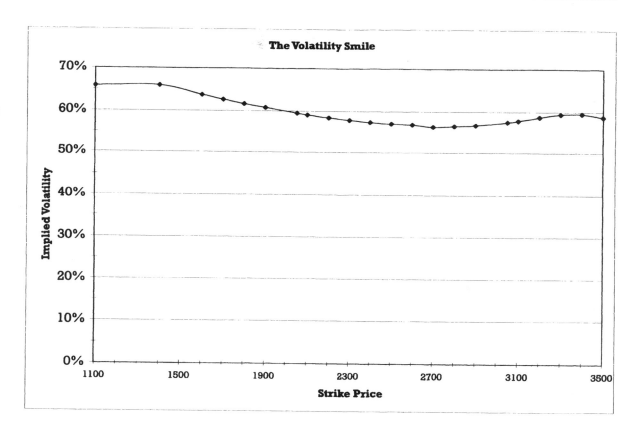

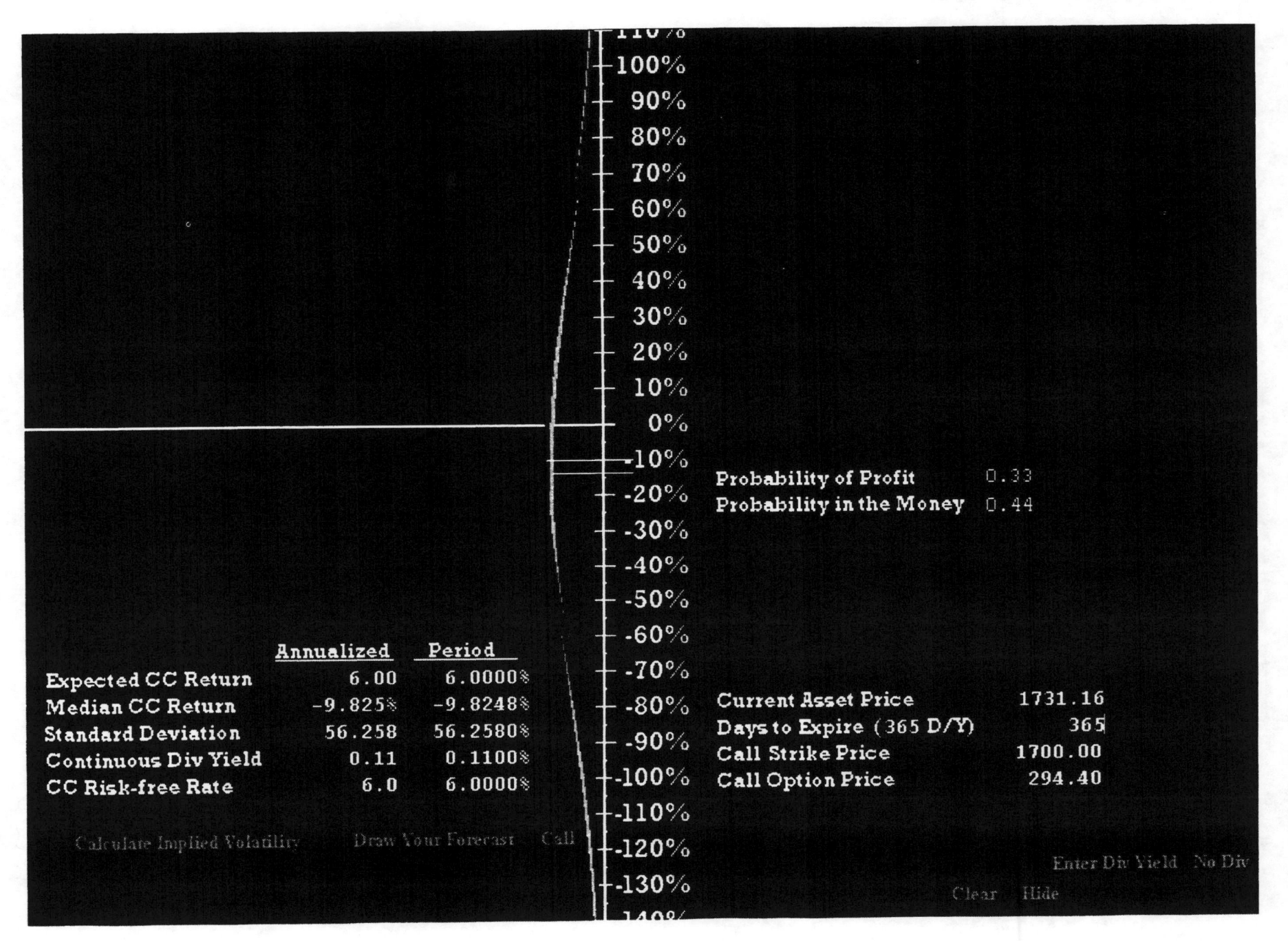

	Annualized	Period
Expected CC Return	6.00	6.0000%
Median CC Return	-9.825%	-9.8248%
Standard Deviation	56.258	56.2580%
Continuous Div Yield	0.11	0.1100%
CC Risk-free Rate	6.0	6.0000%

Calculate Implied Volatility   Draw Your Forecast   Call

Probability of Profit   0.33
Probability in the Money 0.44

Current Asset Price	1731.16
Days to Expire (365 D/Y)	365
Call Strike Price	1700.00
Call Option Price	294.40

Enter Div Yield No Div

Clear   Hide

For a given strike price, different expiration dates give us different implied volatilities. This is the term structure of volatility.

It may be tempting to extract an implied volatility from an option and then extend or contract that volatility to a different investment horizon. This technique doesn't work.

Options with different expiration dates usually give us different annualized implied volatilities. This difference is referred to as the term structure of volatility.

To analyze the term structure, practitioners use the implied volatilities for at-the-money strike prices.

1. Click three times on Clear.

2. Click twice on Hide.

3. Click on Call.

4. For Current Assest Price, enter 1731.16.

5. For Days to Expire, enter 74.

6. For Call Strike Price, enter 1700.00

7. For Call Option Price, enter 217.90.

8. Click on Calculate Implied Volatility.

9. Click on Enter Div Yield.

10. For Continuous Div Yield, enter 0.11.

11. For CC Risk-free Rate, enter 6.0

12. Click on Calculate Implied Volatility

For the June call, the annualized implied volatility is 62.617%.

13. Click on Draw Your Forecast.

14. For Expected CC Return, enter 6.00.

15. For Standard Deviation, enter 62.617.

16. For Days to Expire, enter 365.

17. Click on Draw Your Forecast.

The animation draws the annualized implied volatility for the option that expires in 74 days.

18. Tab to Days to Expire. Enter 166.

19. For Call Option Price, enter 294.40.

20. Click on Calculate Implied Volatility.

For the September call at the same strike price, the annualized implied volatility is 56.258%.

21. For Standard Deviation, enter 56.258.

22. For Days to Expire, enter 365.

23. Click on Draw Your Forecast.

The animation draws the annualized implied volatility of the option that expires in 166 days.

Be sensitive to the ways in which the financial markets may not conform to the Black-Scholes assumptions.

If you go back and review the other Black-Scholes assumptions, you'll be aware that the financial markets may not conform to a number of them:

■ Stock returns expressed as geometric rates of return may not be perfectly normally distributed.

■ Price changes may not be perfectly lognormally distributed.

■ Geometric Brownian motion may not perfectly characterize potential price paths.

■ The volatility of a stock's price path may not be constant over the investment horizon.

■ Stock-price paths may not be continuous. Prices may jump.

■ Traders and investors may not be able to trade continuously.

■ The financial markets may not be perfectly liquid.

■ Traders and/or investors may not be able to borrow at the risk-free rate.

■ The risk-free rate may change over a given investment horizon.

■ Traders and investors incur transaction costs.

■ Arbitrage opportunities may crop up.

■ Many investors probably are not risk neutral.

Given the fact that the financial markets do not conform to many of the Black-Scholes assumptions, you might expect traders and analysts to abandon the Black-Scholes methodologies altogether. However, they have not done so. They have developed additional methodologies, but Black-Scholes is still very much with us.

The Black-Scholes way of thinking gives you tools with which to analyze relationships among forecasts, hedging costs, probability distributions, expected return, and potential price paths.

The Black-Scholes model usually is the take-off point for developing other option-pricing models. Understanding Black-Scholes makes it easier to understand alternative pricing models.

In many respects, the markets behave in ways that are close enough to the Black-Scholes assumptions for the methodologies to prove useful. The central premises of the theory hold true. Volatility drives the cost of hedging options positions. The cost of hedging drives options prices.

When you use the Black-Scholes model, be sensitive to the ways in which financial markets may not conform to the underlying assumptions.

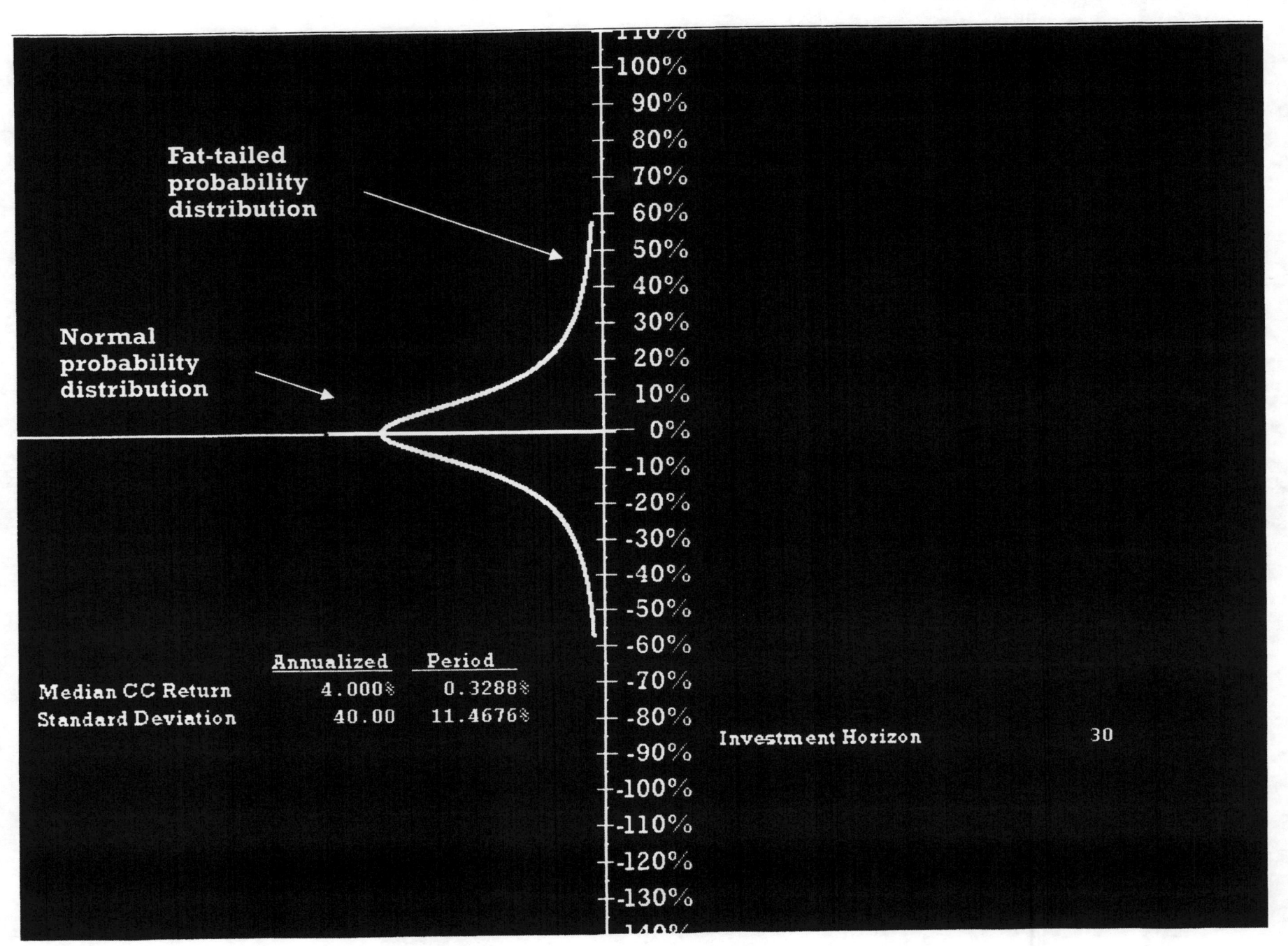

Theoreticians keep building models they hope will model the financial markets more accurately than does Black-Scholes.

Many theoreticians and practitioners object to a number of the Black-Scholes assumptions. Accordingly, they keep building models that seek to remedy their objections.

The Black-Scholes model prices easily only European options and American calls on underlyings that pay no dividends. To price other American options, binomial models are much easier to use than Black's approximation. Binomial models look automatically at the potential value of early exercise.

Black-Scholes assumes that stock returns expressed as geometric rates of return are normally distributed. Many theoreticians argue that the actual distribution of geometric rates of return are more fat tailed than in a normal distribution. In their models, they may use more fat-tailed distributions. The graphs above show the difference between a normal distribution and one type of more fat-tailed distribution.

Black-Scholes assumes that the potential price paths of a stock can be characterized by a geometric Brownian motion model. This approach assumes that at any given instant the probabilities are equal for an up or down percentage change about a stock's average return. Some alternative models assign or allow the user to assign different probabilities to up ticks and down ticks.

Black-Scholes assumes that the volatility of a stock's price path is constant over the investment horizon. Alternative models may adjust expectations about future volatility to the outcomes of price-path simulations. If a volatile potential price path increases a model's expectations about future volatility, the pricing result may be similar to using a fat-tailed distribution with a constant-volatility assumption.

Black-Scholes assumes that the risk-free rate of interest will not change over the investment horizon. Alternative models may incorporate interest rates that vary in keeping with the yield curve.

Theoreticians generally assume that the market prices of options are the correct prices. That is they assume market prices accurately embody consensus expectations about future stock prices, interest rates, volatility, and the nature of a stock's potential price paths.

In this view, the goal of an option-pricing model is, from a given set of inputs, to produce option prices that are consistent with market prices across all strike prices and expirations. Going in the other direction, from all the options on a given stock, the model would extract the same implied volatility. Such a model would make the Black-Scholes volatility smile go away.

When you began your study of Black-Scholes, you may have thought the model complex and difficult. Compared to the alternatives, Black-Scholes is simple, elegant, and easy to use.

If you have a good understanding of how option values change as all those little squares move around relative to the strike price, you'll be able to understand what the theoreticians and self-appointed experts are arguing about. You'll even be able to join in the fray.

As *Black-Scholes Made Easy* goes to press, the author has begun to experiment with animations that would allow an investor to draw probability distributions of whatever shape he or she believes best describes the market behavior of underlyings. If you are interested in keeping abreast of those experiments, on the *Black-Scholes Made Easy* website double-click on StayInTouch.htm and send the author an e-mail.

(The animation is not programmed to draw the illustration above.)

Using the Animations to Assess Option Opportunities

This section assumes that you are familiar with the concepts, assumptions, and computer routines covered in the previous sections.

If you disagree with the forecast implied in an option's price, you can use the option to leverage your expected return.

An option price implies a risk-neutralized, market-equilibrium forecast for the underlying. If you disagree with the forecast implied in the option's price, you can use the option to leverage your expected return. If you are right and the market is wrong—or if you are lucky—you can make a lot of money.

Given your forecast and different options structures, the animations show you the expected returns, probabilities of profit, and potential payoffs of the options.

To use this capability, you have to come up with your forecast for an underlying over a specific investment horizon.

If you're not absolutely sure what your forecast is, you may want to begin by looking at the risk-neutralized, market-equilibrium forecasts for the underlying in which you're interested.

Let's say it is March 19 and you believe the latest Nasdaq tumble was just a hiccup. You say to yourself, "Dub-yuh's going to get this economy rolling!"

You wonder, "What do the risk-neutralized, market-equilibrium forecasts for Nasdaq-100® look like over the next couple of months?"

Let's see.

Nasdaq-100® Index Options
Current Price: 1731.16
Annualized Nasdaq-100® Index Dividend Yield: 0.11%

NDX
European

Mar 19

Calls	Bid	Ask	Mid
Jun 1100. (NDV FB-E)	643.1	665.1	654.1
Jun 1400. (NDV FH-E)	396.0	418.0	407.0
Jun 1600. (NDV FL-E)	262.2	284.2	273.2
Jun 1700. (NDV FN-E)	206.9	228.9	217.9
Jun 1800. (NDV FP-E)	161.8	179.8	170.8
Jun 1900. (NDV FR-E)	122.6	140.6	131.6
Jun 2050. (NDX FA-E)	80.1	92.1	86.1
Jun 2100. (NDX FB-E)	68.1	80.1	74.1
Jun 2200. (NDX FD-E)	48.3	60.3	54.3
Jun 2300. (NDX FF-E)	36.3	42.3	39.3
Jun 2400. (NDX FH-E)	25.2	31.2	28.2
Jun 2500. (NDX FJ-E)	18.6	21.6	20.1
Jun 2600. (NDX FL-E)	12.8	15.8	14.3
Jun 2700. (NDX FN-E)	9.0	10.5	9.8
Jun 2800. (NDX FP-E)	6.3	7.8	7.1
Jun 2900. (NDX FR-E)	4.7	5.7	5.2
Jun 3050. (NDY FA-E)	2.9	3.9	3.4
Jun 3100. (NDY FB-E)	2.5	3.5	3.0
Jun 3200. (NDY FD-E)	2.0	2.7	2.4
Jun 3300. (NDY FF-E)	1.5	2.3	1.9
Jun 3400. (NDY FH-E)	1.0	1.7	1.4
Jun 3500. (NDY FJ-E)	0.5	1.2	0.9

Puts	Bid	Ask	Mid
Jun 1100. (NDV RB-E)	15.0	18.0	16.5
Jun 1400. (NDV RH-E)	58.6	70.6	64.6
Jun 1600. (NDV RL-E)	119.2	137.2	128.2
Jun 1700. (NDV RN-E)	162.7	180.7	171.7
Jun 1800. (NDV RP-E)	212.3	234.3	223.3
Jun 1900. (NDV RR-E)	271.8	293.8	282.8
Jun 2050. (NDX RA-E)	374.3	396.3	385.3
Jun 2100. (NDX RB-E)	411.7	433.7	422.7
Jun 2200. (NDX RD-E)	490.7	512.7	501.7
Jun 2300. (NDX RF-E)	574.4	596.4	585.4
Jun 2400. (NDX RH-E)	662.0	684.0	673.0
Jun 2500. (NDX RJ-E)	752.6	774.6	763.6
Jun 2600. (NDX RL-E)	845.5	867.5	856.5

What do market-equilibrium forecasts for the investment horizon look like?

The table above shows data on some of the Nasdaq-100® Index Options being traded on March 19.

They are European style. They pay an annualized dividend yield of 0.11%.

You're interested in the June options. They expire in 74 days.

We want to take a look at the risk-neutralized, market-equilibrium forecasts for the Nasdaq-100® Index over this investment horizon.

To calculate implied volatilities for this series of options, we will use the midpoints of the bid-ask spreads on the call options.

(Calls and puts with the same strike price and expiration pretty much have to give the same implied volatilities. Otherwise, market participants could structure positions that would allow them to earn risk-free profits.)

To draw the forecasts that the options imply, we will combine the implied volatilities with the risk-free rate of return.

1. Click three times on Clear.

2. Click twice on Hide.

3. Click on Simulate Price Change.

For what we're doing, we do not need an expected return estimate.

4. To get rid of the Expected CC Return field, click once on hide.

5. Click on Call.

6. Click on Calculate Implied Volatility.

7. For CC Risk-Free Rate, enter 5.00.

8. For Current Asset Price, enter 1731.16.

9. For Days to Expire, enter 74.

10. Click on Enter Div Yield.

11. For Continuous Div Yield, enter 0.11.

12. For each strike price on the June Call series:

A. Enter the strike price.

B. Enter the midpoint option price.

C. Click on Calculate Implied Volatility.

D. Click on Draw Market-Equilibrium Forecast.

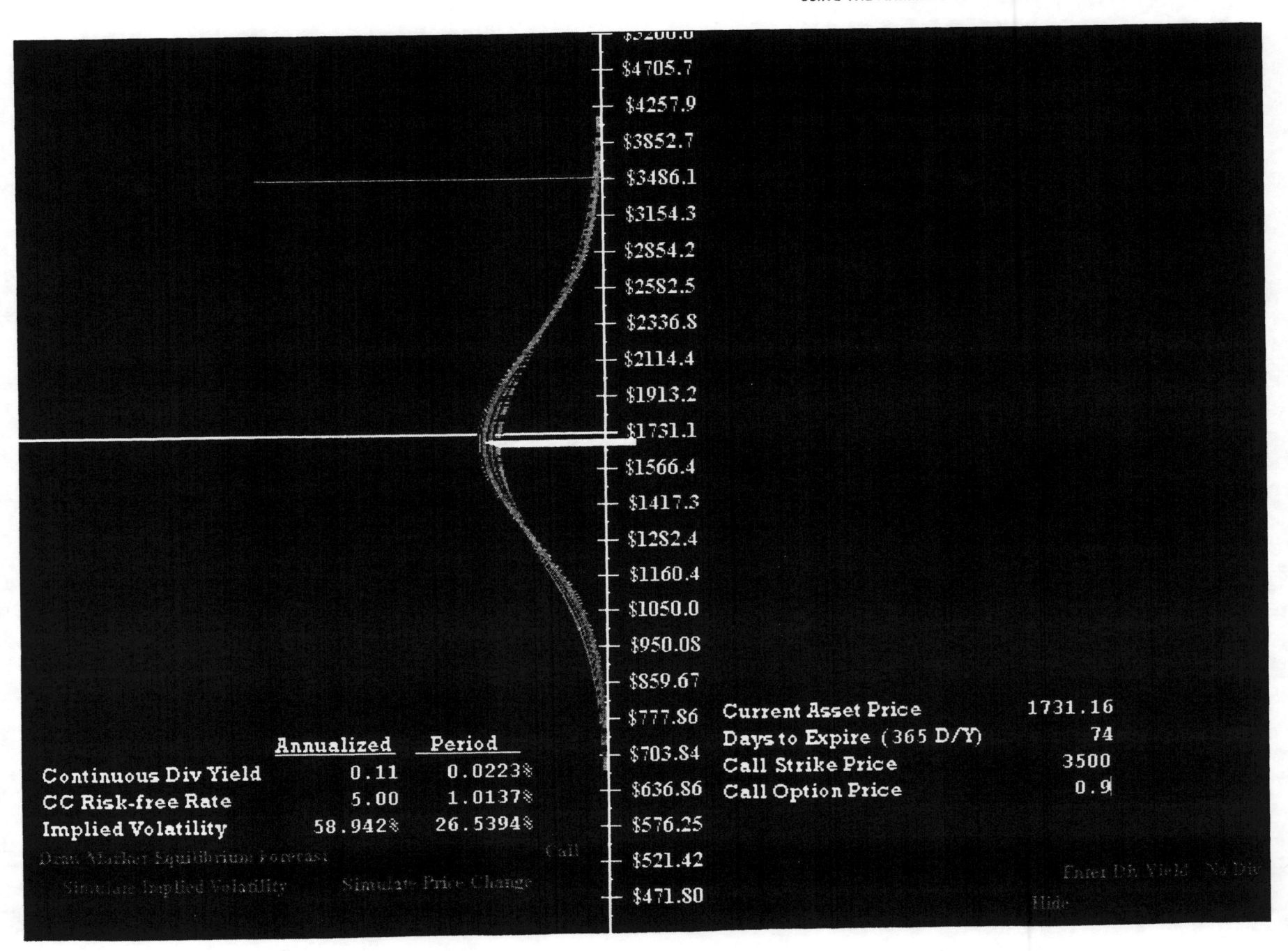

$5200.0
$4705.7
$4257.9
$3852.7
$3486.1
$3154.3
$2854.2
$2582.5
$2336.8
$2114.4
$1913.2
$1731.1
$1566.4
$1417.3
$1282.4
$1160.4
$1050.0
$950.08
$859.67
$777.86
$703.84
$636.86
$576.25
$521.42
$471.80

	Annualized	Period
Continuous Div Yield	0.11	0.0223%
CC Risk-free Rate	5.00	1.0137%
Implied Volatility	58.942%	26.5394%

Current Asset Price	1731.16
Days to Expire (365 D/Y)	74
Call Strike Price	3500
Call Option Price	0.9

Draw Market Equilibrium Forecast   Call

Simulate Implied Volatility   Simulate Price Change

Enter Div Yield   No Div

Hide

Looking at the series of market-equilibrium forecasts may make it easier for you to decide what your forecast is.

The option prices at the different strike prices produce a cluster of forecasts. The forecasts give end-of-period prices that range from around $700 to around $4000.

You believe that the Nasdaq has bottomed out. Why, it's just as you told your teammate while you were waiting for the ball return last Thursday night. "No way on God's green earth the Nasdaq 100's gonna go below $1,000 between now and June," you said. "Yeah! It'll stay volatile. But it's going to be going back up, up, up. June 1, it could be as high as $5,000."

When you got your spare, you both knew you were right.

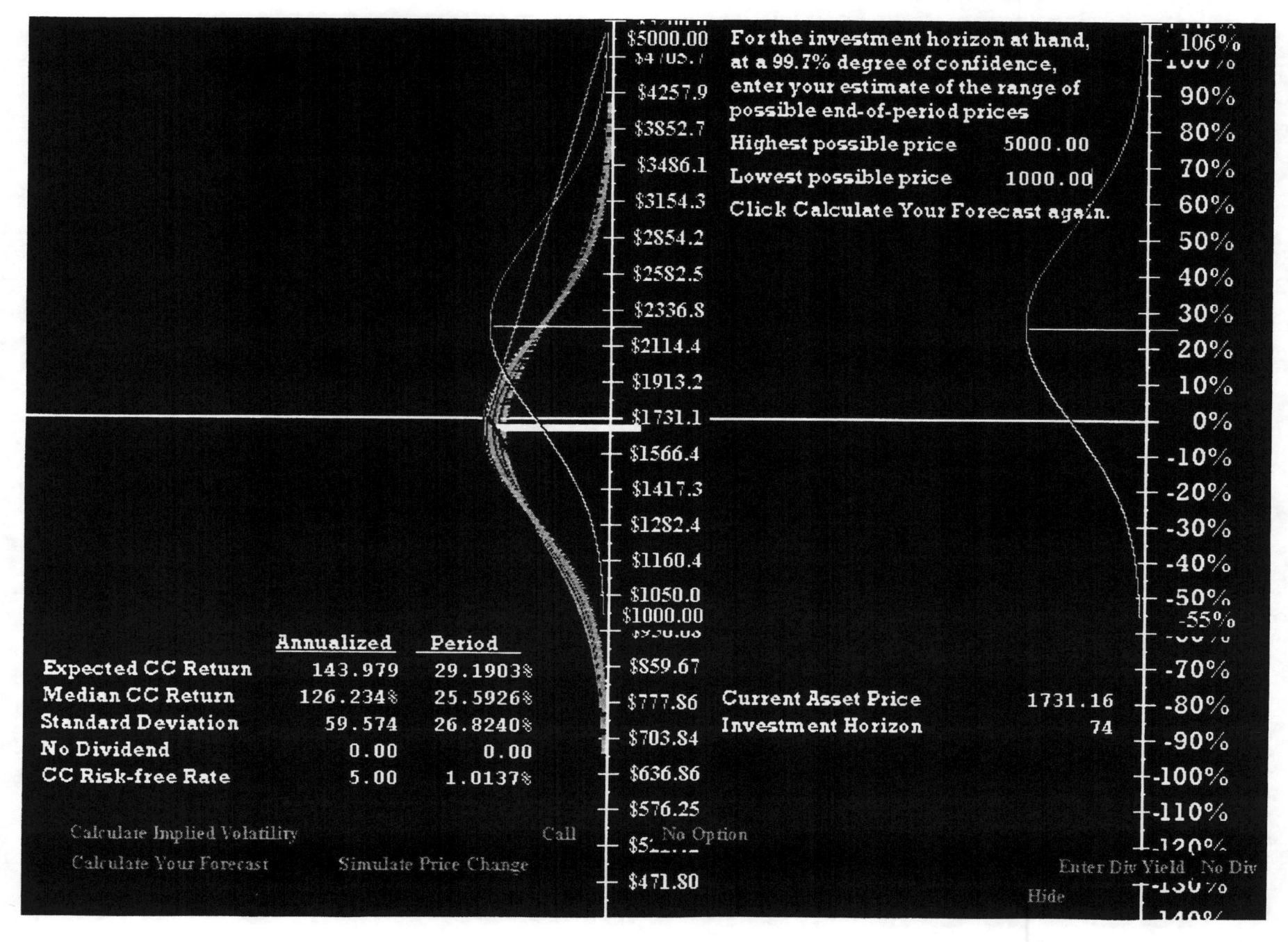

For the investment horizon at hand, at a 99.7% degree of confidence, enter your estimate of the range of possible end-of-period prices

Highest possible price   5000.00

Lowest possible price   1000.00

Click Calculate Your Forecast again.

	Annualized	Period
Expected CC Return	143.979	29.1903%
Median CC Return	126.234%	25.5926%
Standard Deviation	59.574	26.8240%
No Dividend	0.00	0.00
CC Risk-free Rate	5.00	1.0137%

Current Asset Price   1731.16

Investment Horizon   74

Calculate Implied Volatility

Calculate Your Forecast   Simulate Price Change

Call   No Option

Enter Div Yield   No Div

Hide

$5000.00
$4257.9
$3852.7
$3486.1
$3154.3
$2854.2
$2582.5
$2336.8
$2114.4
$1913.2
$1731.1
$1566.4
$1417.3
$1282.4
$1160.4
$1050.0
$1000.00
$859.67
$777.86
$703.84
$636.86
$576.25
$471.80

106%
90%
80%
70%
60%
50%
40%
30%
20%
10%
0%
-10%
-20%
-30%
-40%
-50%
-55%
-70%
-80%
-90%
-100%
-110%

To calculate your forecast, you can use your best guesses of how high and how low the prices might be at the end of the investment period.

Let's calculate your forecast. (To calculate your forecast, the animation uses your estimate of highest and lowest possible prices assuming the underlying pays no dividends. We add back the dividend yield later.)

13. Click on No Option.

14. Click on No Div.

15. Click on Calculate Your Forecast.

16. For Highest Possible Price, enter 5000.00. (No $ or commas.)

17. For Lowest Possible Price, enter 1000.00.

18. Click again on Calculate Your Forecast.

From your view of the potential end-of-period prices, the animation calculates and draws your forecast for the period—assuming no dividends.

To help pick a strike price, we can look at where the deciles of your forecast fall.

19. Click on Color Deciles.

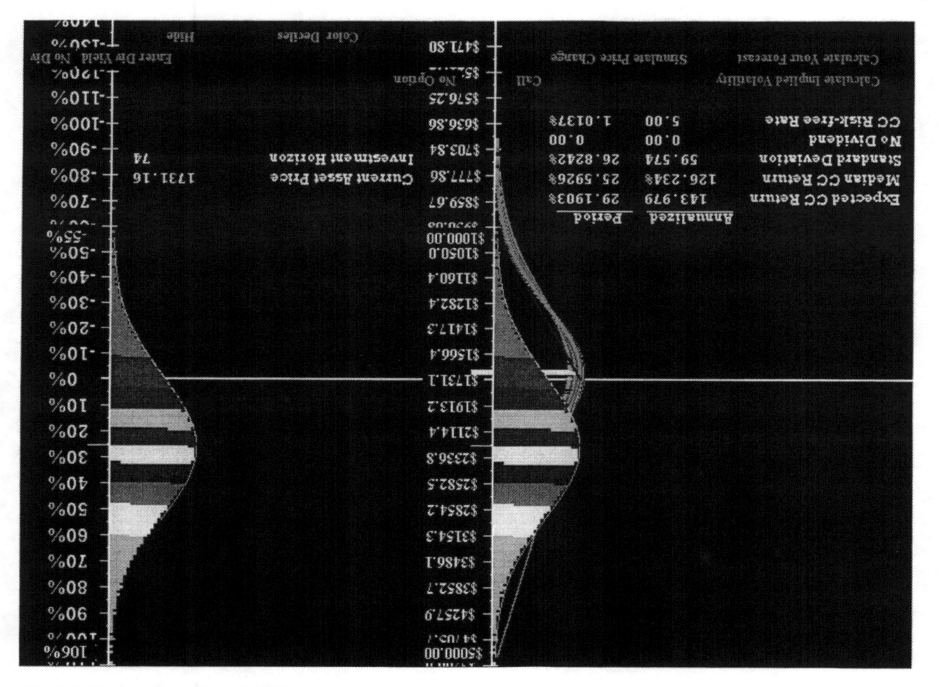

When you're buying an option, don't worry about the annualized forecast. Focus on your forecast for the investment period.

You see that the middle of your forecast has an end-of-period price of around $2,200.

Your forecast has an annualized expected return of 143.979%. This may seem absurdly high, but the annualized expected return is irrelevant. The question is: Is the period expected return of 29.1903% consistent with your beliefs?

The same consideration applies to the standard deviation. Your forecast's annualized standard deviation is 59.574%. It's close to the volatilities implied in the midpoint prices that we looked at. At the same time, we're only concerned with the period standard deviation. Does a period standard deviation of 26.8242% make sense?

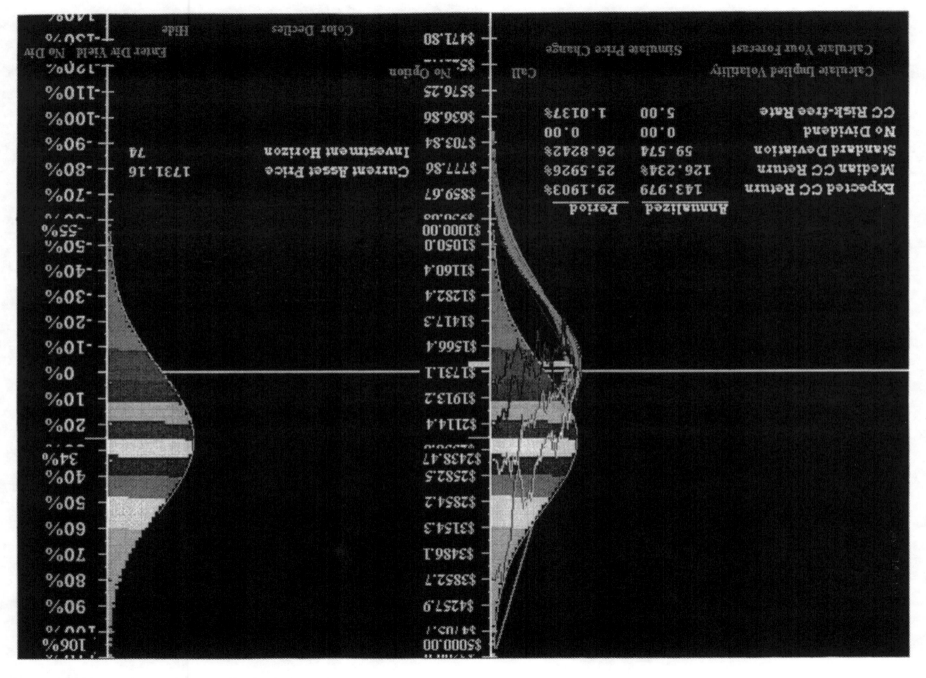

To see if the forecast feels right, simulate potential price paths.

To get a feel for whether this is the forecast you want to go with, you can simulate potential price paths based on the forecast.

> **20. Click on Simulate Price Change as many times as you want.**

If the forecast seems to be consistent with your beliefs, go with it.

If not, you can keep adjusting the expected continuously compounded return and the standard deviation until the forecast is what you want it to be.

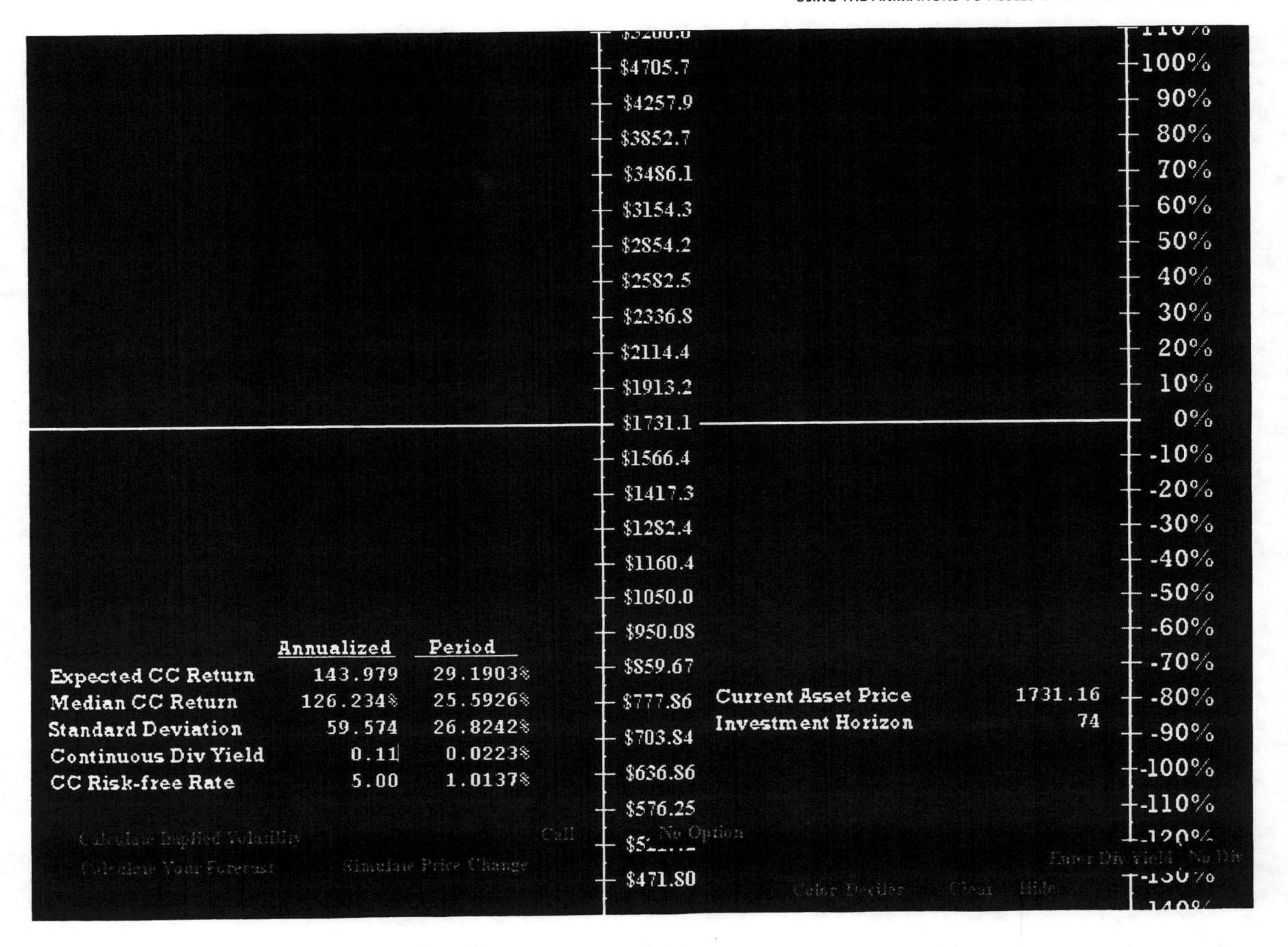

	Annualized	Period
Expected CC Return	143.979	29.1903%
Median CC Return	126.234%	25.5926%
Standard Deviation	59.574	26.8242%
Continuous Div Yield	0.11	0.0223%
CC Risk-free Rate	5.00	1.0137%

Current Asset Price   1731.16
Investment Horizon   74

To go from a return forecast to a price forecast, enter the dividend schedule or dividend yield.

There are many ways in which you can come up with a forecast of return. However you do it, option payoffs are tied not to returns but to prices.

Dividend payments lower prices. If an underlying pays dividends, to go from a forecast of return to a price forecast, you have to factor in the dividend schedule or yield.

If the underlying pays dividends, this is when you enter the dividend schedule or yield.

21. Click once on Clear.

22. Click on Enter Div Yield.

23. For Dividend Yield, enter 0.11.

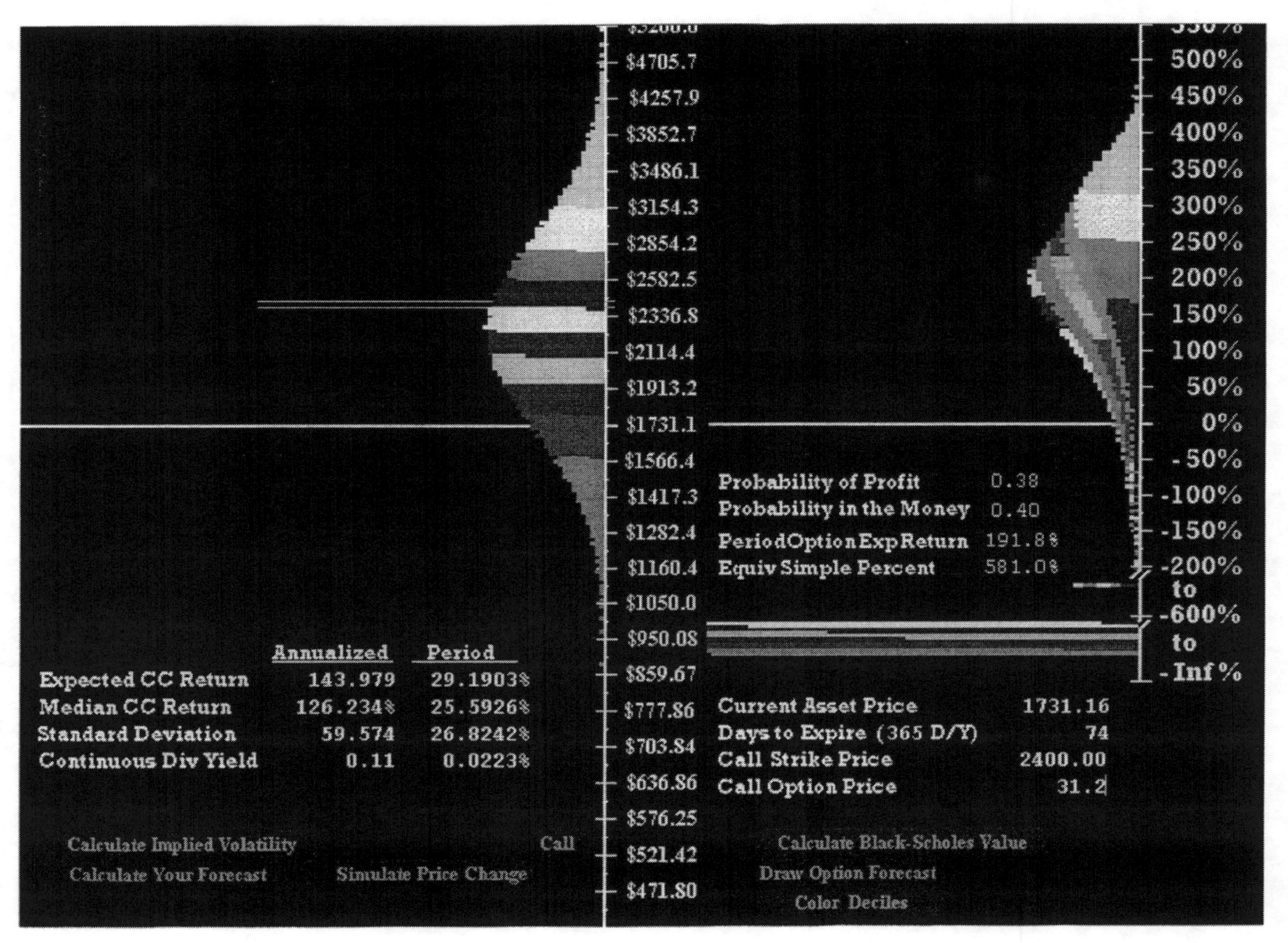

	$4705.7		500%
	$4257.9		450%
	$3852.7		400%
	$3486.1		350%
	$3154.3		300%
	$2854.2		250%
	$2582.5		200%
	$2336.8		150%
	$2114.4		100%
	$1913.2		50%
	$1731.1		0%
	$1566.4		-50%

	Annualized	Period
Expected CC Return	143.979	29.1903%
Median CC Return	126.234%	25.5926%
Standard Deviation	59.574	26.8242%
Continuous Div Yield	0.11	0.0223%

Probability of Profit	0.38
Probability in the Money	0.40
Period Option Exp Return	191.8%
Equiv Simple Percent	581.0%

Current Asset Price	1731.16
Days to Expire (365 D/Y)	74
Call Strike Price	2400.00
Call Option Price	31.2

Calculate Implied Volatility   Call

Calculate Your Forecast   Simulate Price Change

Calculate Black-Scholes Value

Draw Option Forecast

Color Deciles

Once you have a price forecast, you can calculate each option's probability of profit and expected return.

If your forecast disagrees with the risk-neutralized, market-equilibrium forecast, then each option will give you a different probability of profit and expected return.

(Remember: An investment's expected return is the average of all the returns in its probability distribution. See page 105.)

You're looking for a probability of profit of around .50.

24. Click once on Clear.

25. Click on Hide twice.

26. Click on Simulate Price Change.

27. Click on Color Deciles.

Looking at the underlying's end-of-period color deciles, you see that an option with a strike price around $2,200 will give you that probability.

We'll evaluate the call with the $2,200 strike price, the two above, and the two below. We'll use the ask price because that's the price you have to pay.

28. Click on Call.

29. Click on Draw Option Forecast.

30. For each strike price:

A. Enter the strike price.

B. Enter the ask price.

C. Click on Color Deciles or Draw Option Forecast.

Strike Price	Ask	Probability of Profit	Period Option Expected Return	Equivalent Simple Percent
2050	92.1	.56	144.4%	323.9%
2100	80.1	.54	150.3%	349.4%
2200	60.3	.48	161.8%	404.4%
2300	42.3	.43	179.7%	503.1%
2400	31.2	.38	191.8%	581.0%

Here's your quandary: The options with the highest expected returns have the lowest probabilities of profit. They give you a shot at making the most money—but they also give you the highest probability of losing all your investment.

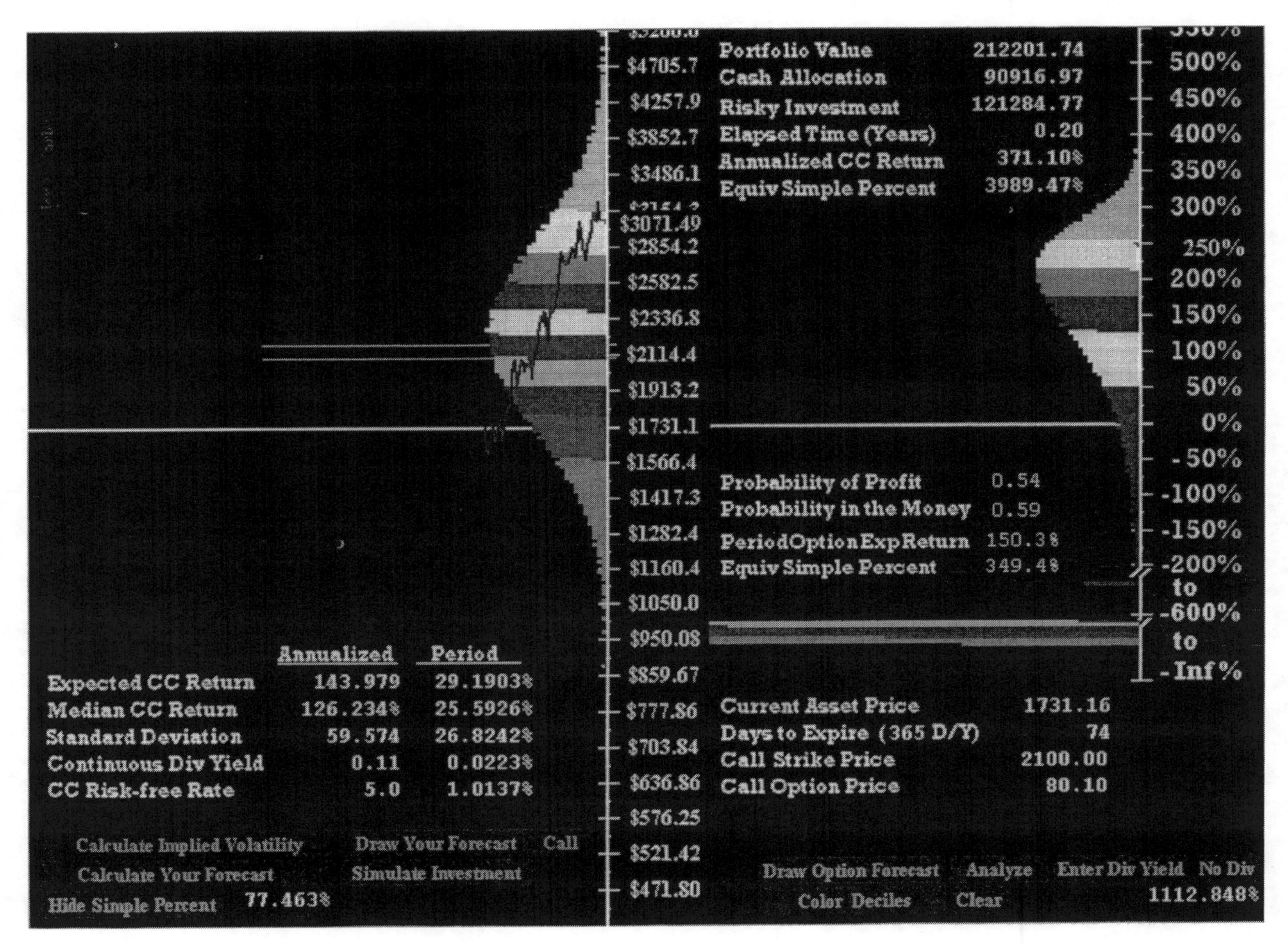

Portfolio Value	212201.74	
Cash Allocation	90916.97	
Risky Investment	121284.77	
Elapsed Time (Years)	0.20	
Annualized CC Return	371.10%	
Equiv Simple Percent	3989.47%	

Probability of Profit	0.54
Probability in the Money	0.59
Period Option Exp Return	150.3%
Equiv Simple Percent	349.4%

	Annualized	Period
Expected CC Return	143.979	29.1903%
Median CC Return	126.234%	25.5926%
Standard Deviation	59.574	26.8242%
Continuous Div Yield	0.11	0.0223%
CC Risk-free Rate	5.0	1.0137%

Current Asset Price	1731.16
Days to Expire (365 D/Y)	74
Call Strike Price	2100.00
Call Option Price	80.10

Calculate Implied Volatility   Draw Your Forecast   Call

Calculate Your Forecast   Simulate Investment

Hide Simple Percent   77.463%

Draw Option Forecast   Analyze   Enter Div Yield   No Div

Color Deciles   Clear   1112.848%

Left axis (prices): $5200.0 $4705.7 $4257.9 $3852.7 $3486.1 $3154.3 $3071.49 $2854.2 $2582.5 $2336.8 $2114.4 $1913.2 $1731.1 $1566.4 $1417.3 $1282.4 $1160.4 $1050.0 $950.08 $859.67 $777.86 $703.84 $636.86 $576.25 $521.42 $471.80

Right axis (percent): 550% 500% 450% 400% 350% 300% 250% 200% 150% 100% 50% 0% -50% -100% -150% -200% to -600% to -Inf %

To decide whether to buy an option, you can use the option's expected return and probability of profit or you can simulate potential investment outcomes.

Let's say you want to give yourself at least a 50% chance to make a profit based on your forecast. You think you might go with the option with a strike price of $2,100 and a probability of profit of .54. You wonder what kind of outcomes it might give you.

> **31. Click on Clear.**
>
> **32. For Strike Price, enter 2100.00.**
>
> **33. For Call Option Price, enter 80.10.**
>
> **34. Click on Color Deciles.**

The animation draws your forecasts for the stock and the option.

> **35. Click on Invest.**
>
> **36. For CC Risk-free Rate, enter 5.0.**

You've got $100,000. You're thinking of putting $10,000 in the option.

> **37. For Portfolio Value, enter 100000. (No commas. No $.)**
>
> **38. For Risky Investment, enter 10000.**
>
> **39. Click on Show Simple Percent.**
>
> **40. Click on Simulate Investment.**

The cash allocation earns the risk-free rate of return. The option payoff depends on the end-of-period stock price.

See if the outcome is one you can live with.

Regardless of the outcome, try it again. Put another $10,000 in the option.

> **41. For Risky Investment, enter 10000.**
>
> **42. Click on Simulate Investment.**

What happened this time?

Keep putting $10,000 in the option and clicking on Simulate Investment.

Chances are that much of the time you will lose all the money you put in the option. On the occasions when you make a profit, the payoffs probably will more than compensate for your previous losses.

Of course, for a given option, you only get one chance. The idea is that if on many occasions you are able to come up with better forecasts than the market-equilibrium forecasts, then over time the payoffs you get will more than compensate for your losses.

Keep in mind that the animation generates the potential price paths and payoffs from your forecast. If your forecast is flawed, so are the potential price paths and payoffs.

Nasdaq-100® Index Options
Current Price: 1731.16
Annualized Nasdaq-100® Index Dividend Yield: 0.11%

NDX
European   Mar 19

Puts	Mid
Jun 1100. (NDV RB-E)	16.5
Jun 1400. (NDV RH-E)	64.6
Jun 1600. (NDV RL-E)	128.2
Jun 1700. (NDV RN-E)	171.7
Jun 1800. (NDV RP-E)	223.3
Jun 1900. (NDV RR-E)	282.8
Jun 2050. (NDX RA-E)	385.3
Jun 2100. (NDX RB-E)	422.7
Jun 2200. (NDX RD-E)	501.7
Jun 2300. (NDX RF-E)	585.4
Jun 2400. (NDX RH-E)	673.0
Jun 2500. (NDX RJ-E)	763.6
Jun 2600. (NDX RL-E)	856.5

If you think somebody's bubble is about to burst, buy puts. Make money.

Let's say that it's March 19. Instead of thinking the Nasdaq is about to rally, you think the real plunge is yet to come. If you're right, by investing in puts you could make a lot of money.

You wonder, "What do the risk-neutralized, market-equilibrium forecasts for Nasdaq index options look like over the next few months?"

To draw the forecasts that the options imply, we calculate the implied volatilities, and for the market-equilibrium expected return, we use the risk-free rate.

> 1. Click three times on Clear.
>
> 2. Click twice on Hide.
>
> 3. Click on Simulate Price Change.

For what we're doing, we don't need an expected-return estimate.

> 4. Click on Hide.
>
> 5. Click on Put.
>
> 6. For Current Asset Price, enter 1731.16.
>
> 7. For Days to Expire, enter 74.
>
> 8. Click on Calculate Implied Volatility.
>
> 9. Click on Enter Div Yield.
>
> 10. For Continuous Div Yield, enter 0.11.
>
> 11. For CC Risk-free Rate, enter 5.00.

> 12. For each put strike price in the June series:
>
> A. Enter the strike price.
>
> B. Enter the midpoint option price.
>
> C. Click on Calculate Implied Volatility.
>
> D. Click on Draw Market-Equilibrium Forecast.

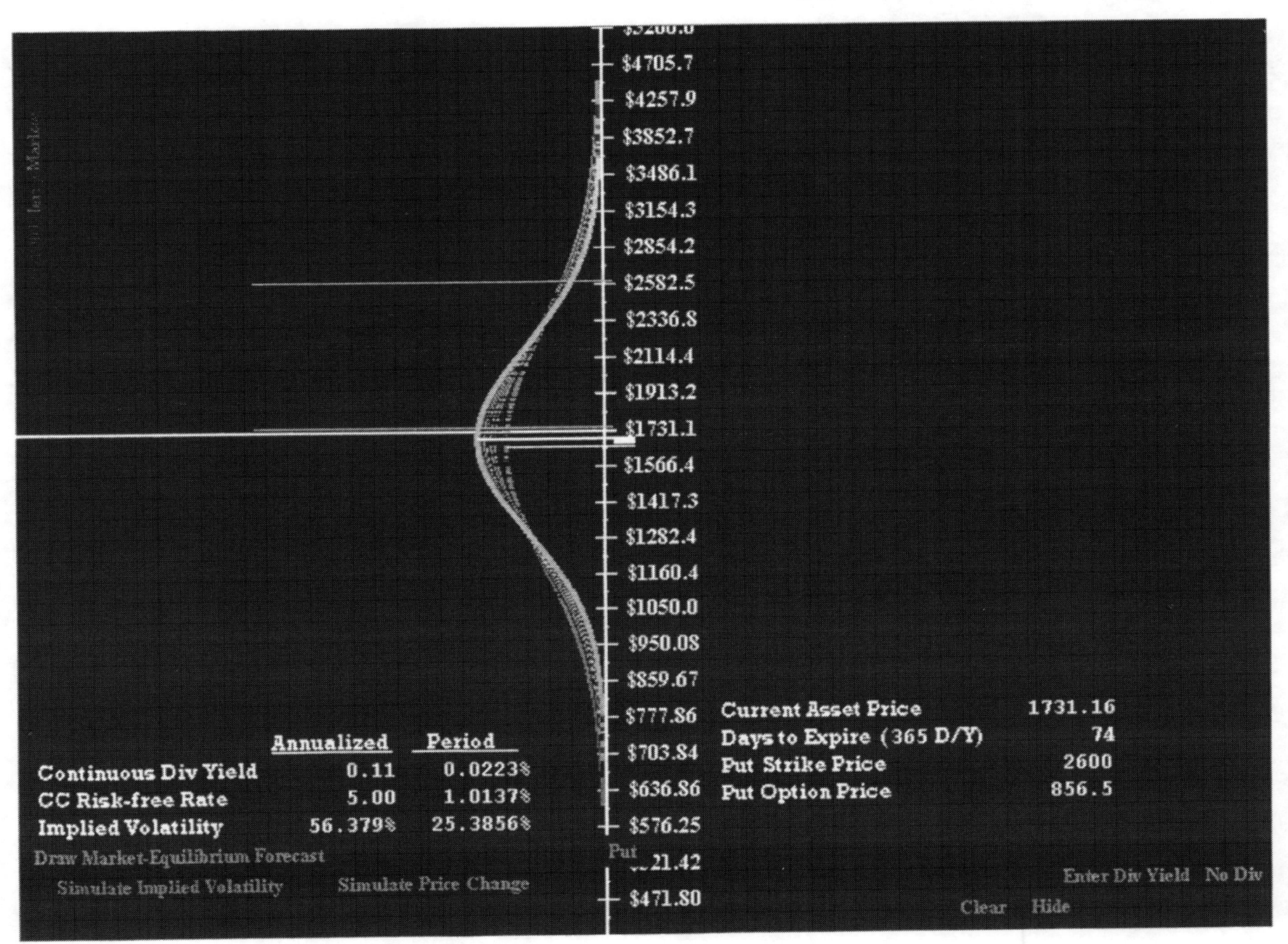

	Annualized	Period
Continuous Div Yield	0.11	0.0223%
CC Risk-free Rate	5.00	1.0137%
Implied Volatility	56.379%	25.3856%

Draw Market-Equilibrium Forecast

Simulate Implied Volatility   Simulate Price Change

Current Asset Price	1731.16
Days to Expire (365 D/Y)	74
Put Strike Price	2600
Put Option Price	856.5

Enter Div Yield   No Div

Clear   Hide

Looking at the series of market-equilibrium forecasts may make it easier for you to decide what your forecast is.

The option prices at the different strike prices produce a cluster of forecasts. The forecasts give end-of-period prices that range from around $600 to around $4,000.

You figure that the only direction the Nasdaq 100 is going in is down. By June 1, it may not go below $600, but it certainly isn't going above $2,300.

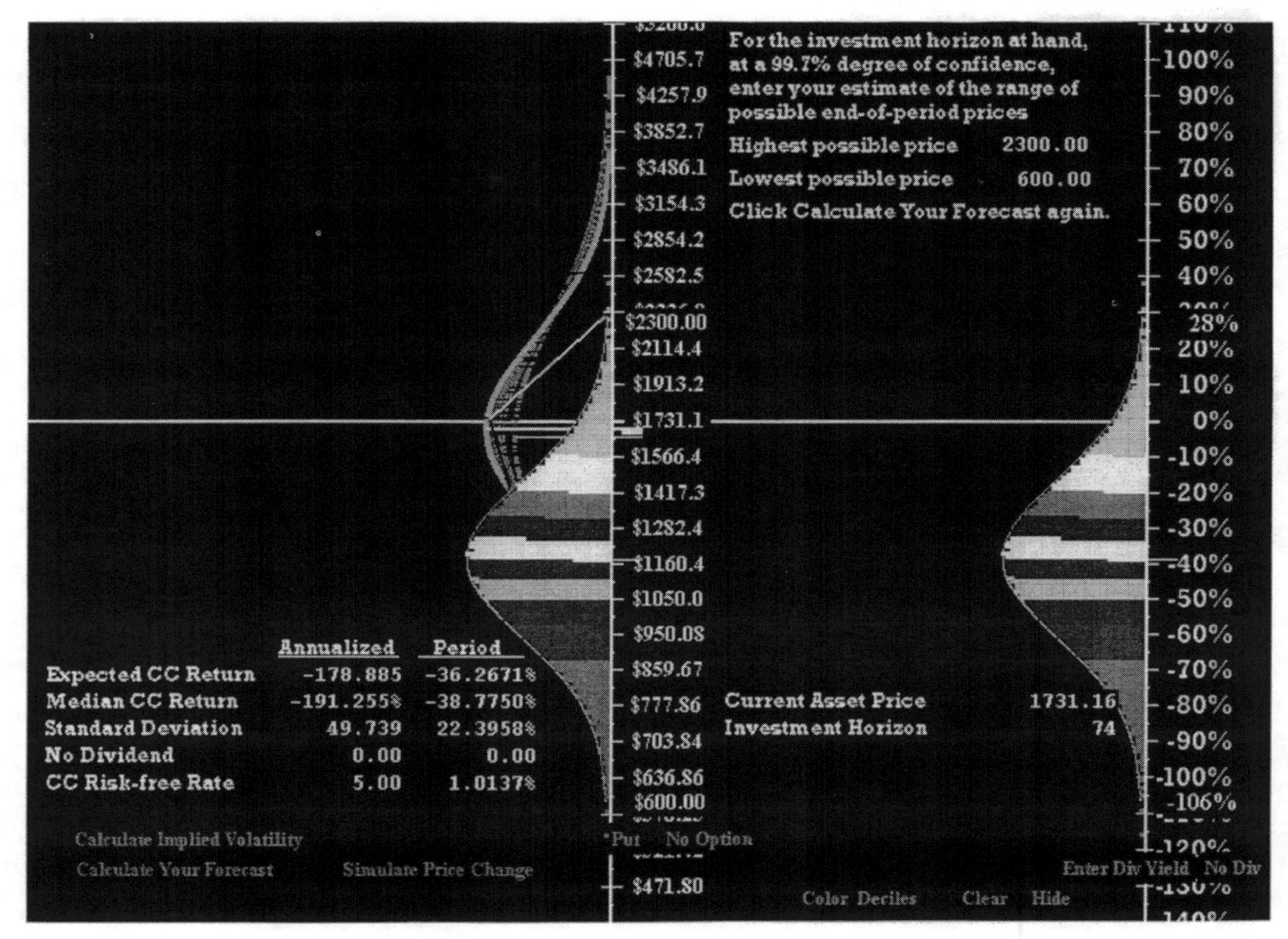

For the investment horizon at hand, at a 99.7% degree of confidence, enter your estimate of the range of possible end-of-period prices

Highest possible price   2300.00

Lowest possible price   600.00

Click Calculate Your Forecast again.

	Annualized	Period
Expected CC Return	-178.885	-36.2671%
Median CC Return	-191.255%	-38.7750%
Standard Deviation	49.739	22.3958%
No Dividend	0.00	0.00
CC Risk-free Rate	5.00	1.0137%

Current Asset Price   1731.16

Investment Horizon   74

Calculate Implied Volatility

Calculate Your Forecast   Simulate Price Change

*Put   No Option

Enter Div Yield   No Div

Color Deciles   Clear   Hide

$4705.7 — 100%
$4257.9 — 90%
$3852.7 — 80%
$3486.1 — 70%
$3154.3 — 60%
$2854.2 — 50%
$2582.5 — 40%
$2300.00 — 28%
$2114.4 — 20%
$1913.2 — 10%
$1731.1 — 0%
$1566.4 — -10%
$1417.3 — -20%
$1282.4 — -30%
$1160.4 — -40%
$1050.0 — -50%
$950.08 — -60%
$859.67 — -70%
$777.86 — -80%
$703.84 — -90%
$636.86 — -100%
$600.00 — -106%
$471.80

To calculate your forecast, you can use your best guesses of how high and how low the prices might be at the end of the investment period if the underlying paid no dividends.

Let's calculate your forecast assuming no dividends.

> **13. Click on No Option.**
>
> **14. Click on No Div.**
>
> **15. Click on Calculate Your Forecast.**
>
> **16. For Highest Possible Price, enter 2300.00.**
>
> **17. For Lowest Possible Price, enter 600.00.**
>
> **18. Click again on Calculate Your Forecast.**

From your view of the potential end-of-period prices, the animation calculates and draws your forecast for the period—assuming no dividends.

You get a period expected return of −36.2671% and an annualized expected return of −178.885%. You get a period standard deviation of 22.3956% and an annualized standard deviation of 49.739%.

Your estimate of standard deviation is less than that of the market-equilibrium forecast.

> **19. Click on Color Deciles.**

You see what your period forecast looks like. You can decide if you want to change it.

To get a feel for whether this is the forecast you want to go with, you can simulate potential price paths based on the forecast.

> **20. Click on Simulate Price Change as many times as you want.**

If, excluding dividends, your forecast seems to be consistent with your beliefs, go with it.

If not, you can keep adjusting the expected continuously compounded return and the standard deviation until the forecast is what you want it to be.

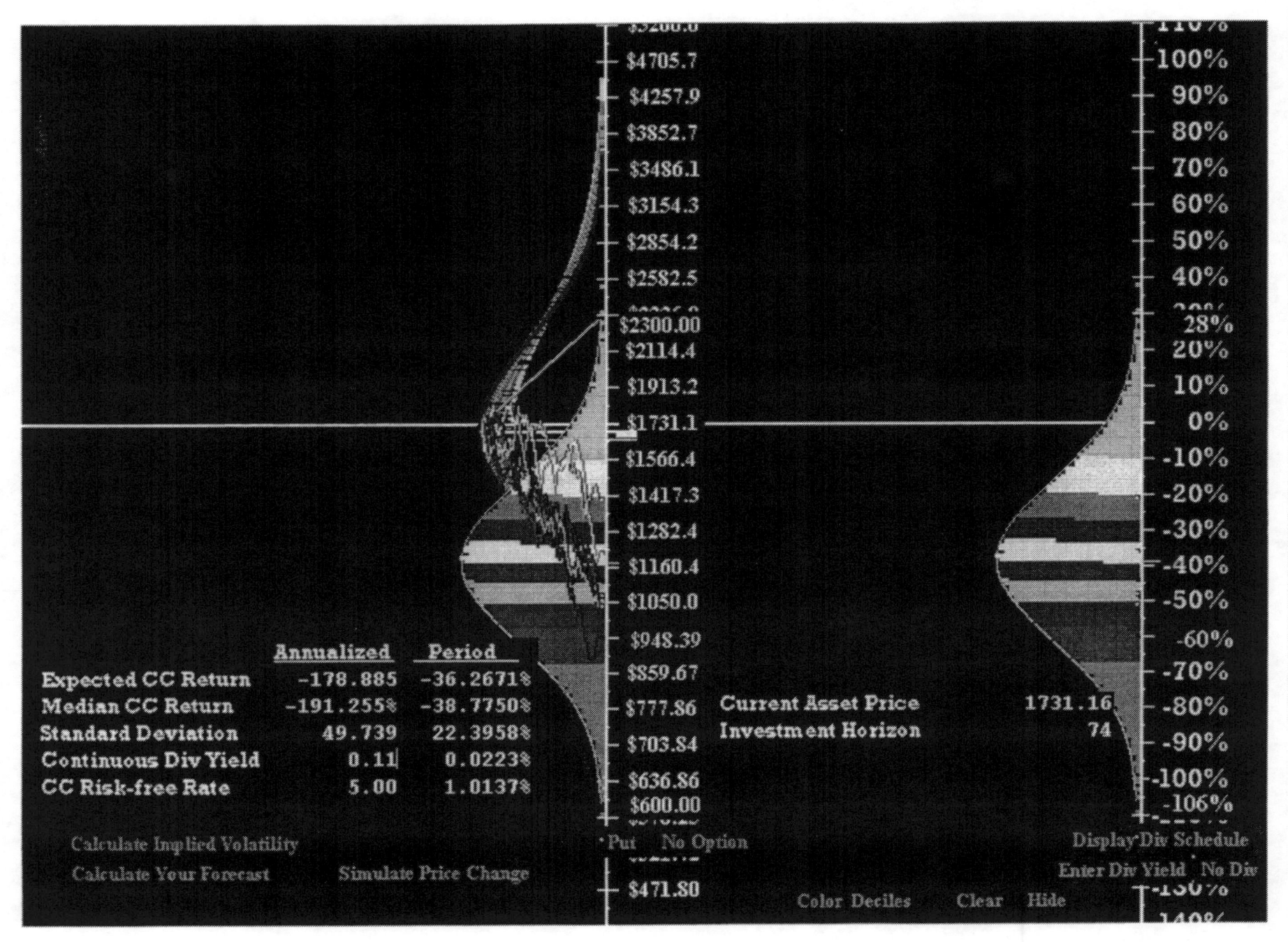

To go from a return forecast to a price forecast, enter the dividend schedule or dividend yield.

If the underlying you are working with pays a dividend yield or dividends, this is when you enter them.

In our example, the Nasdaq-100® pays an annualized dividend yield of 0.11%.

21. Click on Enter Div Yield.

22. For Dividend Yield, enter 0.11.

If you want to compare your forecast's potential price paths with potential price paths from the market-equilibrium forecast, click on Put, Calculate Implied Volatility, and Simulate Implied Volatility.

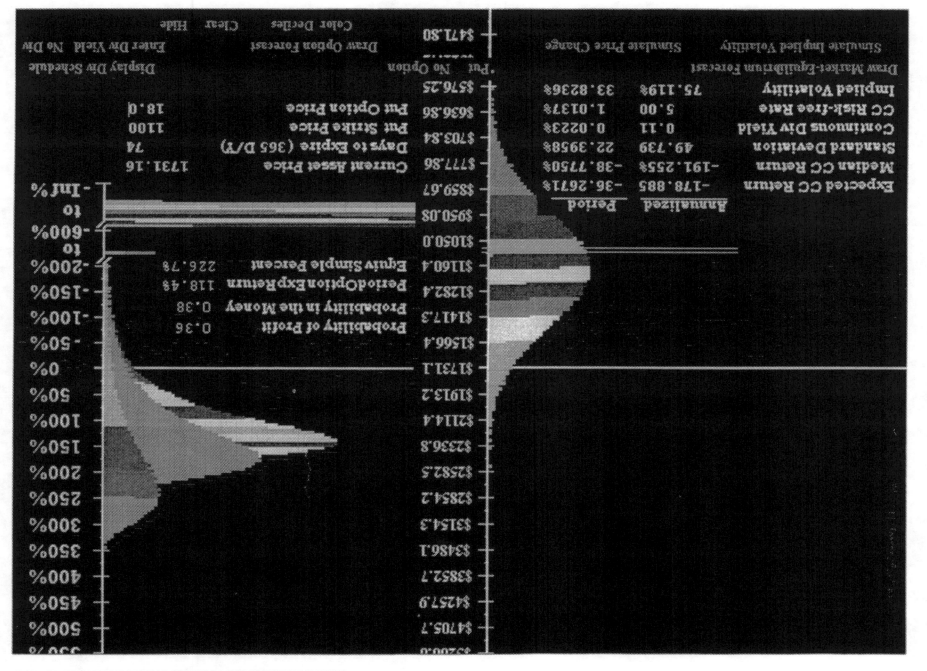

Once you have a price forecast, you can calculate each option's probability of profit and expected return.

If your forecast disagrees with the risk-neutralized, market-equilibrium forecast, then each option will give you a different probability of profit and expected return.

In our example, the lowest strike price offered is well within your forecast. We'll evaluate the three options with the lowest strike prices.

---

23. Click on Draw Option Forecast.

24. Click on Clear.

25. Click on Put.

26. For Current Asset Price, enter 1731.16.

Strike Price	Ask
1600	137.2
1400	70.6
1100	18.0

---

27. For each strike price:

A. For Put Strike Price, enter the strike price.

B. For Put Option Price, enter the ask price.

C. Click on Color Deciles or on Draw Option Forecast.

D. Click on Calculate Implied Volatility.

Strike Price	Ask	*Implied Volatility	Probability of Profit	Period Option Expected Return	Equivalent Simple Percent
1600	137.2	68.3%	.84	109.7%	199.4%
1400	70.6	70.9%	.71	122.0%	238.7%
1100	18.0	75.1%	.36	118.4%	226.7%

*Implied volatilities computed from ask price.

We quickly notice that the option at the strike price of $1,100 has a lower probability of profit and lower expected return than the one with the strike price of $1,400. This option's ask price also gives a higher implied volatility than the other two.

Together, the low probability of profit, low expected return, and high implied volatility indicate that this option, relative to the other two, is overpriced.

The option with the strike price of $1,400 with a probability of profit of .71 looks good to you. The prospect, on average (if your forecast is right), of getting back two and a half times your money appeals to your sense of what constitutes a fair return.

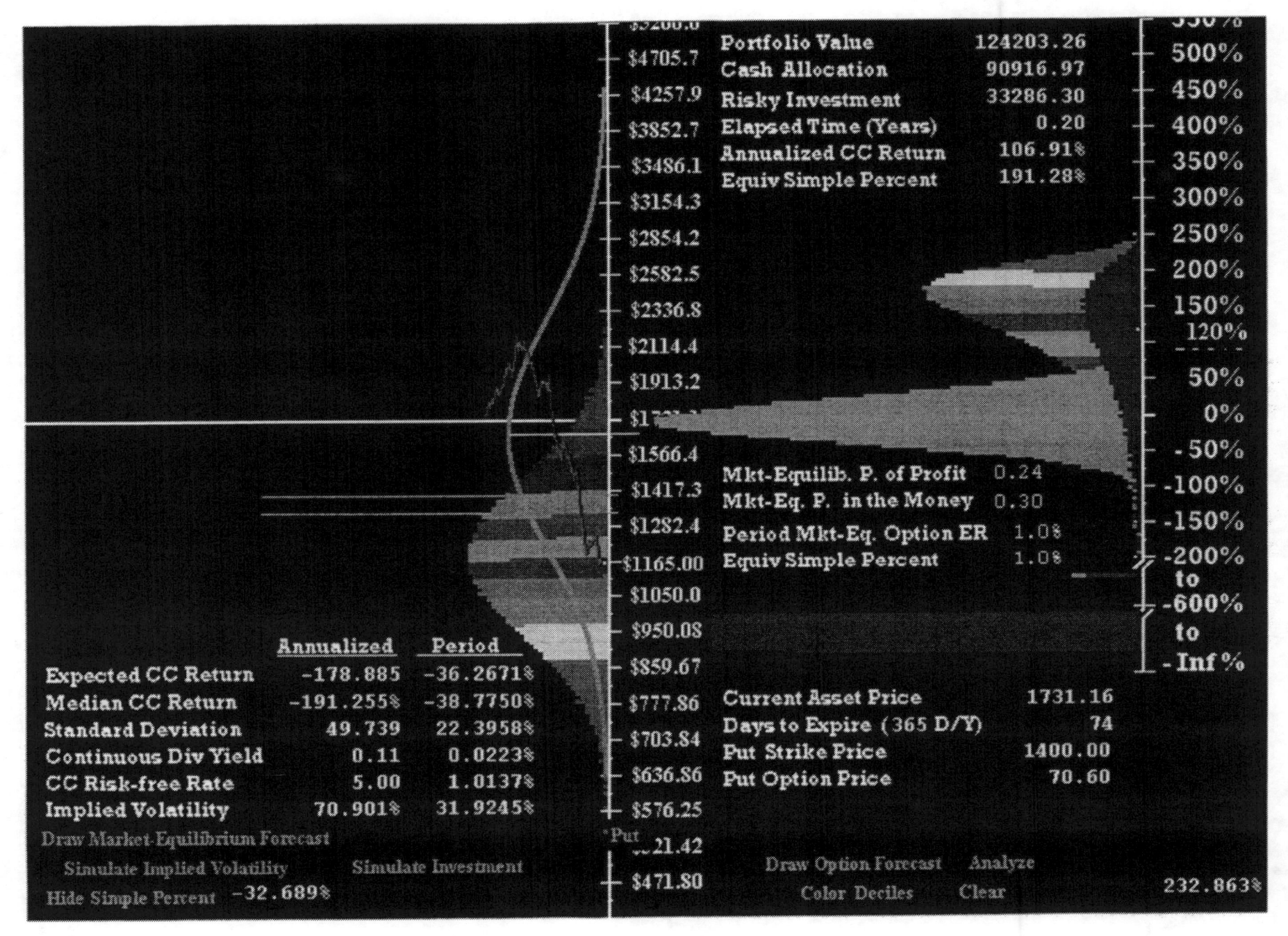

To decide whether to buy a put, you can use the option's expected return and probability of profit or you can simulate potential investment outcomes.

Let's say you think you might go with the option with a strike price of $1,400. It seems to give you the best trade-off between probability of profit and expected return. You wonder what kind of outcomes it might give you.

> 28. Click once on Clear.
>
> 29. For Put Strike Price, enter 1400.00.
>
> 30. For Put Option Price, enter 70.60.
>
> 31. Click on Color Deciles.

The animation draws your forecasts for the stock and the option.

You can compare your forecast to the forecast implied by the ask price.

> 32. Click on Calculate Implied Volatility.
>
> 33. Click on Draw Market-Equilibrium Forecast.

First, on the option axes, the animation draws the implied forecast for the underlying.

Next, on the price axes, it draws the implied price forecast.

Finally, on the option axes, it draws the implied option forecast.

Now we'll see what kind of investment outcomes your forecast might produce from this option.

> 34. Click on Invest.
>
> 35. Click on Show Simple Percent.

You've got $100,000. You're thinking of putting $10,000 in the option.

> 36. For Portfolio Value, enter 100000.00.
>
> 37. For Risky Investment, enter 10000.00.
>
> 38. Click on Simulate Investment.

The cash allocation earns the risk-free rate of return. The option payoff depends on the end-of-period stock price.

Regardless of the outcome, keep putting $10,000 in the option and clicking on Simulate Investment.

> 39. For Risky Investment, enter 10000.00.
>
> 40. Click on Simulate Investment.

As was the case in our example with call options, chances are some of the time you will lose all the money you put in the option. On the occasions when you make a profit, the payoffs probably will more than compensate for your previous losses.

The idea is that if on many occasions you are able to come up with better forecasts than the market-equilibrium forecasts, then over time the payoffs you get will more than compensate for your losses.

To see how your option might fare under the market-equilibrium forecast, put some money in the risky investment and click on Simulate Implied Volatility.

What We Didn't Tell You

and Aren't Going To

You can sell what you've got. You can sell naked.

The animation and book focus on simulating and evaluating potential end-of-period payoffs of options. The Black-Scholes model is designed to price European options—options that can be exercised only at maturity.

Just because the animation focuses on end-of-period values, don't think you have to hold onto an option until then. You can exercise American options prior to maturity. You can sell your American and European options at any time.

If your forecast is for an underlying change, you can use the animations to evaluate option performance over investment horizons other than to maturity.

Not only can you sell options you own, you can sell options you don't own. In the jargon, you can write options. If, when you sell options, you own nothing to hedge the exposures you create, you're selling naked. You can lose money big time.

The animation and book show you how to calculate expected return when you buy options. Calculating expected return on selling options is an altogether different proposition.

When you sell options naked, you're not really making an investment, you're making a funny kind of loan. You make a loan at the risk-free rate. You collect the interest payment up front.

At the end of the term of the loan, or, in the case of an American option, whenever the borrower wants, you may have to buy some stocks at the market price and sell them at a money-losing lower price. Or, at an agreed-upon price, you may have to buy stocks that sell for less on the market. You may lose more on the stock transaction than you received in "interest."

It's hard (or perhaps impossible) to calculate a return or an expected return because, in this loan, we never know what the principal is. Even if we came up with a theoretical value, there's a good chance that on a given transaction the loss would be greater than the principal.

In that case, as a simple percent, you would lose more than 100% of your investment. As a continuously compounded rate of return, your rate of return would be less than negative infinity. Your computer can't compute numbers less than negative infinity.

Selling naked options is akin to borrowing on terms that some banks have been known to use in mortgages.

In the 1970s, interest rates were volatile. Some banks occasionally gave homebuyers a mortgage that had this structure: The interest rate floated with market rates. The homeowner made monthly payments of a fixed dollar amount. At the end of the term, the homeowners made a balloon payment of any unpaid principal and interest.

In some cases, when interest rates shot up, the monthly interest charge was greater than the monthly payments. At the end of the term, the balloon payment due was larger than the original loan amount.

Banks called these loans neutron-bomb loans. They could wipe out occupants and leave buildings standing.

You can sell covered. You can construct butterfly, bull, bear, and calendar spreads. You can construct strips, straps, and strangles.

In the animations, we restrict ourselves to looking at single instruments in depth. Based on market-equilibrium forecasts and based on your forecasts, we show the probabilities of different outcomes for underlyings and for the options written on them.

Most books on options dive right into investment strategies that combine buying or selling options with being long or short the underlying. They show you strategies that combine different maturities or strike prices of the same option. They show you strategies that combine different types of options. Authors draw payoff diagrams with lots of different shapes.

Payoff diagrams show how you can profit if spot prices go up or down. They show how to sell some of your potential gains and buy your way out of some of your potential losses. They show how much money you'll make if certain things happen.

Funny thing is, the diagrams usually don't tell you the probability of any of these things happening.

For example, you can sell covered calls. That is, you can sell call options on stocks that you own. If the stock goes down or doesn't go up much, you get to keep the proceeds of the option sale at what may seem like no cost.

Keep in mind the Black-Scholes assumption that the probable payoff of any investment is the risk-free rate. That assumption applies to complex positions as well as to simple ones.

If you accept the assumption, it suggests that when you write a covered call the probability-weighted net present value of your potential losses offsets most of the value of the premium you received.

What are your potential losses?

The stock may go up beyond the strike price. If it does, you'll have to sell it at the strike price and forego some of the gain that would be yours had you not sold the option. You incur an opportunity cost.

The stock may go down. If it does, you'll be stuck with the loss.

For now, the author leaves payoff diagrams, complex strategies, and complex positions to others. Future works may include joint probability distributions of complex positions.

Using the Animation to Sell Options to Others

Imagine for a moment that you're out in the world selling stock options.

Or you're a financial advisor to a wealthy investor who has been putting most of her money into mutual funds.

Here's what you might find yourself saying to your client:

"Dr. Quelquechose, the last time we spoke, you expressed an interest in buying some stocks of pharmaceutical companies. I think that could turn out to be a very advantageous strategy.

"I checked with our analysts who specialize in that sector. We're quite bullish on Pfixo La Rush right now. They're especially strong in psychopharmaceuticals. And, hey, you know, that's a product most of the people I know could benefit from.

"Our analysts are so confident this stock is going to go up that we're recommending that our more sophisticated clients consider buying call options."

"Aren't options risky?" she asks.

"Depends on your investment strategy. A better way to look at them is as a way to leverage your investment.

"Here, let me show you how call options work and the profit potential associated with Pfixo La Rush."

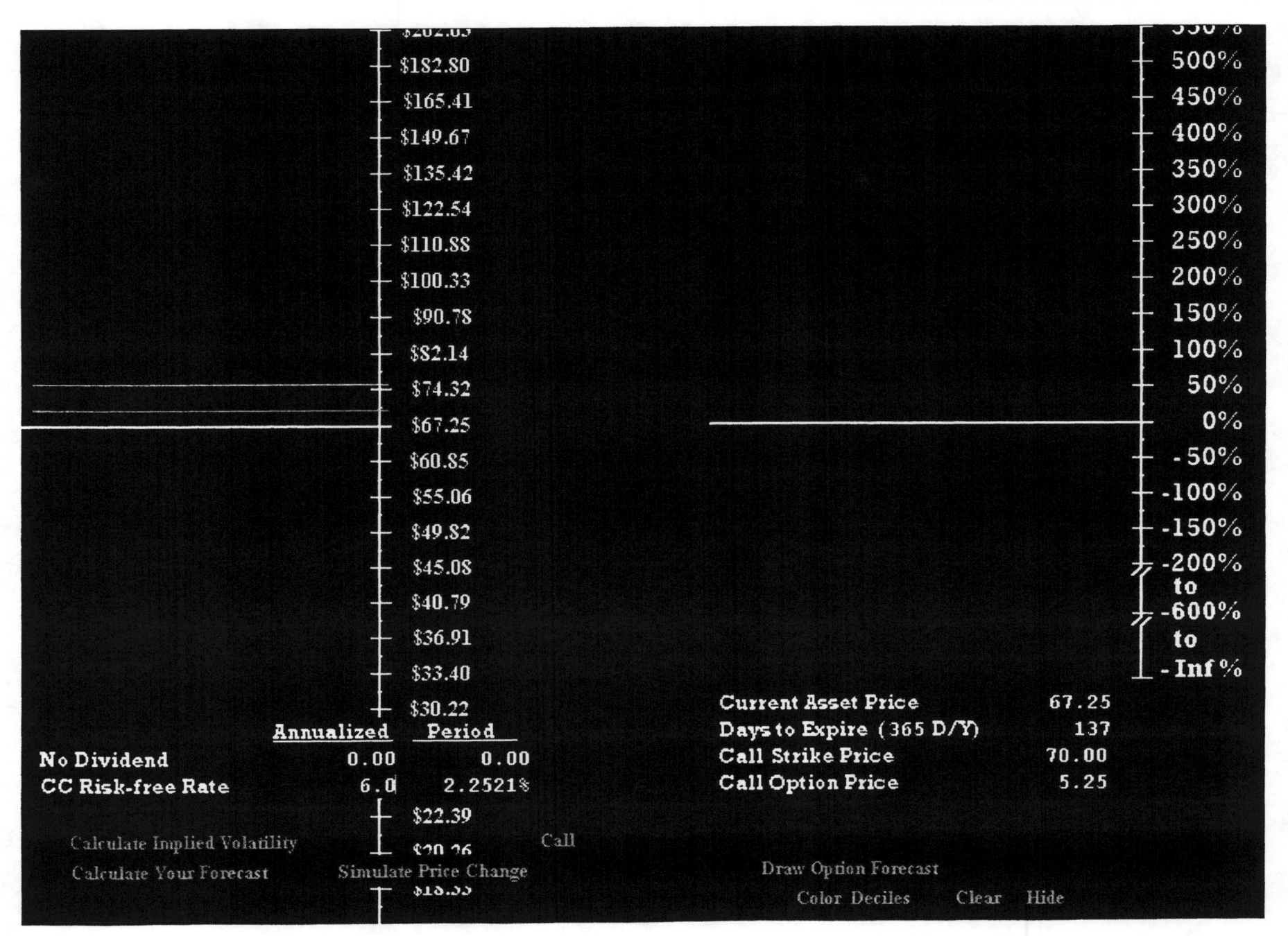

$202.03				350%	
$182.80				500%	
$165.41				450%	
$149.67				400%	
$135.42				350%	
$122.54				300%	
$110.88				250%	
$100.33				200%	
$90.78				150%	
$82.14				100%	
$74.32				50%	
$67.25				0%	
$60.85				-50%	
$55.06				-100%	
$49.82				-150%	
$45.08				-200% to	
$40.79				-600% to	
$36.91					
$33.40				- Inf %	
$30.22					

	Annualized	Period
No Dividend	0.00	0.00
CC Risk-free Rate	6.0	2.2521%

Current Asset Price	67.25
Days to Expire (365 D/Y)	137
Call Strike Price	70.00
Call Option Price	5.25

$22.39

$20.26   Call

$18.33

Calculate Implied Volatility

Calculate Your Forecast   Simulate Price Change   Draw Option Forecast

Color Deciles   Clear   Hide

1. Click three times on Clear.

2. Click twice on Hide.

3. Click on Draw Option Forecast.

4. Click on Simulate Price Change.

5. Click once on Hide.

6. Click on Call.

7. For Current Asset Price, enter 67.25. (No $.)

"Right now, Pfixo La Rush stock is selling for $67.25.

8. For Days to Expire, enter 137.

"On the market, there are a number of stock options available that expire in 137 days.

9. For Call Strike Price, enter 70.00. (No $.)

"The one we're most excited about has a strike price of $70.

10. For Call Option Price, enter 5.25.

"Right now, it's selling for around $5.25. When we're finished, if you're interested, I'll get the up-to-the-minute quote for you.

"This is what the stock and option look like on a price-forecast axis.

"The yellow line represents the option's strike price. For the option to be in the money, the stock price has to go above the yellow line.

"The distance from the yellow line to the green line represents the price of the option. For you to make a profit on the option, the stock price has to go above the green line.

"To decide whether you want to buy this option, you might want to consider these questions:

"What is the probability of making a profit?

"What is the expected return on the option?

"To figure that out, what we need is a financial forecast for the stock itself.

"In fact, what we're going to do is compare two different forecasts: the market-equilibrium forecast and my investment firm's forecast.

"As I'm sure you're aware, a few years ago, Myron Scholes and Robert Merton won the Nobel Prize in Economics for their work in developing the theory and the mathematics that—among other things—lets us extract financial forecasts from option prices.

"That's what we're going to do.

11. Click on Calculate Implied Volatility.

"To extract the market-equilibrium forecast for Pfixo La Rush, we need two additional pieces of information: the stock's dividend schedule—if it pays dividends—and the risk-free rate of interest.

"This stock doesn't pay dividends, so we don't need to enter a dividend schedule.

12. For CC Risk-free Rate, enter 6.0. (No % sign.)

"To draw a price forecast for the stock, we need estimates of the stock's expected return and potential volatility.

"According to Black-Scholes, the market-equilibrium expected return for any stock is the risk-free rate, which right now is around 6%.

"With this information, we can extract the market-equilibrium forecast for Pfixo La Rush.

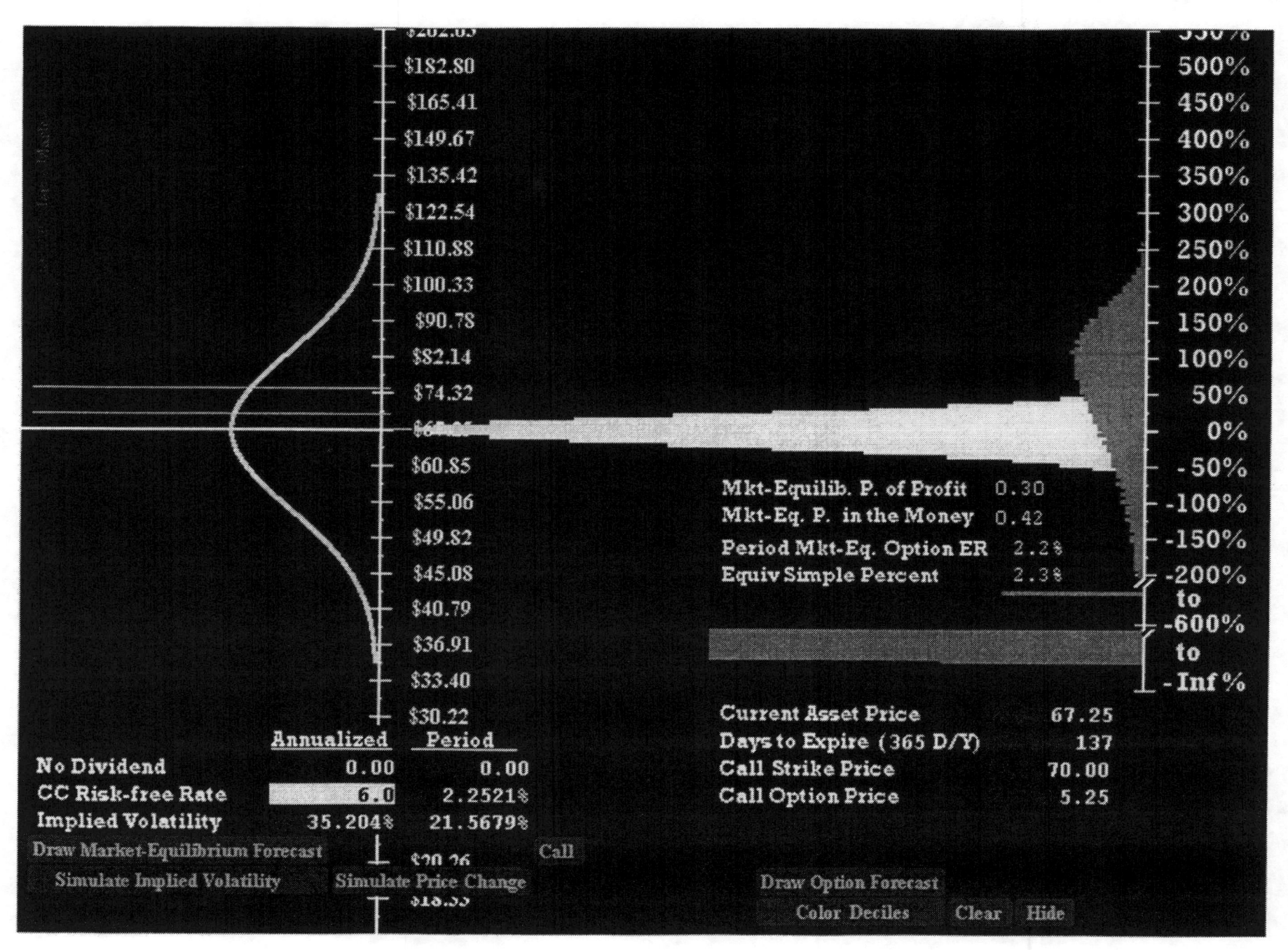

13. Click on Calculate Implied Volatility.

"The annualized implied volatility is just over 35%.

"For the 137-day period until the option expires, the implied volatility is about 21.6%.

"Let's see what that forecast looks like.

14. Click once on Draw Market-Equilibrium Forecast.

"In this case, the market-equilibrium forecasts for the stock and the option looks like this. The probability of profit is .3. The option's expected return for the 137-day period is 2.2%, the same as for the stock.

"If you agree with this forecast, you do not have much incentive to buy the option.

"However, let's look at my firm's forecast for the stock and for the option.

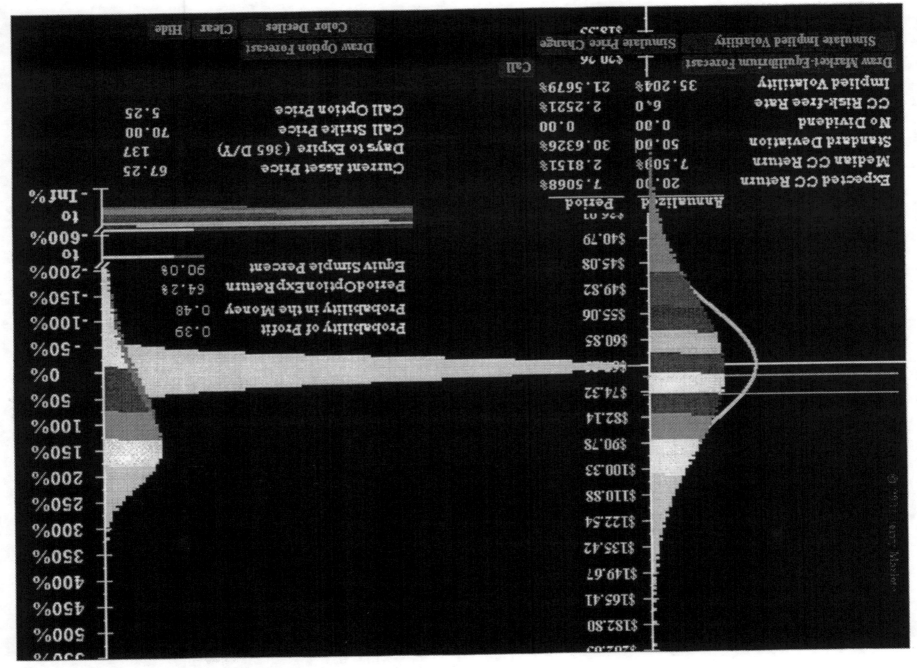

15. Click on Simulate Price Change.

16. For Expected CC Return, enter 20.00.

"Over the next quarter, we project Pfixo La Rush to have an annualized expected return of 20%.

17. For Standard Deviation, enter 50.00.

"We think there is the potential for a significant increase in the volatility of this company's stock. We're projecting an annualized volatility of 50%.

"When we draw the price and option forecasts for our projections, they look like this.

18. Click once on Color Deciles.

"We see a .39 probability of profit and a 137-day expected return of 64.2%.

"Expressed as a holding-period expected return, that's a 90% return.

"Granted, you still have an almost two-thirds chance of losing money, but if the price direction and volatility break your way, you can make quite a killing.

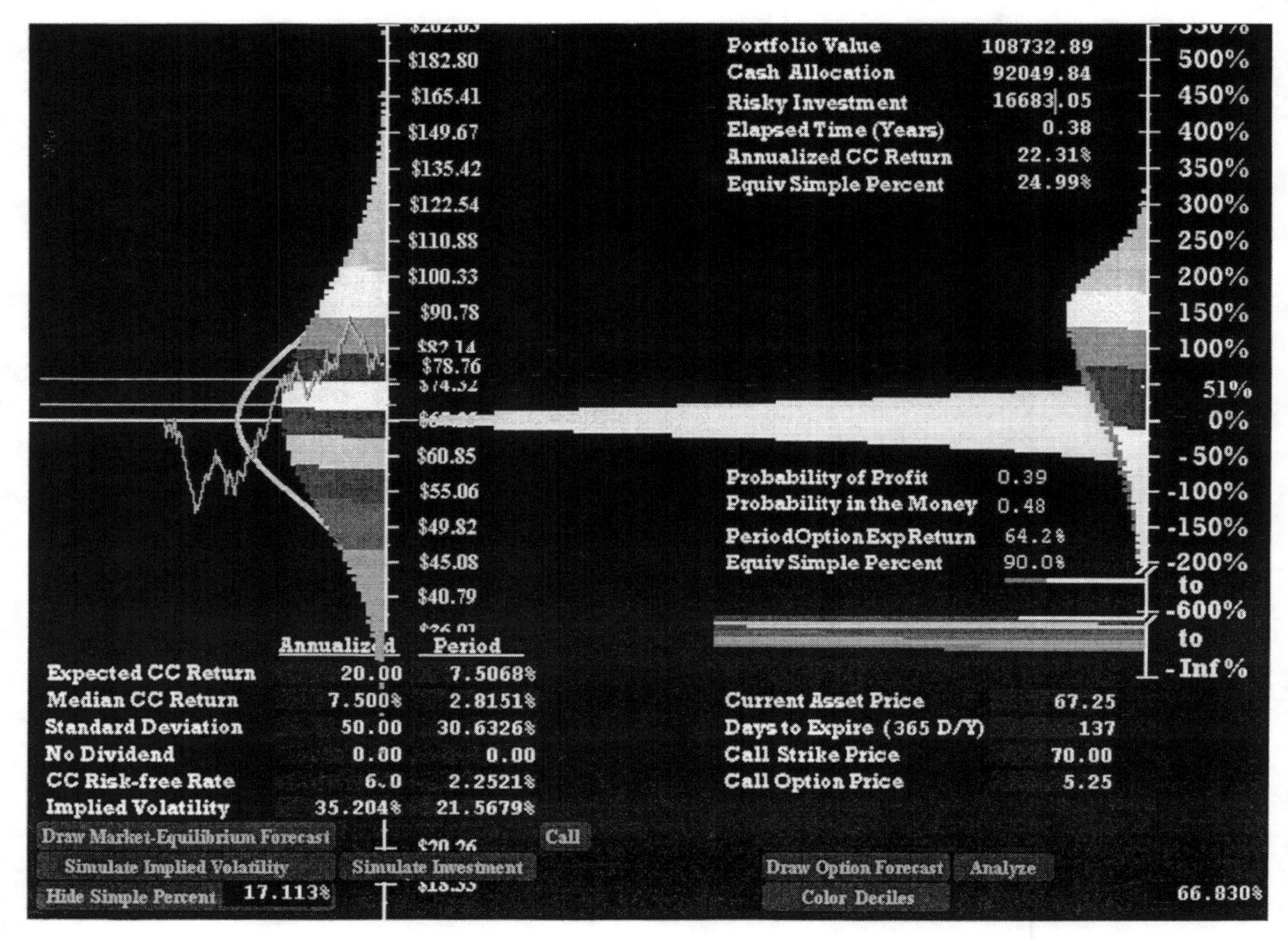

"We can simulate the kind of payoffs you might get.

> **19. Click once on Invest.**
>
> **20. For Portfolio Value, enter 100000. (No $ or commas, please.)**

"Let's say you have $100,000 that you're working with. You might want to put $10,000 in an option like this.

> **21. For Risky Investment, enter 10000.**

"How's it going to turn out?

"We don't know. To get a feel for what might happen, just click on the Simulate Investment button.

> **22. Client clicks on Simulate Investment.**

(Depending on outcome.)

"That's great! Your $10,000 in the option just paid $____.

> **23. Click on Show Simple Return.**

"That's a holding-period return on the option of _____%.

(Or:)

"No excitement there.

(Or:)

"Okay, we're not pulling any punches here. You could lose your $10,000.

(Then, regardless of outcome:)

"Let's put another $10,000 into the option."

> **24. For Risky Investment, enter 10000.**
>
> **25. Hit Simulate Investment again.**

	Strike Price	$0.00
100%	$271.83 — End-of-period Asset Price	53.90
90%	$245.96 = Payoff	$0
80%	$222.55 Payoff	$0
70%	$201.38 x Probability	0.00059172
60%	$182.21 = Probability-weighted Future Value	0.00000000
50%	$164.87 Probability-weighted FV /	0.00000000
40%	$149.18 (exp(Period Expected R))	1.12749685
30%	$134.99 = Probability-weighted Present Value	0.00000000
20%	$122.14 Cumulative	
10%	$110.52 Probability-weighted Net Present Value	0.0000000
0%	$100.00	
-10%	$90.48	
-20%	$81.87	
-30%	$74.08	
-40%	$67.03	
-50%	$60.65	
-62%	$53.90	
	$49.66	

	Annualized	Period		
Expected CC Return	12.00	12.0000%	$44.93 Current Asset Price	100.00
Median CC Return	4.000%	4.0000%	$40.66 Days to Expire (365 D/Y)	365
Standard Deviation	40.00	40.0000%	Put Strike Price	
No Dividend	0.00	0.00	$36.79 Put Option Price	
-100%			$33.29	
-110%			.30.12	

Draw Your Forecast   Put

Simulate Price Change

Calculate Option Value   Fast   Fastest   Color Deciles   Clear

Risk Management and Value at Risk

Value at risk—How much you might lose at a given confidence level.

The animations were not designed with risk management or value-at-risk measurements in mind. Nonetheless, many of the assumptions and techniques that go into risk-management modeling are at work in *Black-Scholes Made Easy*.

The central concept of risk management is value at risk. This is the largest amount of money you might possibly expect to lose at a given confidence level over a specified investment horizon.

Usually, value at risk is specified at the 95% or 99% confidence level. The animation's color deciles can give you a rough idea of your value at risk at a 90% confidence level.

Let's say that you have $100,000 in a portfolio of stocks. For a one-year investment horizon, the expected return of your portfolio is 12% and the standard deviation of the forecast is 40%. (Make sure that the forecast you are using is expressed in continuously compounded rates of return.)

1. Click three times on Clear.

2. Click twice on Hide.

3. Click on Simulate Price Change.

4. Click on Draw Your Forecast.

5. For Expected CC Return, enter 12.00.

6. For Standard Deviation, enter 40.00.

7. For Current Asset Price, enter 100.00. (We'll let this be a proxy for $100,000.)

8. For Investment Horizon, enter 365.

9. Click on Color Deciles.

Look at the color deciles. The break between the ninth and tenth deciles is at around $62 or, in this case, $62,000.

The idea is that you have 1 chance in 10 that at the end of the year the value of your portfolio will be below $62,000. Expressed another way, you have 1 chance in 10 of losing more than $38,000.

To put this into the language of value at risk: At a 90% confidence level, your value at risk over the next one year is $38,000.

If you want a more precise estimate of value at risk, you can torture the animation a bit more and get it.

10. Click on Put.

11. Click on Calculate Option Value.

The first little square appears at $26.34. It takes 1,690 little squares to fill in the entire probability distribution. Hence, there's one chance in 1,690 that your end-of-year portfolio value will be below $26,340. At this confidence level, your value at risk is

$100,000 − $26,340 = $73,660

1/1,690 = 0.06%
100.00% − 0.06% = 99.94%

Hence, at the 99.94% confidence level, your value at risk is $73,660.

12. To get to the next little square, it takes four clicks on Calculate Option Value.

13. After that, each click on Calculate Option Value fills in another square.

The table below shows the number of little squares that correspond to selected confidence intervals and their values at risk for this example.

Number of Little Squares	Confidence Interval	Value at Risk in Example		
		Beginning Value	− Possible End-of-Year Value	= Value at Risk
1	99.94%	$100,000	$26,340	$73,660
8	99.53%	$100,000	$36,540	$63,460
16	99.05%	$100,000	$40,510	$59,490
85	94.97%	$100,000	$53,900	$46,100
169	90.01%	$100,000	$62,290	$37,710

An Investment Strategy

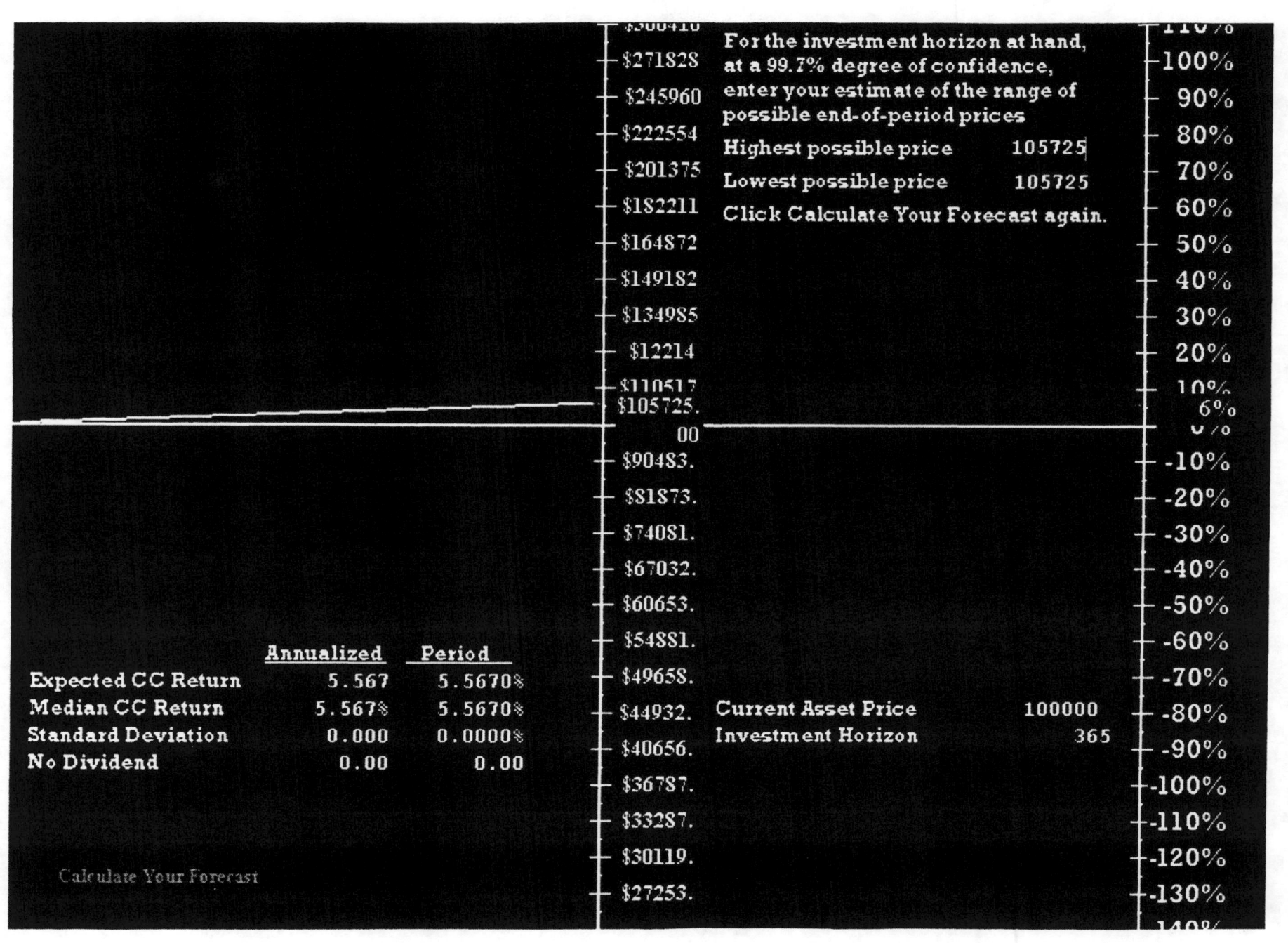

For the investment horizon at hand,
at a 99.7% degree of confidence,
enter your estimate of the range of
possible end-of-period prices

Highest possible price   105725

Lowest possible price   105725

Click Calculate Your Forecast again.

	Annualized	Period
Expected CC Return	5.567	5.5670%
Median CC Return	5.567%	5.5670%
Standard Deviation	0.000	0.0000%
No Dividend	0.00	0.00

Current Asset Price   100000
Investment Horizon   365

Calculate Your Forecast

$300410
$271828
$245960
$222554
$201375
$182211
$164872
$149182
$134985
$12214
$110517
$105725.00
$90483.
$81873.
$74081.
$67032.
$60653.
$54881.
$49658.
$44932.
$40656.
$36787.
$33287.
$30119.
$27253.

110%
100%
90%
80%
70%
60%
50%
40%
30%
20%
10%
6%
0%
-10%
-20%
-30%
-40%
-50%
-60%
-70%
-80%
-90%
-100%
-110%
-120%
-130%
140%

An investment strategy that lets you express your point of view and ensures that the value of your portfolio will never go down.

By themselves, options are risky. You have a high probability of losing 100% of your investment. However, you can combine options with other investments and create a portfolio that has a very low value at risk. At the extreme, you can create a portfolio with zero value at risk. The value of your portfolio will never go down and you will have the opportunity to earn exciting returns.

To execute this extreme strategy, you put almost all your money into a risk-free investment and put the rest into deep out-of-the-money options. Over the term of the options contract, the risk-free investment grows back to your starting portfolio value.

If the options do not pay off, you're back where you started from. Your only loss is the opportunity cost of the money you put in the options.

If you've chosen your options shrewdly (or luckily), you earn your option premium many times over. Your portfolio earns a healthy return.

Let's look at an example.

Let's say you have $100,000 to invest. You're interested in some European-style options on the Nasdaq 100 that expire in 166 days. The annualized, simple risk-free rate of return on six-month Treasury bills is 5.725%. The six-month rate should be a reasonably close rate to use for 166 days.

First, you need to figure out the continuously compounded equivalent of 5.725%.

1. Click three times on Clear.

2. Click twice on Hide.

3. Click on Calculate Your Forecast.

4. For Current Asset Price, enter 100000.00.

5. For Investment Horizon, enter 365.

6. For Highest possible price, enter the value of $100,000.00 a year from now at the risk-free rate. In this example, it's 105725.00.

7. For Lowest possible price, enter the same amount, in this example, 105725.00.

8. Click again on Calculate Your Forecast.

The expected return that the animation calculates is the continuously compounded equivalent. In this example, it's 5.567%.

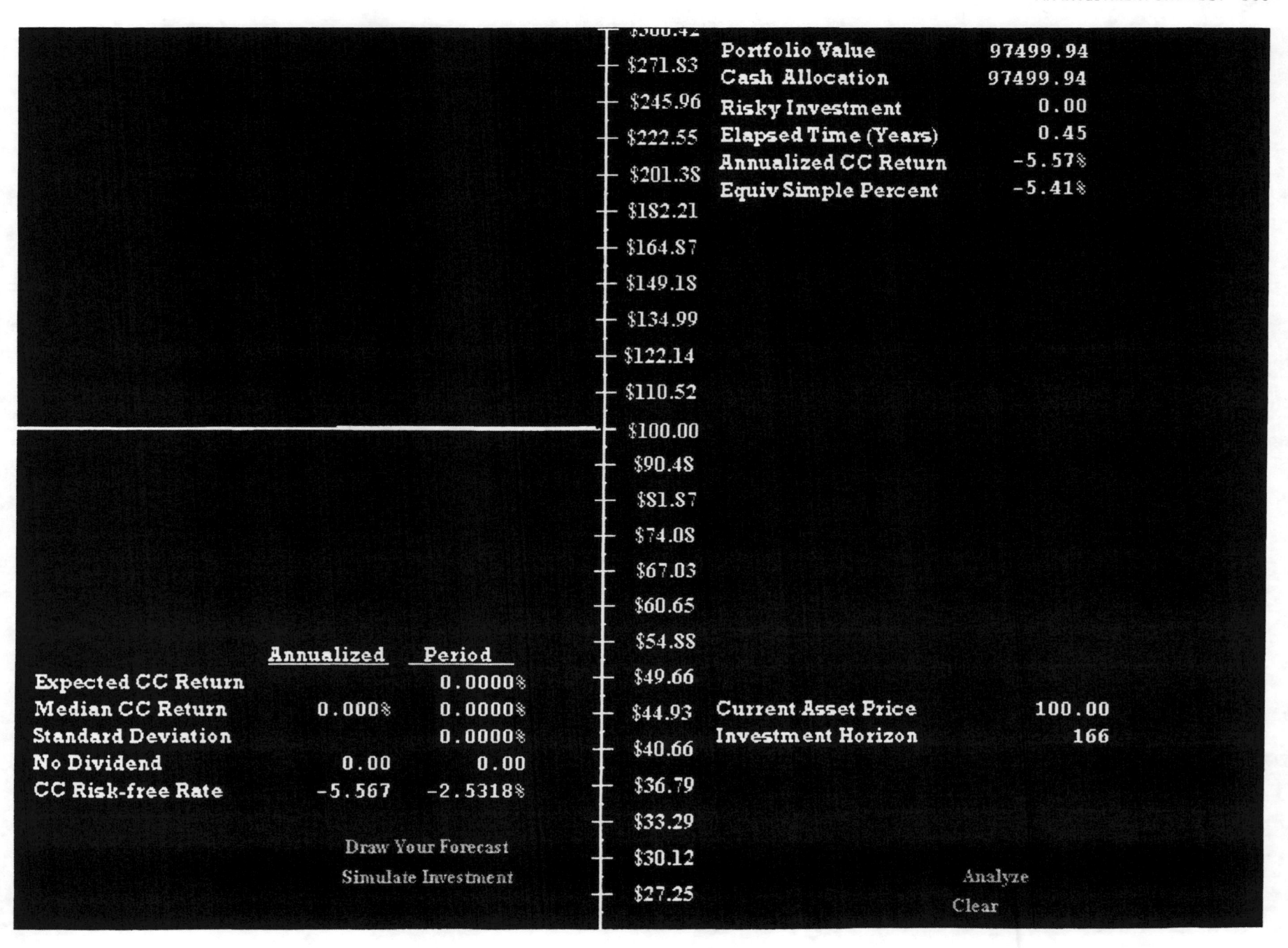

	Annualized	Period
Expected CC Return		0.0000%
Median CC Return	0.000%	0.0000%
Standard Deviation		0.0000%
No Dividend	0.00	0.00
CC Risk-free Rate	-5.567	-2.5318%

Draw Your Forecast

Simulate Investment

$300.42
$271.83 Portfolio Value   97499.94
$245.96 Cash Allocation   97499.94
$222.55 Risky Investment   0.00
         Elapsed Time (Years)   0.45
$201.38 Annualized CC Return   -5.57%
         Equiv Simple Percent   -5.41%
$182.21
$164.87
$149.18
$134.99
$122.14
$110.52
$100.00
$90.48
$81.87
$74.08
$67.03
$60.65
$54.88
$49.66
$44.93 Current Asset Price   100.00
        Investment Horizon   166
$40.66
$36.79
$33.29
$30.12
        Analyze
$27.25
        Clear

Put into a risk-free investment an amount of money that will grow back to your original portfolio value. This way, worst case, you get back to where you started from.

Next, you need to figure out what amount of money invested at the risk-free rate will grow to your original portfolio value in 166 days. In our example, we want to find out what amount of money invested at 5.567% for 166 days will grow to $100,000.

1. Click three times on Clear.

2. Click twice on Hide.

3. Click on Invest.

4. Click on Simulate Investment.

5. For Portfolio Value, enter 100000.00.

6. For Current Asset Price, enter 100.00.

7. For Investment Horizon, enter 166.

8. For CC Risk-free Rate, enter the continuously compounded interest rate preceded by a minus sign, in our example, –5.567.

9. Click on Simulate Investment.

This continuously compounded interest rate with the minus sign in front drops the portfolio value to $97,499.94. That means at 5.567%, $97,499.94 in 166 days will grow to $100,000.

Rounding to an even amount, you invest $97,500 at the risk-free rate. That leaves you with $2,500 to invest in options.

In periods of low interest rates, this strategy does not give you a lot of money to invest in options. Even so, keep in mind the Black-Scholes assumption that the expected return of every investment is the risk-free rate.

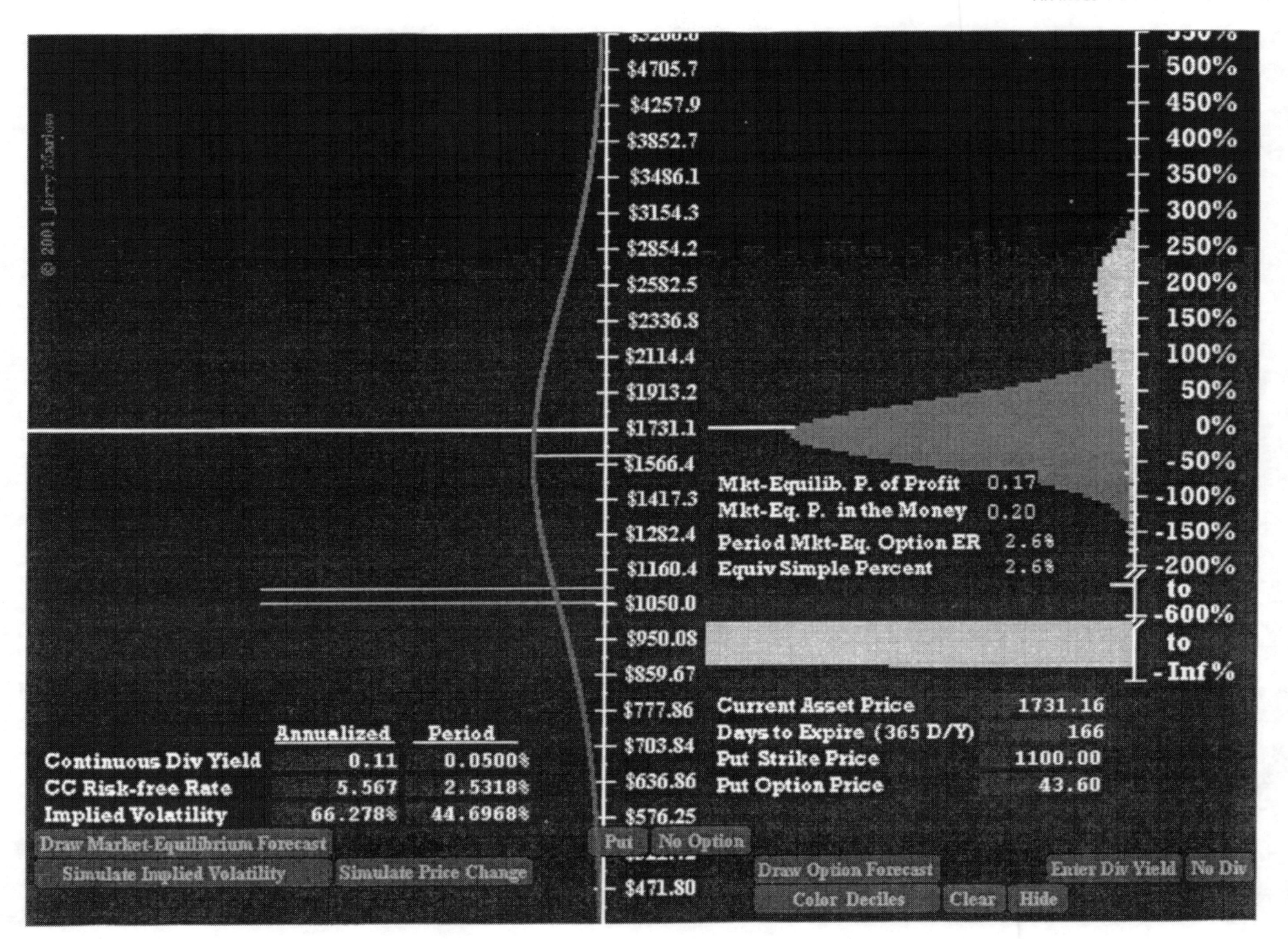

On a stock or index about which you have strong beliefs, look at market-equilibrium forecasts for deep out-of-the money options.

Let's say you think that sometime over the next four or five months the bottom is going to fall out of the Nasdaq. If you're right (or lucky), you could make a killing by investing in puts.

Today the Nasdaq-100® Index option is trading at 1731.16. You're looking at puts that expire in 166 days. At the moment, the lowest strike price for which puts are being sold is $1,100. The ask price is $43.60.

You take a look at the market-equilibrium forecast implied in the option price.

(Here we'll do our analysis on just one instrument. To evaluate an option series, look at several in the strike range in which you're interested. For the steps to follow, see the chapter on using the animations to assess option opportunities.)

1. Click three times on Clear.
2. Click twice on Hide.
3. Click on Simulate Price Change.
4. Click on Draw Option Forecast.
5. Click on Hide.
6. Click on Put.
7. Click on Calculate Implied Volatility.
8. For CC Risk-free Rate, enter the rate you calculated: 5.567.
9. For Current Asset Price, enter 1731.16.
10. For Days to Expire, enter 166.
11. For Put Strike Price, enter 1100.00.
12. For Put Option Price, enter 43.60.
13. Click on Enter Div Yield.
14. For Continuous Div Yield, enter 0.11.
15. Click on Calculate Implied Volatility.
16. Click on Draw Market-Equilibrium Forecast.

You see that under the market-equilibrium or consensus forecast you have a probability of profit of only .17. You have roughly one chance in six of making a profit. The option's expected return, of course, is the period risk-free rate.

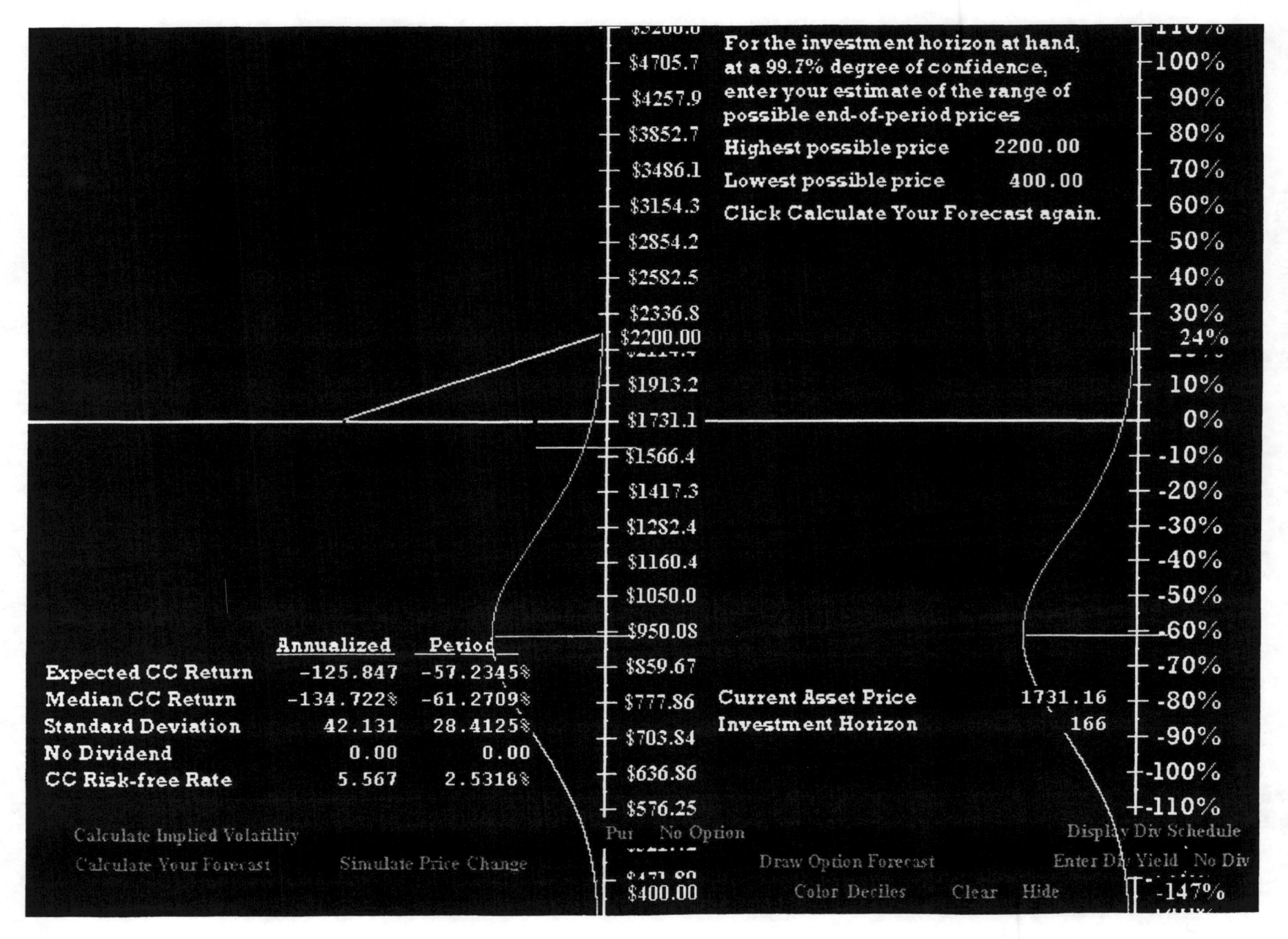

For the investment horizon at hand, at a 99.7% degree of confidence, enter your estimate of the range of possible end-of-period prices

Highest possible price 2200.00

Lowest possible price 400.00

Click Calculate Your Forecast again.

	Annualized	Period
Expected CC Return	-125.847	-57.2345%
Median CC Return	-134.722%	-61.2709%
Standard Deviation	42.131	28.4125%
No Dividend	0.00	0.00
CC Risk-free Rate	5.567	2.5318%

Current Asset Price 1731.16

Investment Horizon 166

$3200.0
$4705.7
$4257.9
$3852.7
$3486.1
$3154.3
$2854.2
$2582.5
$2336.8
$2200.00
$1913.2
$1731.1
$1566.4
$1417.3
$1282.4
$1160.4
$1050.0
$950.08
$859.67
$777.86
$703.84
$636.86
$576.25
$400.00

110%
100%
90%
80%
70%
60%
50%
40%
30%
24%
10%
0%
-10%
-20%
-30%
-40%
-50%
-60%
-70%
-80%
-90%
-100%
-110%
-147%

Calculate Implied Volatility

Calculate Your Forecast   Simulate Price Change

Put   No Option

Draw Option Forecast

Display Div Schedule

Enter Div Yield No Div

Color Deciles   Clear   Hide

Translate your beliefs into a forecast.

Looking at the market-equilibrium forecast, you figure that, ignoring the tiny dividend yield, in 166 days the Nasdaq-100® will be somewhere between $2,200 and $400. You translate your beliefs into a forecast.

17. Click on No Option.

18. Click on No Div.

19. Click on Calculate Your Forecast.

20. For Highest possible price, enter 2200.00.

21. For Lowest possible price, enter 400.00.

22. Click on Calculate Your Forecast.

Excluding dividends, you have your forecast in a form you can work with.

We add in the dividends—in this example, the dividend yield of 0.11%.

23. Click on Enter Div Yield.

24. For Continuous Div Yield, enter 0.11.

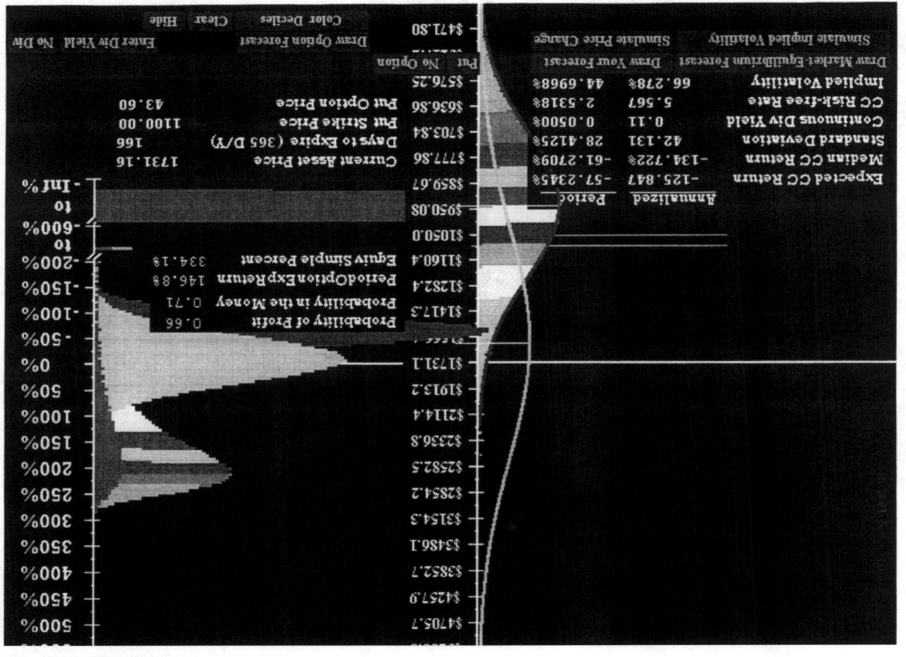

Look at the probability of profit and expected return under your forecast.

Now you want to see the expected return and probability of profit based on your forecast.

> 25. Click once on Clear.
>
> 26. Click on Hide.
>
> 27. Click on Put.
>
> 28. Click on Draw Option Forecast.
>
> 29. Click on Color Deciles.

In this example, the probability of profit based on your forecast is 0.66. The period option expected return is 146.8%.

> 30. Click on Draw Your Forecast.

For comparison, we can redraw the market-equilibrium forecast.

> 31. Click twice on Calculate Implied Volatility.
>
> 32. Click on Draw Market-Equilibrium Forecast.

The animation shows you the option's market-equilibrium probability of profit and period expected return.

> 33. To replace the market-equilibrium probability of profit with your forecast's probability, hold down the Ctrl key on your keyboard and hit the A key.

The drawings let you compare your forecasts for the underlying and option with the market-equilibrium forecasts.

Under your forecast, a probability of profit of .66 gives you a two-out-of-three chance of making a profit. If you were buying options with money you couldn't afford to lose, these still could be nerve-racking odds. With your protection money invested risk-free, these odds are merely exciting. Based on your forecast, on average, you can expect the options to pay more than four times the money you put in them.

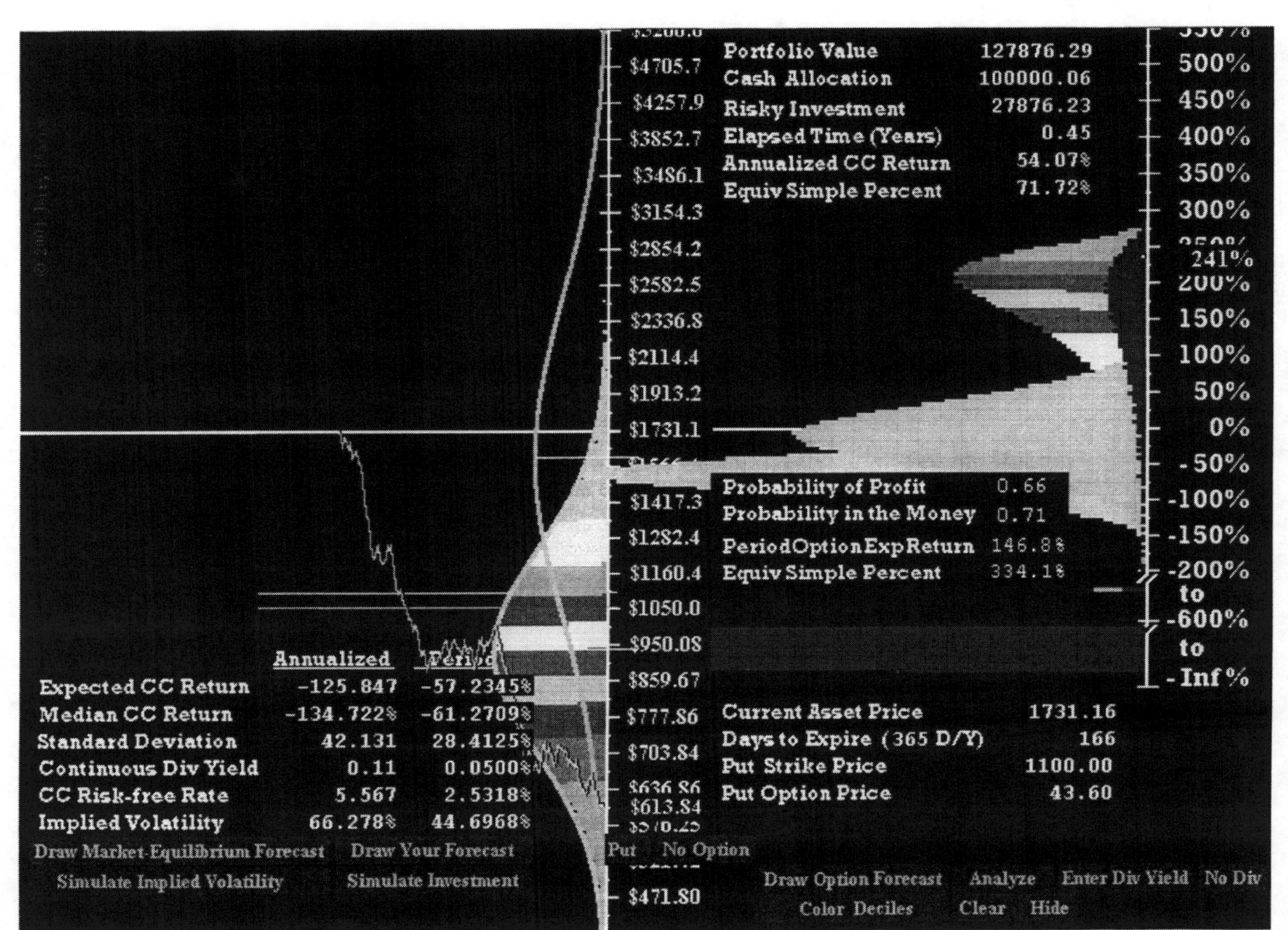

	Portfolio Value	127876.29
	Cash Allocation	100000.06
	Risky Investment	27876.23
	Elapsed Time (Years)	0.45
	Annualized CC Return	54.07%
	Equiv Simple Percent	71.72%

	Probability of Profit	0.66
	Probability in the Money	0.71
	Period Option Exp Return	146.8%
	Equiv Simple Percent	334.1%

	Annualized	Period
Expected CC Return	−125.847	−57.2345%
Median CC Return	−134.722%	−61.2709%
Standard Deviation	42.131	28.4125%
Continuous Div Yield	0.11	0.0500%
CC Risk-free Rate	5.567	2.5318%
Implied Volatility	66.278%	44.6968%

Current Asset Price	1731.16
Days to Expire (365 D/Y)	166
Put Strike Price	1100.00
Put Option Price	43.60

Draw Market-Equilibrium Forecast   Draw Your Forecast   Put No Option

Simulate Implied Volatility   Simulate Investment   Draw Option Forecast Analyze Enter Div Yield No Div

Color Deciles   Clear Hide

Simulate potential investment outcomes for your portfolio.

Now you're ready to simulate potential investment outcomes for your portfolio.

(While options are sold in round lots, for simulations we'll use the full $2,500 as your risky investment amount. It's easier to track mentally.)

> **34. Click on Invest.**
>
> **35. For Portfolio Value, enter 100000.00.**
>
> **36. For Risky Investment, enter 2500.00.**
>
> **37. Click on Simulate Investment.**

In the simulation example above, we see that:

- The Nasdaq-100® has gone to $613.84.
- The $97,500 cash allocation invested at the risk-free rate has grown back to the original portfolio amount of $100,000.
- The $2,500 invested in puts has grown to $27,876—a more than eleven-fold return!
- In 166 days, the portfolio value has grown from $100,000 to $127,876.29.

All without the risk of the value of your portfolio ever going down!

One interesting thing about the outcome in the example is that it falls within the market-equilibrium forecast. Your friends (and enemies) could say, "You weren't smart. You were just lucky!"

What's more, you could not prove them wrong!

Maybe that extra 20,000 or so dollars you put into the bank would be of some comfort to you.

Does this strategy make sense?

Compared to what?

Many investors do not address head-on the psychological aspects of making investment decisions. Very often where they put their money bears little resemblance to what they say they think and believe. They suffer from an anxiety that might be called schizo-dinero: Their beliefs are in one place. Their money is in another.

If an honest appraisal of your portfolio shows that it accurately reflects your beliefs, then God bless you!

If, however, you frequently find yourself saying, "I knew that was going to happen! Why didn't I do something?" then you may

want to combine risk-free investments with options in a way that lets you act on your beliefs in a risk-free way.

Right or wrong, you'll probably feel better about your investments. You can alternate between glory and despair. You will learn from your wins and from your losses.

Chances are your anxiety level will go down. You will be less likely to pay for and rely on investment advice that you neither understand nor, in your heart of hearts, trust.

All the while, the value of your portfolio will never go down.

Not only might this strategy make sense for you, it may set you free.

What makes life interesting?

Winning and losing make life interesting.

To win or lose, you have to play the game.

—*Alan Watts*

Navigating through the Animations

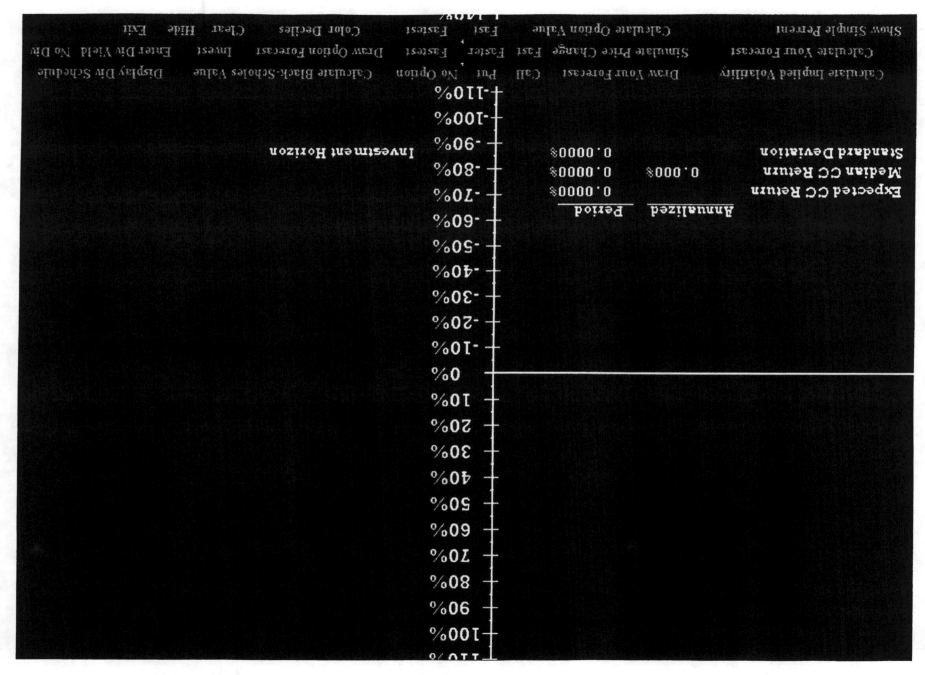

To make command buttons visible, mouse around on the bottom and top left of the screen

The animation interface follows several general design principles. If you spend a few minutes to become familiar with these now, later you won't wonder why your screen is such a mess.

Command buttons remain invisible until you move your mouse cursor over them. To make buttons visible, move your mouse cursor around on the bottom of the screen. To make the Lock-Random-Seed button visible, mouse around at the top left of the screen.

To bring a set of axes on-screen, click on any of these buttons:
■ Draw Your Forecast
■ Simulate Price Change
■ Draw Option Forecast
■ Calculate Your Forecast

1. Click on Draw Your Forecast.

The animation brings a set of axes on-screen. It prompts you for the data entries it needs to do what the button calls for.

2. Fill in the data boxes that are displayed.

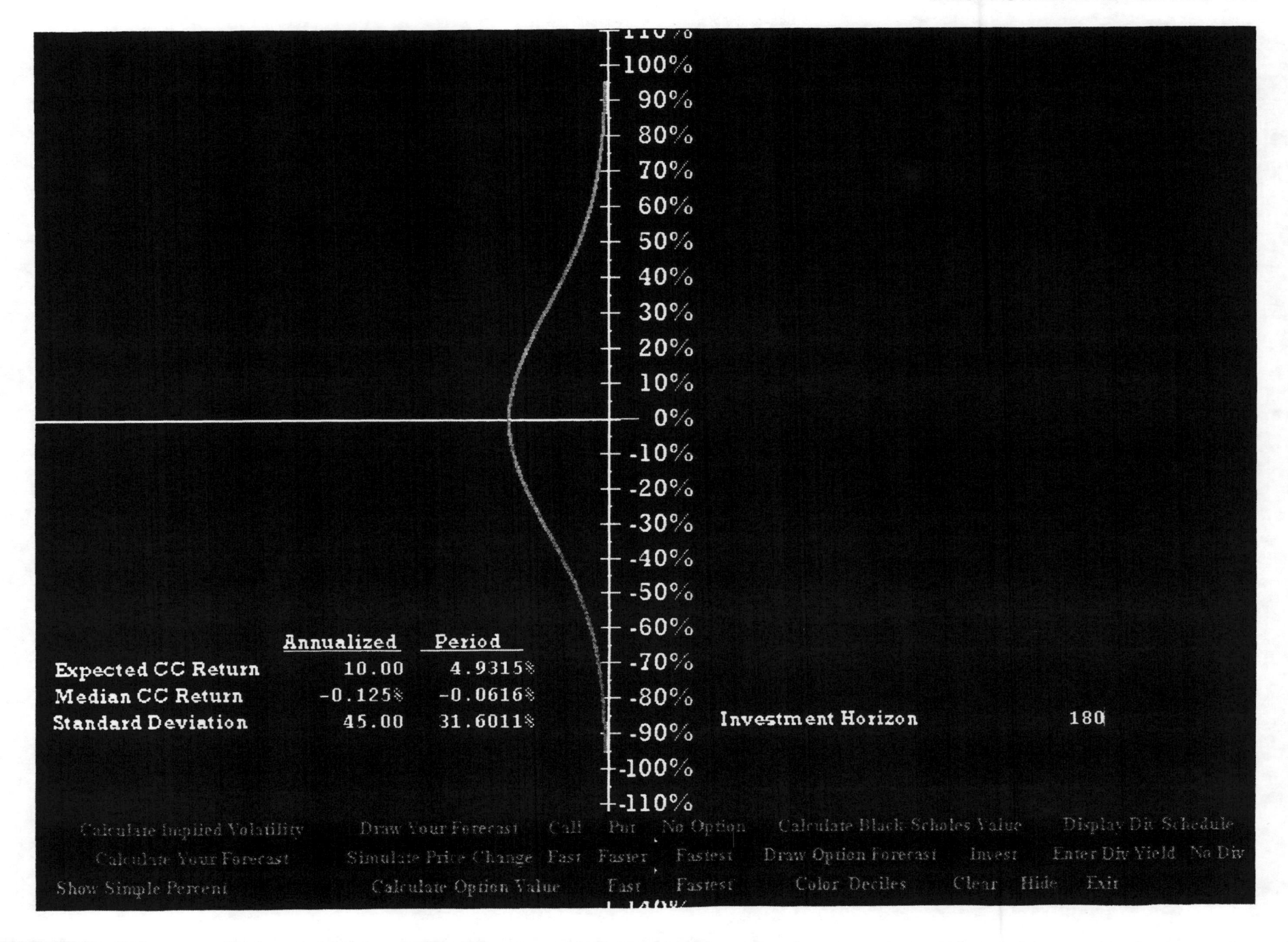

	Annualized	Period
Expected CC Return	10.00	4.9315%
Median CC Return	-0.125%	-0.0616%
Standard Deviation	45.00	31.6011%

Investment Horizon 180

Calculate Implied Volatility   Draw Your Forecast   Call   Put   No Option   Calculate Black-Scholes Value   Display Div Schedule

Calculate Your Forecast   Simulate Price Change   Fast   Faster   Fastest   Draw Option Forecast   Invest   Enter Div Yield   No Div

Show Simple Percent   Calculate Option Value   Fast   Fastest   Color Deciles   Clear   Hide   Exit

Click the same button a second time and it does what it says it does.

If you click the same button again, it does what it says it does.

3. Click again on Draw Your Forecast.

If you just keep clicking buttons without ever bothering to tidy up, an amazing amount of stuff will pile up on the screen. You'll lose track of where you are and what you're doing. Anyone trying to follow what you're doing will be twice as lost.

Therefore, tidy up early and often. It's easy.

To use Color Deciles, first use other buttons to get the axes and required data fields on-screen.

The Color Deciles command button draws color deciles for whatever axes and data fields you have on-screen. To get the axes and data fields on-screen, you have to use other buttons.

4. Click on Color Deciles.

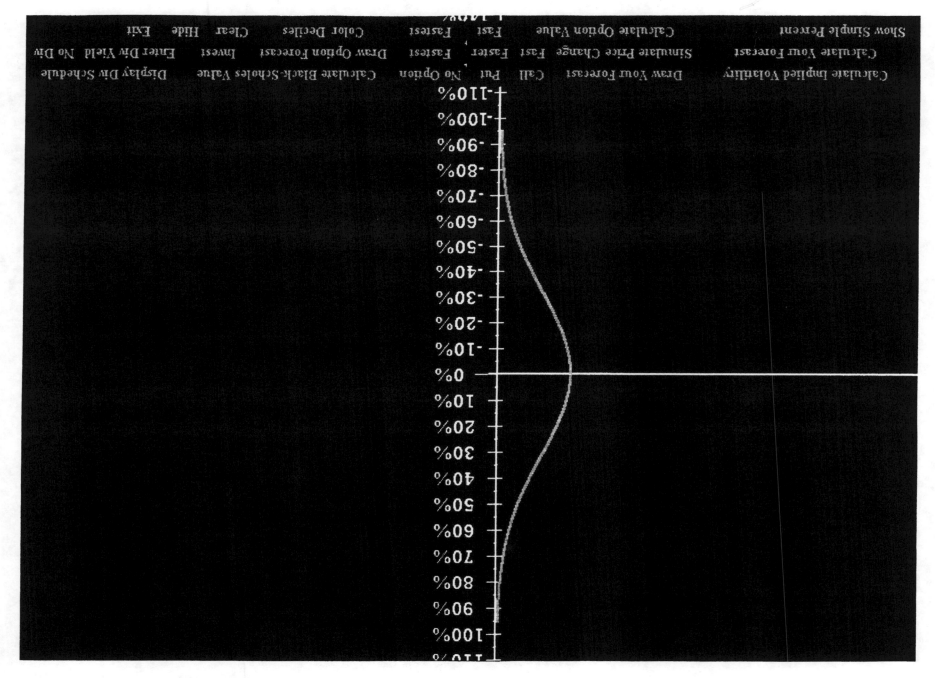

Click the Hide button once and the data boxes go away.

5. Click on Hide.

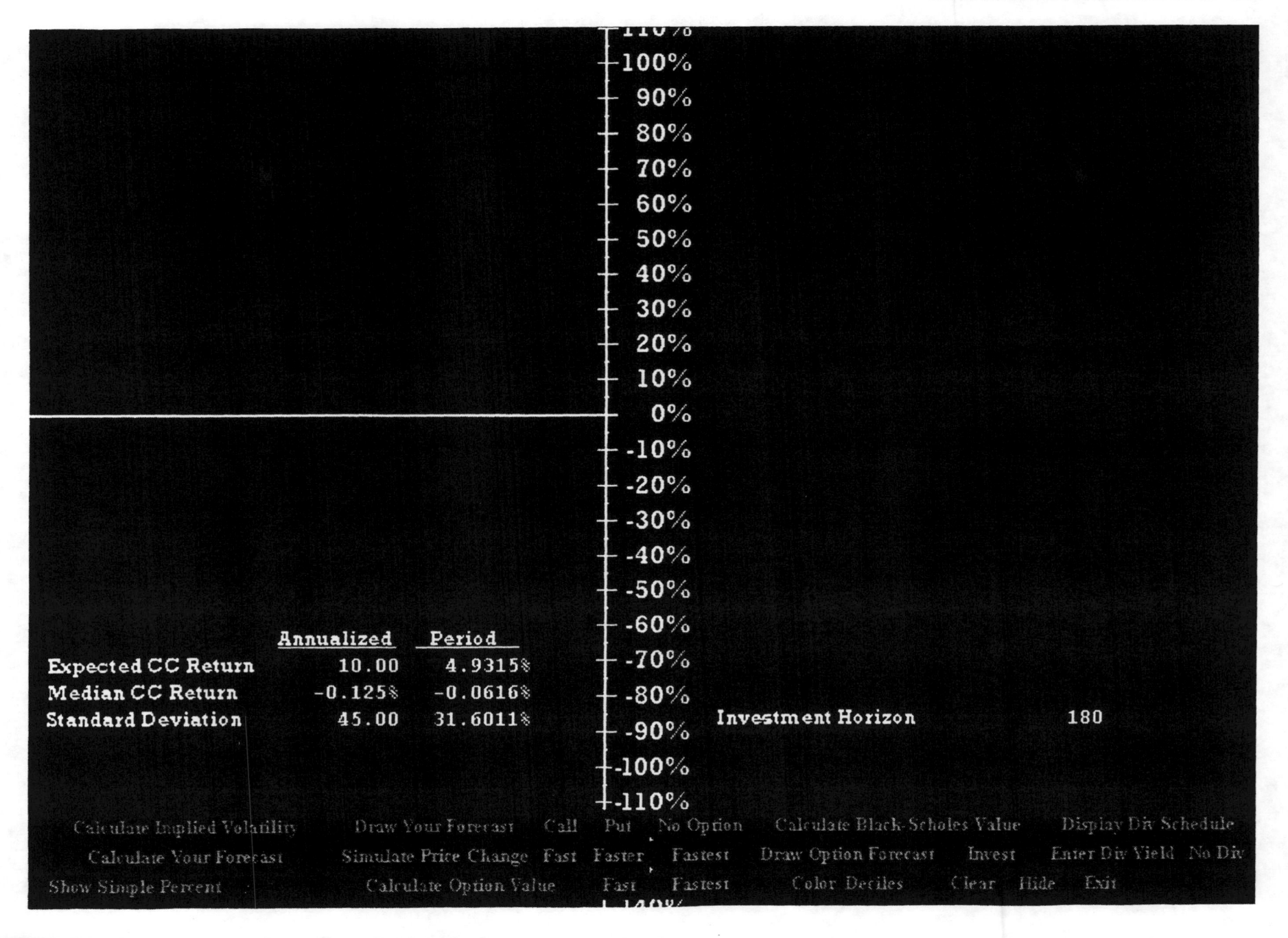

Click Clear once and what you drew goes away.

6. Click on Clear.

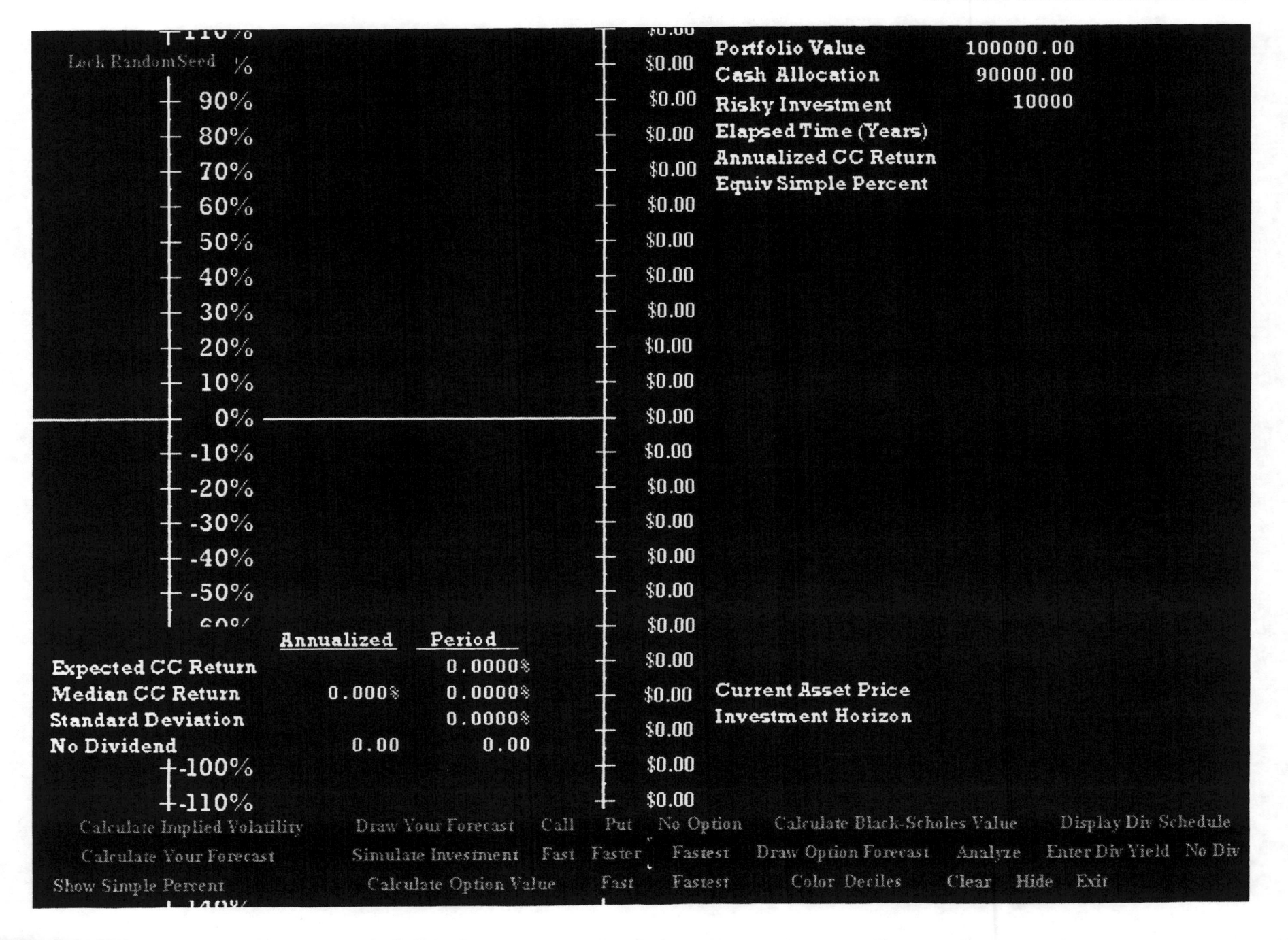

110%

Lock RandomSeed %

90%

80%

70%

60%

50%

40%

30%

20%

10%

0%

-10%

-20%

-30%

-40%

-50%

60%

	Annualized	Period
Expected CC Return		0.0000%
Median CC Return	0.000%	0.0000%
Standard Deviation		0.0000%
No Dividend	0.00	0.00

-100%

-110%

$0.00
$0.00
$0.00
$0.00
$0.00
$0.00
$0.00
$0.00
$0.00
$0.00
$0.00
$0.00
$0.00
$0.00
$0.00
$0.00
$0.00
$0.00
$0.00
$0.00
$0.00

Portfolio Value	100000.00
Cash Allocation	90000.00
Risky Investment	10000

Elapsed Time (Years)
Annualized CC Return
Equiv Simple Percent

Current Asset Price
Investment Horizon

Calculate Implied Volatility   Draw Your Forecast   Call   Put   No Option   Calculate Black-Scholes Value   Display Div Schedule
Calculate Your Forecast   Simulate Investment   Fast   Faster   Fastest   Draw Option Forecast   Analyze   Enter Div Yield   No Div
Show Simple Percent   Calculate Option Value   Fast   Fastest   Color Deciles   Clear   Hide   Exit

140%

Click Clear twice and zeroes and blanks fill in all the data boxes.

7. Click twice on Draw Your Forecast.

8. Click on Invest.

9. Fill in Portfolio Value and Cash Allocation.

Click Clear three times and zeroes and blanks fill in the investment-portfolio data fields.

10. Watch what happens as you click once, twice, three times on Clear.

Click Hide twice and everything but the command buttons goes away.

Click Hide three times and the command buttons go away.

1. Watch what happens as you click once, twice, three times on Hide.

Mouse around and you'll find the buttons again.

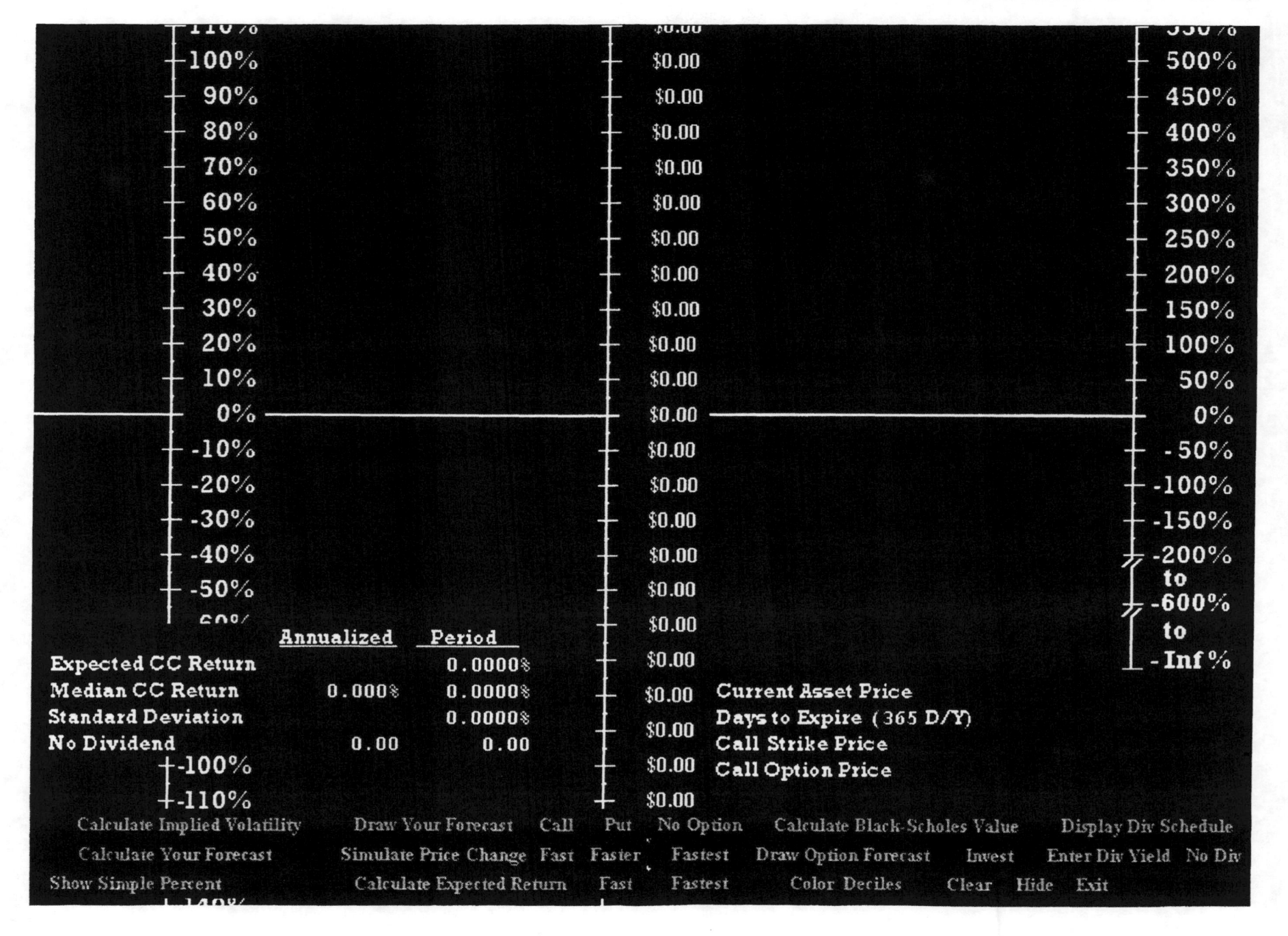

110%
100%
90%
80%
70%
60%
50%
40%
30%
20%
10%
0%
-10%
-20%
-30%
-40%
-50%
60%

$0.00
$0.00
$0.00
$0.00
$0.00
$0.00
$0.00
$0.00
$0.00
$0.00
$0.00
$0.00
$0.00
$0.00
$0.00
$0.00
$0.00
$0.00
$0.00

550%
500%
450%
400%
350%
300%
250%
200%
150%
100%
50%
0%
-50%
-100%
-150%
-200%
to
-600%
to
-Inf%

	Annualized	Period
Expected CC Return		0.0000%
Median CC Return	0.000%	0.0000%
Standard Deviation		0.0000%
No Dividend	0.00	0.00

$0.00
$0.00

$0.00 Current Asset Price
$0.00 Days to Expire (365 D/Y)
$0.00 Call Strike Price
$0.00 Call Option Price

-100%
-110%

$0.00

Calculate Implied Volatility   Draw Your Forecast   Call   Put   No Option   Calculate Black-Scholes Value   Display Div Schedule

Calculate Your Forecast   Simulate Price Change Fast Faster   Fastest   Draw Option Forecast   Invest   Enter Div Yield   No Div

Show Simple Percent   Calculate Expected Return   Fast   Fastest   Color Deciles   Clear   Hide   Exit

The order in which you click on the buttons determines the positions of the axes.

When you bring axes on-screen, the order in which you click on

- Draw Your Forecast
- Simulate Price Change
- Draw Option Forecast

determines the positions of the axes.

For example, click on the three buttons in this order:

2. Draw Your Forecast

3. Simulate Price Change

4. Draw Your Forecast

5. Draw Option Forecast

Notice where the axes are.

6. Click Hide twice.

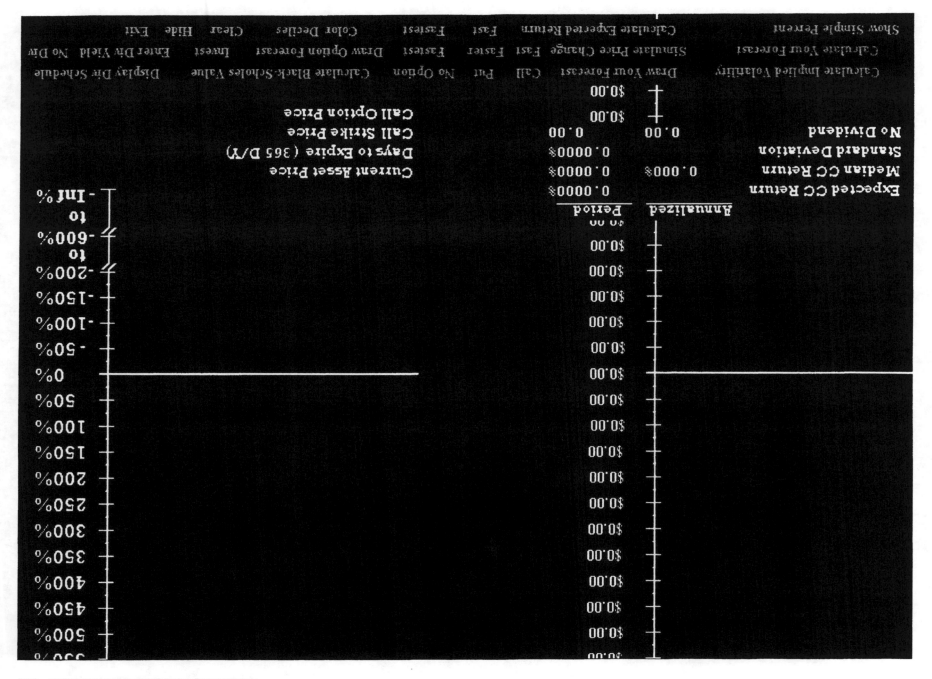

Now click on the three buttons in this order:

7. Draw Option Forecast

8. Simulate Price Change

9. Draw Your Forecast

That's right. You have more room for the option return axes, but the underlying return axes refuse to appear.

The animation gives the most room to the button you click on first.

If you don't like the way the screen is laid out, click Hide twice and bring on the axes in a different sequence.

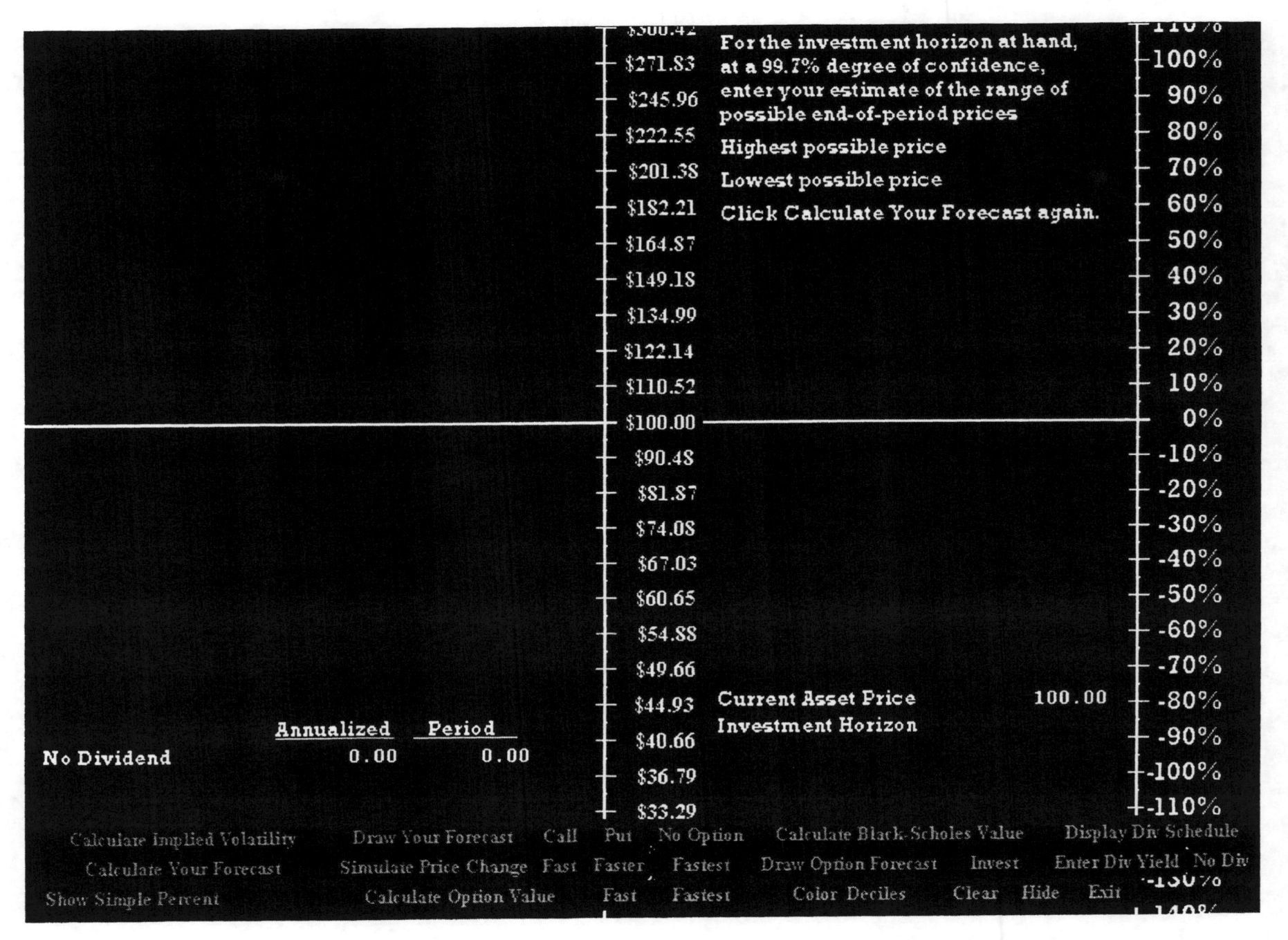

$300.42

$271.83   For the investment horizon at hand,
   at a 99.7% degree of confidence,

$245.96   enter your estimate of the range of
   possible end-of-period prices

$222.55   Highest possible price

$201.38   Lowest possible price

$182.21   Click Calculate Your Forecast again.

$164.87

$149.18

$134.99

$122.14

$110.52

$100.00

$90.48

$81.87

$74.08

$67.03

$60.65

$54.88

$49.66

$44.93   Current Asset Price   100.00

   Investment Horizon

$40.66

$36.79

$33.29

110%
100%
90%
80%
70%
60%
50%
40%
30%
20%
10%
0%
-10%
-20%
-30%
-40%
-50%
-60%
-70%
-80%
-90%
-100%
-110%

No Dividend   **Annualized**   **Period**   0.00   0.00

Calculate Implied Volatility   Draw Your Forecast   Call   Put   No Option   Calculate Black-Scholes Value   Display Div Schedule

Calculate Your Forecast   Simulate Price Change   Fast   Faster   Fastest   Draw Option Forecast   Invest   Enter Div Yield   No Div

Show Simple Percent   Calculate Option Value   Fast   Fastest   Color Deciles   Clear   Hide   Exit

Neatness counts. Whenever you do anything with a different emphasis, click Hide twice and start over.

1. Click on Hide two or three times.

2. Click on Calculate Your Forecast.

The return axes for the underlying asset appear on the far right. That's because the animation will derive your rate-of-return forecast from your estimates of potential end-of-period prices.

If you calculate your forecast and then do lots of other stuff and leave the axes in these positions, you can create a real mess. Whenever you do anything new, click Hide once.

Whenever you do anything with a different emphasis, click Hide twice and start over.

Neatness counts.

To get to the data fields, you can either click in the fields or tab your way to them.

If you're working along and suddenly tapping the tab key no longer moves you through the data fields, that means the cursor was in a data field when you got rid of the data field. The cursor is out in cyber-space somewhere.

If this happens, use the mouse to highlight one of the data fields on-screen. After that, you should be able to tab from field to field.

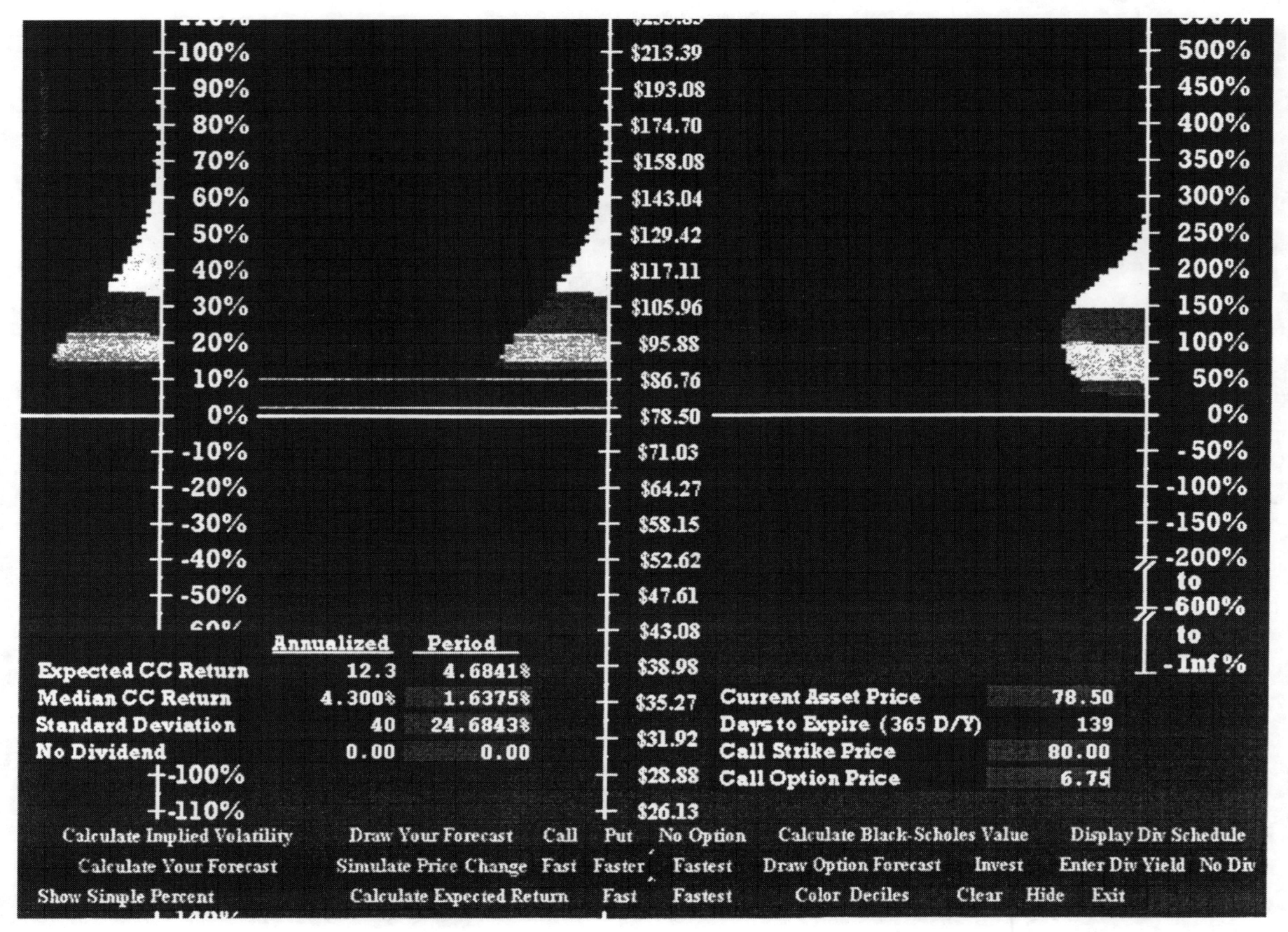

	Annualized	Period
Expected CC Return	12.3	4.6841%
Median CC Return	4.300%	1.6375%
Standard Deviation	40	24.6843%
No Dividend	0.00	0.00

Current Asset Price 78.50
Days to Expire (365 D/Y) 139
Call Strike Price 80.00
Call Option Price 6.75

Calculate Implied Volatility   Draw Your Forecast   Call   Put   No Option   Calculate Black-Scholes Value   Display Div Schedule

Calculate Your Forecast   Simulate Price Change   Fast   Faster   Fastest   Draw Option Forecast   Invest   Enter Div Yield   No Div

Show Simple Percent   Calculate Expected Return   Fast   Fastest   Color Deciles   Clear   Hide   Exit

To stop an animation once it is in progress, click long and hard on a blank area of the screen.

Fairly often you will start an animation and realize you're not doing what you meant to do. To stop an animation once it is in progress, click on some unoccupied area of the screen. To interrupt the animation, you may have to hold the mouse down for a moment or two.

If you're running your laptop on battery power and the animations are running sluggishly, set the battery-operation mode to high performance.

Unlike many applications, the animations actually use a lot of the power built into your computer. They are calculation intensive.

If you're running the animations on a laptop computer and the computer is running on battery power, you may discover that the animations are slow and sluggish.

On many laptops, the default setting for battery-operation mode is low speed or low performance. While this setting saves battery power, it slows down the animations.

If you find the animations running sluggishly, go into your laptop's battery-power-management dialogue and change the power setting to high speed or high performance. The animations should run just as fast on battery power as they do when you're plugged in.

To exit the animation, click on the Exit button or hit the Esc key on your keyboard.

Index

System Requirements

Made in the USA
Lexington, KY
17 April 2010

5219476R0